D1319244

What does the year 1960 mean to the Chinese people?
"Three-Years of Natural Disaster", in which it is said more than 30 million Chinese lost their lives.

A surviving boy aged six, is taken from his extended, countryside family with whom he has been living for four years, by a "total stranger" to Changsha, the capital city of Hunan Province.

This was the first time DanJiu ever met his father, for that matter, it was the first time he had ever heard the word "father". This first meeting marks the beginning of a decade's long bid for his father's love.

Second son of a not so high ranking, not so low ranking Communist Party Member, he was born in response to the Party's call to, "have as many children as possible for the use of war". The seriousness with which the world around him presents itself demands he fit in.

DanJiu learns quite early that he is a square peg. The desperate bid for his father's love seems unattainable as he overhears Father say, "I dislike that child by nature." heartbreaking words that will haunt his life as he questions, "Why 'by nature'?"

The blissful discovery of violin at age twelve leads to a lifelong passion, love, obsession and a major problem. It's 1966 and the Cultural Revolution is in full swing meaning that anything WESTERN is evil, including his beloved violin. How will he persist in his pursuit?

Time marches on and DanJiu becomes Daniel. In the early 80s he follows his passion for violin to the west where he lives for his dream in a violinist's world with a beautiful Norwegian wife, about to take the next step to the USA. Everything sold, money in hand, packed and ready to go, Daniel receives a desperate letter from China pleading for his help.

His long estranged father lay dying in a hospital unable to pay for his medical care. Daniel is the family's only hope. What will he do? Having come so far in pursuit of his passion, will he give it all up for his father who dislikes him by nature?

What would you do?

From award winning Mandarin language author Daniel Olsen Chen, comes his first (but not last) English language book, **"Father, Son & Violin"**, a Memoir of his life growing up in Mao's China is a poignant, amusing and shocking journey about courage, passion growth of spirit and character, but above all, the quest of a son for the love of his father.

FATHER, SON & VIOLIN

A Personal Life Story Tells The Vivid History Of Mao's China

Daniel Olsen Chen

E-mail: danielolsenltd@gmail.com
Website: www.danielviolins.com
YouTube: AV Daniel Violin

Trade paperback ISBN 978-4-9909899-0-3
E- Book ISBN 978-4-9909899-1-0

Designed by Mercedes LaBenz

Dedicated to my parents and all of their generation.

My special thanks to Ms. Mercedes LaBenz, without her encouragement and inspiration, hard work in editing, artwork and publishing assistance, this book would never have been made public.

1: MY EARLIEST MEMORIES OF MY FAMILY

A Terrifying White Balloon

Everyone has one's own memory of childhood. My memory of childhood starts on a cobble stone paved road called "Blue Stone Road" (Qing Shi Jie in Chinese), the main road fifty years ago, and still today, of Xinhua County in Hunan province, Southern China. I lived in a house close to the road with my family.

When I say "*my family*", it was not the customary nuclear family consisting of parents and their children, but rather grandparents, an aunt plus two uncles and I. As the only child, it shouldn't be hard to imagine my position as the core center of the family.

Even now there are things I can clearly remember from when I was as little as 3 or 4 years old. One such memory takes place on the day I found a small, white, rubber tube in a rubbish-pile, hastily picked it up and blew it into a balloon. I found it amusing and swiftly ran back home asking my aunt to tie the balloon up with some string. As soon as my aunt, who was in high school at the time, saw the "*balloon*" in my hand, her cheeks flushed bright red, panic stricken! She looked as if the sky were falling and immediately called my younger uncle, Xi. Uncle Xi came quickly with some used newspapers in his hand. He forcefully snatched my treasure away and quickly ran towards a toilet. At the same time, my aunt pushed me back towards a wash basin, cautiously avoiding my hands.

Twice Uncle, and then three times my aunt vigorously washed my hands. Being the "center" of the family, how could this be tolerated? Straight away I employed my typical method of resistance and glued my bottom to the ground! No matter how hard my aunt coaxed, I refused to get up, instead, yelling, "I want my white balloon! I want my white balloon!" over and over at the top of my lungs. My screams were finally quieted when Uncle Xi came running to me with two big colored balloons in his hands.

It must have been more than ten years after that event, I had continued wondering, why my aunt was so terrified of that small white balloon. Until one day I suddenly realized that that white balloon was in no way a child's toy. It is of great importance when two adults exchange their love, and today, an absolute necessity, more to prevent getting disease than for contraception. Sorry, my poor aunt!

I became a six-year-old by the year 1960. It was the most horrible time throughout all of Chinese history, if not the whole history of humankind. The entire Chinese nation was suffering from starvation yet I had little memory of hunger when I was with that family. Until one day, I was taken by my father from this hometown to Changsha, where I would grow up.

Leaving Xinhua For Changsha

I vividly remember the day, after the usual nap, I went to Zijiang River again with my two uncles. I played with sand and stones at the riverbank while my uncles were swimming.

When the suns glow dyed everything golden, again I heard my elder uncle Din's self-satisfying but out-of-tune singing. "The twilight is declining to the western hill…", then, as always and with a much softer voice, he changed the lyrics to, "The eastern sun is declining down the western hill."

Just when I was about to plug my ears with my fingers I heard my aunt shouting, "DanJiu (my Chinese name) your father is here! Quickly let's go home!"

That was the first time I had heard the title "*father*" in my life. With no time to think, I was taken home and placed in front of a complete stranger. He was very thin, emaciated even. Forgive me if I overemphasize a bit how hollow his cheeks looked, as if he were a skeleton covered by a sheet of skin. His side-glance at me through his glasses made me shiver; quickly I hid myself behind my aunt.

However, my aunt pulled me out gently and pushed me in front of the man again! In addition, she asked me to call him "*Baba*" (Father).

Every member of the family sat around the dining table, except for grandpa. Being the symbol of family authority, grandpa's absence was rather unusual. (I wondered why, suddenly, grandpa said he felt a little uneasy) My father took grandpa's place. Deadly silence made the sound of peeling candy paper and chewing extraordinarily noisy. Uncle Xi placed another into his mouth before he had even finished his first. In a muffled voice he whined, "Better than nothing."

"What?" Father responded.

Uncle Xi swiftly swallowed what was left in his throat and moaned, "No more than a small bag of candy! I thought after so many years my big brother coming home would bring us some rice or meat."

"What do you think we are, kids?" Uncle Din was the only one who withstood the lure of this sweet, tasty candy. He lost control at this stage, "The whole family has had no rice for a long time! Every day we eat vegetables, sometimes even grass, tree leaves and bark!"

Aunt captured the last two candies and handed them to Uncle Din, "Take them before nothing is left."

Uncle Din did not accept the loss-of-dignity. The two candies on the table in front of Uncle Din captured all eyes in the room, particularly the two belonging to Uncle Xi.

In an attempt to maintain a family-like atmosphere, Aunt voiced her complaint in a very peaceful, soft tone, "Though they are noisy, what they say is true. Our family has been suffering from hunger for more than a year now. You are the eldest son of the family; you are the only one who works for the government in the capital city of the province. In any way possible, you ought to do something to help the family."

Aunt's words were like oil pouring on Uncle Din's fire, he shouted, "That's right, that's right! Not only doing nothing to help the family, but also added *your burden* (me) for us to carry!"

"My burden?" My father disagreed in a low voice: "Yes, the boy is my son, but he also belongs to the country." Father's voice was growing louder and more emphatic little by little, "It is our great leader Chairman Mao who called on our nation to have as many children as possible for the use of war. We followed his great teaching to have four children, that's why I say they are not only *our* children but also children of the country. In this sense, everyone in this country has an obligation to raise them."

"Nonsense! You make children for the use of war? Animal!" Uncle Din was now furious.

Grandma saw things were getting too intense. She stood up endeavoring to strike a balance, "Stop! Stop. That's enough. It's not easy for us all to sit together around the same table. Can't we be more like a family?"

As soon as she finished having her say, grandma calmly collected the two remaining candies, making eye contact with Uncle Din to be sure he in no way wanted them for himself, "I'll put them into a jug so that we can all share some sweet water."

After everybody was quiet for a while, my father slowly, deliberately, cut a letter heading paper into eight small, equally sized pieces. He then opened a small, old, iron box, took out a bit of loose tobacco, put it in the middle of a small paper and rolled himself a horn shaped cigarette. He lit the cigarette and deeply inhaled it three times.

As he couldn't find a good excuse for not helping the family, he decided to make his voice half official jargon like, "Now our nation is temporarily in difficulty due to three years of continual natural disasters, plus the Soviet Revisionism and other imperial countries that have us by the neck. Not only our family but the whole country, including the capital city of the province, even the central government, everybody is short in food. Haven't you heard? Our great leader, Chairman Mao, also has stopped eating meat after he heard many of our class brothers and sisters lost their lives from starvation!"

(It is said from 1958 to 1961, 36 million Chinese lives were lost as a result of starvation or related reasons. Though some intellectuals doubt the accuracy of the number, a couple of million more or less dead bodies, seems not to bother the Chinese much.)

"What should we do? Wait to die?" Uncle Xi's voice worsened the mood.

Silence again, this time without even the noise of peeling candy paper or chewing.

My father took one last deep inhale of his cigarette until his lips felt burnt. He changed his tone to a more domestic one, "Exactly because we know you are also in difficulties, Xiwan (my mother's name) and I decided to release your burden by taking DanJiu back. I'm afraid this is the only thing we could do to help at this moment."

After a little pause, my father obviously tried to cheer everybody up by saying: "We must trust our great leader Chairman Mao and always-correct Communist Party. Our country will be better and better from now on."

As no one seemed to be cheered up, my father's effort was in vain. Uncle Xi moaned again, "If our eldest brother had finished his university degree instead of taking part in the Communist Party's revolutionary activity before liberation, at least he could now earn some money by some other related work. If he had done that he would be able to do his share supporting our old parents."

Capturing the gap before my father's response, Uncle Din poured out with grouse, "If revolution can't bring our family a better life but results in hunger for the whole nation, what's the meaning of it? Gas! "

"Be careful, be careful!" Father raised his voice with authority, "What I have just heard was anti-revolution. It's dangerous, especially from a non-working-class family."

Uncle Din was outraged by his brother's words, he jumped up and shouted: "Remember? Just like most of your Party members, you cut all ties with your family a long time ago when you joined the Party. Whatever happens to us, you've got nothing to worry about."

Aunt also looked quite anxious, she clarified: "Our father's class is self-*employed & small-land-renting.* It is 'self-employed' before 'small-land-renting'. In addition, after the victory of the Revolution, our father was once elected to be the people's representative of the country. Therefore, our family is in no way anti-revolutionary class. If not, how could the people's enemy represent the people? Right?"

The above dialogue must be nonsense to most nations on earth, but was absolutely of great, *the greatest* importance, to every single Chinese family at that time. It was so vital that it could mean the difference between, "to be or not to be."

Such an important debate was of course, not suitable for a child of 6. Grandma saw things getting out of hand. She took my hands and dragged me into the kitchen. She made me promise to stay there until being called. Then again, she went into the battlefield endeavoring to extinguish the fire.

My sensitive nose led me to a small aluminum lunch-box. Guess what I discovered? Two boiled eggs and two baked Chinese sweet potatoes! As my mouth was still busy with some candy, I decided to let them be for a little while longer.

The quarrelling of the adults was getting louder and louder. Curiosity forced me to put my face against the kitchen door. Through the gap I saw my father standing up, saying to grandma: "Where is DanJiu? We've got to go at once otherwise we'll be late for the train."

"Won't you have something to eat before..." grandma hinted for Father to go into the kitchen.

"Eat? Eat what?" Uncle Din cut in: "He brought nothing home! What have we got for him to eat?"

The kitchen door again was opened. My father quickly walked towards me and grasped my hand dragging me out. My instinct was to bite him! Fortunately, he avoided my teeth in time. I got away from him and quickly hid myself behind Aunt as always. To my immense surprise, a thousand, thousand million surprises, she pushed me away!

My aunt, the woman who had always kept her arms open to me, in any case at any time had always been my protector, was not this time. For the first time in memory, she pushed me away. This unthinkable action turned my surprise into anger. I decided to make her pay for what she had done to me by going away with this stranger. "Without *me*, she must be sad to death." I imagined with a bit of satisfaction.

The next thing I remember, I was on a train. I leaned against the window, anxiously expecting Aunt to take me back. But when I saw her with the lunch-box in her hand, running beside the train, back and forth searching for me window-by-window, again I felt like playing a game. Every time Aunt passed by my window, I lowered my head so that I was invisible until the train started to move. I stretched my head up and waved my hand to Aunt. When Aunt saw me she hastily held up the lunch-box yelling "DanJiu, DanJiu, take it, take it!" but that was too late. The train moved faster and faster.

5

The figure of Aunt's body became smaller and smaller, until it faded away. When I realized it was no longer a game but real, my aunt and I were apart, I "Wa..." burst into tears, "I want sweet potato, I want sweet potato!" I clamored. My father showed no response to my crying, only changed seats with me. Now he replaced me, sitting by the window.

After I gave up the hope that my aunt would appear again, I turned my eyes to my father. He avoided eye contact by turning his face to the window and gazed out. My crying got softer and softer, gradually becoming like a little monk chanting Buddhist scriptures.

When I felt a little tired and sleepy, a noodle salesman passed by with a cart. My father hastily searched his pockets seeking every single coin, he put all the coins together in the middle of his left hand counting them twice by the first finger of his right hand. In total he had thirty-six fen RMB (about five US cents. I could be wrong. I was after all no more than six years old). His expression suddenly changed to what seemed to be a little pleasantly excited.

He called the noodle vendor with a rather positive tone. Father counted the coins again in front of the salesman and carefully handed them to him. As soon he took a bowl of noodles from the salesman he slurped the soup, loudly, I suppose partly because he was afraid I would spill the soup if it were too full. He then passed the bowl to me very carefully.

I nipped the noodles one by one by means of chopsticks, feeding them into my mouth. My father again turned his face toward the window. I looked at him and felt the blue veins on his neck appeared somewhat like blasted tree roots. I tried to observe his facial expression by looking at the window reflection. My father seemed to have noticed my intention; purposely he blew some hot air on the window glass. Instantly my father's face became obscured.

I squeezed the noodles and chewed them very slowly, deliberately making as much noise as I could, attempting to draw his attention. In fact, I was chewing my father's thoughts more than the noodles. Nevertheless, from the beginning to the end, he showed no response. Finally, I felt rather full. Though my stomach was filled, I quickly ate whatever else my chopsticks could catch in the bowl and then handed it over to my father. This time he responded right away. He took the bowl and poured what was left into his mouth at once.

When we arrived at Changsha (the capital of Hunan province) and got home, (when I say "*home*" it was actually one of Father's office rooms) the first person and also the only person I met, was a boy who looked only a little bigger than me. Father said something to the boy I could not understand then he turned to me telling me that that boy was my elder brother. Our father left us alone soon after this brief introduction and went to work. The next time I saw Father again was quite some months later.

My Brother DanXin Took Me To Meet Mom

My elder brother DanXin is only a year and half older than me. However, at that time his status seemed to be a generation higher, especially every time I saw the room key hanging around his neck. You see, being a seven-year-old boy, he was literally the "_key-man_" of our home.

What about other members of the family, my mother, and other brothers? Only a few minutes after I had been home, my elder brother DanXin, told me that it was time to go see our mother and younger brother at a hospital.

We went out. He had an aluminum lunch-box in his left hand and me in his right. Being a country boy's first time in a big city, I grasped his hand tightly enough to cause pain.

Endlessly we walked and walked. I couldn't remember having ever walked so long a distance. DanXin was constantly switching hands between the lunch-box and me. I wasn't aware it was I causing his hands pain, but instead thought the lunch-box was too heavy. I suggested that I could help him with the lunch-box from time to time. Honestly, I offered my help not because I felt sorry for him, but because I felt the lunch-box somehow symbolized a sort of privilege, and partly I thought taking the lunch-box might be kind of fun.

After he refused me, I tightened my hand even harder forcing him to change hands. I caught a chance and tried to seize the lunch-box by force. Undoubtedly he strove to avoid me. Back and forth a couple of times resulted in the lunch-box dropping out of his hand. Noodles were pouring out from the lunch-box onto the ground. With no time for him to show his anger to me, he quickly crouched down trying to get the noodles back into the lunch-box.

At exactly that moment, a man dashed to the spot where the noodles fell, and soon more men were down too, on the ground, like dogs! Soon that portion of the earth was licked clean once, twice and more times.

The scene shocked my vexed brother causing him burst out crying. It was his crying that shortened the distance between my brother and I, and made me realize that my brother was, like me, no more than a boy.

He picked up the empty lunch-box and ran away in despair. I didn't believe he would really leave me alone in the middle of nowhere; at least I did not _want_ to believe. Therefore, instead of following him I stood still, until the view of his back disappeared in the distance, then I started to worry. I hastily chased him. When I saw him on a corner waiting for me, I relaxed, pretending not to see him and walked my unnaturally slow steps like a Beijing Opera actor, as if nothing had happened.

When we finally arrived at the hospital, my brother's face was jammed again with new snivels and tears. My mother, a pretty woman with golden color framed glasses on her nose, looked quite elegant.

When my brother narrated the lunch-box adventure I hid myself behind him. My mother appeared not to pay much attention to my existence (but I knew she anxiously wanted to see what I looked like), putting all her attention toward a pile of bones, bones that were wrapped by a sheet of human skin in her arms. That *thing* was my youngest brother.

The only reason I could think why Mother showed little affection to me was that I had destroyed her lunch-box. There might be some other reasons, for taking the bait of The Party's call to have four children for instance? Anyway, if there WERE other reasons, they must be reasons beyond the comprehension of a six-year-old boy.

I remember that I *could* understand my mother's language. She didn't ask me to call her "Mom". Instead, she pushed me to call DanXin "Gege" (elder brother). Being shy perhaps, I refused. DanXin took out a small toy frog from his pocket, saying he would only let me play with it if I call him "Gege". But my objective was to play with the lovely toy frog without calling him "Gege". Just like all other international affairs, when negotiations get nowhere, the war begins. That was the first of many fights between DanXin and me.

After we pushed each other back and forth a couple of times I felt I was likely going to lose. I turned my eyes to Mother, hoping to get some kind of support but Mother was busy with my little brother's diaper and acted as if we boys did not exist. Finally I lost the battle (as I did all other battles later). I was shamed into anger. I called Chinese national names. "F u c k your mother!"

I wondered why was it so funny that I said "F u c k your mother" to my brother? Everyone, regardless if they were doctors, nurses or patients, all burst into laughter. That hit my mother at last. She immediately showed her attention to me by smacking my face, both sides. That action of hers did not correspond with her urbanely golden color framed glasses, indeed not at all. And yet to me, I had finally caught her attention, which was a kind of victory.

My face revealed a little smile with the tears. But that facial expression lasted only a very short moment, because I instantly decided to utilize my usual game, I "Wa...!" hit my bottom to the ground, and as loudly as I could shouted, "Aunt! Aunt!" until my bottom felt ice cold, my hundreds of miles away aunt certainly did not show up. Going through that experience I began to be aware, that unlike my other family with my grandparents, in this family, I was by no means the center of attention.

Fortunately, DanXin was, after all, a good hearted boy. He threw the toy frog in front of me, which gave me the perfect excuse to get my bottom away from that ice-cold ground, compared, this was much more important than playing with the toy frog.

To hit both sides of my face was the present my mother gave to me the first time we met after being apart for four years. But thinking twice, what else could she give me, a bar of milk chocolate, after I jeopardized her lunch and called out dirty names embarrassing her in front of so many?

Introduction Of My Parents

Now, allow me to give a very brief introduction of my parents. My mother was born in 1922, the same year as the establishment of the Chinese Communist Party. She was from a poor family and lost both parents at a very young age. Nevertheless, she had a very strong will to be an educated woman and somehow managed to reach high school (that was rather rare at the time in China). Influenced by communist ideology during her high school years, she took part in some underground revolutionary activities.

My father, on the other hand, had a much different story. His father (my grandpa) was a medical doctor. After receiving his education in Japan, Grandpa came back to his hometown and established his own private hospital. Additionally, he inherited some land so that he was well off enough.

Being the first son, my father was spoiled. He had a considerably good education beginning with private school all the way up to university, studying English literature. It was during the second year of his university life that his head was filled with Shakespeare. By chance, he met my mother at a school party. That meeting changed his life.

I have always wondered if it was really my mother's revolutionary enthusiasm or her ardors as a pretty girl that aroused him. Whatever! Unbelievably, he gave up his university education, cut all ties with his family and followed his girlfriend (who later became my mother) to join the communist revolution.

After the liberation, my parents, as intelligentsia class, became a small portion of the new government. They both worked for the Hunan Provincial Government. Since the day they walked into their office they were classified as those who *"could be used but never trusted by the Party"*. My father soon became a Communist Party member, while my mother never managed to get herself into the Party, I think mainly due to her "too-straightforward" personality and bad temper.

In response to the Party's call to, *"have as many children as possible for the use of war"* they got married and produced four sons: my elder brother DanXin, me (DanJiu later adapted to Daniel by my American English teacher), my younger brother DanPi and the youngest brother DanHen. (DanHen was the one being treated in the hospital as I wrote above) I was sent to my father's hometown before I reached age two, and my younger brother DanPi was sent to my mother's hometown not long after he was born. (For some difficult-to-explain reasons, this book avoids talking about my younger brother DanPi).

My Younger Brother DanHen's Miracle

1960 was the worst year of China's so-called, *"Three Years of Natural Disaster"*. People gone from hunger or hunger related reasons became a part of everyday life. We were the lucky ones as our parents worked for the government; regularly we received carrots, white potatoes and sweet potatoes, etc. as a result.

Unlike many other families, the biggest problem for our family was not a daily struggle between life and death, but my youngest brother's health issues. He suffered from bad dysentery a few months after he was born. Several times, Mother was informed by the hospital that the little boy had very small chance. All other kids in the same sickroom suffering from the same killer didn't make it but my mother refused to give up.

Every day she held the pile of bones, persistently hoping for a miracle and a miracle did happen! One day, my brother DanHen smiled. That earned the hospital a big celebration. Combined with a letter of congratulations, my mother received a very expensive bill of three hundred renminbi (maybe one hundred USD at that time). Seeing as the monthly salary in China was around thirty RMB, paying back the three hundred renminbi debt was a heavy burden pressed on our family for quite some years to come.

My First Days In Changsha Were Among The Loneliest Days In My Life.

As I mentioned before, after Father took me back from his hometown, he disappeared from us for several months. As one of the, *"could be used but never trusted"* Party members, he was constantly sent to the countryside from one place to another to carry out the Party's endless political campaigns.

Neither was Mother ever at home since she had to be in the hospital twenty-four hours, full time, nursing my sick brother. The result was my seven-year-old brother DanXin, being totally in charge at home.

But even DanXin was unable to look after me as he had his own school to go to.

In the very first days, DanXin locked me up, alone, at home during his school hours. Perhaps I stole too much food to eat; he eventually had to lock me out! Once free, all day I spent my time using my fingers to dig in the ground where sweet potatoes used to grow, together with other hungry kids. The best sweet potato roots we could possibly gain were those as thick as half a small finger.

One day I had to quit digging as I felt an extreme pain in my stomach. What I really needed was to lie down on a bed, yet I had to sit outside of our home for hours yet, waiting for DanXin to open the door.

When DanXin came back from school and saw my mouth was full of mud, again, he changed his policy on me, this time taking me with him during his school hours. I played on the school sports ground while DanXin had his classes. I must have made quite a hell of a noise as some troubled teachers suggested enrolling me as a pupil though I was under age. The awkward thing was when DanXin took me to the enrollment office, neither of us knew how to write our father's name. After everything, DanXin managed to get me into the school. Being six and a half, I became an elementary pupil.

Above are my earliest memories of my family.

To end this opening chapter, I would like to mention my feelings towards DanXin. Though his existence to me was almost the paterfamilias, and also in spite of the fact that we were getting closer and closer, I was still not totally willing to admit he was older than me, at least not on the surface. That is, until the later, "*cigarette ends incident*" happened, then things started to change.

2: A Few, Wish-To-Forget, Unforgettable Experiences

Every single family is a miniature of a society, and almost all families have at least one reactionary. I was born the reactionary in our family. The following are examples.

Cigarette Ends Conflict

The *"cigarette ends incident"* happened during the end of my first elementary school year, 1961.

The distance between where I lived and the school, was about three kilometers. It took a seven-year-old child more than thirty minutes to walk. When I say "thirty minutes" that only meant in the morning on my way to the school. But in the afternoon, from school back home could take me hours. The reason being, I wanted to pick up cigarette ends to meet the need of my father. (My father was a heavy smoker and, for a period of time, back home from countryside errands.)

When I say, "pick up cigarette ends" it was not in all cases that I simply picked them up from the ground. Instead, I would follow a smoker, sometimes for quite a distance, wait until they finished their smoking, and then pick up what was left, if there *was* any left.

Back home from school, the first thing for DanXin and me to do was put our booty on the table. I always wanted to compare his with mine, to see who the winner was. The pity was that he seemed not so enthusiastic in such competition. "OK, you're the winner again" was what he said most of the time. That very much weakened my feeling of satisfaction. Next, we would separate tobacco from papers and mix the tobacco together before

12

handing it over to our father.

Father put the "second mouth" tobacco in a frying pan infusing a little alcohol and then heating it up for a few seconds, for the purpose of disinfection I suppose. Then, the loose tobacco was ready for my father to roll his own speaking trumpet shaped cigarette.

One day, I invited a classmate to do the "pick-up" together with me. Although older than me he looked younger as he was smaller. Our deal was to put our pick-ups together and split it 50/50 in the end. That day business was unusually bad. I put the blame on him and broke the deal by saying I could only give him thirty percent. He disagreed. I ran away. He chased me tightly all the way to where I lived.

My brother DanXin appeared by chance. After listening to his complaint of my wrongdoing, through tears and snivels, DanXin gave all the cigarette ends that he had collected during the whole day, to my classmate! In addition, DanXin walked him back for about ten meters comforting him by promising, "I will report my brother's wrongdoing to our parents."

While I was thinking what my brother did was extremely stupid, especially towards such a small fellow, something unexpected happened. My classmate turned his head, staring at me. As soon as our eyes met he threw a cigarette end on the ground. I pounced on it like a tiger. He walked some distance and threw another. Again, I dashed up. Again and again it repeated. Half an hour passed and we weren't far from where he lived. Then he laughed with victorious satisfaction and poured everything he had left in his hands on the ground!

Though I was exhausted when I got home, I showed off my achievement to DanXin with excitement. I thought I deserved praise, yet DanXin made no comment. Later he told me coldly, "Your classmate's father does not smoke, not at all." I was woodened with no words, only second thoughts that I should not have taken advantage of a smaller classmate in the first place.

In the evening, DanXin kept his promise to report my wrongdoing to our parents. As a result they doubled my housework as punishment. I was very badly affected, and decided to quit the pick-up business forever. I imagined Father running at his nose caused by lack of smoking, I could not help laughing. Somehow I had my moment!

In fact, what I really should be proud of were those speeches written by my father for some important provincial leaders. Speeches such as, *"The situation of our country is not only good, but also getting better and better!"*, for sure derived from my picked-up cigarette ends, at least a part of them.

My Red Rain Shoes

It was some days before the Chinese New Year. 1961 was before global warming; everywhere in Changsha was covered by snow and ice. The temperature was below zero, even inside. Therefore the outside temperature I dare not remember. In spite of that bloody cold, everyday my brother DanXin still walked with me all the way to the school.

Walking was bad. But the worst part was the pair of old rubber rain shoes I had. Because the shoes were without insoles, my mother put a little haulm inside instead. Also because I possessed no socks, my father found two rags to wrap my feet. Again, because the shoes were too old and a little too small for me, I had to fit my feet in by force. This caused one of my dear old shoes to open its mouth like a dead fish.

Counting the days, the Chinese New Year finally drew near. I bowed to my mother with my big toe. Immediately Mother replied without taking a good look at my polite toe, "I know, I know, I'll do something before the Chinese New Year."

At last, the day before New Year came and Mother handed me a pair of red rubber rain shoes when I got up in the morning. I threw myself on them with great joy and happiness! But when I held the shoes in my hands, I felt they were not new.

After a second look, to my great disappointment, they were the same, broken shoes I had worn for years. Why did they look new at first glance? Because a layer of bicycle inner tube had been glued onto them. A romantic description would be, "my black shoes were wrapped by a red coat."

Nevertheless, still I couldn't help but feel excited. I put the shoes on at once and ran out of the house. Outside, the ground was frozen. When I found a place with comparatively thin ice, I hit my heel on the ice to break it. Then, very bravely I trampled my right foot completely submerging it under the water with the satisfactory thought, "Water, water, I'm no longer afraid of you anymore from now on!" Yet, to my enormous despair, the water seeped into my shoe, as always. Pathetic, isn't it?

I limped back home. Mother tweaked my painless frozen ear, "Among the four brothers, only your shoes could I afford to repair this time of the year! How could you step into dirty water with such a precious pair of rain shoes? You deserve no valuable things. From now on, you go out with your bare feet!"

At the same time, Mother removed my red shoes. She did it very gently, on the shoes, but not my foot and tried to dry the wet one carefully by putting it at a not-too-far, not-too-near proximity to the coal stove, adjusting the distance back and forth a couple of times, leaving my foot wet.

The whole day, my brothers were in and out seeing friends and bringing friends back to the house frequently, but poor *me* had to stay in bed just to keep my feet warm, although sometimes I did get up and jump with one shoe, inside of course.

The New Year Eve's family dinner (just like Christmas dinner for westerners) used to be and still is the most important event among the Chinese. It is our tradition to get everyone in the family to sit together around the dinner table on that specific day at that particular moment. In Chinese it is called "*Tuan yuan Fan*" meaning "Reunion Meal".

No matter how horrible the poverty, our stomachs deserved to be fed fully, once a year.

But that evening, Father had received an invitation to an event held by the Communist Party. The party took place at Xianjian Hotel, which was the highest building (as high as nine floors) with an elevator being built after the liberation in Hunan province. Father read the invitation proudly in front of the entire family and then announced there would be no family dinner on that evening because of this much more important party. Everybody cheered up. They all went out for the party with Father, except me.

When they were at the party eating, drinking, singing and laughing, I was hopelessly gazing at my half-dry, half-wet shoe by the stove with desolation. It was all I could do to comfort myself by fantasizing, "I'm not particularly fancy about parties. But about the elevator, when I grow up, I'm going to live in a higher building with a better elevator. Every day I shall take the elevator up and down, up and down all the time. You folks will not be welcome to visit me."

By mid-night after I got over my hunger, my people came back with full stomachs. Immediately I decided not to give them a chance to show their penitence to me. I covered my head with a quilt, pretending to be in a deep sleep. Maybe my performing grunt was better than reality, everybody seemed to be amused. Father deterred their laughing; spoke with a loud-enough-low voice, "Don't wake him up." Soon after that I heard the sound of opening a package. Father's voice again, "Look at this, the Party leader gave it to our family!"

"Rice-cake! My goodness! We haven't had it for a long time. Thank the great Party!" my mother's voice said with excitement and gratitude.

"We'll only have a little, just to get the taste for now, and leave the rest for tomorrow." Father ordered.

Next I heard the chewing sounds of my brothers.

"How about DanJiu (me)?" Mother reminded. "He should wake up if he would like to join us." Father teased.

A piece of cake to a seven-year-old boy, what a cruel temptation! Suddenly I felt my mouth full of hands (an expression meaning, "so eager to eat") extending to take the cake. From the bottom of my stomach, I would like very much to join them. In one word "eat, eat". I really wanted to eat, but what about my face, my pride, my self-respect? Yes, I stood the lure of the piece of cake by swallowing my constantly flowing sour slobbers.

Until everybody went to bed and the room was dark, my elder brother DanXin poured a bit of rice-cake into my mouth. The wonderful taste kept me awake the whole night.

Next morning, though my shoe was dry, I volunteered to be home alone again. When the whole family was out to do New Year's greeting to our neighbors door by door, I called one of my die-hard pals to come to my home. Together we broke the lock of the only food box our family had, and shared all the rice-cake left in it.

Tong Hao, That Changed The Destiny Of Our Family

Tong hao, chrysanthemum greens in English, is a kind of edible wild plant (similar to grass). Apart from picking up cigarette ends for our father, DanXin and I spent much time every day looking for tong hao. The tool that we used to cut tong hao was our father's old shaving blade.

One day, DanXin and I went to the usual place searching for tong hao among all the other wild grasses. While I was busy working, our neighbor Wang-Pang, a fat boy three years older than DanXin, came over to me. (His father was Provincial Minister Wang, my father's superior. Precisely, my father was his father's secretary.) He said to me, "Jiu boy, work harder. But when you finish, you must give me half of what you get from this area." I asked him why? He explained to me that yesterday he declared ownership of the tong hao in this area by putting a wooden sign here. Therefore, anyone who picks tong hao from this entire area ought to hand half to him.

What he had said was completely against the communist ideology that his father fought for, but I was too young to reason this. All that I could do was to walk away. Of course, he wouldn't let me. The fight occurred. Wang-Pang was not only four or five years older than me, but also much larger. Therefore, in no way could I be his rival. Soon he was riding on me.

I called for help by shouting, "DanXin, Gege!" (In that period of time I would call DanXin as "Gege (elder brother)" only when in a desperate situation and needing his help.)

DanXin rushed over to us, trying his best to drag me out from Wang-Pang's arms. Beyond my expectations, Wang-Pang gave me up; instead replacing me with DanXin as his horse, punching my brother's face again and again! At the same time he yelled at me, "How dare you call your brother! Call your brother for what, for being beaten?" The situation made me crazy. I decided to fight with him, to the death! I dashed up and bit his arm like a wild dog! Wang-Pang overcame the pain, punching me down. Now DanXin and I were BOTH under him!

Someone must have told our father what was happening down there. Father ran to us hastily. He pulled both of his sons out from under the fat boy (meanwhile DanXin started to cry. Unthinkably, Wang-Pang was not afraid of an adult, not a bit; on the contrary, he became MORE overbearing! He chased us all over in order to continue punching us! Our father could only use his body as a shield to prevent his sons from being beaten.

Meanwhile, our mother had arrived. When she saw such a little fat boy daring to attack three men of hers, she tweaked the boy by the back of his collar and lifted him up into the air, "How overbearing you are! Let's go see your mother." Suddenly, Wang-Pang, "Wa…" burst out crying as loudly as he could.

Finally I felt I was in safe hands; felt the power of Mother's backing. Taking advantage, I ran away from Father towards Wang-Pang, "f u c k your mother. You're a son of bitch."

Immediately, Mother rewarded me with a big blow to my head.

At exactly that moment, Wang-Pang's mother appeared. She must also have heard my words, "son of bitch". She dragged her son back home with snivels and tears.

The same day at dinner hour, Mother was working overtime. I went and washed the tong hao I collected that day in a public water place (at that time most Chinese homes were without private water supply). After I cleaned up the tong hao, I went back home. I saw minister Wang (Wang-Pang's father) was sitting on the only chair with a back in our home. His right leg crossed over his left, toes pointing to the ceiling. Watching me walk in, Wang did not stop playing with a box of cigarettes in his hand.

My father was sitting on a small wooden bench looking up at his boss (like a, a… if he were not my father, I would have described him as looking like a Pekinese dog).

Minister Wang must have been quite disappointed when he saw I was not so frightened. He looked at me again. Very slowly he said, "Jiu boy, how dare you to call your fat brother (his son) names. If your fat brother is a 'son of bitch', what am I? Bitch?"

I looked at him asquint and did not say he was not a bitch nor explain to him that "bitch" is a she-dog, therefore he was not qualified.

Wang continued, "Suppose I'm a bitch, what would that make your daddy? Bitch secretary?! Your mom would be bitch secretary's wife. And you all would be sons of bitch secretary."

Not knowing what to say, my father's smiling face appeared uglier than if he were crying.

Then Wang turned his face to Father, talking with a rather official tone, like he always did at the office, "This, this, *You*, not only the children, you should also criticize your wife, you, should not be afraid of wife, and, and, this, this, kids quarrel, adult get involved, what is that? This, this…"

Father clapped his hand with adulation, "Today I discover that you, respectable Minister Wang, can give considerably good speeches without my manuscripts."

"Well, well…" Wang was obviously very pleased. He took out two cigarettes from the cigar-boxes, clipped one between his lips, and flipped one towards my father.

Father failed to catch the cigarette from his boss and the cigarette rolled under a table.

Father hurried down under the table, picked up the cigarette, blew dust once, twice, and handed it back to Wang, "This is not strong enough. It would be a waste for me to have it."

Wang took the cigarette without hesitation and put it back into the box, "That's right, that's right, to save every single coin, for the sake of the war and revolution."

I was glad that Father did not take his cigarette, a sugar coated bomb.

Then, Wang turned his tone to be much more personal, slowly he said to my father, "This, this, I mean the one, your sister-in-law (Wang's wife) who is in charge at home, is still angry at me. She is from the North, not well educated, ill tempered, nothing I could do. Perhaps, may be, we could invite comrade Xiwan (my mother) to my home, give a self-criticism, that could calm her anger. The affair would be over. Otherwise, she is very stubborn, and the complaining would be endless with me. Hey, after all, kids quarrel, no big deal."

My father echoed, "Right, absolutely right, kids quarrel, no big deal." At the same time Father must be thinking that, "your wife stubborn one inch, my wife stubborn one meter. If my wife could make a self-criticism to your wife, she wouldn't have lifted your son up in first place."

All the while in my mind I was laughing, laughing at this pair of old fellows afraid of wives, one worse than the other.

Hence, Father must come up with an idea, an idea of losing minor to save major. He stood up from the little bench, turned to me and ordered, "Bring the bunch of tong hao to Uncle Wang's home and give it to Aunt. Don't forget to apologize."

By then I was still grieving. Father's unbelievable order was like pouring hot oil on my burning heart. It is human nature (animal nature too) to protect one's own children. While my father not only spoke no justice; he actually stood by the enemy! I jumped up to the bench to make myself taller, "Why should I apologize? Why should I give my tong hao to them? What are they? Landlord? Collecting rent?"

Wang must have been quite shocked. He, slapped his hand on his leg, "Pa!", stood up, stared at my father, "You see, you see, such a son you have, scolded me, an old revolutionary, as 'landlord'! This, this, lack of domestic education. Let's forget it old Chen, I did not come here. We'll see each other in the office tomorrow." Wang said with despair walking toward the door.

Father quickly followed him. On the way he slapped my face loudly and shouted at me, "How dare you talk back. Go, hurry up!"

I knew, though Father looked terrible, if it were not to save face as minister's secretary, he would probably rather kneel down to me.

I was not born as a patient man in nature. My father's unusual action pushed me to the limit! To step higher I jumped up to the table, like a flood breaking a reservoir, I roared with fury, "You are working for what? *Bread winner*, ha? Can't give us enough to eat, in addition force me to give the wild grass picked up by my own hands to others!"

I got off the table and placed myself before Father, "Beating your child to please your landlord! What kind of a father are you? Beat me! Beat me again and you better beat me to death! I'm not afraid of death! Having a father like you, I would be starving to death anyway... You, no more than a running dog slave!"

Father woodened.

Wang was outraged. He trembled, walking to the door. Repeatedly, "Anti anti, rebel..." he opened the door.

Father caught the last chance, picked up a piece of bamboo and lashed my bottom. I moved my bottom quickly enough to avoid being beaten. The piece of bamboo hit my heel; a small piece of flesh was sliced off, not totally but connected to my foot with a piece of skin.

That stopped Wang from going out. He had a look at me, half stunned.

Father kept his eyes on his boss, raised up the piece of bamboo towards me again. He stopped there, as if waiting for the order from his boss. Wang quickly responded by holding Father's hand, "Stop, old Chen..."

At that very moment, DanXin got up from bed with all the pain and injuries all over his body, took the bunch of tong hao and walked resolutely, straight to Wang's home.

From that point on, our brothers had no problems with Wang-Pang for a long time.

Later, the area where we used to pick tong hao was divided, piece by piece, equally to all families. As our little bit of land had no tong hao left, Father grew some vegetables. Even this, was later forced to be shared with some other Party members.

About a year after, my mother was removed from her work position and transferred to a much lower working unit, far away from where we lived. Though there was no hard evidence that Mother's transfer was to my credit, everyone in the family knew it deep down in the bottom of their heart. In my memory, all during that period, Father's only facial expression was a tight scowl.

After the "Tong Hao Conflict", my position as the family's *apple of discord* was in unprecedented consolidation.

Now when I think about the whole situation in retrospect, I have no complaints but rather a sincere appreciation for my father's chopping a slice of flesh off my foot. If it were not for that "piece of meat" which saved Father's job, we all could have ended up dead from starvation ages ago.

My Competition With Brothers

As I mentioned before, my younger brother DanPi (the third son of our parents), was sent to Mother's hometown right after he was born, therefore in everyday life, we had only three brothers at home.

Both DanXin and DanHen had a little privilege. So did I.

Besides the house key around the neck and taking care of DanHen and me, DanXin's privilege was to receive a reward of two fen from Mother every evening. He established himself a small private treasury by means of a section of thick bamboo. Every day after he put a coin through the cut into the bamboo container, he shook it for a little while. The sour sound caused my constant toothache.

My youngest brother DanHen's privilege, was to have a bottle of milk every morning. Every time he drank the milk he made a kind of, "xu,xu" sound. That, "xu,xu" too, was as sour as DanXin's bamboo container shaking. Every day after DanHen finished his drink, I would always wish to use my own tongue to clean up his white mustache.

My privilege was simple. It was to boil DanHen's milk. The reason that I so eagerly did this was of course not for DanHen's benefit, but instead my own interest in monopolizing the surplus during the pot washing. Perhaps because of the concept of milk formed back then, no matter what brand milk I drink today, they are all too dense to me.

I always wanted to be number 1 at home. The sadness was, every time I exchanged blows with DanXin, I had to hope for my victory the next time. Though the great Chinese teaching says, "For a real man to get revenge after 10 years, is not too late." When the time finally came in which I was confident enough, I also became an adult, too embarrassed to perform such childish games.

Although I was not strong enough to beat DanXin for the time being, I always had a weaker one to fight with, my youngest brother DanHen. Besides being six years younger than I, DanHen was very weak during his childhood caused by his illness, therefore to conquer him I needed only a little finger. However, the pity was that there was a powerful mountain backing that little monkey! The mountain was our mother.

Every time I laid a finger on him, he would fall apart on the ground crying, huckstering his bones until our mother came back from work.

Inescapably, I would be pressed by the mountain for quite some time. The result being, that to lay a finger on DanHen was far worse than to fight and lose against DanXin.

Where there is oppression, there must be resistance. I did not want to believe that I could only be clamped between, sandwiched. Thus I decided to win the battle with my brothers and to be number one at home by some means other than physical fighting.

First of all, I wanted to be taller than DanXin. For that purpose I often hung myself from a horizontal bar as long as I was able. I sometimes also tied my feet to one bedside and used my hands to pull the other, endeavoring to stretch myself longer like a twisted dough-strip before being put into an oil pan

I remember it was during second grade, DanXin brought back a horizontal bamboo flute from school. Immediately, I borrowed a vertical bamboo flute from a friend that was longer than DanXin's.

Sometime later, DanXin brought an Erhu (a two stringed Chinese musical instrument) home; I looked everywhere until I found myself a Sanxian (a three stringed Chinese musical instrument) to compete with him. The extra string made my victorious feeling last quite a while.

When I saw DanXin was learning how to ride a bicycle on a field, I soon appeared on the same spot with a tri-cycle that I borrowed from a little kid, with a bit of reluctance on his part. I waved at my brother, beaming with pride, "What do you think? Even by riding, mine is one wheel more than yours!"

Finally, one day DanXin had a terrible fever. Even my fever, I wanted to be higher than his! I took the thermometer and put it into a glass of boiled water. When Mother came over, I quickly put the thermometer into my mouth and lay down on a bed. After examining the thermometer, Mother said I must be sent to a hospital at once, not exactly inside the hospital, but somewhere behind the hospital, the morgue behind the hospital to be precise!

All those days I had been thinking of doing something big, earth shattering if possible, for that would make me very special among my family members, make DanXin call *me* "elder brother", make my father look at *me* with a respectable eye.

That's right, "RESPECT" was what I was longing for.

3: THE CULTURAL REVOLUTION

Home Moving

From six up to ten years old I lived with our family at Father's working unit. Though most of the time he was not home as I mentioned in chapter one, my father, as one of the 'could be used but never trusted' Party members, was constantly sent to the countryside from place to place to carry out the Party's endless political campaigns.

My little head was filled with all the communist jargon. Jargon such as, "*Four Liquidating*", the "*Stay at One Spot*", the "*Socialist Education Movement*", the "*Three Anti's Five Anti's*", the "*Anti Right Wing*" the "*May 7 Cadre's School*" etc, etc. Anyway, if I list all the Chinese Communist Party's political movements, I can't say that my father had contributed to every single one of them, but most of them for sure.

As I also wrote in chapter two, not long after the "Tong Hao" instance, my mother was removed from her working position and transferred to a much lower working unit located at the edge of Changsha city, far away from where we lived.

For saving money, everyday Mother woke up with the chickens to go to her work place at the crack of dawn, by foot. The distance even today, takes me, a strong man, over an hour. Coming back from work she was also walking in the dark. I can still clearly recall the scene, every evening, three hungry brothers sitting together in darkness, anxiously awaiting the sound of our mother's footsteps.

Father was away from home; Mother had to work; DanXin and I went to school; the only person left home was our youngest brother DanHen. Actually the youngest and weakest was not exactly "left" home, but locked up at home, the same as DanXin had done to me during my first days in Changsha.

One day I had a fight with a classmate at school. DanXin had to accompany me while I stayed at school over time. He apologized to my classmate in our parents' stead. Meanwhile, our four-year-old little brother must have been in extreme hunger, he poured an entire bottle of oil and a bag of green lentils into a pan and put the pan on the stove. Fortunately, there was no fire in the stove, otherwise that could have resulted in a bloody tearing tragedy.

Through all these years DanHen's *"Frying Oil Bean"* as a butt has been one of our families standing jokes. It was also from then that DanHen decided to become a cook when he grew up so that he would never suffer from starvation again. Forty years later, he did become a cook at a Chinese restaurant, in London.

The, "Frying Oil Bean Incident" forced Mother to choose to move the entire family from the provincial government fence, to her countryside-work place, a place called Panjiaping.

1964, we moved to a temporary one-story house at Mother's workplace. The house consisted of eight units. That means eight households shared the building. Each unit of the house had a front and back room; the third room was a kitchen. Two households shared the same back door, that is to say there were eight front doors in the building, but only four back doors. Because the building was meant to be temporary, nothing had been done to the ground, no cement, no wood floor, no nothing. That natural fertile soil "floor" consequently resulted in grass growing inside our home, under the bed for instance. We lived in that temporary one-storied building, "temporarily" for eight years, until I became an adult and went out to make my own living. For this reason, quite a portion of my following stories take place on this scene.

An Ugly Phoenix Dropped Into A Chicken Nest

I said goodbye to my first elementary school , "Da Tong Wan Xiao" which was supposed to be the best elementary school in the city and transferred to fourth grade at the "New River School", absolutely among the worst in the city.

During my years in "Da Tong Wan Xiao" I had always been one of the troublesome pupils in class. When I left, there were only four in the class who were not members of the Youth Pioneers , and I occupied twenty-five percent. At that time, I had a lack of self-questioning ability, therefore would only put the blame on Father for being without any official title, but rather a secretary. For the atmosphere at that school was, if someone's father possessed no color-faded old army uniform, it equaled shame.

On the other hand, things changed dramatically once I moved to Panjiaping. Among all those countryside boys, I was just like an ugly phoenix dropped into a chicken's nest, suddenly becoming the favorite pupil of the whole school. I was accepted to be an Advanced Youth Team member within my first week. Next, I was chosen to be the leader of the class! And soon after that, I was appointed to play a major role in a school drama! Later I was selected to be a member of various sports teams, such as dash, ping-pong, and swimming. As one of the representatives of the school swim team I was even sent to the Provincial Sport School to be trained. I also took part in a few sporting events. Yet the results were all disappointing. For I had always been number one, counting from the back.

All these efforts and failures meant little to me, for what I really wanted, was not to be special at school among my classmates, but to be special at home, among my brothers.

My Neighbor Sister Hu MeiMei

Hu MeiMei was our next, front door neighbor. Our two families shared the kitchen and the back door. She had an elder brother from the same mother and a younger sister from her step-mother. Her own mother passed away while giving birth to her. For that, she was blamed by her father, therefore, no need to explain more about her position in the family. She was one or two years younger than I. As we were both the middle child in our families, we met often in the kitchen which is very easy to understand.

MeiMei was an ordinary looking girl, a sweet girl is more accurate than a beautiful girl. My memories of her started when our family moved from Father's working unit to Mother's unit. The very first day, it was MeiMei who showed me how to get to school. Of course we did not walk shoulder to shoulder, but with her about five meters in front as I followed. Though we shared the same kitchen, we had no significant contact at that time, until one year later when I was about eleven years old, MeiMei was nine or ten, and we went to take our neighbor's banana.

The story goes like this. Not far away from where we lived, there was a banana tree which was planted by one of our neighbors. In order to protect the bananas from being stolen, the neighbor named Qi, made a fence surrounding the tree. We passed by the tree from time to time, and saw the bananas grow from tiny to small and then bigger and bigger.

One day we saw a small banana had been bitten by a bird and was almost falling off the tree. We couldn't help but want to get hold of the banana and try the taste. We got ourselves inside the banana tree fence with no difficulty, but how to get to it remained a problem as the tree was too high for us to reach.

I had to let MeiMei ride on my shoulders to reach the banana. As soon

24

as she got the almost falling banana, the owner of the banana tree, Qi, showed up. We got out of the fence and ran away as fast as we could, but MeiMei was caught by Qi. I had to throw the half dead banana toward them.

Qi was so angry that he picked up the green, hard banana and tried to force it into MeiMei's mouth! MeiMei desperately tried to avoid the banana being squeezed into her mouth by keeping her mouth closed and lowering her head. This resulted in the banana hurting her nose.

Seeing this, I had to come forward and face Qi to claim the guilt. I felt very sorry for MeiMei's nose being hurt. That was the beginning of our teamwork, our friendship started from there.

It was about a week later, we met Qi's wife. She gave us a yellow banana, and told us, "To eat a banana, you have to wait until it is ripe, then peel the skin off and eat it bite by bite." I think that was MeiMei's first banana ever, I guess.

The second instance of teamwork brought us even closer. That happened when the Chinese Cultural Revolution started. I will tell the story in the next episode.

The Cultural Revolution Begins (Bodhisattvas On Fire)

In 1966, as soon as I reached the grade six, our great leader Chairman Mao, launched the Historically Unprecedented, Cultural Revolution.

Everyone who experienced the Cultural Revolution knows the movement began with, *"Breaking Four Olds"* (old thoughts; old culture; old tradition; old habits). Our school was situated in part of an old nunnery, a nunnery of historical significance.

One day, when the whole class was criticizing our teacher, we overheard someone shouting, "Everybody put on action! Let's burn all the bodhisattvas in the temple!" Hence, people moved out many bodhisattvas, big ones, small ones, heaping them in front of the temple then pouring asphalt on them. One match and immediately a thick smoke, rolling with fire twisted into the sky. The one who lit the fire was a man we called Uncle Huang.

As an eleven-year-old boy I didn't know what to be afraid of, and so went to see the crowd for fun with a neighbor about ten years my elder. He showed off his knowledge by telling me, "This is just like before liberation when the foreign devils burned our Circle Brilliant Garden in Beijing." Now I know, just one match, and one match only, with madness, hundreds of years of heritage was burned.

Meanwhile, a few women's voices (the nuns) shrieked, "My Bodhisattva, my Bodhisattva!" as they rushed into the fire.

What followed was chaos. I was too small to see anything behind all the adults, only hearing the comments, "Good miserable God! Being burned like that…"

Amidst the chaos, I happened to see a very tiny Buddha dropped on the ground. To me it was just a toy, a doll, like Barbie dolls in other countries. I picked it up and quickly hid it in my school bag.

On our way home, we happened to walk close to Uncle Huang and a couple of his colleagues.

One man said, "All these kinds of people are blocks to the great revolution, therefore we should not save them. Let them burn to death. As our great leader Chairman Mao taught us, 'There is revolution, there must be sacrifices'."

Immediately after the man, a woman commented, "That's right, that's right. Look at them, being burned like ghosts! How can they go on living? Better to let them be dead without pain than be alive with endless suffering. Ai, Bloody miserable!"

The opinion of Uncle Huang was however wiser, "Let them die? That would be too easy for them. Can't die and can't live. Not human, not ghost. Let them be worse than not to exist. This would be the best retribution and what they should get."

Back home, I wanted to give the little Buddha to MeiMei as a doll but MeiMei was not at home. Instead, I placed it on their side of the kitchen. I just wanted to give MeiMei a surprise, to please her.

However, at that time, to adults, Buddha's were considered to belong to the 4 olds, and to have them was absolutely unacceptable, as serious a crime as possessing drugs is in most countries today.

Next thing I knew, it was after MeiMei was badly beaten by her father. Stripped of her clothes by her step-mother, she was left alone in the kitchen almost naked, only in her underpants. It was very cold. MeiMei was in great pain and freezing. As soon as the adults went to work, I let MeiMei into our home and lie in the bed of my brother and I (I shared the bed with my brother). She was so cold and terrified. I had to hold her tight to keep her warm inside the quilt. This was how we got closer to each other.

Later, somehow, I managed to get the small Buddha back. I will tell more about this little Buddha story in later chapters.

The Death Of The Secular Bird Wang

Like everybody in China during the Cultural Revolution, I too personally encountered lots of difficult-to-comprehend events. For example, those who used to be looked down upon, suddenly became mounted on a high horse, while those highly respectable people, like Party leaders and school teachers, were suddenly down at the bottom of society! Some of them were even forced to parade around with a placard of bad names hanging on their necks.

For a period of time Father was at home, I mean staying AT HOME, not going to work in the office. The whole country was paralyzed, the Party, the government, the police... all except the army.

There were red guards everywhere. They had absolute power to do whatever they wanted, searching anyone's home for 4 olds. They could beat anyone or even kill if they regarded them as an enemy (Mao shook hands with a red guard named Song BingBing at the Tiananmen in front of Billions. That girl, a red guard, had just killed her teacher by beating the teacher to death. And the rumor has it, she is now living in the USA).

One day, Father found a piece of five-layered plywood. He cut it and made a board, drilled two holes. Trying different ropes, he picked the best one and hung the board around his neck.

"Too heavy." Father said to himself.

Then Father changed to a piece of three-layered plywood and started all over again from the beginning.

"Are you also going to parade with that?" Mother worried.

"I'm not qualified." Father smiled bitterly, "This is for my superior, Minister Wang." Next, Father wrote on the board, "Down to the capitalist-road-going Wang".

I thought Father must have also joined the rebels, taking advantage of the timing to get revenge on Wang for what he did to my mother (transferring her to a much lower working unit). Recalling the hatred of his son from the instance of the tong hao, I was actually quite excited about Father's activities.

But later I learned that Father was entrusted by Wang to make that board, as he couldn't make his own because he was handicapped. Wang was one of Mao's followers and had been shot several times during various battles. Until the day Mao announced the establishment of the New China, Wang also made an announcement, that he was a secular bird and would never die. It must have been far beyond Wang's expectation, that during his lifetime, in the country he fought for, one day, he would suddenly lose everything.

Under the circumstances, all of his family members declared the cutting of all ties with him. My father, being his faithful old secretary, was the last and only person left in the world he could turn to for help.

Wang was an optimistic person. Even under such pressure, he comforted my father by saying, "Don't worry old Chen. I'm not afraid. I've gone through everything in my life. I'm a secular bird. Remember?"

But, the secular bird's day finally came. That day, Father's working-unit held a criticizing meeting against Minister Wang. Wang was tied up and forced to kneel on the stage. People jumped up onto the stage, one after another, to make their accusations. That was an age of *"Class Above Family"*.

Wang's own son Wang-Pang, as a Red Guard member, shouted slogans together with the others to knock down his father.

More unexpectedly, Wang's wife too, jumped on the stage accusing Wang of cheating and forcing her to be his wife when she was young and innocent, working on an army propaganda team. That accusation certainly brought the meeting to a high climax.

Wang was made to wear a high paper hat and the board my father made, while escorted to the parade. Though the board was not really heavy, Wang was handicapped. Coupled with the agony, there was no way he could walk with that board all the way through by himself. So, from time to time, Father took turns replacing him, carrying the board.

After some distance, Wang was dragging his feet rather than walking. When the procession passed by a small garden pond, Wang broke loose and dashed into the pond. He had his final words, "Anti! All anti!" In front of everybody's eyes, he threw himself into the garden pond. The revolutionary sunk down to the bottom.

Wang's wife fainted on the spot, like a dead tree trunk, and dirtied her trousers with natural relief.

Wang's son Wang-Pang, was nowhere in sight, for the time being. Only Wang-Pang's younger sister was crying like hell for her daddy and mom.

My father was shocked of course. He instinctively rushed into the pond a few steps and then stopped, turned around, making every effort to conceal his emotion behind his eyeglasses. Reluctantly, he followed the ebullitions, shouting the slogan, "Knock down the capitalist-road-going Wang! Wang is guilty, guilty for ten thousand deaths!"

The political conclusion to Wang was, "Betray the motherland, betray the Party and betray the people."

It is said that from 1966 to 1976, within those ten years, around two million people died unnaturally, due to political reasons. Besides a huge number of suicides, they were killed not directly by the Communist Party, not by the government, not by any authorities, but by ordinary people themselves such as students killing teachers, civilians killing Party leaders, workers killing their work leaders, farmers killing surviving landlords and their families, the rebels and the loyalists killing each other…

Old Revolutionaries Encountering New Problems

"*Old revolutionaries encountering new problems*" was a popular expression during the beginning of the Cultural Revolution. It is a literal, vivid description of the situation. My parents were of course, among those who encountered the new problems. The biggest problem among all, was how to adopt oneself to the incomprehensible happenings.

After Wang's death, back home my parents had a heated debate. My mother was one of the most loyal. She was very angry with her husband for shouting slogans with the others to knock down Wang, especially after Wang's death.

"Not to mention he used to be your superior, how could you betray such a good comrade, an old revolutionary?" Mother asked.

I was a bit surprised by Mother's words, wondering if I should remind her who sent her to Panjiaping causing a life change for our whole family.

But Father reasoned, "Being a revolutionary, we can't let our emotions control our reason. The purpose for Chairman Mao launching the Cultural Revolution is to knock down those *'capitalist-road-going'* leaders in the Party. Wang used to be a revolutionary, he was our comrade, but today the political situation changed. He has become a capitalist-road-going leader, therefore he is no longer our comrade but an enemy. I did betray my small landlord father and follow you on the revolutionary road before, why can't I betray my capitalist-road-going superior today? This is called *'continuous revolution under the dictatorship of the proletariat'*."

Father was getting more and more excited. He recited Mao's quotation. The words were more like crying out rather than speaking out, *"What is Revolution? Revolution is not inviting someone for a meal. Revolution is riot, is a violent activity for one class to overthrow another!"*

"This, is too ruthless!" Mother cried out.

"Revolution has always been ruthless." After Father finished, he swallowed the phlegm in his mouth.

After a little pause, Mother emphasized again, "Everything is mad. White becomes black, and black becomes white."

"Exactly. This is what today we call, *'box-up'* or *'snafu'*. Everything we see is opposite, which means, whatever was good is bad and whatever was bad is good." Although Father's tone sounded positive it clearly could not cover his perplexity.

"Whatever you say, still I feel that it's all wrong." Mother's voice became weak and full of despair.

Father changed his tone to be more negotiable, "Right or wrong, let history make its conclusion. The only thing we can do right now, is to listen to our great leader Chairman Mao."

The family political debate ended. Father put the board he made for Wang on the loft, in front of Chairman Mao's quotation book and a lighter. The lighter that Father received from Wang as a private gift many years ago, the lighter that Father carried with him everywhere, every day and showed off before people from time to time.

Quite a few days after that debate, Mother not only refused to talk to Father, but also refused to have a meal with Father at the same table.

Despite being similar to most youth, I was also extremely perplexed. In addition, similar to many others, the biggest desire for me at that time was to take part in the Red Guard, so that I could wear a self-made army uniform, a red chevron on my arm and leather belt at my waist.

Unfortunately, or should I say fortunately, I was too young. There was nothing I could do. Could I rebel against my parents for that, could I?

The worst thing was my brother DanXin, only one and half years older than me, had been accepted by the Red Guard. What made me even more jealous was he, together with a few other older neighbors, visited the Revolution Holy site, Jinggangshan.

While poor little me, with no school to go to, no nothing to do, every day nested at home, cooking. If it were not that we shared the kitchen with Hu MeiMei and the fact that with her I could boast about anything I liked, I would probably have died of boredom.

Fortunately, that situation didn't last long. Finally, I found something very special, that I love and more importantly I believed could help me reach my ultimate goal of gaining the respect of my whole family, especially that of my father.

What could that be? Please find out in the next chapter.

4: THE VIOLIN THAT CHANGED MY DESTINY

Falling In Love With Violin At First Sight

No school to go to, and too young to participate in any revolutionary activities, to me those days were the most mind-numbing time in my life. But one day, a miracle happened.

A neighbor who lived on the second floor of the building next to us had a teenage visitor called Li. That handsome young man soon had a chemical reaction with my neighbor sister Lan. Every morning when sister Lan visited him, he would keep the window open and play a violin. How romantic it was! I was rather drawn to that violin sound, then, inebriated. Every morning I kept my eyes wide open, anxiously waiting for the window to be opened.

One day, Li's window opened only for a very short while and then closed without playing the violin. I couldn't help but rush up to the second floor of their building and peek inside through the keyhole.

Oh my God! Guess what I saw? I saw both brother Li and sister Lan naked, holding and rolling together on the bed! Back to my kitchen, I described vividly what I saw to Hu MeiMei and added my wise comment, "If they were cold they should not be naked, if they were hot they should not hold so tightly on to each other, they should open the window."

Hu MeiMei's face turned flush and she ran away into her room before I finished my blowing.

Later I met Hu GeGe, (Hu MeiMei's elder brother, a Red Guard) again I repeated the story, not forgetting to add my comment. Hu GeGe too, did not wait until I finished and walked away.

The next morning, a small group of Red Guards broke into Li's home.

A moment later, brother Li and sister Lan were brought out from the room, naked. Li suppressed his bird tightly with his violin, as if the bird would fly away if not held down tightly enough. Lan too, though her two big breasts were completely revealed, both front and back of her lower parts were covered by Chairman Mao's portraits. I felt those were two of the most attractive portraits of Mao's. However, if I could choose, I would rather take the violin.

From then on, I never saw brother Li again. And sister Lan couldn't find a man to marry until the Cultural Revolution ended ten years later.

By that time in China, sex was considered to be ugly, and for people to sleep together naked before marriage was a shameful crime.

Although brother Li was no longer there, every day I would look at that window, hoping the violin would sound again.

Hu MeiMei, seeing I was so obsessed with the violin, told me Li's violin was placed together with all of the other Four Olds trash, in a huge storehouse. Again and again, I begged MeiMei to ask her brother for help. MeiMei must have been annoyed to death and in the end she lied to her brother, claiming that she herself would like to see the violin. Hu GeGe took the violin secretly and ordered his sister, "Only touch it at home and never make any sound out from it."

Every day, when everyone of both our families were out, MeiMei brought the violin to the kitchen and let me play with it. I carefully took it as a fragile treasure. Although the violin had no bow, I still put it to my neck, playing with sound from my mouth, mostly Li's favorite tune, "*Jian Gege, Mo luotuo*".

One day when MeiMei went out to wash vegetables, (there was no water supply in most Chinese households, we all had to do all washing in public places) I was in such high spirits that for a moment I forgot the promise to stay inside without sound. I took the violin to the back yard and played with an empty right hand but sound from my mouth, under brother Li's window. That bold action resulted in the violin being taken away immediately, plus Hu GeGe's name being deleted from the Red Guard list.

Though in reality I had no violin, my head was filled with nothing BUT violin.

A Violin In A Shop's Glass Cabinet

One day, I happened to see a violin in a glass cabinet at Changsha May-First Cultural Goods Store. Beside the violin there was a little notice written, "*A propaganda weapon of Mao's thoughts*". I flattened my nose against the glass cabinet for a long, long time until the heat of my nose melted the glass and I got the violin. Of course that was only what I day dreamed. In reality I was scorned out of the shop.

After that, I grew a habit of running a marathon every day, from home to the shop (about 5 kilometers one way) just to take a look at the violin again, from a safe distance.

One day, the two shopkeepers were debating. The short fat man had a red chevron and the words, "Xiangjiang Wind & Thunder" (one of the extreme rebel organizations) on his arm. While the slim, tall lady had a red chevron on her arm and the words, *The Protector of Mao's thoughts*" (one of the loyalists). The debate went so rigorously that they didn't notice me at all as I approached the violin. Again, I flattened my nose.

This time, I even checked the price, twenty-eight RMB, about seven USD at that time, and half the monthly salary of my daddy or mom. I stood there for a long time, in fact as long as I could, fantasizing how wonderful it would be if I had had twenty-eight RMB. After some time, I started to believe that I did have twenty-eight RMB! To avoid their eyes, I faced them and requested with all my courage, "Please, that violin, pass it to me. Let me take a closer look."

The lady stood up from her chair and opened the glass cabinet without looking at me. But the man recognized me right away and roared at me, "Valuable goods, no show to kids!"

My feelings were hurt, but like a civilian facing a Chinese policeman, there was nothing I could do, except comfort myself, "Big deal! Wait till my father comes back…"

That rebel didn't let me finish my self-soothing-talk, chasing me with a flyswatter brandished in his hand. I saw trouble and put my dash training to good use. Running out of the violin store, I turned around to check if he was still after me.

When I felt I was a safe distance, I shouted toward the violin store again, "Big deal! Big deal! Wait until I grow up! I'll run a violin shop a hundred times bigger than yours!"

That dwarf once more chased me , this time not with a flyswatter but a big broom in his hand!

Even after such an unpleasant experience, the habit of running this marathon every day from home to the shop did not stop, for the temptation of the violin was too strong to resist. The difference between before and after was that I was no longer able to flatten my nose against the glass cabinet. Now, I was forced to imagine the shape of the violin from outside the store, constantly comforting myself by thinking, "Wait until my father comes back…"

One More Crack Between Father And Me

Father did come back, at last.

He not only came back, but also bumped into my twelfth birthday. It was our family's tradition that the birthday person would be specially treated with a bowl of noodles covered with a poached egg.

When a bowl of warm noodle with steam floating up into the air was placed in front of me, and especially when we saw the yellow coming out of the white poached egg, there is no need to mention how terrible the temptation was.

My elder brother DanXin kept swallowing his slobbers and younger brother DanHen kept his eyes tightly shut. To me, that was a great moment, the only brief moment I looked forward to for a year was that particular day and that time I could feel above all my brothers and be special among the family. Conversely, that must always be the moment that turns my folks' stomachs the most.

Usually I would make the moment last as long as possible, one second longer if I could. But on that day, I behaved to the opposite.

Unexpectedly, I clipped the poached egg with my chopsticks, placed it in front of DanHen's eyes and quickly put it into his bowl before my parents could stop me from this practical joke. Next I clipped a few noodles, raising them up into the air and then pushed the whole bowl of noodles in front of DanXin.

"That's wonderful! You have become so much more reasonable. You've grown one year older after all." Mom praised.

"Is the noodle poisoned or are you sick, which?" DanXin asked me without moving his eyes away from the noodle.

"Neither." Father answered. "I think this has to be a new trend of *class struggle*. If you don't tell us what kind of drugs you want to sell in your bottle in time, the egg will be gone."

After all, Father was more experienced. What a deceitful fox!

"If you force me." I borrowed the birthday courage requested, "What I want is an instrument, a musical instrument, but not an ordinary musical instrument, it is the queen of musical instruments. It is the most elegant and the most..." I wanted to go on.

"Blow your gas out quickly. What do you want?" Mom was out of patience.

"OK, to cut it short. The most elegant and the most beautiful thing I want..."

Meanwhile, DanHen clipped the poached egg with chopsticks and placed it in front of his mouth.

"Okay, okay." I got nervous, "*Violin*. That's right, Father and Mother, I want a violin." I made a violin-playing gesture in the most elegant way. I brought out my wish in a way not as I had rehearsed many times.

"What ...*lin*? What was that? For what use?" Mother kept asking questions without giving me a chance to answer.

"How much?" Mother asked the last but not least, in fact it was the most important question of all.

"Twenty-eight RMB." I had decided to buy it a long time ago. hence I started to imagine Father taking me to the store. We would wait until that dwarf was present and Father would throw twenty-eight RMB on his face. Then the man would know how strongly my father was supporting me. With that imagining, I broke into a satisfied laughter.

"*What?* You must be out of your mind! twenty-eight RMB to buy you a *hand…lin*! Later I'll have to pay two hundred and eighty RMB to buy you a piano when you grow even older!" Mother must have been very irritated as she raised the pitch of her voice high enough to be a Beijing Opera singer.

"*What* kind of musical instruments?" Father intentionally pronounced "what" as "Hwat" to show his despise.

"But…"

Mother did not let me go on with what I wanted to say. She shouted again, as if she was being robbed, "No matter what you say, I have no money to buy you a hand…lin!"

"Violin!" I also raised my voice up, "It is such an elegant violin, and from your mouths it becomes '*hand…lin*'! Country folk!"

Mother opened her mouth again, but before her words came out Father took over, "Whether it is called a violin or hand…lin doesn't matter. What matters is that our family does not raise (educate) THAT. This is what we call, '*prefer proletarian's grass rather than capitalist seedling*' " In finishing his statement Father added, "*Hwat* (what) violin, GAS!"

"G A S", those were the three letters given to me as my twelfth birthday present, by my father.

I was speechless, watching DanHen devour the egg voraciously, I responded quickly, clamping his throat forcing him to open his mouth. At the same time DanXin took the opportunity and quickly filled his mouth with noodles and soup, then pushed the bowl back to me before I could do anything to him.

That was my birthday, my poor twelfth birthday, full of melancholy and sadness.

My birthday party (if I may call it a party), was quickly over, more quickly than ever before. I couldn't get to sleep until very late that night. I kept thinking of the violin, the disaster that had happened to brother Li and brother Hu, the dwarf salesman, the loss of my poached egg… and quietly I overheard my parents' conversation in the next room.

Mother's voice, "Twenty-eight RMB, almost half of my monthly salary, it is really too, too expensive, if it were eight RMB…"

Father's response, "Even if it were five RMB we shouldn't buy it for him. The question is not '*how much?*' The question is, why is he thinking of playing the violin? Who influenced him? We all know in the present situation, anything to do with the west is politically sensitive. That includes a violin, of course."

Just like millions of Chinese people at that time, Father was a complete revolutionary, even when in bed with his wife.

Mom laughed and she asked, "The reason you dislike DanJiu is because he looks like me more than you?"

"Hey Hey Hey," Father asked a rhetorical question, "Like you what?"

"For example, my nasty temper, stubbornness, straight forward…" Mother pointed out all her shortcomings.

Meanwhile, I heard Father turn over. I imagined that he was facing or had his back to Mother, and then Father's voice turned low and heavy, sounding somewhat like self-criticism. Though the whole content I cannot remember, the last sentence I can't forget and would never forget, ever.

The sentence from my father's was, "I DISLIKE THAT CHILD BY NATURE."

That statement aroused storms and waves in my mind and heart. Being afraid of waking the other two brothers, I did not release my crying with sound, I literally drank my tears.

Perhaps because of that silent crying, after all these years, every time I remember those words I feel like crying out. No matter how many times I have done so, I just cannot heal the wound completely.

That night, I had a dream. The dream brought me to a fairy tale world. I walked into a small wooden house, a house with violins hanging everywhere. I myself turned into a violin; pulling a bow across me caused beautiful music to come out.

Suddenly, the door fiercely opened and Father appeared in front of me. He yelped at me loudly with heavy breath, "I DISLIKE YOU BY NATURE!"

I cried out with my broken heart, "Why *by nature*?" My emotion turned into a strong wind blowing all the violins up to the sky. I myself became a kite, a huge kite gone with the wind further and further away from Father. But I could not escape him completely as the string of the kite was held firmly in his hand. After making my every effort to get away from him, I, as a kite without a string to take control, headed straight to the ground.

I woke from the dream, asking myself the same question over and over, "Why does my old man dislike me… *by nature*?"

5: I WANT TO PLAY VIOLIN

To Play Violin, Joining The Mao Propaganda Team

1968, after the astounding Chinese Cultural Revolution had been going on for two years, the schools re-opened. It was called, "*Restart School to do Revolution*".

DanXin entered *Changsha No. 3 Middle School* (formerly, "*The Clear Virtue Boy's School*"). I however, entered *Changsha No. 4 Middle School* (formerly, "*The Zhou Nan Girl's School*").

With over thirty students in our class, only six were boys, therefore it wouldn't be too hard to imagine my popularity among the girls in class. However, not long after being elected as the class leader, I lost interest in class affairs and fixed my eyes on the school *Mao Propaganda Team* (Mao Propaganda Team is a select group of people who praise Mao and his thoughts by means of singing and dancing). The reason was simple; besides that admirable gray uniform, I discovered a violin, *a-n-d* that charming little girl with a small nose named Ma, playing on the violin.

My mind was made up. I wanted to join the school Mao Propaganda Team.

I talked to Teacher Lao, who was in charge of the team. (Later Lao played a very influential role in my music career) Teacher Lao asked me, "What can you do?"

"Anything, as far as I can publicize Mao and his thoughts." That's what I said, but what I thought was, "*Anything, as far as I can touch the violin.*"

Lao smiled, "If anything can publicize Mao and his thoughts, you do not need to join the team." Before I could plead further, he walked away from me for some, "*urgent matter*" as he said.

The first semester at middle school, I was often together with those who were good at singing and dancing, outside of the school, during school time. I also started to practice bamboo flute which was the only musical instrument I possessed. That resulted in my going from the class head to the class tail, by the end of the semester.

The second semester started at last. At the new team member's audition, I said to Teacher Lao this time, "Please don't ask me 'What can you do?' but ask me 'What have you learned?'"

"That's better." Lao smiled again, a better smile. "OK, show us."

After singing and dancing, I played the bamboo flute.

Lao's comment was that my singing and dancing were good but not enough, only the flute sounded somehow interesting. The pity was that I held my flute towards the left which is the opposite direction of a western flute, meaning it would be difficult if I wanted to learn western flute later. In addition, there was already a good bamboo flute player named Chan, in the team. All appeared hopeless, again, for one more semester.

A few days later, the names of the new Mao Propaganda Team (from now on let me call it *Mao Team*) members were posted on the wall at the school entrance. To avoid being hurt again I dared not check it. Beyond my expectation, when I quietly entered my classroom from the back door, the whole class congratulated me! The new class leader Xiao Ping even said, "This is not Chen DanJiu's honor only, but the honor of the whole class."

The fact was, that Teacher Lao worked on Chan Flute (his nick name) saying it would be good to have one more flute so that he could concentrate on Sola, (a very noisy Chinese traditional musical instrument) in addition, he could help by doing more administrative work as a prospective leader of the team. It must have been the final words, *"prospective leader of the team"* that worked, as Chan Flute had been a competitive rival to the present leader, Captain Lee.

One more fact I discovered was that I was accepted to be a team member not because of my flute playing skill, but my passion to join the team. Teacher Lao was absolutely right about my passion, but not my purpose.

The *first* thing I tried to do after I got into the Mao Team was to get close to Ma, the little violin girl. The main reason was not the girl but *the violin* in her hands obviously. Obvious in my mind but not others. For instance, every time we would go out to give a performance, I would offer my help in carrying her violin with the excuse that, "My flute is very light." But Chan Flute had always reserved such a luxurious task in advance. Ma apparently did not get my real purpose for *"helping"* her.

One day, when Chan Flute was close to us she made her announcement, "I have no interesting in bamboo flutes, no matter what kind, they are all country bumpkins." She made it loud enough so Chan Flute could share with me. Chan Flute and I were both hurt, in different aspects.

"No big deal, someday I will learn to play the violin, as good as you, may be even better than you." I thought, not said.

In spite of her unfriendly attitude, I still worked hard to keep our amity. When she realized my interest was more her violin than her, she became relaxed in one-way and disappointed in another. She was just like all women, don't have to like all men, but hope to be liked by all men.

After this, we became closer and closer. Sometimes I could even feel her intention to capture me in a prison of her loveliness as a girl. Through this accident I learned that if a man wants to get a particular woman, never make her fully contented, unless one does not really want to get her in the first place. Anyway, that great discovery was too early for me as the only desire at that time was to touch a violin, not a woman.

Everything seemed to be working okay until one day I got myself into huge trouble. That day, we gave a performance in a factory.

After arriving, Chan Flute put Ma's violin on a table and walked away to help organize. Meanwhile, Ma was busy in a dressing room. Seeing nobody around, I lost my power to resist touching the violin. I meticulously opened the case and took the violin out. My heart was beating more quickly than after finishing a sports event. Yet not until I put the bow on the string did I see worker's representative Chuan *(by that time, it was the workers from the factories who were in charge of all schools, not the professors, teachers nor administrators of the school)* walking towards me. I hid the violin behind my back immediately. This action certainly did not escape the sharp and shining eyes of the working class.

The Representative Chuan kept walking toward me as he asked, "What's in your hands?" I counter-marched myself once, twice and again, a third time. I felt my body was against the wall, of course with the violin in between. I heard "Pa" and a jangle sound. "Oh my God!" But it was too late. I took the violin out of hiding to realize the sound had come from the violin bridge having broken.

When the bad news, "The violin is broken." spread, Ma rushed out from the dressing room, "Who allowed you to touch my violin! You think you deserve that? Never! You, country bumpkin!" She looked at the bridge, broken in half in my hand and the loose strings on her violin and wept, "Now what? Now what?"

Though I found Ma's language of contempt towards me in public very offensive, I felt it was in balance, as I knew my wrongdoing was enormous and unforgivable.

In the meantime, almost all of the team members had gathered around us, taking turns blaming me, one after another, among the most aggressive was Chan Flute. He pointed at my nose with his finger as he accused, "You did it on purpose!"

After hearing that, Representative Chuan's spirit rose, "That's right, to break the tool used to publicize Mao's thoughts intentionally, is an *anti-revolution* behavior. We should convene the criticize meeting right away."

"That's right!"

"Let's do it." team members echoed.

Teacher Lao, who had kept quiet the entire time, opened his mouth at this point. "For sure Chen DanJiu should be criticized, but we are here to give a performance. We should publicize Mao's thoughts first. Representative Chuan, the working classes are all waiting for us. How about we move the criticize meeting to after the performance?"

"But without a violin how can I play the violin solo part of the ballet, 'The White Hair Woman'?" Ma cried out.

"Use bamboo flute to replace it. No violin solo, I can dance just as well." said the sweet voice of a girl.

Everybody turned their eyes toward the voice. The owner of the voice was called Lu XiaoBing; the prettiest girl on the team and also the one who plays the main role in the ballet, *"The White Hair Woman."* She usually liked to chat with me during free time at rehearsals, particularly liking to cut in when I was with Ma alone. She smiled at everybody, and then again toward me and repeated, "I can dance just as well to bamboo flute. The White Hair Woman was a country bumpkin too. Everybody, please get ready."

"That's impossible!" Captain Lee shouted with his voice out of tune. Captain Lee chasing after Lu was an open secret. He looked as if he wanted to say more but was silenced by Lu's glance. This scene made Ma cry even more than the broken violin.

What a disaster!

It was many years later that I finally realized there was a little love circle going on there, Chan after Ma, Ma after Lee, Lee after Lu, Lu after me and me... after *Ma's violin.*

That night, the performance went as usual. When it came to the violin solo, I replaced it with my bamboo flute. Lu threw smiles at me a couple of times during her performance. I of course, politely smiled back, expressing my gratitude towards her. All of these small actions were closely monitored by Captain Lee and Ma.

After the performance and before the evening meal, the criticizing meeting was held. Chan Flute followed Representative Chuan's order and took me to a separate room. He said to me callously, "This is your last day. Wait to be dismissed."

I waited there for a short while, thinking, *"If I have no more chance to touch the violin it won't be a big deal to be fired. Actually, what's the point of waiting to be fired? Isn't it better to walk away right now?"* I suppose I stayed there instead of walking away due to the expectation of that free bowl of noodles.

Unexpectedly, the one who came to take me back to the meeting room was Ma. She suddenly turned friendly toward me as she asked a peculiar question, "You *also* like Lu XiaoBing?"

"What do you mean by 'ALSO'?" I didn't get the point behind her sentence. Did she mean, "Lu XiaoBing likes you, you also like Lu XiaoBing?" or "Somebody likes Lu XiaoBing, you also like Lu XiaoBing?", or perhaps both? Ma did not answer my counter-question, just smiled and smiled, saying, "For the violin, it's alright this time, but be careful next time, when you touch my violin again."

Do I have a next time? That's wonderful!

When we walked to the doorway of the meeting room Chan Flute was waiting for us. Ma said she needed to have a few words with Chan and asked me to go into the meeting room first.

The *"court"* was ready to start. To be frank, the atmosphere was somewhat scary for everyone was so, so serious. Chan Flute jumped up as the first speaker. I was waiting to be scolded. Surprisingly he started to self-criticize by saying, "It was my fault too. I should have put the violin personally in classmate Ma's hand. I failed to do so. That is an irresponsible attitude towards the weapon of publicizing Mao's thoughts. Therefore I apologize."

Following, was Captain Lee whose attitude was even higher than Chan Flute, "I, as the captain of the team…" so on and so forth…

Next, it was Ma's turn to apologize. And then all of the team members apologized individually, one after another, even Teacher Lao!

Lu XiaoBing was the only one who did not apologize. What the pretty princess said was, "Let's forget the whole thing as far as Chen DanJiu promises never to touch the violin again." She paused, and added, "I suggest that from now on we use the bamboo flute to replace the violin solo just as we did today."

"That's impossible!" Captain Lee remarked. What he meant was, *"How can bamboo flute replace the violin solo?"*

"That's impossible!" I also shouted, meaning, "How can I promise never to touch the violin again?"

I looked at Lu with mixed feelings, about to make my speech. In my speech I wanted to declare that if I was not allowed to touch the violin anymore, I may as well quit the team. But at that exact key point an exciting voice was heard, "The noodles are ready!"

Representative Chuan stood up first like a released spring. Teacher Lao asked him, as I was the last speaker, "Should we let Chen finish what he was saying before eating?"

Representative Chuan did not wait for Lao to finish his words, "Give him a little more time to think the whole thing over. We should not let one person's mistake influence the whole team. Good health is the capital of revolution. Comrades, towards the dining hall, rush!"

I immediately jumped up after Representative Chuan. Sadly, Chuan turned his head to me and said, "Not you. You stay here, go on self-questioning."

However, afterwards, I had not only noodle to eat, but also more meat in it than anybody's, because that bowl was specially made for the main actress Lu XiaoBing.

As I pointed out above, there was a dramatic relationship circle going on in the team. The bumpkin Chan Flute, was in love with the noblest Ma; the noblest Ma admired the tall and handsome Captain Lee; Captain Lee was crazy about the beautiful Lu; Lu liked to make fun of me, "a man full of passion and energy" as she remarked; But *I* was only obsessed with Ma's violin. To reverse the circle, Chan Flute hated Captain Lee over Ma; Ma was jealous about Lu for Captain Lee; Captain Lee was sick of me for Lu and Lu disliked Ma's violin.

After that incident, Ma changed her attitude towards me completely. During rehearsal, she often prepared something like a small towel or drink, asking me to pass it to Lu in front of Captain Lee. In return she would allow me to play her violin. Sometimes, when my violin playing appearance was just too awful to look at, she would even take the trouble to correct me a bit.

One day after the rehearsal, only Ma and I were left in the room. She again let me play her violin. After I finished a tune, applause with "bravo" woke me from my fantasy. That was Teacher Lao. Before I could hide the violin, Lao praised me, "Your progress is really quick. You will be a good violin player for sure in the future." At the same time, Lao showed me a huge book, the western violin Method, "Hohmann". "You may borrow it later, when you need it. But you must promise to take very good care of it." Then Lao put his finger against his lips meaning, "This is a secret only among the three of us."

Lao added, "Practice more and harder. We are applying for some money from the school to buy new instruments. When you are good enough, we plan to buy a new violin for Ma. By that time, this violin will be for you to use."

Lao's words encouraged me tremendously. I was speechless and felt an enormous hope ahead of me. By then I understood that Ma had let me play on her violin not only to repay me for the things she asked me to do so that Captain Lee might give up Lu for her, but also for the new violin Lao promised her.

A Palace Of Art

The bad news was, the school decided to delay the money to Mao Team for one semester. Thus Ma's fever of helping me to play the violin dropped abruptly.

One day, as soon as the rehearsal ended, Ma hurried out with her violin. I intercepted her at the doorway and asked, "Why in such a hurry?"

"Don't bother me, I'll be late." Ma pushed me away and ran out.

"Where are you going?" I asked again to her back.

"That's a secret." Ma answered without turning her head.

It was that, *"secret"* which aroused my curiosity. I could not help tailing her. I hid myself every three or five steps. In fact, that was unnecessary, because Ma was too busy running to look back.

After following her for a while, I saw that she went into a side door beside a Christian church. I stopped in front of the church, hesitant to follow her in, as in China by that time churches were similar to temples, both belonging to the *Four Olds*. Seeing nobody around, I kept my heart beat under control and gathered the courage to walk closer to the church.

The main gate of the church was marked with red paper seals. As the seals were old and ragged it was indistinguishable *which* revolutionary organization's revolutionary activity it was. I stood there, raised my head, looking up to the top of the church; I wondered about the existence of God. It was at that moment that I heard a sound from God! The sound, so soft, so harmonious, so beautiful, so elegant, so touching and moving that I had never heard the like in my entire little life! My ears led my feet to the side door, beside the Church. I walked through the door, following the sound. I found there, behind the Church, was an old one-story house. The sound, the sound of two violins came out from the house.

I squatted down by the window, joyfully devouring the music. After a while, I felt time had stopped, my soul separated from my body and drifted freely into the endless universe. Without knowing how long the music had stopped, I heard a conversation between Ma and a man. That gentle conversation and the sincere mirth, were also a novelty to me.

When I heard Ma say, "Goodbye" in English, immediately I ran away.

I tailed Ma to the Church quite a few times. Later, I discovered besides Ma, there were others too with violins who went into the side door beside the church. It was like I was addicted, often waiting somewhere close to the church for people to go into the side door. Then, I would enjoy myself quite a while under the window outside.

One day I must have caught a cold and I could not help sneezing. The window opened. The kind smile of a middle-aged man stopped me from running away.

"If you like to listen you may come in, though the room is a bit small. It's terribly cold out there." the man said to me.

His name is Li ZengTao, and he used to be a priest before the Cultural Revolution. He was the teacher of almost all the young violin players in my city during that period in time. He certainly became the first of my violin teachers.

The teenage man having a lesson was called Wang ShiYi, the son of a former professor at Hunan Medical College, now at Yale University. By that time, just like all other professors, his father was not teaching in classrooms but working at the hospital, sweeping floors and cleaning toilets. Wang ShiYi later became one of my best violin pals.

That day, after Wang's lesson, Teacher Li opened his treasure, a manual gramophone. Teacher Li put a record on the gramophone and wonderful violin music came out. That was the first time in my life I heard Kreisler's magical performance, *"The Beautiful Rosemary"*.

After that Li told me a word that was also a first to hear in my life, *"Christmas"*. Yes, that was Christmas Eve. Li played *"Silent Night"* with his violin and followed it with a piano tune, *"A Maiden's Prayer"* (Modlitwa Dziewicy).

The whole scene was far away from reality. To *me*, Li's violin sound came from another world, a world totally different from the violent brutal Cultural Revolution. That violin sound made me drunk, made me *crazy*. To use an inappropriate but very accurate figure of speech, I was drugged.

On the way home, I walked shoulder to shoulder with Wang ShiYi. (It was not exactly shoulder-to-shoulder as Wang was one head taller than I.) Wang told me that because Teacher Li was very kind and never offended anyone, nobody gave him a hard time. Though the church was sealed, it needed someone to take care of it. That's why nobody fussed about Teacher Li going in from the back door to do some cleaning from time to time.

After Wang became aware of my desire to learn the violin but having no instrument, he told me he knew someone named Zhou who had the knowledge of making violins. "Once I watched your school's performance." Wang suddenly changed subjects, "The girl who dances the roll as the 'White Hair Woman' looks, looks, hen... not really that pretty."

"I think she's pretty...*enough*. Her name is Lu XiaoBing, a very good friend of mine." I said proudly.

"Good on you." Wang laughed, dry and jealously. "You know what, Master Zhou is also a very good friend of mine."

"OK, you introduce me to Master Zhou, I introduce you to Lu. How's that?" I raised my head looking at him jokingly. He immediately stretched out his little finger. When two little fingers bundled, a dirty business deal was made.

The First Violin Of Mine

In accordance with the deal, I invited Wang to watch our rehearsal at school.

"How dare you chase me up here?" Ma was very surprised to see Wang there.

"No, you misunderstand XiaoMao, I'm not here for you today. It is your teammate Chen who dragged me here to see his rehearsal." Wang quickly explained.

Wang and Ma both took violin lessons from Teacher Li so naturally they knew each other well. But by the way Wang used Ma's nickname, "XiaoMao" could mean that their relationship was closer than normal, or at least Wang wanted it to be. Whatever, that wasn't important to me. But I did learn Ma's nickname, "XiaoMao" and that was important to me. After then, whenever something unpleasant happened between us, I would threaten to call her "XiaoMao" in public. This often resulted in a favorable compromise.

On that day, Wang's pair of eyes were as busy circling as Lu's pair of legs. When the rehearsal finally ended, as usual, Lu came to ask me to look after her schoolbag while she changed her clothes.

I caught the chance to introduce Wang to her. Suddenly, not knowing why, I felt uneasy and somehow ashamed, as if having sold something that I did not really possess, (I had no intention to possess her in the first place), or I traded something that I did not possess with someone for something that I wished to possess? I guess when people are young and naive, they all would do anything, even something stupid, to get what they desperately want.

"My name is Wang. I have been a faithful fan of yours, your dance, for a long time." Wang bowed to Lu as he introduced himself. At the same time he quickly swallowed his slobbers caused by loss of control.

Lu raised her head to take a look at Wang. Then she dragged me to a corner and bit my ear, "So tall, will the rationed fabric ticket be enough for him?" After the statement of her first impression, Lu nodded her head greeting Wang and went off to change her clothes laughing.

"What did she say to you, anything about me? " Wang asked anxiously.

"Nothing important." I tried to get away.

"Tell me quickly, otherwise …" Wang threatened.

I knew what his *"otherwise"* was. Otherwise he would not introduce me to Master Zhou. It was not that I was not good at making stories. In fact, I have always been quite good at it. It was just that I was not used to replacing truth with stories, or perhaps not willing to do so. Therefore I told Wang the truth, the absolute truth, whole truth, nothing else, "She said you were so tall, how could the rationed fabric ticket be enough for you?" At that time in China, almost everything was on quota strictly by folk registration (registration at birth of where you reside, this cannot be changed, EVER). *Everything* had a ticket, rice ticket, oil ticket, tobacco ticket, tofu ticket, match ticket, etc.

Wang heard that and turned from excited to sentimental. He expressed his feelings with tears filling his eyes, "How kind of her to put thoughts on me, so concretely and so far away! She would be a very good wife."

Ma kept watching closely at the ensuing drama for the duration. She rewarded me with a bright look, probably meant to thank me for doing such a good job of, *"killing two birds with one stone"* for her.

And then, as always, she went to glue Captain Lee with some smart excuses.

On the way to Master Zhou's home, Wang sang a song loudly. The lyrics were something like, "I remember that moment of wonder. You appeared at my present, just like an illusion written in water..." That scene if it were today or in a movie, must be, "I am in love!"

I was not at all in the mood for poetry, on the contrary I felt somewhat lost. The only way to recover my feeling was to get to Master Zhou's home as quickly as possible and watch him making a violin for me at once.

In front of Master Zhou's home, Wang suddenly held me up. He said to me, "You don't have to say anything. I will tell Master Zhou that Teacher Li told you to see him. Though they have been friends for many years, they dare not see each other since the Cultural Revolution, therefore Master Zhou wouldn't find out the truth." Seeing my look of reluctance, he persuaded, "Don't you worry, this is not the first time I..."

Master Zhou's door opened from the inside. The first words that came out from Master Zhou were, "You must be little Chen. Priest Li told me about you. Come on in please."

Both Wang and I were embarrassed by Zhou's unexpected welcome speech.

The result of our negotiation was, Zhou, under pressure from the society, dared not to make violins anymore. The only possibility left was that I bring my own wood and borrow his tools and workshop to make one by myself, at least namely by myself.

Back home, I took apart the family's only wooden chair with a back, using the excuse that there was a crack in the chair already. Next, I took a piece of pine from my own bed (actually the bed I shared with my brother DanXin).

After that, every day I ran to Zhou's home after school. Three weeks passed, under the guidance of Master Zhou, or should I say partly under the "hand" of Master Zhou, as I cut my forefinger by the very end of the violin making. A violin shaped wooden box formed.

On the day of the violins completion, I used my two day's lunch money, twenty fen Renminbi, to buy a bag of cookies and rushed to Zhou's home. "It's not varnished yet." Zhou said to me as he pushed the bag of cookies back.

"Later, Later, I can't wait one minute longer!" I wrapped the violin shaped wooden box with a few used newspapers, and rushed home merrily.

Nobody was home except our next-door neighbor MeiMei, cooking in the kitchen. I waved my treasure at her excitedly. But Hu MeiMei seemed not to be interested. She didn't even stop cutting her firewood. A short moment later, she went into her home and walked out again with a very old violin case, saying, "Remember my elder brother took the violin from the Four Olds trash place? The Red Guards smashed the violin and left only this ragged box."

I was so pleased to see the case, *"Recycle the waste. Recycle the waste."* I repeated, a popular revolutionary slogan at the time.

I repaired the case with violin glue and plastic tape. Then I took apart DanXin's old broken Erhu (two stringed Chinese musical instrument); put the rusted strings on the violin shaped wooden box, and some rosin on the Erhu bow. *Soon after that my newborn baby cried for the first time!*

No doubt it was an ugly sound from an ugly violin made by a fourteen-year-old ugly boy. But, THAT WAS MY VIOLIN!

Just like that, I took my first step forward, toward my life's career.

6: PRELUDE TO MY LEARNING THE VIOLIN

My Hand-Copied Violin Method Book, Hohmann

Once I possessed my own violin, I could not contain my excitement and ran straight to Wang ShiYi's home. Wang took a glance at my dear ugly baby and burst into laughter with a sneeze. He made some very unpleasant comments, saying my unvarnished treasure, *"looks like a naked woman"*. As for my poor Erhu bow, No language could be found in the dictionary strong enough to taunt.

How could anyone in this situation tolerate it? I put my baby back into the old case and walked away. Up to the doorway I felt it would be too easy for him if I just disappeared like that. I turned back to him, "You're not a good man."

Wang laughed even more, first with his face to the sky, and then bent over towards his navel. I would have jumped out of his window if I had a parachute. I opened his door indignantly, *"I'm going to tell Lu XiaoBing."*

I said that only to express my anger. Unexpectedly, it worked! Wang chased me and dragged me back to his home. He took out a broken violin bow and explained to me with sincerity, "Once my younger brother sat on it. If you can, or find someone who can fix it, I can let you use it for some time. It's a broken bow, but it is a violin bow, much better than your Erhu bow, for sure."

Wang took the "Hohmann" violin method book from his music stand and turned it back to the first page. Next he taught me a little about how to read scores and even demonstrated a couple of times.

I was so very excited that I forgot all of the humiliation from only a few minutes ago. When I packed up my violin, together with his broken bow and walked to the door, Wang again blocked my way. He took out a crinkled letter from his pocket (it looked like it had been in his pocket for quite some time) and handed it over to me mysteriously, "We're friends right? Friends help each other. Hand it over to her, Lu, you know what I mean, secretly...*Please?*"

"Make sure nobody sees it." he reminded me again from his window.

The next morning I went to see Teacher Lao as I remembered he had the Hohmann book and had once said he could let me borrow it when the time came. What I found out was that the method Hohmann was not his property but the property of Ma. "I will talk to Ma again next semester when we are going to buy a new violin." Lao comforted me.

Nothing more I could do, I turned to leave when Lao asked me if I would give him a hand sorting out some recording tapes (big tapes) as well as some records as we still had two hours to go before the rehearsal. He played the tapes on a recorder and the records on a phonograph. When the music started, Lao would tell me the title of the music as well as the name of the composer and I would label them. I remember there were symphonies by Tchaikovsky, Beethoven, etc. Rimsky-Korsakov's *Capriccio Espagnol* drove me crazy and became my most favorite orchestral work.

The music went on and on. Time made no sense to me anymore. My spirit soared to a completely different sphere until Teacher Lao turned off the music and told me, "All these are called *'non-title music'* (a Chinese political name for western classical music). When we have time later we can do more *criticizing* together."

Since then, "to help Teacher Lao sort out the tapes and records" became the best excuse for me to see him often.

Before rehearsal, Lu XiaoBing asked me to look after her schoolbag as usual. I caught the opportunity and passed Wang's letter to her, secretly. Lu looked excited. Her face turned red when she took the letter. She even rubbed my hand a little. To avoid a misunderstanding, I quickly told her it was not I, but my friend Wang ShiYi who wrote the letter to her. Immediately her face turned blue and she returned the letter back to me without opening it, looking very disappointed, "Since when did you become a postman?"

When Lu was about to walk away from me, she bumped into Captain Lee. (I believe Lee was somewhere observing us the entire time.) Lee seized the letter from my hand and quickly opened it, then read very loudly, *"If you were the sun, I wish to be the earth, turning around you forever. If you are the Earth, I wish to be the moon, turning around you forever ..."*

Meanwhile, more and more people came closer to Lee, forming a little circle, among them also Ma. Lee looked at everybody, and again, more importantly, looked at Lu. He found Lu didn't really look offended, to Lee that was Lu's tacit consent, therefore he courageously went on with his reading, *"I think the best would be I become your ballet shoes, let you trample my body whenever you wish …"*

Inevitably, a huge burst of sneers poured on me after Lee's performance. Lee waved the letter in the air with great satisfaction and asked, "Who wants to see more? Who wants to see more?"

As I hesitated as to whether I should take the letter back, Lu stretched her little finger towards Lee. The letter was soon in the hand of Lu. Lu looked at me remarking, "A man with courage should be respected." Lu moved her eyesight to Lee and again remarked, *"Unlike* someone else." Then to me again, "Go to thank him, but also don't forget to tell him, unfortunately his shoes may be too big for me."

After that, Lu carefully folded the letter and instead of giving it back to me, put it into her schoolbag. My subconscious ordered my hand to take her schoolbag as always. But this time, she wouldn't let me.

As soon as Lu left, Lee suddenly became unusually friendly to me. He tried to find out from me, who that, "man with courage" was. His hot attitude looked as if he wanted to form an, "ally of anti-love rival" with me.

Seeing that Lee left me to go find Lu, Ma said to me in a disdained tone, "The same letter I also received before, only the last sentence was, *'I think the best would be I become your violin case, let you lie inside my body whenever you wish …"*

After that Ma added her comment to Wang, "That tall guy is really not a bad fellow. Not bad at all, only does silly things sometimes. What a big boy!"

Ma's mouth was talking to me, but her eyes were busy looking at somebody, something else. Suddenly, she intentionally provoked me by grabbing my bamboo flute and running away.

"Give it back to me at once; otherwise I will call you…" I threatened her with my usual weapon, to call out her nick name.

"Call me whatever you like, better let everybody hear it." Ma said as she quickly ran in Lee and Lu's direction.

I chased her up and caught her before everybody's eyes, "What are you doing!? Are you crazy!?" I shouted.

I thought she might be embarrassed or even angry, but on the contrary when she saw Lee, Lu, Chan and all others were watching us, she leaned her body towards me exaggeratedly, and bit my ear saying, "Mission completed. Good job!"

With Lu's wide-open eyes, Lee's wide-open mouth and Chan's wildly standing hairs, Ma returned my flute back to me and slowly walked away with a smile of some kind of satisfaction.

During that day's rehearsal, I was pushing the rhythm from beginning to end. Afterwards there was no need to look for Ma as she was waiting for me outside of the rehearsal room. The place she stood was so obvious, as if she wanted us to be seen by all others.

"What do you mean by 'mission'? *What mission?* What's the matter with you today? " I had a million questions to ask but didn't know where to start.

"The feeling in my heart, that dancer should have half." Ma said sourly.

"What do you mean? You mean? *You and me?"* I felt totally lost.

"From now on you might as well call me XiaoMao. I mean, I only allow you to call me XiaoMao, temporarily." she ordered.

"But, but you said you dislike bamboo flute, of any kind." I reminded her.

"You can reform yourself to be a violin player. Can't you?" she stressed.

Later, after I reviewed the whole thing, I realized that that was the instance Ma decided to give up hope for Lee, therefore she wanted Lu to share part of her broken heart by means of pretending to be my girlfriend. At the same time she wanted to pass a "stop trying" message to Chan Flute.

Additionally, I think she probably had a little change in taste by taking me as her new boyfriend, temporarily, or as a kind of anesthesia for her lovelorn heart for the time being.

But my brain was filled with violin and *violin only*, with no room, no room at all for this romantic nonsense, or anything else. That meant I could reject Ma easily, but I couldn't reject Hohmann, the violin method book she possessed.

I traded my little dignity for the violin method book, Hohmann, temporarily. I took it home and hand copied it, note by note, line by line, page by page, day by day and month by month. During the athletics lessons at school I pretended I had a stomach-ache and hid myself in the classroom copying the notes. Back home during cooking time I asked MeiMei for help, so that I could copy the notes. After supper, I occupied the only table at home, along with the excuse of copying notes for publicizing Mao's thoughts.

(Father was again away from home being reformed at the May 7 Cadre School. No one in the rest of the family understood what I was copying, especially as I changed all the titles to revolutionary names, such as, "Praise for Mao's Thoughts") Even late at night, after my brothers went to sleep, I sometimes got up and used a flashlight to copy the notes.

Hohmann is a duet written for two violins. In practice, I only need to copy the notes for one violin, but I did both. That passion and effort, I had only applied *once* before, in the year 1960 when I desperately tried to prevent myself from death by starvation as I dug Chinese potato roots to eat. I worked so hard that my hand was blistered. Finally, I finished my copy of the violin method Hohmann, completely, from book one to book five.

Bow Issuer

Now, about the broken bow Wang lent me, I luckily found an acquaintance who worked as a car repairman to fix it for me using a hollow copper tube. Although the bow was very heavy, just as Wang said, "Much better than the Erhu bow." For the sake of clipping the violin steadily between neck and shoulder, adopting the same theory as Chinese Gongfu, I made myself a sandbag to hang over the scroll of the violin head. Compared with that, the overweight bow became insignificant.

Unfortunately, the prosperity did not last long. One day, when I was tired after a long hard practice, I put the bow on a bench. Just a few minutes later, back from the public toilet, I found my brother DanXin was rubbing his bottom from pain. Before I could feel amused I saw my bow stick was divided again, into MORE than two pieces!

"Oh My God!"

Now what? To fight with him, I couldn't win and scolding him wouldn't put my bow back together again. Though DanXin hinted he wouldn't hit back, I stood there, still, miserable. Seeing me begrudgingly saying good-bye to the remains of my dear bow, in fact not my bow, but a bow I borrowed from Wang, as we agreed.

Looking at me with such sadness and remorse, my brother asked, "How much would it cost to buy a stick like that?"

DanXin had no alternative but to painfully brake two of his bamboo made dummy cash boxes he saved every day for many years.

While we were busy counting the money, coin by coin, the younger brother of our mother came to see us from Zunyi, the holy revolutionary site that was Mao's base during the civil war but then and now, still among the poorest places in China. This explains why for him, "coming to see us" was less important than, "coming to buy some pork fat for frying oil." By that time, each Chinese head was rationed very limited plant oil per month.

For the sake of buying fat pork for Uncle, I had to get up at four o'clock, in the dark the next morning to line up in the cold. After 5 hours, Uncle was very pleased with the fat pork in his hand, but at the same time disappointed that the pork was not as oily as he would have wished. All the same he repeated, "I don't know how to reward you?"

"But I know how you can reward me." I captured that, *"once in a lifetime"* opportunity and requested, "In fact, you don't have to reward me, just lend me fifteen RMB." (At that time fifteen RMB was one third of his monthly wage) Looking at Uncle's frozen facial expression, quickly I pleaded, explaining how important the money was to me. To put the importance concretely, "To buy a violin bow for me now will change my life."

Repeatedly I promised that he would get his money back with a tremendous profit when I grow up. Immediately following, I handed over a letter to him, a beg-to-borrow-money letter. In the letter, I also begged him to keep it secret from my mom.

Ladies and gentlemen, think about it, how a fourteen-year-old boy could do such a thing. How strong his desire to play the violin must be!

I don't know whether my uncle was moved by my passion, that's not important. What *was* important is that he gave me the money, although not directly in my hand, but into the hand of my mother. Mom did not only put the sum in my hand, but also a severe scolding. Frankly speaking, not to mention the scolding, even a severe beating would have been worth the value.

Luckily, I bought a nice used violin bow at a second-hand shop with the money. But, to my extraordinary bitterness, only a few days later, Wang saw my new bow and said to me, "Since you already have your own bow, how about returning my broken bow to me."

When he was told that his broken bow was even more broken, his face turned very serious, again and again he emphasized the importance of that broken bow of his. To me, the meaning was obvious; he wanted my nice new bow to compensate for his old broken one.

I felt I was being cheated and trapped! I ran straight to Lu XiaoBing's home to express my fury. But when I got Lu's home, I happened to see her father was severely ill.

"Why not take him to the hospital?" I asked.

"We just got back from the hospital. The doctor says he's not sure from which disease my father is suffering." Lu said to me with tears.

At that time in China, it was the same throughout the whole country, doctors who could actually cure diseases were sent out to be labor reformed. The remainder, those left in the hospitals, were those who could not cure diseases.

"Don't worry, don't worry, let me think." I comforted Lu, and then went for a three kilometer marathon again, back to Wang's home since I knew Wang's father was a medical professor.

Wang heard the bad news and revealed his unimaginable excitement, excitement obviously for the chance of a profitable achievement, profitable not for money, but for beauty. Together we raced to Lu's home again.

At Lu's home the way Wang called Lu's parents, "Lu Mom, Lu Daddy" made my teeth ache so badly they felt as though they would soon fall out. That vinegar flavor proved that I did in fact like Lu, quite a bit perhaps. But that was a very critical moment, a moment not to fight for a girl, but for the life of Lu's father.

Wang took an old notebook out from his pocket and wrote down all the details about Lu's father's symptoms. Then, ignoring Wang's, "No thank you." I took a marathon again, for the fourth time, back to Wang's home with him.

Wang's father was waiting for us. Hearing his son's report, the professor anxiously said Lu's father might be suffering from a kind of acute inflammation, if not treated in time his life could be in danger.

The professor quickly covered his face with a big hat and carried a common army bag on his shoulder. Together, the three of us hurried to Lu's home, for me the fifth marathon in the same day.

As soon as we arrived at Lu's home, the professor took some medical instruments out of his bag and examined Lu's father. Quickly the professor wrote a letter and asked Lu's family to take the father to the recommended hospital and talk to a specific doctor at once.

Afterwards, the professor reminded me, "Don't blather to anyone about today." Wang explained to me that as his father was supposed to be a *knocked-down anti-revolutionary scholar*, the professor did not wish to bring trouble to others for his underground medical activities. That's why only in darkness would the professor see the patients who shouted, knocking him down during the day.

This also explained why my friend Wang ShiYi needed a notebook with him at all times.

Just like that, the life of Lu's father was saved. A few days later, when Lu's father recovered, the working class mother said to her daughter Lu XiaoBing, "Who said your tall friend comes from a bad family? I think his family is very good."

The mother's words made Lu blush with shame. She explained, "His name is Wang, not my friend, but a friend of my schoolmate Chen. In fact, I don't even know that tall Wang much at all."

Lu's father's incident alleviated the crisis of the bow problem, yet it remained unsolved. I checked almost all the musical instrument shops in Changsha, hoping to find a bargain. One day I passed the Changsha May-First Cultural Goods Store. The memory of being chased out by that little fat man made me nervous. I finally encouraged myself enough to walk in again. To my surprise, that twenty-eight RMB violin was *still* there, only the price was reduced to twenty RMB.

With the excitement, I decided to contact my dear aunt who used to be the closest to me in the world. I wrote a letter to her, the same letter I wrote to my uncle (Mom's brother), with the content, "to buy a violin bow for me now could change my life…you will get your money back with a tremendous profit when I grow up" etc. etc. etc. Finally, I also added the request, "to keep it a secret from my parents."

Two weeks later my aunt came to see me from her hometown Xinhua, *"to exploit the working convenience "* as she explained.

I took my aunt to the Changsha May-First Cultural Goods Store right away, partly as I was looking forward to meeting that short fat fellow again. After we arrived, Aunt gave me twenty RMB, twice explaining that five out from the twenty were given by my Uncle Din. I threw the sum on the counter as I dreamed of doing for such a long time! What a pity the short fat man wasn't there, only the thin lady was present.

When I opened the violin case I found the neck of the violin was off of the body. The sales lady argued, "Because of that we reduced the price. Find someone to glue them together, it will be as good as new."

"No need to find someone, *that* I can do myself." I replied proudly.

I noticed the sales lady trying to avoid eye contact with me the entire time. Purposely I asked, "You do remember me, don't you?"

"No, I don't." she denied coldly. Seeing me disappointed she changed her tone, "Nowadays what good does it do to remember so many things?" she paused, "You are much taller now. You used to come here very often, how could I forget you?"

"That's very nice of you to remember me." I was half satisfied, "But do me a favor, please send my regards to that fat man and tell him that the *'child'* has bought the violin." I spelled that out with great pleasure.

"Xiao Gao, you mean my Xiao Gao." Her voice trembled, "Alright, I'll forward your greeting to him when I also go there."

"Go where?" I puzzled.

"He is gone." she answered in an undertone.

"Gone where?" I asked again loudly.

"Dead, D E A D, dead!" she shouted.

"What? How?" I was shocked, but did not give up questioning. To put it in a Chinese saying, *"breaking an earthenware pot to inquire the bottom."*

"Do you have an end? *How?* Gun fight of course." She lost control and cried out, "My poor husband did not even take a look at our child…" she lowered her head down and never lifted it up again.

During the Cultural Revolution, there was a period of time called *Wudou* (militant). The rebels and the loyalists both had arms. They fought war with real bullets. If you Google it, you will find the number of deaths in the year of Wudou is between *three-hundred-thousand and five-hundred-thousand.* As always, a hundred thousand more or less, does not bother my people very much. This man named Gao, who used to chase me out of the music store with a broom, was just one of them.

I felt a total emptiness in my brain, quietly leaving the store with the violin. On my way home, I decided not to hate that poor short fat fellow anymore, actually he was shapeless, no longer short nor fat anymore. Being frank, I even felt a little sorry for him. Who said, "Death concludes everything." ?

Back home, I compared the new bow with the second hand bow, going back and forth over and over; finally deciding the second hand bow was the better one. Hence, I endured my pain and gave the new bow to Wang as compensation. After that heavy burdened was removed, I felt much relaxed. From then on, I could play my violin, in peace.

Just like THAT, the prelude to my learning the violin, started.

7: TEACHER LI TAUGHT ME HOW TO BE A MAN AS I LEARNED TO PLAY THE VIOLIN

By then I had my self-made violin, a nice used bow and the hand-copied Hohmann. What else did I need apart from time and practice?

In fact, I did have enough time and much practice as at that time school was not so busy and to me, practice itself gave me the greatest pleasure and happiness. Every early morning I practiced my violin by the side of a garden pond close to home so as to avoid waking my neighbors.

During the summer, every afternoon my brothers went swimming with other kids and that was my chance to monopolize our home to practice.

With the temperature rising to around forty degrees in a not-well-ventilated bungalow house, I was always showered by my own sweat. Though the temperature became much more friendly in the evening, I was forced to go outside to practice. Outside, the mosquito cluster was my major enemy, particularly when I played the A string. The mosquitoes would attack me like the Japanese Kamikaze pilots during World War II! Later, I found a favorite practice spot near a railway where there were fewer mosquitoes flocking.

In those days, although I ate with my brothers at the same table and slept in the same room, my spirit lived in an entirely different world. I had almost no friends but *many* unfriendly neighbors.

We quarreled from time to time for one reason and that reason alone, *"the strident noise out from that wooden box, endlessly, from morning till night."* Due to this, few neighborhood kids talked to me, except one girl, the next-door neighbor Hu MeiMei.

Back then my greatest grievance was that nobody recognized my genius. Now when I think back, I feel sorry and shameful for having caused so much headache to my neighbors with that dreadful violin sound.

Forgive me, my poor neighbors. Now I apologize to you in front of the whole world.

I took lessons with Teacher Li once a week in the beginning. Later, I went to see him more and more often. After the lessons we always played some duets from the method Hohmann. Gradually, violin lessons became art and enjoyment for both of us. This is how, within one year, my violin playing took a, *"great leap forward"*. It gave me the confidence to compete with Ma or even Wang. The pity was, Ma was not interested in competing with me as she was a girl and more importantly, she was supposed to be my girlfriend, temporarily. Therefore, of my rivals, this left only one, Wang ShiYi.

Speaking of Wang, for the sole purpose of chasing Lu XiaoBing, he transferred to our school. That resulted naturally, in adding one more violin to our Mao Team. That is to say, the Mao Team now had three violins, Ma, Wang and me.

As I mentioned previously, in the ballet, "The White Haired Woman", there was a violin solo passage that used to be played by Ma. But one day, just before the performance, Ma's face looked longer than usual. After questioning, I found it was Wang who requested to substitute her and play that solo paragraph himself. That fact gave me very confused feelings.

"What a guy. Not only did he take Lu away from me, but he also wanted to take the solo from Ma, or should I say my *'XiaoMao'*." From that moment, I decided to contend with him for the solo.

The performance started. When the dance got close to the violin solo passage, I saw Wang had stopped playing, constantly wiping his sweaty hand on his trousers getting himself ready to play the solo. When the time came, I could not help myself, I rushed to play the solo paragraph, half a beat earlier than the rhythm, causing trouble on the stage.

The untimely violin solo confused Lu's steps and made her inclined body fall down on the stage. Fortunately, the people sitting in front of the stage were all Liberation Army Soldiers; who most likely had the discipline not to laugh at any and all incidents.

After the performance was over, Lu was circled by teammates in a corner backstage; receiving handkerchiefs as one after another was passed to her. I felt extremely lost; the only way to ease myself was by thinking of something else, such as, "How can a women's eye store so much water."

Wang looked at me with great disappointment, rebuking me in an undertone, "You are not a good friend, so selfish and full of arbitrariness…"

I gave tit for tat, "What? You say *I'm* selfish! That solo passage used to be XioaMao's; I mean teammate Ma's. Why did you want to take it over?"

"Why are you so furious about the violin solo thing? Whoever plays, it will not be your turn." Unexpectedly Chan Flute interjected, a remark full of vinegar, obviously because I called Ma, XiaoMao.

Wang ShiYi nodded his head echoing, "So so so." I ignored Chan Flute and challenged Wang directly, "Let's compete playing the solo passage or Hohmann, YOU name it. The winner will play the solo paragraph from now on."

Ma heard that and quickly pulled me aside, whispering to me, "To play Hohmann, he finished that a long time ago, now he practices Kayser." (Kayser is a violin teaching method a step higher than Hohmann). Seeing me speechless, Ma comforted me, "Why compete with him? I'm positive that *you* are the No. 1 violin player among the Changsha amateur violin players."

Ma's action irritated Chan Flute, he rushed forward and pushed Ma away from me, "Look at you two pull and drag. There should be a division between boys and girls!"

How could that be tolerated? I acted like a little rascal and pushed Chan Flute against the wall.

Wang was shocked, keeping his mouth half open he rumbled repeatedly, "How can it be like this?"

Ma was on the side unable to help but laugh.

Lu however, walked towards us, "Stop it, both of you. It was my fault. I didn't follow the music closely enough. I'll be more careful from now on."

At that moment Teacher Lao and the workers representative Chuan, came to inform us that the noodles were ready.

Seeing us entangled together, it was inevitable to be questioned and judged. When they found our key problem was the violin solo, Lao expressed his opinion, "From now on, you three take turns playing the solo. Is it worth quarreling over such a trifle?"

Representative Chuan, on the other hand, had a totally different idea about the issue. He suggested, "Why does the solo have to be played by one person? Bad individualism! From now on, you three comrades play the solo together. More people, bigger strength. *Good.* This matter is settled. Go, go, go, let's go eat."

"A solo, a solo, how can three play a solo together? Art has its own rule and form." Teacher Lao said, opposing representative Chuan publicly, which was the first for any of us to see.

"What rule? Art obeys publicizing Mao's thoughts, you obey me and we working class lead everything. *That is the law above all.*" After Chuan showed his absolute authority as a working class, he again urged us, "Let's go eat quickly everybody. As Mao said, 'good health is the capital of revolution'."

During the whole night's meal, Teacher Lao was constantly explaining that the solo must not be played by three. He even told Chuan that the solo passage in the ballet, "White Haired Woman" was an imitation of Tchaikovsky's magnum opus from the ballet, "Swan Lake". It was classical literature that could not be and should not be changed.

Representative Chuan nodded his head showing he was listening while he was busy working on his noodles. After he finished the noodles he drank all the soup left in the bowl, then he put the chopsticks on the empty bowl looking at Teacher Lao and sighed with regret, profoundly, "The noodle today was a little lacking in oil."

The very next day, I went to see Teacher Lao at his home. First, I showed my regret for taking over the solo passage, soon after that I asked, "About the, 'Swan Lake' you mentioned yesterday, could you also let me criticize it?"

"That's what you come here for, isn't it?" Lao smiled and continued, "I don't think I have the, 'Swan Lake' tape here, but you can find that solo passage in the movie 'Lenin in 1918'."

Seeing me looking greatly disappointed, Lao added, "I happened to have a few classical music records, in them there are a few fascinating violin solos. The problem is, the school phonograph is at the moment, in the hands of the Worker's Propaganda Team at the broadcasting room.

"My violin Teacher Li has a gramophone. Please lend the records to me at once." I begged anxiously.

"That's too risky. How can a teacher lend the 'Four Olds' to a student? That's simply too risky!" Lao looked truly worried.

After entangling him over and over again, and more importantly convincing him of the complete safety of Teacher Li's place and my promise of this being kept an absolute secret, Lao responded, "As I said, those things cannot be *lent*. However, it would be a different story if you picked them up from the trash."

Lao carefully wrapped the records with a few used newspapers, and then wrote, *"cultural trash"* on it. Together, the records were placed with all other music tapes. Staring at that pile of, "cultural trash" Lao groaned, "What a pity."

When I was so pleased to pick up the records and about to walk away, Lao warned me again, "Just in case someone sees, say you picked them up from MY trash. Don't bring trouble to others, understand?"

I opened the package as soon as I got out of Lao's home. The records were not something else, but my most favorite, *"Spanish Fantasy"* by Rimsky Korsakov! I hurried myself straight to Teacher Li's home right away with the records and excitement.

When I got to Li's home, he was in bed. He slowly got up and said, "Just a little headache, not bad enough to remain in bed."

We immediately enjoyed the music, "Spanish Fantasy". Li woke me up from that inebriating musical dreamland, and gave me an introduction to the composer, "Rimsky-Korsakov who used to serve in the navy. He was an amateur musician without having studied composition systematically.

Because of his outstanding gift, he was invited to be the director of the St. Petersburg Music Conservatory. Being a director, he however, appeared in classrooms with some first grade students to study harmony and other music theories."

I was amazed by Li's story, as always. Also, as always, I thought Li was randomly telling a story, a story only. But this time, Li went on with his "story". He said to me in a very sincere tone, "Therefore we should always be modest and prudent, always think of learning from others, even when we become a real master of violin playing."

I started to realize that Wang ShiYi had talked about the solo issue to Teacher Li. To avoid more criticism, I admitted, "Alright, alright I was wrong. I promise that will not happen again."

Li smiled gently and went on with his sermon, "Music is a gift given by our Lord. It's meant to purify our soul and enrich our spirit, therefore should never be used as a means to show off."

"I have already said I wouldn't do that again. What else do you want from me?" I was a little inflamed.

"Look at you, the way you talk is the same way you play the violin. Too much emotion and lack of reason. Whenever you get excited, the rhythm gets quicker and the intonation inclines higher." Li paused. He washed a cup again and again, indicating he was afraid to pass his cold to me. Then he passed a cup of tea to me.

Seeing I cooled down, he added, "As a young man like you, with character and talent, I'm sure you will be a violin soloist, a good one in the future. You do have some technique problems though, but that can be solved gradually, with time. What I'm saying is, you can learn to be a good violinist and at the same time learn to be a *good human being*."

"You mean I'm *not* a good human being? I don't steal, don't rob and I love the always great, glorious and correct Party and Chairman Mao." This time I was more exasperated than inflamed.

Teacher Li shook his head a little and stood up, "Come, let me show you something." We went out of his room, passed through a small path and then from the back entrance, we entered the church.

It was rather dark inside the church. The sunlight cut through the colorful glasses, brilliantly filtering upon the portrait of Jesus. That was the first time I was in a church, an experience that had no precedent. I felt like my soul got away from my body and was placed in front of God.

Li looked at Jesus and said to me devoutly, "We should not only love the Party and Chairman Mao, but also love the people, not only the people around you, but also the people all over the world."

"Love people all over the world?" I questioned, "Including our enemies?"

"That's right, *including* our enemies." Li looked at my puzzled face. He

61

explained softly, "Maybe it is not appropriate to talk about the love of Christ nowadays, but at least you should be able to be generous enough to love those who quarreled with you. For example, to love Wang ShiYi, not only because he is your friend, your schoolmate and the one who has helped you before, but also as a human being. You should learn to be grateful. We all should learn to understand the meaning of thanksgiving, for we all were born with sin. You know why Christ was put on the cross?"

Just like that, apart from the violin lesson, Li was also often evangelizing, preaching the gospel, talking about God, love and kindness, forgiveness and thanksgiving, the way he did was as if the astounding Cultural Revolution outside did not at all exist.

Being educated by Li, quite a few times I wanted to say "hello" to Wang, but after all, I could not put down my face. I guess Wang felt the same. During the Mao Team's performance, every time it got close to the solo passage, Wang put the violin down, as did Ma, leaving me no choice but to play the solo section. On the surface I was the winner of the solo conflict, however, since then, Lu stopped asking me to look after her schoolbag. The successor was no one other than Wang ShiYi.

One day I caught a chance to show my warm temperature to Lu, but in return I received a few cold words, "I'd rather you blow your bamboo flute." was exactly what she said to me.

I finally made up my mind to reconcile with Wang. I waited outside the rehearsal hall. When I saw him come out I intentionally bumped straight into him, my head colliding with his chest. Immediately I apologized. He however, repeatedly said, "Never mind."

"Painful?" I asked.

"Very painful." Wang covered his chest with a hand, quickly explaining, "Pain not caused by you, but from a heart broken." Wang suddenly looked awful.

"Hey, don't you scare me!" I was truly a little scared.

At the right moment, Lu walked out of the rehearsal hall... Wang fell toward me and whispered, "Say I'm dying."

I embraced Wang and loudly shouted to Lu, "I'm Dying. No, I mean he's dying. Please help me–*him.*"

Can you imagine? The most sympathetic and kind-hearted Lu XiaoBing laughed at us, saying coldly to me, "Ask him if he wishes to be buried or burnt."

"You, how can you be so heartless, he is not dead yet." I yelled at Lu. "No, not dead yet, not in a hundred years." Lu laughed. Waiting until Lu disappeared; Wang stretched his arms twice and soliloquized, "Again, a fruitless effort." Then he shook hands with me very exuberantly to express our reconciliation and walked away whistling a tune.

"Hey, are you still mad at me?" I confirmed.

"How could I be? On the contrary, very grateful." Wang said cordially.

I believe what he said was true. Because if it were not for me taking over his violin solo, how would he have gotten the chance to look after Lu's schoolbag!

8: MY NOT-SO-SWEET HOME TURNS SOUR AND BITTER

Seeing My Status In My Parents Heart Through A Fight With Schoolmates

In a preceding chapter I mentioned how during the first year of my learning the violin, my father, just like most of the time, was *"the family man rarely with the family"*. He was still at the May 7 Cadre School being reformed, for better or worse. Therefore, at home was only the "family woman" and we three kids.

As I also wrote, I always wanted to be number 1 at home. Unfortunately, DanXin seldom took my provocation bait and even if he did, it always resulted rather quickly in, "to win or to lose is a common occurrence to fighters" (a Chinese proverb for losers to excuse themselves).

Although I do have a younger brother, that little monkey had a powerful backer supporting him. Whenever I laid a finger on him, Mom always punished me by beating my flesh and hurting my feelings. That continuous abuse made me feel I was not being treated fairly at home. Therefore, home to me had never been very sweet.

My not so sweet home took a turn for the worse, becoming sour and bitter from my physical fights with schoolmates.

In chapter five I introduced my middle school as a former girls' school, we were historically the first boys to attend that school. There were only six boys out of the thirty students in our class and half of the six were "girlish". On the other hand, the class next to us not only had more boys, but each of them were like tigers, like lions, and they all lived on the same street. They soon became the overlord gang of the school.

One day without knowing why, my male classmate Jiang, had a quarrel with the boys in the next class. That group of tigers and lions incredibly, chased Jiang up to our classroom. Watching, Jiang was punched and kicked severely as all the male classmates backed away in fear, leaving the girls desperately trying to moderate the violence with words.

At this point one of my female classmates, Ou YangMin shouted at her boy classmates, "Come on, how can you guys watch our classmate get beaten? Where are your balls?" (I know where their balls were, all pressed tightly between their legs, mine too were between my legs but not pressed as I squatted at a toilet.)

Ou YangMin had the nickname "tomboy", she showed braveness at this key point. Her shouting encouraged the boys. They tried to stop the fight but it ended before doing so as nobody took the lead. Seeing the boys pressing their balls even more tightly, Ou shook her head and rushed forward into the crowd herself but was blocked by another female classmate, Yu Bing.

Yu was our class flower, the prettiest girl in the class. She looked delicate, fragile and unobtrusive, but beyond everybody's expectation, her bell ringing voice sounded, *"Stop!"*

Do you believe that? The gang stopped and watched as the flower poked her way into the crowd to help classmate Jiang stand up from the ground. She instantly won a burst of acclaim.

The aggressors looked at each other in blank dismay. The head of the gang felt a huge loss of face and therefore became more aggressive from the embarrassment. He ordered loudly, "Why stop? Come on!" The punches were falling like rain on Jiang's body. The flower Yu, tried to protect Jiang with her outstretched arms, but was pushed down by the gang. Seeing the flower down, the tomboy Ou rushed up with fury, "Does it make you heroes by beating girls? I will fight you guys to the *death*."

At almost the same time, I heard the news and dashed back to my classroom from the water closet. Seeing the invaders had trampled our flower on the floor, I lifted up a chair overhead and rushed into the crowd. A couple of the other boy's saw my, "fight to the death" attitude and also raised chairs. The head of the gang realized the situation had changed and the odds were now against them. He ordered, "Withdraw, wise fellows don't care about a short-term loss!"

I put the chair down. Hurrying to embrace Yu, I didn't notice at all that I had stepped on the buttock of classmate Jiang, only felt the ground was not quite flat. Hence, the entire class burst into applause, again for the second time. Instantly, I became the class hero, admired by more girls than before. To me, more importantly was that was the moment Yu and I became the best of friends in the class, and we've kept in touch (never physically) even to this day.

Despite all of this, the conflict wasn't over. On that day after class, the gang was waiting for me outside the school entrance. The cruel strikes and severe kicks... I still feel pain when I recall it. I remember the only words I said to them repeatedly were, "I have an elder brother and he won't let you get away with this!"

Mentioning my "elder brother" was evidently my consolation, since how could it be possible for my gentle, kind-hearted brother DanXin to fight, especially, for *my* problems?

Back home, Mom was very upset to see my ripped pants (instead of my deformed face and colorful body), "You are the only trouble maker in this family! You see, you see, you made two holes in your new pants that I made only two years ago! Today your father will come home. You talk to him *yourself!*"

Almost a year since I saw my father last and he chose *this* moment to come home, must be God's will. I purposely did not clean my wound in order to make him feel pain and sympathy for me. Yet I completely miscalculated. Father came back very late that night. He was eating as he listened to my grievance. To express my pain, I, "hun, hun" while narrating, expecting he might feel sorry for me. But all my efforts seemed to be in vain, as he had no response throughout my entire story, only one sentence at the end, "You are troublesome".

"Your flesh and blood has been abused. You do not help me, but criticize. Are you really my father?" I queried.

"What can I do to help you? Go to your school to fight with your schoolmates? Children fighting with each other is a common matter, that happens all the time. Ask your mother to write a letter to your school tomorrow. Only the school authority can deal with such matters." Father put his chopsticks on the bowl, meaning the issue was concluded.

"You don't help me now, wait until you are old, on whom can *you* rely?" I rumbled to threaten him.

Father, "Ha" sneered. He took off his glasses, wiped them clean, put them back on his nose and stated very seriously, *"When I'm old, I will not need to rely upon you. I don't need to rely upon anyone. I'm a Communist Party member. I can only rely upon my Party, the great glorious and correct Party. Since I joined the Party, I have wholly committed myself to it. I do nothing else, nothing else at all except what the Party asks me to do."*

"Did your *Party* ask you to manufacture so many children and ask you not to take care of them ?" I assailed him.

"That's right." Mom chopped in, "It was the Party that called to have as many children as possible, for the sake of war. At that time every woman wanted to be a heroic mother. 'More people greater strength' as it says. If it were not for those words …"

Though Mother did not finish her notion, from her tone I understood that she somehow regretted having gotten into the Party's trap and giving birth to four products.

Father immediately caught Mother's words as if he wanted to cover up the Party's scheme, "Good kids, many are not enough, bad kids, one is too many. In our family, there is just one too many." As soon as he finished, he gave a sign of "meeting over", and arranged his body in bed.

My heart was smashed and torn into pieces by his disdainful words. Compared with that, the pain from my wounded body became insignificant. I loudly roared at him, "I swear I will overthrow your dog-shit Party! I want you and your nonsense Party to realize what a great mistake you people have made having manufactured me as the one too many."

At that time I found no other way to pour out my emotions but to fiercely curse his Party, that so-called *"great glorious correct and everlasting Party"*.

Seeing me sorely enraged the old man revealed his satisfaction as the winner with a quiet sneering "ha", followed by a yawn and then turning his back to me. When I was about to leave him he soliloquized, "Overthrow my Party? Hen! The Chinese Communist Party can never be overthrown, unless, it falls down itself!" Soon after that he fell down horizontally in his bed.

The next day, Mother gave me a letter and asked me to hand it over to the school authority. I really didn't want to go to the school; to be more precise, I really *dared* not go to the school. I wandered a few circles outside the school and then accepted there was nowhere else to go but the school.

Painstakingly I walked to the school entrance but still dared not go in. Meanwhile, I saw my classmate Ou YangMin with her father, walking towards me, I mean towards the school entrance. She looked just like me, with a swollen face and colorful arms, most probably legs too.

"Are you too being beaten?" Ou looked at me in surprise, "Alright, let's go tell the Worker's Propaganda Team together. (the Worker's Propaganda Team was the authority in all Chinese schools at that time)"

I learned I was not the only one beaten by the gang. Ou's father was a worker, the highest-class rank in Chinese society during the era. Immediately, I felt to have caught a powerful ally. I took my mother's letter from the schoolbag and held it in my hand, vigorously following them to the school administration office.

On the way I made a chance to boast to Ou, "My father also wanted to come with me. It was *I* who stopped him, because I knew he had an important meeting to attend."

Before I even finished my hot air, my face turned hot, hot enough to burn an egg, hotter than being beaten the day before.

After a few words between the workers (Ou's father with the leader of the school Worker's Propaganda Team), the four representatives of the gang were kneeling on the ground in the school administration office. The leader of the worker's team asked the four boys what social class their families were. Three out of the four were from worker's families, only one from a Right-Wing family (Right-Wings were anti-revolutionaries).

Instantly, the leader of the worker's team slapped the face of the Right-Wing-Family boy, twice. An old worker simply removed one of his shoes and whipped the boy's back repeatedly, "How dare you beat a working class junior!" The other three boys were scared to death.

"To use violence against violence." that was the sort of education the workers taught us. Unfortunately I don't think that was the worker's patent, as my Mom also did that to me to stop me abusing my baby brother. Doesn't this also apply to world politics?

Though I was gloating in the beginning, soon I couldn't stand the fact that adults were beating a teenager, especially when I remembered Teacher Li's voice, "love and forgiveness". I subconsciously raised my right hand (the hand with my mom's letter) to show my opposition.

Classmate Ou noticed the letter and asked, "What's in your hand?"

I quickly scrunched the letter into a paper ball, stalling, "You mean this? Nothing, just some paper, for the toilet."

While I was saying those words, I was very jealous of my classmate Ou YangMin, envying her to have a father willing to protect her.

The gang of four was brought to our classroom to admit their guilt and forced to apologize. When Ou and I went into the classroom, we received a huge welcome of applause, like heroes. But there was one classmate who didn't applaud. That was Yu Bing. She not only did not applaud, but did not even show her face, instead bending her head to the table the whole time.

When the lesson was over, I went to talk to Yu and found that she also had a panda eye. Ou rushed to ask her, "Why don't you ask your father...?" Yu turned her face away from us to avoid the question. Her blood brother, or should I say, "blood sister" Wang XiaoAn stopped us from further questioning.

Later, she told us Yu was from a capitalist class family and her parents were killed by the proletariat class a long time ago. Yu was brought up by her maternal aunt. She had always been a good, sensible girl. No matter what happened, she would always keep it to herself, never wanting her aunt to worry about her.

Though I really felt sorry for Yu, still I thought I was worse off. After all, there was nothing Yu could do about the fact that she had no father, yet I *did* have a father but there was no difference from being without, in fact it was worse. That makes a big difference between Yu and me!

Why Play The Song, "Home, Sweet Home" Away From Home In The Rain?

A direct conflict between Father and I because of the violin.

My father stayed home for a few days. In that period I couldn't practice my violin because my hand was enlaced with a bandage.

Although I felt wronged and acted rashly toward my father, I was afraid of losing the opportunity to show off my violin playing ability in front of him. I didn't forget that that was a part of my very original purpose of playing the violin, to impress him, make him acknowledge my talent, and respect me.

There were only two days left before Father was to return to his May 7 Cadre School. I played truant and returned back home in the afternoon. I took the gauze off of my hand and endured the pain, trying to practice an old European folk song, "Home, Home, Sweet Home".

I stood by the window, peeping outside, all the time expecting Father to show up while I practiced the violin. A surge of satisfaction gushed from my heart when I imagined the surprised face of my father.

At last, I saw my parents walking towards home. I quickly moved to the back room lest Father realize my intention to show off. I forgot the pain and concentrated all of my technique and musical feeling on playing the song, "Home, Home, Sweet Home". Perhaps I was too excited; I could not keep my bow from trembling. I dreaded so much the thought of being laughed at by him.

The door, "peng", pushed open. Hastily I asked to be excused, "I didn't do well. I'll do it again."

My father was certainly surprised, though _not_ in the way I had hoped. He did not praise me, nor criticize me, but uttered very seriously with his eyebrows wrinkled, "What nonsense are you doing?"

"Not nonsense." I was still in my intoxicated mood, "It's a European song called 'Home…'"

"What 'Sweet Home'?" Father didn't wait for me to finish my explanation; obviously he wanted me to know that he knew the title, "Home, Home, Sweet Home". Then he fixed his eyes on my hand-copied violin method Hohmann on my bed.

Just then, I started to realize that this thing could go wrong. I used my buttocks to cover the Hohmann by sitting on it. But that was too late. Father not only seized the Hohmann, but also found the music records I picked up from Teacher Lao's, "trash dump".

Father quickly glanced at all of the things and jawed, "Where did you get all this rubbish from? Mozart, Beethoven, Liszt, Tchaikovsky, all the bourgeoisie nonsense."

Originally I wanted to impress my father, but now was being impressed by my father. Since he could recite so many great names so smoothly, he should be bourgeoisie enough himself. Wrong?

Father took my hand-written copy of Hohmann and the records to the front room and slammed them down on the dining table like booty. Oddly, his anger was not towards me, but directed at my mother. He demanded, "Look what he's doing at home! Why haven't you done anything to stop him?"

Mom looked unconcerned. She replied, "He never listens to me, what could I do? I know it's noisy. The neighbors complain a lot. But he's a member of the School Mao Propaganda Team. His playing the hand-lin (violin) has not cost the family so much. Why not let him be?"

"Comrade…" Father paused, perhaps not finding the appropriate vocabulary to criticize Mom, if there were any. He swallowed his mouthful of phlegm, changed posture and continued his bureaucratic jargon, "Money, money, money, all you know is money. Where has your class consciousness gone?"

Father started to turn the pages of my hand-written Hohmann, "Look, look what, Aida, Carmen, Serenade? How could he learn all these if no one taught him? This is the new tendency of class struggle happening in our family, and it is a concrete phenomenon of capitalism fighting with us for the next generation!"

"Alright, alright, alright! I'm no good at educating him, I entrust you to do the job, totally, entirely and completely. He is *your* son too." Mom poured out her chagrin, "You are never home. I have to work and at the same time take care of the kids, all of them, their eating, drinking, shitting, sleeping and going to school. When have I got the time to look at his… his bean sprouts (music notes)? Now you are home. You do whatever *you* want."

Mom's speech shut Father up. Therefore he diverted his spear, pointing it directly at me. Very sternly he interrogated me, "Give me a black or white answer. Where is this rubbish from?"

"From a rubbish place?" I pretended.

The old ginger is always more spicy than the young. By the end, Father found out the Hohmann was from Ma XiaoMao and the records were from Teacher Lao. He wrapped the Hohmann and records up together with a few used newspapers and was about to walk out."

"Where are you going? It's supper time." Mom tried to stop him.

"This is far more important than eating." Father said to Mom and then to me, "*You*, come to the school together with me."

"I'm not going at supper time. There is nothing more important than eating. 'The good health is the capital of revolution', our representative Chuan always reminds us." I rejected my father.

Ladies and gentlemen, think of that, when I was beaten, he, as the strongest man in the family refused to go the school in my defense, but now he wanted to go to my school to accuse me because I played the violin. What on earth *was* this? Of course this is what I'm thinking today, while at that moment I thought nothing but to protect my Hohmann and records.

I stepped toward Father and scrabbled to release my treasures from his hands. Father was not in the mood to contend with me like someone of my age would be, he released my treasures and left.

"Go with your father and take the chance of also sorting out the fight with your schoolmates with your school authority." Mother ordered me.

"No, no, NO, I'm not going!" I obstinately back talked.

"You, trouble making son, you, stubborn little devil..." Mother's pinching and beating on my wounded body turned those spots from blue to red again.

Far worse was when she started to grab my treasures out of my hands.

To me, being beaten by Mother was an everyday meal that I was very much used to, but to take my music away from me was something absolutely intolerable. Mother made her best endeavor to pull my Hohmann. I desperately clung to it not letting go. During the dire struggle, Mother lost her balance and toppled over, her hands still griping my music book.

DanXin quickly went to help Mom stand up. My eight-year-old baby brother rushed out shouting loudly towards Father, "Baba, come back, the number two is beating Mother!"

Seeing Father was turning, the baby swooped in on me like a little lion, opening his mouth and biting my arm! Both of my hands were employed as they tightly held my music book. I had no extra hand to fight with the lion, all I could do was try to get his teeth off by swinging my arm.

The result was just the opposite! The more I swung, the more painful it was. So I had no alternative but to go to my last resort. However, regardless of how hard I kicked; the baby lion would not take his teeth off me!

Meanwhile, Father strode in. He asked Mother to let go of her grip and helped her sit by the table. He then ordered the little lion to release his weapon and embraced him for standing by his mother. Then, he took my music treasures from my hands with a sudden force and *smashed* them on the ground.

"You, get out, our family doesn't have such a son!" Father shouted heavily as he pushed me towards the doorway. Mother took this opportunity to pick up my hand-copied music notes and tear them page by page. That sound was simply worse than a knife cutting my heart out.

Just as I was pushed out of the house, I heard the smashing sound of my records. That sound too, just like a bomb blowing up inside my body.

I was outside of my home away from my family, peeping through the window and saw my baby brother bringing the bed-wetting basin. Mom put all the torn pieces into the basin. Father lit a cigarette with a match, and quickly passed the left over burning match to Mom. Mom did not catch it but rather pushed Father's hand, the match dropped into the basin, instantly, a red terror growing.

That was how I saw my hand-written Hohmann, my months' of painstaking effort, that hard work day and night, stroke by stroke and page by page emotions, my joy and love, burning to ashes in front of my eyes.

I yelled with all my strength, "Stop! Don't!..." But nobody heard the sound but me as I bit my lip so tightly it started to bleed.

My brother DanXin witnessed the whole process. He was in a state of shock and stood there with his mouth half open.

I waved my hand to him, the only person in my family I might turn to for sympathy. DanXin took my hint and quietly moved to the back room. I quickly ran to the back door. Without asking, DanXin opened the back door with my violin in his hands, "You come in now you will be *dead*. Take your stupid thing and run."

Before I could even show my appreciation, DanXin shut the door with an angry sentence, "They burned my Foreign Folk-Song 200 book too. All your fault."

I held my violin and ran straight to the Xiang Jiang River.

The flowing river water brought me back to my childhood. I could hear my Uncle Din's out-of-tune singing with the wrong lyrics, "The eastern sun is declining down the western hill...". I could also hear my aunt's calling, "DanJiu, the supper is ready."

Talking about supper, a band started to play in my stomach and sour water gushed into my mouth. It started to rain. I'm not making a move. The rain really poured down, and was getting heavier and heavier.

Though I was very cold, I *had* to take off my over coat to wrap up my violin. I hid myself under the extended eaves of a storehouse. "To suffer from cold and hunger" under a roof to cover my head, was a literal and vivid depiction of my situation.

It turned to complete dark. The rain was getting gradually weaker. I left the riverbank and walked subconsciously toward home.

"If you could go back, why run out in the first place?" a voice asked me.

"If not home, where else could I go?" I replied to that voice, rascally.

When I reached the railway where I used to practice my violin near home, I stopped. Not because I was too tired, but too afraid, and of course, did not want to lose face. Looking at the faint light from that home window, I was trembling from incomparable cold.

The rain finally stopped. I sat on a railway track and my rain soaked body began to feel the pain of my schoolmate's punches, Mom's nail marks and little brothers bite marks. I needed to do something to anesthetize my body. I opened my violin case. With my shivering hands I played the unfinished song, "Home, Home, Sweet Home".

I hoped someone in my family would hear, wishing one of them, or even a neighbor would come to call me back. A tiny little call in the distance would be enough. I extravagantly imaged my returning home to a bowl of steaming hot noodle waiting for me. If so I would certainly put in more peppers and an extra spoon of lard. Please don't laugh at me. I had just turned 14, a boy at his awkward age.

When I write this section today my heart bleeds again from these old wounds. But please, save your tears for later.

On that night, I waited and waited; the dream of "someone calling me back" never did happen. I held my violin and lay my head on a pillow, sorry, on a rail; slowly I brought myself into a dreamland.

9: The Intellectual, The Flight, The Chaos

Encounter A Bosom Friend - Jiang LangSha

I fell asleep on the railway and dreamed I fell into an ice hole. I was shivering from the frigid cold until I couldn't shiver more as I had turned into a corpse.

I saw someone walking towards me. He looked familiar, resembling my Uncle Din, or my aunt, but when I took a close look, unexpectedly that person was *my father*! He bundled me with a big quilt, took me home, and put me on my bed.

Though I was totally conscious, my body could not move. By then, my younger brother DanHen came towards me with a lighter in his hand. He made a fire with the lighter and started to burn my quilt! I yelled desperately, "Don't burn my violin, don't …"

"I'm not burning your violin; I'm just burning some rotten rail-wood to dry your clothes." My baby brother's voice had changed to that of a young man.

I woke up from my dream to find myself in bed, not alone but together with an unknown young man! I jumped down from the bed with alarm, then realized I was naked, *totally*, not even wearing underpants! I was soon trembling again.

"They should be dry now. Quickly, put them on, or you'll catch a cold." The young man pointed to my clothes by the fireplace.

I put my clothes on as quickly as I could, took a look around and recognized it as the wooden hut by the rail crossing where a senior rail-and-fence-switchman used to stay. I remembered when I was in primary school I used to pass this place twice a day, from home to school and back. How did an old man became a young man?

"My name is Jiang LangSha. My master told me that from time to time he asked you to buy tofu and vegetables for him. Do you remember?" That young man introduced himself to me.

"LangSha?" I thought, "In English it should be 'river sand wave'. How can a rail-switchman have such a romantic, capitalist, 'four olds' name?" I felt a little amazed.

Seeing me more relaxed, he went on, "Recently I've grown a habit. After supper I always wait for you to play the violin. I can tell you are progressing very fast. When you didn't show up for a week I wondered why, thought you might have moved away. Luckily I heard you again yesterday. But your unusual playing of the song 'Home, Home, Sweet Home' (he also knew 'Home, Home, Sweet Home!) made me a little worried. But not until I went to switch the rails did I find you were falling asleep on the railway. *Very* dangerous you see."

I felt very grateful to him, not only for his saving my life, but also equally if not more importantly, for his appreciation of my violin, which was *vital* to me, particularly at that moment, under such circumstances.

To be with a confidant I surely could, "make myself at home."

"Can I have some hot water? A-n-d do you have something to eat?" I asked casually.

"I baked a sweet potato for you. It should be ready by now." Jiang got off the bed, took out the sweet potato from the fireplace, peeled off part of the skin and passed it to me.

The baked sweet potato was truly sweet and hot, so was Jiang and his hospitality.

Watching me devour the sweet potato voraciously like a hungry tyke, he looked sympathetic and hesitant, but still asked, "You've got wounds all over your body. Did your parents do it to you?"

"No!" I immediately denied, "How could they, my parents love me very much, they would *never* do things like that …" I couldn't talk more. In China there is a proverb, "The ugly domestic affairs can't go outdoors". In English it might be, "Don't air your dirty laundry in public." Therefore I could say nothing, just chew my sweet potato with ketchup of sour and bitter snivels.

After my emotions cooled down a bit I began to think that I could actually survive by staying here for a couple of days, but my mother couldn't. She must be worried to death over my whereabouts.

Imagining my mother quarreling with Father, I started to be happy again.

Jiang looked tired. He wrapped himself with an army coat and sat on the wooden armchair. After being recharged with hot water and sweet potato, I became energetic again. I felt I should do something to entertain him in return for his kindness.

But as soon I started to talk, like a vehicle with a break out of order, I couldn't help making stories far away from, or even opposite to the facts. Stories such as, "my parents love me the most of all the brothers in the family, they forced me to learn the violin and put all their hope on me to become a dragon (to be rich and famous)," Bula bula.

The alarm clock rang. Jiang suddenly stood up, cut my hot air and said to me, "I have to go switch the rail. I think you are tired too. If you can't go home tonight, you may stay here. 'Tomorrow, we will have milk, we will have bread'." He imitated the tone of Lenin in the movie, "Lenin in 1918", smiling with a sense of humor.

Like that, I made Jiang LangSha an acquaintance. Later he became one of the most important figures in my life, influencing my thoughts and impacting my life.

I Became A Devil Harming Everyone Around Me

Let me continue my story about staying overnight with Jiang LangSha.

When I woke up the next morning, I found myself again in Jiang's little plank bed.

Jiang, no longer a stranger but rather a friend, was still sitting on the wooden armchair wrapped in his army overcoat. (Army items were the most popular and most common among the civilians during the Cultural Revolution. Just imagine how much money the army made from the civilians?)

Seeing me come back to the real world, he mixed some herbs with alcohol and daubed it on my wounded spots, "I learned this when I was at the so called *'vast world'* (countryside). I don't believe the drug will perform some kind of miracle or wonder, but surely better than doing nothing."

"You also have been one of the educated youths?" Thus the scene of sending-off the elder brothers and sisters to the countryside appeared to me again. (In the late 60s and early 70s, almost all middle school and high school graduates, the formal red guards, were sent to the countryside as so-called, "educated youth" to be re-educated by the peasants.)

"As a man of my age, who could escape that glory? However, I was unlucky. I stayed only a short period before I managed to come here." Jiang narrated, with a playful smile from his small narrowing eyes.

"Our great leader Chairman Mao teaches us, 'Great achievements can be made in the vast world', while you hide yourself in such a little hut, not bored?" I teased him.

"Bored? No, not at all, just the opposite." Jiang looked rather serious, more serious than needed. "There was nothing I could do in that vast world, but in here, this little hut, I can read numerous books. The world in the books is far more vast than the *'vast world'*. It's infinitely vast, endless with no limitations."

Jiang pulled out a book from beneath his bed, "Look, see what this is, 'David Copperfield' by Dickens". He passed the book to me with excitement.

I, as a boy having grown up under the red flag, had never read a foreign book. I turned the pages randomly to show my politeness and disapprovingly passed it back to him.

He did not take the book from my hand, but added, "This was my favorite book when I was your age. I have gone through it quite a few times. Every time I've read it, I felt I was the little David. Thanks to it, I overcame all my loneliness and sadness..." Seeing me still hesitating he insisted, "Take it home and read it. But promise me not to damage it or dirty it and make sure you return it to me when you finish reading."

In response to his fervency I just had to turn the pages again, this time, taking a look at some illustrations. I did that for I felt I had to give him some respect, especially when the sweet potato I had in last night was not yet out.

Jiang looked at the wounds on my face and hands sympathetically, hesitated for a moment but still suggested, "How about I take you home? I will try to talk to your parents. We've got thirty-six minutes until the next rail switching, thirty-five minutes I mean." He paused, and then complained with anger, "What gives them the right to beat a kid like that, just because they are parents?"

Immediately I explained again that my parents were not responsible for my wounds, at least not entirely. I also made up another story that I was just betting with my brother DanXin that I could stay outside all by myself without going home for two days.

"Right, I see, and understand." He imitated a tone of someone from a movie, as he did before when showing that he was saying one thing but meaning another.

I went on staying with Jiang as it happened to be Sunday and I had no school. At lunchtime, he let me share some food from his lunch-box.

After lunch, he joked seriously, "You have had my food, you should work for me too, as the book says, 'There's no such thing as a free lunch'." After that announcement he went out to pull the rail fence down at the road crossing. After the train passed, I gave him a hand pulling the fence up. To my surprise the fence was much heavier than I thought.

Close to 3:00 pm I stood by the road crossing, stretching my neck like a duck, expecting my family to pass. I remembered the whole family planned to go see a movie at 4:00 pm, a movie with the only "film star" in Chinese cinema at that time, the Prince Sihanouk from Cambodia.

Half an hour later, my family showed up. The little lion (my younger brother DanHen) was the vanguard, followed by my parents, then at the tail, my brother DanXin. I waved a little yellow rail-flag to draw their attention but failed. The little lion thoughtlessly looked at me like an unknown distant star in the universe. They were followed by the parents, whom also showed little concern, as if I were someone else's dog or cat.

This led me to believe that they had agreed to have the same attitude towards me before they went out. I was so anxious that I yelled out, *almost* yelled out I mean. Meanwhile, my wisdom prompted me to pull down the rail fence, blocking my brother DanXin. He stopped; staring down at his toes. Seeing that, the little lion retreated. He bent down to get through the fence, and dragged his oldest brother, "Come on, let's go, or we'll be late for the movie."

Seeing two sons were on the other side of the fence, Mother also stopped. Father walked forward a few more steps, realizing he had lost his function as the family locomotive and turned his head around. Instantly a kind of joy, a joy of victory and hope emerged in me. Hence I made a decision, make sure they do *not* see the movie!

Until then, Jiang had not noticed I put the fence down by myself. He rushed out with an ugly face to scold me for taking work as play and quickly pulled the fence up. Then he noticed that he was surrounded by my family. His ugly face suddenly turned much friendlier. My mother stared at him enquiringly and questioned, "Who are you? What are you? What's the relation between you and my son?"

Jiang LangSha immediately introduced himself, including "although not old enough yet to be a leading class, (working class was regarded to be the leading class at that era) surely not an anti-revolutionary."

Seeing Father approaching him Jiang added, "I'm an old friend of your son. It was me who invited him to stay overnight, it's not his fault. I'm sorry to have caused your worry, I sincerely apologize."

Father intentionally avoided eye contact with Jiang. Very impatiently, he urged Mother to go to the cinema. Mother looked troubled and her eyes turned red, however unwillingly she followed Father and walked away.

My father's attitude toward me must have enraged Jiang. He suddenly raised his voice shouting, "Just because you are parents you can abuse your child like that?"

Those words were like an electric shock to my mom. She turned back and rushed in front of Jiang, "Who abused him? Let's make it clear." Again Father pressed Mother, "It's not worth wasting our time here. Watching the movie is the main issue today. Let's go."

"Sorry, you don't abuse your son, only consider him *less* important than a movie." Though Jiang used sarcastic language to keep a sense of humor, his seriously congested facial expression revealed his agitation and anger.

Obviously, Jiang's sarcasm incited Mother a great deal. She neglected

Father's pullback, stepped closer toward Jiang and argued, "How do you know I take my son as less important than a movie? Who has been feeding him and raising him every day up until now? How much do you know of my family affairs? Today, I may as well *forget* the movie. Let's talk until it becomes absolutely clear!"

Hearing Mother say, "forget the movie" a joyous victory flooded my mind. Now is the time to please Mom by turning my spear on Jiang. I roared at him, "How dare you talk to my mom like that? Who invited you into my family business? You stop sticking your nose in other people's affairs like, "dog bites rat.""

My, "turning my weapon around" ingratiated Mom a little but not Father, not a bit. He made his last effort to hasten Mom to get going with him to the cinema but failed, he walked away all by himself. My baby brother followed Father at a distance and frequently turned his head back toward us.

I dared not check Jiang's reaction towards my abnormal attitude of, "biting the hand that feeds me". Thank God at that moment a train was drawing near. Jiang pulled down the road-crossing fence with Mother and DanXin on the other side.

Through the successive clearance between moving carriages, I saw the silhouettes of Mother and DanXin get smaller and smaller as they moved toward home. Combined with the rhythm of the train wheel rumble, my heart palpitated intensely, "Bang bang, bang bang, bang bang …"

After the train was gone, I thoughtfully offered my help to pull the fence up. Soon after, I apologized for the crude and reckless words just spit from my mouth and expressed that for atonement, I was willing to work there for two days for nothing except rice and bed.

Jiang paid little attention to what I was saying as he was in a state of profound thinking, "Your parents too, are intellectuals. How can they also…" He breathed, bewildered. Like that I stayed with Jiang for two more days. Little by little he told me about himself.

Jiang LangSha was from an intellectual family. In the year 1957, his father was given one of the Right-Wing headgears. The same as all the other million Right-Wings, his father was sent to be transformed far away from home.

Immediately, the mother had to draw a distinct boundary between herself and the Right-Wing husband by divorcing him and throwing herself into a working class's embrace. After the family's reorganization, Jiang LangSha suffered much maltreatment from the new family man, to put it into clear words, frequently suffering from beatings.

When family contradiction rose to a non-reconciliatory level, Jiang, as an elementary pupil had to give up the family, or more correctly, leave his mother. Through the introduction of his school teacher, he was adopted by a working class family, a family with only a daughter, that wanted a son very badly. Jiang had not seen his parents since.

When he was a high school freshman the Cultural Revolution started. He stayed inside and immersed himself passionately in his book world, without taking part in any revolutionary activities until he was sent to the countryside as an "educated youth".

After a short while he found it to be a pure waste of time and life, so he made excuses to return back to the city. Somehow he got himself acquainted with the former master of the little hut, the one I used to know, and replaced him in the job. (Afterwards I discovered Jiang had concealed a portion of the facts, which I will explain in later chapters.)

His story made me understand why he yelled so furiously at my parents for their ill-treatment of me, as he too used to be a severely abused child. In a way, we were two bitter gourds on the same cane.

Jiang also told me his father was a writer, and his dream was to follow in his father's footsteps and become a writer. Very confidently he said, "The most important book I want to write in my life is, 'My Father', because I'm very proud of him." Jiang's small narrowing eyes shined when he said that.

Jiang's words shook my heart, and also aroused a kind of jealousy. Yes, how wonderful if one has a father that he can be proud of, even though that father may not be a Communist Party member but a Right-Wing.

Two days later, Father went back to his May 7 Cadre School. I, as a little bird with immature wings, returned to the nest. Another, few days had passed. Gradually my wounds were recovering. But, just when everything seemed to go back to normal, another mishap started in school.

I Got Teacher Lao In Trouble

Before I go on about Teacher Lao, I have to tell a little story about our Mao Team. As I described in earlier chapters, the school and the Mao Team were governed by factory workers. The one in charge of our Mao Team was representative Chuang.

Though Teacher Lao made every effort, they could not get along well. There were just too many disagreements on too many fronts. Teacher Lao compromised as much as he could regarding all issues except one, Chuang trying to abuse our team girls, sexually.

One day after rehearsal, representative Chuang ordered Lu XiaoBing to go to his office, alone, to have a heart–to-heart talk. Teacher Lao knew exactly what was going to happen, therefore, as soon as Lu went into Chuang's office, he told me that Lu wanted me to look after her school bag and of course Lu's whereabouts.

It had been a long time since I had the chance to look after Lu's school bag. I was so delighted that I rushed to representative Chuang's office. I didn't bother to knock on the door but pushed straight in. Yet the door was locked from inside. I shouted, "Lu XiaoBing, I'm here, pass your school bag to me!"

A few seconds later the door opened. Lu looked uneasy with red face and eyes. Lu avoided eye contact and quickly ran away.

I was completely puzzled as representative Chuang shouted at me with great fury: "Who asked you to come here?!" I was such a naive boy that I answered this unnecessary-to-answer question, "Teacher Lao asked me to come here to take teammate Lu's school bag." That was it. Teacher Lao was in trouble for sure, it was only a matter of when.

Lu XiaoBing left the Mao Team suddenly, just like a few of our other former female teammates.

It was just a few days after my father had gone to the school with the music records I got from Teacher Lao, more precisely from his cultural trash. Lao called me to his home. He closed the window, put a mute on my violin, and then asked me to play the Balada by the Romanian composer Ciprian Porumbescu, repeatedly.

I stopped playing when I noticed Lao's eyes were turning red. After a moment of dead silence, Lao started to tell me a story about Ciprian Porumbescu. He then said, "If someone has no forethought, he must have immediate worries. You are a young man full of talent, passion and ambition. Therefore I hope you will always think about the future and not entangle your time and energy in those everyday trifles."

"Teacher Lao, if you have no other more important things to talk about, I'll have to go home. Today it's my turn to cook, one of the everyday trifles. If I'm late for cooking, I will surely be scolded again."

Just as I got out of Teacher Lao's door I bumped into his wife. I greeted her as usual, but she did not greet back as usual, worse than usual, much worse.

I would never have thought that that was the good-bye moment between me and dear Teacher Lao.

The truth was, after my father went to talk to the school authority, he handed a record of Beethoven's No. 9 symphony to the Worker's Team. One of the workers played the record on the school phonograph, and the whole school was amused by that powerful chorus. The worker was very much amused too and said, "Good sound." until my father stopped him and explained how serious the matter was.

It must have taken Father quite some time and effort before the workers understood what they were dealing with. That certainly gave representative Chuang an excellent excuse for revenge on Teacher Lao for what Lao did to him.

Lao's home was immediately searched. Thanks to my father's knowledge and instruction the working class team found all the "cultural trash", the western classical music tapes and records. Teacher Lao was sent to a countryside village school as punishment for his wrongdoing.

Even today when I recall that matter, I feel grief in my heart.

Teacher Lao was not the only one dragged into the trouble caused by my father, Ma XiaoMao's home was also searched. As Ma's father was a so called "Reactionary Academic Authority Intellectual", her home had been searched several times before; therefore nothing significant was found, except the violin method "Hohmann". But, something much worse happened when one of the workers dropped Ma's violin on the ground while conducting his search, "not intentionally" he claimed as he excused himself. The violin had a few cracks on the top, and the neck fell off of the body.

Ma narrated her calamity with tears. I immediately took her to see Master Zhou, the one who taught me how to make my first violin.

Surprisingly, the good and warm-hearted Master Zhou rejected my knocking at his door. On our way back, Zhou's daughter chased up behind and handed me a piece of pigskin hide glue (a special glue for making and repairing the violin). She told us that her father was strongly warned by the school worker's team, though as a worker himself, his home was spared a search.

Zhou's daughter's story scared us. We rushed to the church to see whether Teacher Li was okay. Thank God Li remained untouched. What a relief! I was really relieved I had not exposed anything about Teacher Li to my father.

I used all of my knowledge and craftsmanship learned from Master Zhou, to glue Ma's violin head and my violin body (the one my aunt bought for me at the May-First Cultural Store) together, so that Ma would have a violin to play for the time being.

Without Teacher Lao, the school Mao Team became a group of vapidity. After Lu XiaoBing left, Wang ShiYi also left, so we both quit the Mao Team and concentrated on home practice.

Thanks to my father, calamity fell upon my teachers, schoolmates and friends. This turned my love for him to hatred and a steadily growing desire for revenge.

During that period, I often had nightmares. If it was not the sky falling down it was someone chasing me trying to kill me. Each and every time it came to that crucial moment I could hear others calling, "Mama!" yet I had no one to call for help.

At that point I became clearly aware that I, as one of the communist products, who wanted to be a human individual, different from the Party molded pattern, stood there all on my own. I had no Communist Party to rely upon, nor the Party member parents who manufactured me. No matter what happens to me, obstacles encountered, adversity faced or difficulties to overcome, the one and only person in the whole world I could rely upon was I, me and myself. This fact left me with no choice but to fight my own way out, studying and working hard to make myself strong, strong enough to change my living conditions.

My better, happier life as an individual rather than a product, in the future, would be the best proof of my correctness in the lifestyle I chose to live.

10: The Second Stage Of My Violin Learning

I decided to be a professional violinist by stimulation. If say, my original intention of learning the violin was partly hoping to impress my father and gain his respect, after the incident, (burning my Hohmann and harming the people around me) to learn the violin became only for my love of the violin, though a portion of the fondness to show-off still remained.

Now when I think back, the words, *"love for the violin"* are not strong enough. More precisely, by that time, violin was the only thing and everything to me, my life interest and purpose, life content, spiritual consignment, and more importantly, a road or a bridge that led to the prospect of a better life.

Burned, my hand-copied music notes, I could hand-copy again. Not allowed to practice violin at home, I could go out and hide myself at my secret place close to the riverbank, indulging in self-inebriation.

But one major problem was, I had no money to buy the violin strings, particularly the A string which broke very easily. I remember an A string cost twenty fen RMB, the same amount as two lunches. I received ten fen lunch money from Mom daily. (Note: Here I by no means blame my mother. In fact, it was not easy to give me ten fen per day from her income.)

In that period, if I broke a string, I would go out of the classroom and play basketball during lunch hour. Sacrificing lunch to buy strings was soon discovered by my classmates (girls).

One day, Ou called me back to the classroom from the sports ground, saying that there was something in my drawer waiting for me. I opened my drawer; a bowl of steaming hot wonton appeared in front of my eyes! I felt awkward and embarrassed, but looked at Ou with thankfulness. She laughed and explained, "You think I would be so kind? If it were not for classmate Peng ManZhen putting in the money, I would never run an errand for you."

I searched for classmate Peng, hiding among the others but only saw half of her face, a blushed face. In fact I seldom talked to her. What she did for me that day touched me so much that until today I would never want to forget.

I pretended to be troubled, remarking loudly, "How can I finish such a big bowl of wonton? I ate too much in the morning, and it's still not digested, that's why I had to go out to play basketball."

I took the bowl and ran quickly, but not so quickly as to spill the wonton. I found a place with nobody, took a look around making sure no one was watching, then poured the wonton in my mouth and swallowed it down into my stomach like a hungry prisoner, cleaning the empty bowl a couple of times by means of my tongue afterwards.

The problem was, after that I could not spare lunch to buy violin strings anymore as I had to not only eat my lunch, but eat in front of the whole class, soundly, in order to prevent another, "wonton occurrence" from happening.

This matter soon spread to the ear of Ma XiaoMao. Hence, she gave me violin strings from time to time. What she gave were not cheap strings for students, but expensive, "Red Star" strings for professionals ("Red Star" silver strings were the best China made violin strings at that time).

The odd thing was, the look-new-strings were all broken and needed to be knotted before use. Ma could not stand my incessant enquiring, and finally told me the secret. Her little friend named DuGuo went into the Changsha City Opera and at her request, DuGuo kept all broken strings for Ma. Besides God, only DuGuo knew if those strings broke naturally or with some "help".

From then, I went to see DuGuo very often. Although he was much younger than I, he was half a head taller. The excuses for visiting him began with begging for strings and gradually changed to indirectly learning his violin performing technique.

Although I pursued my violin studies with Teacher Li, after getting to know DuGuo, I somehow started to feel that Teacher Li's method was good for beginners but maybe not the best for people who wish to be professionals. DuGuo was already a member of the professionals. He was taught and closely watched by his professional violin teacher therefore he progressed very quickly.

My trick of learning from him indirectly was, every time I went to see him I would ask for a piece of blank score paper, I would then hand-copy the violin exercise he was working on. During my hand-copying I always paid special attention to his teacher's pencil marks, the bowing, fingering, musical expression or technique hint etc.

After the copy was done I would always request that DuGuo play it a couple of times for me, claiming that I was checking my hand-copied notes for mistakes. The rest was easy. I went back home and would practice, twice or many more times harder than DuGuo, as I believed. Evidently, my violin playing progress was very obvious during this period.

Though I appeared to be very friendly to DuGuo I was truly envious of him. I envied his work and study environment but most of all his "Gold Bell" brand violin that was worth four hundred RMB, when the average monthly wage was forty RMB! Each time I saw the tiger figured maple back of his violin, I couldn't stop the slobber from dropping out of my mouth.

One day I was in DuGuo's room hand-copying Mozart's No. 3 violin concerto. When I had just gotten started, the leader of the orchestra called DuGuo out. "I'll lock the door from the outside. Make no noise. Nobody knows you're here. Take your time."

I copied, rested and copied. When I finished the first movement of the concerto it was time for me to go home, but I couldn't. DuGuo was still not back. I was tired and started to doze off. Though I wasn't even 15 yet, I was aware that it was rude to fall asleep in another person's bed. In order to stay awake I paced back and forth inside his little room.

It was then envy came into my eyes. The twilight through the curtain gap shone on that 4th grade "Gold Bell" making it look like a pile of gold, or maybe more like a beautiful girl with tenderness and affection, winking at me. I could no longer resist my desire, gradually I got closer to her temptation. I touched her neck causing the gold bell to ring. That made me *insane*. I took the bow out from the case. When the bow touched the violin, the sound brought me to wonderland.

From DuGuo's room, a crippled Mozart violin concerto No. 3 sounded. At exact the high climax of my self-satisfaction, a knock on the door, "bang bang" woke me up. Then I heard a man's voice, "DuGuo, your rhythm today is terrible. You need more attention." I immediately stopped playing and kept quiet as DuGuo had asked me to. But the voice did not give up, "How did you lock yourself in? Is there someone pulling your legs?"

I still kept quiet as I promised DuGuo. Another woman's voice from a distance answered for me, "DuGuo's not in. He's out with all the other students. He won't be back until 5 pm."

The man's voice replied to the woman's voice, "If DuGuo's not in, who's playing? A ghost? I heard the violin."

"That's impossible." a women's voice again.

"Don't tell me your conductor has a hearing problem." man's voice.

"Who could that be? Who? If you give no answer we will call the security section." both voices.

I had no choice but to tell them I was a friend of DuGuo, the one that comes very often.

"Alright, please open the window." The woman indicated.

The window opened, a young lady and a man in his thirties appeared to me.

"This is Teacher Xiao, the conductor of our opera and my name is Haung. I'm DuGuo's violin teacher." Teacher Huang's friendly face relaxed me very much. I politely greeted, "Nin Hao (You good), Teacher Huang and Teacher Xiao."

Huang nodded her head and asked me with an affable smile, "Conductor Xiao said you were playing the violin. Could you play it again, for us?"

Hearing that request, plus Xiao's extraordinarily serious face, my relaxed nerves tensed again. I faltered, "Could I play something else instead of the Mozart I just tried?"

So, I played, "The Beautiful Rosemary" by Chrysler that I felt adept at as I had learned it from Teacher Li. However, Xiao walked away before I finished my performance. Thank God Huang didn't leave, instead she started to show me the more correct way of holding the violin.

Meanwhile, DuGuo returned back. Huang left her last words to me, "You are a young man full of potential. But do watch your rhythm when you play."

DuGuo heard what happened when he was away, he said, "I was about to talk to my teacher Huang about you. Rumor has it our opera will recruit new violin students sometime soon."

Immediately my mood helicoptered and repeatedly I begged him to go and ask Teacher Huang and Xiao, ask what they thought about me and my violin playing, to see if I had any chance.

After about ten minutes DuGuo came back again.

"How was it? What did they say about me?" I was too impatient to wait.

DuGuo smiled but made no comment.

"Don't hold me in suspense, *please*! I really can't wait any longer!" I begged him.

"It's not that I am holding you in suspense. It is that I'm afraid you would be hurt to hear it."

"Nothing can hurt me. Say it now." I pressed on him physically.

"Alright alright, it is you who forced me. You face the consequence." DuGuo paused and said, "Our Conductor Xiao said you've got some bad amateur habits, for example bad rhythm, therefore to train you to be a professional violinist would not be easy."

"What?" DuGuo's words not only hurt me, but also shocked me, like throwing an atomic bomb into my mouth! "He said that, that I've got some amateur habits and not good at rhythm?" I roared.

DuGuo's face became longer, "I told you that you would be hurt, but you didn't want to believe me..."

"Hurt? Ha ha ha, No, no, no, I'm not hurt. Go to tell that man, say to be free in rhythm is my style, and I am an amateur and happy to stay an amateur." I made myself an exit to escape from the awkwardness and got out of DuGuo's room. I was in such an upset state that I forgot the Mozart Concerto No. 3 I'd spent the whole afternoon hand copying.

Isn't it true that in everyday life, it is alright for us to grow too tall, too short, too fat, too skinny, or too big a nose, eyes too small, as far as nobody points it out? But if someone does point it out, even though a fact, our feelings would be hurt.

Back home, Mother's scolding for being late getting home was a fruitless labor, my mind was stuffed with Conductor Xiao's words. I was tossing and turning all night until I finally got up and wrote a very emotional letter.

The next afternoon, as soon as my school was over I went to Changsha Opera again. This time I did not go into DuGuo's room but knocked at his window.

DuGuo opened his window, "You forgot your music notes." He passed them to me.

I took the notes with one hand and handed the letter to him with the other, "Do me a favor? Hand it to that Xiao, that man who beats time in your orchestra."

DuGuo looked curious and worried, "May I take a look?"

"Sure, go ahead." I encouraged him.

DuGuo opened the letter and read, *"I swear to you that someday I will become the No. 1 violinist in all of Changsha City. By then you will say I am a professional. When I play the solo in my style, you will have to lead your orchestra, crawling and rolling to follow my rhythm."*

DuGuo stopped reading, as he could not help laughing, "Jiuge (my nickname, means brother ninth), you are amazing. Even though one day you might become the No. 1, how can you say that, especially now? Aren't you afraid to be thought of as conceited and arrogant?"

"That's what I am, conceited and arrogant, extremely. I not only want to be the No. 1 in Changsha, but also No. 1 in the whole Hunan province!" I bragged aggressively and confidently.

DuGuo's window was shut. After that, I stopped going to Changsha Opera begging for broken strings and hand copying music notes. Nevertheless, Conductor Xiao's words continued to stimulate me, functioning as an everlasting power and energy, pushing me forward on my road to be a professional violinist.

11: THE FIRST HIGH CLIMAX OF THE STORY

My Maiden Sex Experience

Any Chinese man, or woman who has gone through the 60s would experience the headache of onerous household chores. For example, cooking rice. There was no electric rice cooker or gas at that time therefore we all had to make a coal fire. To make a coal fire, we had to go to the coal station to buy loose coal. To buy coal we needed to borrow a flatbed cart (a Chinese man-powered trailer). After we got the loose coal back home, we had to make briquettes, later it evolved into making honeycomb briquettes (it was called "oumei" meaning "lotus-root-coal"). Just dealing with the coal formed a chain business.

Also, since we had never even heard of the word "refrigerator", very often we needed to go to the food market. And as we had no washing machine, every item of clothing was dependent upon our hand-brush. Talking about washing clothes, I still remember that feeling, the feeling of acute pain from my carrot like little fingers in the ice cold water. They felt as though they were being pricked by millions of needles. In addition, mending clothes and other chores that were supposedly woman's specialties, us brothers got to do ourselves, as the only woman in our family, our mother, had to go out to win the bread, I mean to win the rice, for us.

There is something that needs to be clarified here. Our family was not an exception, almost all kids my age had to do slave labor to help the family.

I am here and rambling today not to blame my mother, nor the age. If there is something I could blame, anything at all, it would be that my mother made me in the wrong place or at the wrong time. I'm just trying to impart that as a fourteen-year-old juvenile, after school, housework and playing the violin, there was little time left for playing with other kids or childish pursuits. However, up til then, with effort, I somehow managed to keep the balance.

Since I had gotten to know Jiang LangSha, things started to change radically, as from him, I could endlessly borrow books. Works of western classical literature, books like: "Notre Dame de Paris", "Red and Black", "War and Peace", "Anna Karenina", "Spartacus", "Romeo and Juliet" and so on.

Among the piles of books, my most favorite, or as my father would say, the book that *poisoned* me the most, was "Jean-Christophe" by Romain Rolland. Though it is a very thick book, especially to a fourteen-year-old boy, I read it again and again. And I was so much absorbed by the book that sometimes I would imagine I myself was John Christopher.

Quite a few times I burned the rice while in my ivory tower with those books. At times I would keep reciting some of the most fascinating quotations when my mom slapped me in my face.

In return for Jiang's generosity in lending the books to me, I played violin every evening outside his hut near the railway.

"That's my mental food and emotional nourishment." he said.

In addition to reading the books, there was another good thing worth consuming time, eavesdropping on music from a radio station, "The Voice of America".

As I had no short-wave radio set, I would go to a classmate named Ho KeJin's home to do that. Ho KeJin was from a comparatively well-off family and had gotten a Red Light short-wave radio as a birthday present. For the sake of listening to the radio, we were once quite close.

Since "The Voice of America" was regarded as an enemy station and to eavesdrop on it was a serious crime, we usually had to wait until very late at night and then hide in his room covered with a quilt, while listening at a minimum volume.

One night we caught an unknown station broadcasting a violin concerto. That caused me to miss the last bus so I had to go home by the "No. 11 bus" (my own two feet).

During my three kilometer journey home, the rain began to pour down. Recalling the magnificent violin music from the radio I was literally, "singing in the rain."

When I finally reached home I was completely soaked through but was gratified that I could change my clothes and hit my pillow at last. However ... no matter how hard I knocked, Mother refused to open the door. I went around to the back door hoping my brother DanXin would show his mercy but heard Mother shouting at him, "Dare you to open it, you go out together with him!"

Left with no choice, I trembled to the railway hut. More strangely, on that night my buddy Jiang LangSha too ignored my knocking on his door. I was so sure he was inside, as I knew he had to switch the railway several times during the night. His rejection gave me no alternative but to sit outside of his hut dozing.

Not knowing how long had passed, Jiang's door opened. Jiang walked out with a raincoat. Not expecting to see me, he was surprised, "You're still here!"

I yelled at him, "What kind of friend are you?" I stood up and headed straight into his hut.

Jiang tried to stop me, "Don't..." But it was too late as I had already separated myself from my wet clothes.

There was no electricity inside. A faint kerosene lamplight danced with the breeze. I heard the train "Hong hong, hong hong." I was so cold that I couldn't wait for the train to pass, I buried myself in the quilt on his little wooden bed.

"*Ai, my mom!*" A sharp outcry, a woman's outcry was heard, followed by a woman's nude buttocks out of the other side of the quilt. With enormous surprise I quickly held a corner of the quilt tightly to cover my boy's thing. The opposing party too, held the other corner of the quilt tightly to cover her girl's part. However her other two upper parts were revealed, flickering with the rocking lamplight.

Meanwhile, Jiang finished his rail switching and returned back to the hut. Seeing the scene, he couldn't help laughing out. Quickly he controlled himself and introduced us to each other. To me he said, "My sister Chu XiaoLin. In fact I wanted you to meet a long time ago."

And to her, "This is my friend Chen DanJiu. He is the one people call Nine Brother, the violin genius that you said you wanted to meet."

To us he said, "Now you two have met each other, totally, completely, and with no reservation." Soon after the introduction he burst out laughing again. Probably feeling inappropriate, he controlled his laughter and added, "I don't know what to do? You two figure it out yourselves what's best for both of you." He took off his raincoat and wrapped himself in his army overcoat and lay on his wooden armchair sleeping.

We refused to budge for a little while. I told her that all my clothes were wet.

"Mine too, not dry yet." she replied. "I see." I puzzled, with no choice I said, "Ok, I go. Please turn your face around."

"Actually, I don't think I need much space." She said, in a tone of commiseration. She rolled her body up with a small part of the quilt and turned her back to me.

I was really cold and tired, and not yet at the age of needing to pretend to be a gentleman, so I also wrapped my body with a corner of the quilt and went to sleep, together with her feet.

When I woke up next morning, I saw no Jiang LangSha but found myself naked in bed holding a nude girl in my arms. That was the first time I was ever in touch with the opposite sex, physically. I subconsciously released her with astonishment. However, the curiosity and vague longing for a woman made me, a boy in his adolescence, embrace her again, carefully and softly. Her skin was very elastic, though not particularly smooth.

Meanwhile, I felt a baby bamboo growing rapidly between my legs. That getting longer, thicker and harder mysterious little bamboo shoot, pushed against Chu XiaoLin's thigh. Yet at the same time I felt extreme pain as my little banana was not ripe yet therefore the skin was still not peeled.

Suddenly, my whole body was soused like inhaling opium. Chu XiaoLin turned her body; accidentally or not, she touched the extension between my legs and seemed amused. When I realized that she was not really sleeping I was scared off the bed looking everywhere for my life-saving pants.

I returned back home with my half dry, half wet clothes but no one was home, that meant I still could not get into my room. Seeing me running circles to fight the cold, our back door opened. The next-door neighbor Hu MeiMei said to me, "Hurry up and change your clothes, otherwise you'll be just like me and catch a cold, unable to go to school."

I entered the shared kitchen but was still unable to get into my room. I had to ask her to stay in the kitchen while I stripped myself nude inside her quilt and then asked her to take my clothes away to dry in the kitchen.

MeiMei was of course very pleased to do that for me, in return for my favor once upon a time. Remembering back when I helped her after she was abused by her parents and left almost naked in the kitchen, I let her in to warm herself in my bed.

I waited in Hu MeiMei's bed, chewing the cud of the taste of holding XiaoLin's naked body. It didn't help that Hu MeiMei's quilt gushed with the smell of a woman; all of this put me in a state of sexual impulse. I was somewhat befuddled, feeling as if MeiMei walked to me, uncovered my quilt, her quilt I mean and held my life-maker-to-be.

My whole body suddenly cramped, "Wa!!!" I woke up with a throb of excitement and great pain at the same time, feeling moist in my leg junction. With my twitching body I immediately uncovered the quilt and found the moisture was not caused by urine, neither blood. It was a sticky jelly like or bean curd like something, that I had never seen before. I "wa" burst out crying.

MeiMei heard me and quickly came in from the kitchen asking me what was wrong. I hurriedly covered my boy's little thing (by then a middle sized thing) with the quilt, and answered, "There is no use to ask. My vitality of life is gone and I will die soon."

Hu MeiMei didn't get what nonsense I was talking about. After she pushed me repeatedly, I again explained, "My marrow, my bone pith has come out and I won't be able to live for very long."

I showed the part of wetted quilt to her. MeiMei saw it, also unable to figure out what that could be, my snivel, perhaps? Anyway, she went to fetch a few pages of yellow toilet paper (at that time, Chinese toilet paper was called "yellow straw paper") and wiped her quilt as hard as she could. Seeing I was shocked and ashamed, she covered my boy part with the last yellow paper and urged me, "Wipe yourself quickly and get out of here. By noon my elder brother will come back and if he sees you here he will be very angry with me."

That was my maiden ejaculation. My first sexual experience.

Here I have to give a few lines talking about this matter. At that time in China, anything to do with sex was an *absolute taboo*. No one talked about it. Therefore, regarding the knowledge of sex there was no information available. The whole nation was *sex blind*.

I remember we had a female dog. When the dog grew old enough, it started to have its period. The blood could be seen from its back. We brothers were so upset and sure that one of the neighbors was responsible for the injury to our dog. No adults, not our mother, not the parents of that neighbor boy, told us anything about it. So the quarrel between us and our neighbor went on periodically.

My first foreplay education was given to me by my Japanese girlfriend after I went to Australia at more than thirty years of age. Therefore, there will be more stories regarding how naive I was when it came to sex in later chapters.

Now I bring our story back to what happened with me and them.

After all of this, from time to time I met Chu XiaoLin at Jiang's little hut (perhaps I *wanted* to meet her). Occasionally I caught them doing things together. No need to mention how stimulating, yet painful (as my little banana was still green and the skin could not be peeled, every time I became aroused it would cause great pain.) it was to overhear their caterwaul outside the door.

One day, I overheard not their caterwaul but an argument. The voices were getting higher and louder, and Chu XiaoLin rushed out of the hut. I stood there without knowing what to do. Jiang waved at me and I walked into his little castle.

Jiang sat there with soured cheeks. He covered his eyes with his hands and kept silent for quite a while. Just when I started to wonder whether I should go away he suddenly stood, wildly grabbed me and put me down on his bed! I was shocked by his unexpected action and lost my faculty of reaction!

Before I tried to get away, he pressed me onto the bed with my face down and franticly pulled down my pants. I struggled desperately, like a fish out of water! Yet no matter how hard I floundered, as a teenager I was not at all an opponent of his. I felt something hard penetrating inside my back hole! The indescribable pain caused me to cry out miserably. I took a Shakespeare from his bed and pounded over my head!

Jiang immediately let me loose, covered his right eye with his hands and screamed madly. I seized the opportunity to lift my pants up and enduring the back pain, I escaped as quickly as I could.

Back home, I ran to the kitchen looking for MeiMei. As we were the only two left in our homes, I dragged her to my bed with her face down and recklessly took her pants off.

MeiMei too, was puzzled at first. But when she realized what I was trying to do she tried to resist, though not as much as I did but with an excuse, "The rice is going to be burned." I was too excited to care for the rice. However, when I fixed my eyes on her ass, I was more aghast than she was. I did exactly what Jiang did to me, to MeiMei, but only less than half in we both screamed from pain! MeiMei turned her body, and facing me, took the chance to get away from my bed.

Obviously, same as we tried to steal the green banana together when we were around ten, as boy of fourteen my little banana was not ready to be peeled and in her wrong place it was for sure painful! But to me that was the right place as Jiang taught by doing it to me. It took quite a few years before I came to know that human common knowledge.

The Story Of Jiang LangSha And Chu XiaoLin

Henceforth, I dared not see Jiang LangSha again, even when I needed to go somewhere, I made a detour to bypass his hut.

It was okay for me not to see Jiang, yet it was *not* okay not to read books. That put me in a constant state of anxiety, acting like a fly without a head.

One day, I bumped into Chu XiaoLin by chance. Maybe I shouldn't say "by chance", as she was apparently standing there waiting for me. Although she was only two years older than me, she acted like a little aunt, taking me to the Xiang Jiang riverbank and telling me the story about her and Jiang.

Chu XiaoLin's father was a man in favor of boys (a Chinese thinking of "men are superior to women"), yet, the mother's hemorrhage during the birth of XiaoLin cursed her body, leaving her half-paralyzed and living in a wheelchair. That brought her father's boy dream to a dead-end. Hence they decided to recruit a, "home stay" son-in-law when XiaoLin was a little toddler. This explains why the parents joyfully accepted Jiang as their adopted son when he was a primary school kid.

Jiang and Chu got along quite well with each other as brother and sister and had not the slightest idea what their parents plan was, until the day Jiang had to go to the countryside, to the so called "vast world". Their father started to worry that Jiang would be gone forever. Thus the father laid all his cards on the table.

The father handed Jiang a white towel and locked the two up in their room, ordering, "You two will not be let out until the assignment is accomplished. No red on the towel, no chow."

They waited. When they were too tired they went to sleep but when they woke they felt starved. Until Chu couldn't hold out any longer and begged her brother, "Let's do it."

That was the two youngsters' maiden intercourse. Immediately, the father tore the bunk beds apart and put them side by side, saying to them, "From now on, you two sleep together. Ever heard of the term 'child bride'? You are in fact a 'child bridegroom'. If it were the old society, (Chinese refer the time before 1949 as 'the old society') you would already be husband and wife. It's a pity in the new society we have to wait until XiaoLin reaches the legal age of eighteen.

Jiang felt suffocated in such a deformed family relationship and gradually he became abnormal himself. Every time he touched the body of XiaoLin, to him his sister, he felt a strong loathing and guilt, while Chu, a girl in her bloom on the other hand, was gradually getting familiar and accustomed to Jiang's body. That aroused her sexual desire greatly.

The situation developed to the stage that Chu initiatively asked Jiang for lovemaking. That made the days and nights longer and longer for him. If it were not for the loving and caring of the family in his childhood, he would probably have fled in the very beginning.

Fortunately, the time to be away from the family finally came when he had to go to the countryside as one of the millions of educated youth. At the countryside, Jiang avoided being with any women, therefore no need to mention he had no girlfriend. However, he somehow got quite close with a, "barefoot doctor" (self-trained local doctor with no or very little academic education) called, "Small White Face" and the two intimate male friends later became sex partners.

Jiang's foster father, also his supposed father–in–law, heard that his adopted son and son-in-law was mashing with someone else, a man! He stamped with fury and immediately ran to the countryside to get Jiang back.

That was exactly the time Jiang started to realize the countryside was not exactly as Chairman Mao had said, 'Great achievements can be made.', on the contrary, to him it seemed no achievements could be made out there. So, he pushed his boat along with his father's current and returned back to the city.

The father used all his brains, means, and everything in his power to lock Jiang in his pocket. At last, through all kinds of relationships, he managed to get Jiang a temporary job as a railway switch man, an ideal job in which Jiang couldn't go *anywhere*, only walk between the rail switcher and his little wooden hut.

Unexpectedly, Jiang fell in love with my violin playing and gradually moved his affection from the violin, to the boy who plays the violin. When Chu became aware of this, although partly for her natural needs, fundamentally she wanted to rescue her brother, or her husband to be, whoever, and get him out of the deviance and homosexuality.

Hence, she started to visit Jiang more and more often. I just don't want to imagine how dreadful it must have been for Jiang to do things he didn't like with his "sister" each time she visited.

Hearing the story, I had no words to say. Being a fourteen-year-old, these matters surpassed my comprehension.

Seeing I was affected by her story, she brought out the real business, "My brother Jiang is getting more and more crazy because he is unable to listen to your violin or see you. If things go on like this, something awful could happen. I've been talking to him, and he's pledged and gives you his words that he will never ever touch you again. Please go see him from time to time, as a friend, a good friend, just like before. About his abnormal sexuality, I'll do whatever is needed, trust me."

In finishing, she exhorted, "As it says, 'Don't wash your dirty linen in public.' (In Chinese 'the disgrace of a family should never be spread') So promise me you'll keep it all to yourself and never tell anyone else.

"I swear to Chairman Mao I wouldn't..." I didn't finish the sentence, therefore I don't remember if I meant, "I wouldn't tell anyone else" or "I wouldn't keep it all to myself"?

But even after all that, I still dared not go see Jiang LangSha as the memory of the back pain was truly stubborn. Nevertheless, I, a boy at the age of puberty, felt panic about my growing sexual desire. More and more frequently I hid myself under my quilt playing, with pain. My quilt started to look like a map, and every time after, washing it and letting it dry, the map on my quilt gradually growing bigger and bigger.

Although I no longer saw Jiang, I quite often met Chu, for only one reason, to borrow books. Through XiaoLin I got to know that there was a wooden box filled with books under Jiang's bed, the complete and only inheritance from his real father. That's why Jiang regarded the books as precious as his own life.

"Jiang brother had always been very nice and kind to me, but he never let me touch his books. Yet he is willing to lend books to you, that's an obvious sign of your importance in his heart." Chu said with a little flavor of jealousy.

Chu XioLin's words made me feel very heavy. Hence, I decided to give up the method of borrowing books from Jiang through Chu. I even thought of making an effort to quit my addiction to reading. But my effort didn't solve the problem, on the contrary, it put Chu in an awkward position. Almost once every two days she was at the rail crossing waiting for me to pass by, again and again asking me what was amiss with me. When I was forced to tell the truth, she laughed.

"If what you reject is Jiang brother, not books, I may be able to help you both, I mean both my Jiang brother's feelings *and* your reading. You see, my aunt is working at the provincial library. She has had nothing to do for all these years since the Cultural Revolution sealed the library. But recently, the library is thinking of sorting things out and putting them in order before re-opening. I was just considering getting a temporary job as my aunt's helper."

"Really?" Immediately I got excited, "In fact, besides novels, I'm also in *urgent* need for violin music scores."

I soon made a list: Kayser, Kreutzer, Paganini, and many violin concertos such as Bach, Handel, Mozart, Beethoven, Mendelssohn, Tchaikovsky and so on.

Since then, every time I met Chu, she always had a novel and a couple of music scores for me. And each time she handed them over to me she always emphasized the same thing, "No need to thank me, thank my Jiang brother. If it were not for the sake of his happiness, I would never dare to do things like that, although it is said that 'to steal books, one is not considered a thief.' On the other hand, who cares about books nowadays, who has counted how many of them were burned? If you had seen the tons of books piled up there with no one to take care of them, what's the difference from the trash heap?"

Chu's words, and more importantly her actions, made me more and more touched by Jiang's sincerity, which sometimes faded my memory of the back-hole pain. One day, I bought a twenty fen RMB Mahua (Chinese snack), planning to place it outside Jiang's little hut entrance, not to show my forgiveness, but to express my appreciation. Still a good distance from his door, I heard their quarrel.

"What's wrong with you today?" Chu's voice.

"Not today, it was wrong from the very beginning." Jiang's voice.

Chu: "What? You're saying you didn't like me from the very beginning?"

Jiang: "It's not that I don't like you, it's that I don't like to do *those* kinds of things with you."

Chu: "Don't like to do with me, equals don't like me?"

Jiang: "I don't like you, I love you. Let me say it again, *I love you*, very much, because you are my baby sister, my only sister in the whole world. So listen to me carefully. To like you but dislike doing things with you are two separate issues, totally."

Chu: "You mean you are not going to do it with me anymore?"

Jiang: "If it's possible."

Chu: "Not even after we get married?"

Jiang: "Oh, you still don't get it. Do I have to make it so clear to you my silly, that I would never get married, not to you, not to *anybody*?"

Chu: "Why?"

Jiang: "Because sexually I don't like women overall, *not at all.*"

Chu's weeping.

Jiang's comforting.

Chu: "I know your heart is occupied with that little Nine Brother. But he is a man, in fact not really a man yet but just a boy. He scares you to death. I beg you, never harm him again."

Jiang: "I know I know. What I did was disgraceful, as you said he is just a boy. But what you don't know is he is also a man, a man with a great future. That's why I wish to push him a bit with my meager strength, not to redeem my name from wrong done, but for his gift.

Now you understand why I asked you to get close to him? I hoped that you could substitute for me and do things for him. If possible, satisfy all his demands, with all that you can give. You know what I mean? If you really love me, you should do as I wish."

Hearing that, I ran away like a mad man and forgot to leave the bag of Mahua I purposely bought for him outside the entrance.

A few days later, Chu XiaoLin blocked me on my way to see Teacher Li. She said she would show me something to make me very happy.

Following her, we arrived at building ruins burned during the gun fighting at the beginning of the Cultural Revolution. I was led to a room, a room with some loose building materials scattered here and there.

Chu pulled out a sack and opened it. Thus some books and music scores flopped down on the ground. *Oh, my God!* Besides a small portion of novels, it's a whole sack of music scores, not only violin music scores, but also other scores such as piano pieces, operas, symphonies and works for voice etc.

"Loaded a whole bag for you. Should be enough for a while." she said.

"What's wrong? I mean right? *Why?*" I didn't know where to start.

"Why? Because I'm afraid I might not be able to help you with books anymore."

I was too excited by the sight of the books to listen to what she was really saying. Meanwhile, footsteps broke the joyous atmosphere.

She comforted me, "Don't worry, it's Uncle Feng, my acquaintance."

The man called "Uncle Feng", appeared in front of me. He was a tall, strong man in his fifties with longer eyebrows than normal. Chu introduced us to each other. I politely bowed to him, but he returned little response.

Chu finally said to me, "Take whatever you need now and leave the rest here. Whenever you need more, you can always come here to get them. It's absolutely safe here as no one else knows it but me."

Walking out of the building ruins, Chu told me that she got to know Uncle Feng many years ago when she was a little girl. Every time her father beat her, Feng's place was her shelter in which to hide.

Feng was a foreman working for Changsha Construction Company. He lost his wife a long time ago and had no children. Since then he had no fixed home, but lived wherever he worked. Chu repeatedly stressed that though Feng looked crass and uneducated in appearance, inside he was a very good hearted and kind person.

"I have already told Uncle Feng that you are my best friend. From now on if you are cornered, you don't have to see my Jiang brother but turn to him for help instead." she added.

When we reached a road crossing, a place where we were supposed to say goodbye to each other, she suddenly asked me whether I would like to eat a bowl of noodle with her. Seeing me subconsciously searching my pocket, she comforted me, "Don't worry, today it's on me."

I was relieved, "Next time…"

"OK, if there *is* a next time." she smiled, bitterly.

I ordered a bowl of shredded pork noodle. She said she couldn't taste it and so asked for a bowl of sour and spicy noodle. But as the two bowls of noodle were being placed on the table, she said she had little appetite, and only took a couple of spoons of soup, then pushed the bowl in front of me. I kept my nose straight to the noodles.

Watching me gorge, she turned her face away from me and silently wept. She waited until I finished my last string of noodle and then stood and handed over one big yuan RMB (two bowls cost only fifty fen) and said, "Keep the change." Before the noodle man thanked her she uttered, "It's truly tiresome to be alive."

"What?" I didn't get it.

She explained to me and to herself too, "I wish to leave this place and go somewhere else for good, to find another way of existence, in another world."

"I see!…?" I still had not the slightest idea what she was talking about.

"No matter what happens, *promise me* not to see my Jiang brother again." She suddenly looked at me, very seriously.

We said goodbye to each other, just like that. And that was our farewell.

When Chu XiaoLin returned home, before she even entered the door, her father was waiting for her with a chicken feather rod in his hand. (Chicken feather rod is a Chinese dust cleaner, but is commonly exploited as a means of beating children in order to prevent the hands of the parents from getting hurt)

This time she didn't evade but walked straight to the chicken feather rod. The father lashed her with the pitiless rod as he bawled out, "You stole things from the library, you thief! I'll kill you, good for nothing dead devil!"

The mother saw the father was being too excessive and rolled her wheelchair in between the two to defend her daughter, the only daughter.

The father said to the mother, "Get out of my way! You know the old saying 'Spare the rod, spoil the child'!"

The mother made no move, instead she questioned her daughter very indignantly, "How could you do such a thing to disgrace the good name of our working class family, and for whom was it worth taking books from the library? Today your uncle brought a group of people from the Peace Keeper Command Center here…"

She did not wait for her mother to finish. Chu admitted, "For the sake of my Jiang brother, I would do anything. For the sake of someone my Jiang brother likes, I also can do anything."

The father, "You are not my daughter, our family has no such gene, YOU, go die!

Chu replied, "Alright, I know why you hate me. You wanted a boy. That's why you asked Mom to have an abortion to kill me when the doctor said I was to be a girl. Now you have made it so clear you still don't want me to be your daughter after so many years and my Jiang brother doesn't want me to be his wife. Who wants me in this world? My Sky, ("My sky" is a Chinese calling for God, next to Chairman Mao) what's the point of living!?" Chu poured out her tears, together with all that she had wanted to spit out for a long time.

The mother had a hunch that something wrong was going on, she queried, "What do you mean that your Jiang brother doesn't want you to be his wife? Speak more clearly will you?"

"Jiang brother said he would *never* marry me!" Chu XiaoLin sobbed her heart out.

That certainly shocked the parents. The mother tried to comfort her daughter as well as herself and the husband, "I'm sure he was just kidding you. Jiang son is not that kind of ungrateful boy."

The father shouted with fury, "I knew! I knew! I knew it a long time ago, Jiang son is not a good thing, you too, bad stuff! Look, who put your mother in a wheelchair? Ha! You, it was you, little devil! I wish you were all dead! Oh my sky! What a mistake I've made!"

Chu suddenly stopped crying. She bit her lips to control her sobbing, looked at her father fearlessly and very calmly said, "You so much regret your mistake, I'm glad to help you in correcting it. Today, right now, in front of you."

"Hey, how dare you try to scare me! You die, you die!" The father again raised his chicken feather rod, "If you don't die today, I will have to kill you!"

Chu walked to the basin stand, facing the mirror she combed her hair, put a flower in her hair and took a moment to have a good look at herself, then walked into her room to fetch her photo album and walked to the window.

She started tearing photographs piece by piece, throwing the small pieces of her photos out the window. After she watched the last piece wave down from the fourth floor to the ground, she, Chu XiaoLin climbed up to the window.

The mother couldn't take anymore, she yelled to her daughter, "No, no…!"

"Don't buy her bluff, I'm sure she dare not…"

She had heard enough so did not wait for her father to finish his words. She opened the dove cage by the window. The doves, "Pu pu" rushed out toward freedom. Chu XiaoLin took a look at the sky, then shut her eyes, took her last breath, deeply, and launched her wings, with the doves; she flew freely into an infinite time and space.

The father fell, FLOP, down onto a chair, while the mother stood up from her wheelchair and struggled towards the window.

12: A Broken Home & Scattered Family

My Family Situation At The Time

Although things were happening to me one after another, for the other members of our family it was a prosperous period, or even better, a period that could almost be called, "the prime of my family's life".

Mother was given a more responsible position in her work unit, temporarily, due to a considerable portion of her colleagues being sent to the cadre's concentration camp, to be transformed. In fact, my mom, as one of the loyalists (during the Cultural Revolution, people were divided into two distinct groups, loyalists and rebels, you had to be one or the other, there was nothing in between) was on the most wanted list to be transformed, only because the company needed her outstanding working skills to keep things going in the spirit of, "Grasp the revolution and promote the production" was her name waived from the transformation list. Though she was no more than a group leader of about 10 people, temporarily, she felt very honored, satisfied, and had great self-importance, working her day and night willingly, like a horse, a *she-horse*.

My brother DanXin was very fond of school. He had always been, as the Americans say, a "straight A student" and the "teacher's pet", also getting along well with his classmates. He was given a chance to pursue his studies in high school by the school authority. (Only a small portion could go to high school at that time.)

My baby brother DanHen was in his third elementary school year. Accidentally, Hunan Acrobatics picked him up; repeatedly visiting our home to persuade Mother to let her son go. Though indeed Mom had much doubt, "If it were my *second* son you wanted" she said. In the end, she couldn't resist the bitter, sweet and grand words and so agreed to let DanHen have a try.

Regarding me myself, my effort and sweat was rewarded with a quantum leap in violin playing ability reaching a comparatively high level according to the local standard. I was also taken into consideration as a member of a sing and dance unit belonging to the Chinese People's Liberation Army. All I was waiting for was the result of my family background political record checkup to be an army violinist.

This was supposed to be the *highest* honor and almost everyone's dream who learned violin at the time. If that really did happen, it could solve all the problems, well, if not *all* at least most major problems between my family and I.

I was very jealous and curious about DanHen being taken to Hunan Acrobatics. Without asking Mom, I went to see him training. Not even close to the practice hall, I heard children screaming in misery. It sounded like a slaughterhouse!

I gathered my courage and pushed the door open. Various inhumane postures appeared before my eyes! Children were standing on hands, on heads, or on someone's shoulder and someone else's shoulder, others were riding a bicycle backwards and some rolling in the air!

Just when I was starting to feel a kind of novelty about the scene, the horrible screeching of my brother drew my attention. I saw DanHen in a corner, leaning against the wall, legs spread in a line. The coach put his knee against DanHen's chest and gave a deadly push against the wall, at the same time he called two little ones to sit on my brother's thighs and used his own hands to press the trainee's shoulders down!

DanHen was in so much pain that he held his breath, making him unable to cry out. Bean sized sweat was rolling from his forehead, nearly a waterfall. Even when my brother looked faint, the rock-hearted coach showed no signs of ending the torture.

Witnessing this, a sudden impulse of grief hit my heart. It was the first time, so evidently and strongly I felt that this boy in agony was my own *flesh and blood*. I couldn't stand it any longer so I deliberately went to greet the coach. Indeed, as I wanted the coach to let go of my brother!

DanHen shrank, rolling on the floor with pain. A short while later, he crawled to me and embraced my leg, begging me to take him home. It was really rare for him to make me feel like a big brother. *Immediately* I made up a story that our mom was sick and needed him back.

Returning home with a few still functioning yet loose bones, DanHen begged Mother with tears, saying that he'd rather be dead than to go back to the acrobatic business. He also promised to be an even better boy at home from then on. He would listen to Mom and do whatever he was asked to do, even the dishes after every meal.

In actuality, Mom was reluctant to send DanHen to Hunan Acrobatics in the first place, not only because of the bitterness and hardship of training, but because in that era, *nothing* was easy. Mom felt sorry to have a nine-year-old starting work as it sounded like child labor. Besides, if DanHen started working, he would have the remotest possibility of going back to school again.

On the positive side, Mom thought DanHen should learn acrobatics, because it was at that time, Jiang Qing's (great leader Chairman Mao's wife, the one who re-built Chinese show business after the total devastation of Chinese art and literature at the beginning of the Cultural Revolution) show-soldiers with their gray uniforms, were among the top echelon in the social hierarchy.

As for DanXin, Mom decided that he was born to study; therefore she was prepared to use all family resources to support him, up to university if DanXin wanted and could. Very deep in her heart, Mom probably regretted to a certain degree, that she had prompted Father to give up his university studies (English literature) in order to be a full time revolutionary when they first met.

About me, Mom thought it would be the best solution that I join the army, as: a.) Spiritually she would no longer need to worry that I was led astray; b.), Politically, to have a soldier son was regarded as honorable and prestigious. What a shortcut to turn a bad apple into a source of pride! c.) Economically there would be one horse less at the dining table. (I was born in the year of horse.)

One evening, Mom was sitting outside, enjoying one of her rare leisure hours in the gentle summer breeze. Perhaps she felt lonely or more possibly it was intentional, she started to chat with me. She expressed her belief that my elder brother DanXin and I would do okay and that my baby brother DanHen remained her unique concern.

She sighed emotionally, "You brothers will soon be adults. After your independence, in case your father doesn't come back, I think I can manage by myself."

I didn't try to figure out the inner meaning of her words, but was instead busy re-calling the last time she had mentioned my father.

After Chu XiaoLin's Flight To Freedom

Now let me bring our story back to what happened after Chu XiaoLin flew to freedom. The moment she jumped out the window her soul split away from her body, floating in the vast air and observed the body falling down on a truck's canvas top.

The truck driver who was waiting for the traffic light to change, heard a huge *"BANG"*, he scolded, "Who the fuck's throwing things down like that!?"

It wouldn't be hard to imagine how shocked the driver was when he saw Chu's body full of blood on his truck.

Soon, Chu's father wheezed, rolling down from the fourth floor in his pajamas and slippers. He embraced the body of his daughter and shouted at the driver, "Hospital, hospital!"

After an hour of long waiting, anxiously the father rushed toward a doctor who had just come out of the operating room, "H...how is my daughter, do--ctor?" The doctor responded routinely, "We did everything we could yet it's still too early to draw a conclusion. But even if she makes it, her condition will most likely be critical."

The father, "Pa", kneeled by the doctor's feet, "Please, please! You save my daughter, otherwise my wife will also die, *of heartbreak*! I beg you! I pray for you and the happiness of your whole family!"

What happened to Jiang LangSha ?

About Chu's taking books out of the library, her maternal uncle named Zhou, (the husband of her aunt who worked at the library) reacted with the most extraordinary panic. When the news of Chu's suicide reached the uncle's ear it was like pouring oil on fire. The outraged uncle decided to punish the one behind Chu's stealing of books that caused the dreadful tragedy.

The uncle was a small head of the rebels. The whole of China was the rebels' world by the time. They held the *actual* power of government in the country. Therefore rebels' so-called, "Public Order Keeping Command Headquarters" practically replaced the police force and law court.

Uncle Zhou led a group of fully armed "order-keepers" and went to Jiang's little hut. They tied Jiang up without pressing charges. Then implemented the Cultural Revolution routine and seized the little hut, searching it thoroughly. Beneath the bed, they found the box of books.

"I knew you were the apple of discord. Take the criminal together with the booty!" Uncle Zhou ordered.

Meanwhile, a full coal-loaded train approached. Jiang put everything aside, as he was tied up, in desperation he jumped to fall on the wooden box, the only love his father left to him, "These are my books, not the library's books!"

The train was getting closer and closer, but the people present paid little attention.

Order-keeper "A" kicked Jiang's bottom and roared, "How dare you to defend yourself!"

Jiang was struggling in despair and pled, "These are novels I inherited from my father. What XiaoLin took from the library were mostly music scores, not novels."

"Whatever you say, you tell us where those books are, I mean the music sco—books!" Order-keeper "B" demanded.

"I don't know. I really don't." Jiang answered.

Order-keeper "A" kicked Jiang again and shouted, "Tell us the truth now, or I'll beat you to death!"

(Beating people to death happened every day during that period, by "order-keepers". What a tragic paradox!)

I hid myself near the little hut and peeped through, watching the whole process. Until then I knew nothing about what had happened to XiaoLin nor could I clearly hear their conversation, but by instinct I guessed it was something to do with the music scores and books XiaoLin took from the library and left at Uncle Feng's place. I started to fear that Jiang might be compelled to sell his sister XiaoLin out, which I would *never* do. Just as I was thinking of running away, a sharp steam whistle split the air.

"Woo---!"

Based on my earlier observations and knowledge, I knew it was time to switch the rail. I dashed toward Jiang and blared out the warning, "Switch rail, switch rail... train coming!"

Jiang heard me. Like waking up from a dream, he loudly shouted, "Set me loose, or the train will derail!"

Uncle Zhou realized what could happen; he cut the rope to set Jiang free as quickly as he could.

Jiang streaked off toward the rail switcher like an arrow from a bow. When Jiang started to switch the rail, the two order-keepers carrying his bookcase and striding across the railway distracted him from his work. He chased them again leaving the rail half switched. The three of them refused to budge, right in the middle of the railway!

The bookcase slammed down on the ground, books scattered all over. The two order-keepers realized the train was drawing near and fled for their lives while Jiang lay on his stomach covering the bookcase with his body, stretching his arms to cover the dispersed books like a hen protecting her chicks.

"Run away!" I screamed. "Run quickly you bastard! You want to die?" joined Uncle Zhou.

But Jiang was as steady as a statue.

"Woo—Woo----!" The train kept howling.

I knew if I stood there doing nothing the train would derail and Jiang would end up a heap of minced meat, so I rushed to finish the rail switching. I exerted all my strength but as a fourteen-year-old I was just not strong enough to the make the rail switch complete.

The train driver too, noticed the abnormal situation and applied the emergency brake. The train whipped by my side approaching the rail junction, getting close, closer, ten meters, five meters, three meters from Jiang and his books, jangling harshly . . . the train stopped.

The whole thing made my flesh crawl. But Uncle Zhou quickly adjusted himself from the shock, indignantly bawling out at Jiang, "Want to die? Ha! That's too easy for you! My niece XiaoLin, alive is your wife, dead is your ghost! You can't get away from..."

Meanwhile, a steam whistle reached us from a remote distance in the opposite direction. The derailed train driver hurriedly jumped down from his train. With a danger red light, he ran towards the oncoming train.

A Fatal Occurrence 3.3 (3rd Of March), That Affected The Destiny Of Our Whole Family

That same evening, I was too uneasy for my routine violin practice by the railway. Instead, I went close to Jiang's hut to inquire with the prospective of meeting Chu, so that I could find out what all that was about.

From out of the hut came an unknown person somewhat resembling one of the order-keepers, then another and Uncle Zhou. Then, I was sure they were the *trouble-making* order-keepers.

Uncle Zhou said something to the other two, and the three of them headed in the direction of my home with rifles and ropes! Immediately I took a short cut to the house.

Back home Mom was absent, working overtime. I told my two bothers that someone might come looking for me. If that happened, tell them I'm away from home and won't be back for a long time.

While DanXin was doubting my story, a savage knock was heard at our door. Immediately, DanXin asked his two younger brothers to hide back in the kitchen. I did what he ordered yet DanHen refused to leave.

The order-keepers gave our door a mighty kick, it flew open. My little brother blocked the doorway with his emaciated body. Uncle Zhou lifted him up in the air like a little chicken and interrogated, "Where is that boy called Nine Brother?"

My baby brother struggled with his arms and legs in the air and shouted like the little revolutionaries in the New China movies, "I don't know!" and finished by spitting a mouthful of slobber on Uncle Zhou's face.

Uncle Zhou dropped my brother and quickly wiped the slobber with the cuff of his sleeve before it could flow into his mouth. DanHen slammed down on the ground and rolled with pain. DanXin helped his little brother stand up and yelled at Uncle Zhou, "You think you can bully us because we have no adults home?!"

But as soon as my silent little brother rebounded from the ground, he rushed up to Uncle Zhou again. With an uncertain reflex Uncle Zhou tried to grasp him but was firmly bitten by the little lion. The pain was so excruciating that Uncle Zhou screamed to the other two, "What the hell are you guys waiting for? Take him!" simultaneously he punched my little brother's head with his other hand.

Uncle Zhou's action pushed my always gentle and peaceful brother DanXin to the limit. He stepped up to Uncle Zhou and rewarded him with a merciless blow, soon turning Uncle Zhou's face in to a half panda.

When it turned toward violence I decide to go out and fight them to the death. But MeiMei grabbed me tightly and said, "You're stupid. A wise man should not fight when it is an obvious loss. Run." She pushed me out the back door.

My mom heard about what was going on and ran back home. Seeing her nine and fifteen-year-old sons trussed up and escorted by armed order-keepers, she immediately lost consciousness falling to the ground, soiling her pants. Hu MeiMei hurried to take care of my mom. I went to look for a flatbed cart.

Together, MeiMei and I transported my mom to the hospital. MeiMei took my Mother's dirty clothes off and asked me to wash them in a pond outside the hospital. When I was done and back at the hospital, the doctor ordered me, "Ask your father to come here at once." His tone left no room for discussion.

MeiMei also said to me, "Go, go, go. Don't worry I will be here all the while. Go and get your father to come here as quickly as possible." Her tone also sounded as if my father was eating at a restaurant somewhere nearby.

The above happened on the third of March 1971. So our family calls it the 3.3 occurrence, an occurrence so fatal it affected the destiny of our entire family.

To Conquer All Obstacles Looking For Father

Facing such a huge family crises, even if the doctor had not ordered it, I would have had to find my father and get him home. *But where?* I had no detailed address, only the name of the county where Father's May 7 Cadre School was located!

If it were today, I could send him an e-mail, or a fax, or simply make a call from my cell phone, yet the situation then left me no alternative but to go in person. I hitched a night truck to look for my father, the family man who was never very much with the family.

The driver was an open, easygoing young man. He chatted with me all the way, except for asking me if I was hungry. When we reached a resting spot, at last, he asked me if I would like to buy something to eat as he was going to do. I quickly searched my pocket and realized I had only ten fen RMB lunch money. I awkwardly told a story that I wasn't really hungry since I ate too much for supper.

I waited in the truck with my empty stomach, hoping the driver would come back with some leftovers. The truck driver came back without my hope of course. Therefore, I planned to sleep all the way in order to economize my energy.

However, by bad luck, the truck couldn't get started. All the driver's effort spinning the engine handle was in vain. The driver finally gave up and said to me, "It looks like you have to sleep with me overnight, though the truck is a little small for two."

I was too anxious to wait. I jumped down from the truck and walked on. The driver shouted at my back, "Walk along for about ten Kilometers, there's another resting spot. Wait for me there if you don't find another lift."

Ten Kilometers distance in the dark cold, took a fourteen-year-old boy hours to conquer. When I set my feet on the spot it was already dawn.

I inquired at each truck one by one asking their destination and finally found one heading in my father's direction. The driver was a quiet middle-aged man. As he felt uneasy having me sitting together with him in the front, I climbed on the back of his truck and sat on the goods.

I discovered what I sat on was a gunny of Chinese jujubes! I dug a little hole with my fingers and started to cram my gullet voraciously. I was so thirsty that the jujubes got stuck on their way to my stomach, if it had started to rain so I could have a little drink, that would be communism to me.

The truck suddenly stopped and the driver came to me and said, "Come to the front boy, because if you freeze to death I don't want to take responsibility."

When I gratefully and happily jumped down from the back, about to get in the front, my mouth betrayed me. The driver immediately changed his attitude and bawled out, "You're a little thief! Get lost, roll away!"

Besides being in the middle of nowhere, he also left my face smothered in dust from the truck wheels. Again, I had to make good use of my manpower to move forward.

Hours later I passed by a farm. As it seemed nobody was watching, I dug a Chinese sweet potato from the field (I had sufficient practice when I was about six), and hid myself behind a big tree chewing it, together with mud. When I felt recharged I returned back to the road, again I met the second driver who had dropped me off a few hours ago.

On his truck (in front) after driving for some time, he told me that the reason he decided to pick me up again was that my hungry face reminded him of the year 1960, in which he was beaten for stealing flesh from dead bodies, which was his only meat source.

When we were at a rest stop, he bought a bowl of noodle and shared it 50/50 with me. He took me near the county center and then handed me over to another driver, "This boy is my remote relative. Please take care of him."

I finally arrived at the county center, but still didn't know where to find my father. When I tried to get into the county administration bureau to make an inquiry, I was driven out by the doorkeeper, "No beggars allowed in front of the County Bureau."

From the county office I learned the possible location of my father was about a thirty kilometer country road away. In fact, he was closer to where I was handed over to the third driver. I had no choice but to go on foot. When my shoes opened their mouths, I used some tree bark to cover the holes and continued my journey.

By late afternoon I met a small group of educated youth on a hill. One of them said he knew nothing about my father, while another said even *if* he knew he couldn't tell me, and the third said he actually knew where my father was but did not *want* to tell me.

This made me want to cry out in frustration. After I moaned to them the tragedy that was happening in my family, a tall fellow said he might be able to help me, a little. Instantly my sadness turned to happiness.

Then the tall man said, "It's too late to go down there today. Let's wait until tomorrow." Though no one obviously invited me, I followed the group wherever they went.

At the top of the hill the beautiful landscape popped in front of my eyes. The declining twilight reminded me of my Uncle Din's out of tune singing, "The eastern sun is declining down the western hill." Why did he always sing it wrong when the correct lyric should be, "The twilight is declining down the western hill"?

Whatever! My heavy mood was jarred by the marvelous natural scenery.

After a while the tall man covered my eyes with a towel and with his hand, I was led into a clandestine cave. There were five young men and one young woman living in the cave. Watching them cook food, I couldn't control my saliva flowing so much so that I had to utilize my usual technique, sleep. Drowsily, I heard noises. Half sleeping, half-awake I saw one man was doing it with the woman and another two were lining up for their turn.

The next morning, the tall fellow escorted me all the way down. On the way he expressed his envy of me for having a father, unlike he who had no father to care for him since he was very little. He let his tears out while I had to swallow mine down into my stomach.

Little by little he also told me about their group. They are six defecting educated youths out from my father's farm. (the cadres like my father at the May 7 Cadre School, were in charge of the educated youth) The six formed a special family with five husbands sharing one wife.

Meeting Father

After two nights and two days obstacles, I finally reached my father. You know what he was doing? He was blowing a harmonica, taking part in a rehearsal of the Educated Youth Propaganda Team.

He showed little surprise in seeing me suddenly appear before his eyes, as if I was just one of the herd. I couldn't ruin his good mood, I had to sit down and wait. Only a few seconds later I started sawing logs (snoring), which reinforced Father's propaganda noise, sorry, propaganda "music".

When I woke it was time for supper. Father's room was small and simple. A female educated youth was cooking on an alcohol stove. She didn't look so bad except a little over sized, not for the standard today but at that time. What shocked me more was seeing my father's watch on her wrist, the watch Mother gave Father as a keepsake that he said he, "Lost somewhere, maybe it's in more needed hands." The unfamiliar gentleness and kind manner towards the girl made Father *more* of a stranger to me.

Before the meal, Father very briefly introduced the girl to me, calling her …something like "Big Sister", and then they ate and chatted their concerns as if I didn't exist. The whole scene made me feel that without us, the man was more comfortable and happier out there in the farm. If it were true, that Big Sister must be part of the reason. If that was the case then not only me, but the whole family were his heavy burden.

Though my stomach was totally empty, soon it was overflowing with anger by viewing this scene. I shouted at Father, "Something bad is happening back home, hurry up go back!"

Then he asked "Big Sister" to go away and Father listened to my description of the situation back home. Of course I reserved the fact that Chu taking books out of the library might be the basic and direct reason for the entire occurrence, as I still wasn't sure what exactly Uncle Zhou wanted so badly from Jiang and I.

Hearing my report, Father's facial expression returned back to the usual deep frown that I was mostly familiar with.

I stayed at my father's place for only one night, which was one quarter the time I spent getting to him. The next morning he gave me a pair of his used home-made cotton shoes, plus a few yuan RMB, and showed me the way to the long distance bus stop. After telling me how to make my trip, he returned back to his farm and left me alone, hours waiting for the bus to come.

I did all I wanted to do, as well as what the doctor and Hu MeiMei asked me to do, which was to pass the message to my father. I did not expect Father to go back with me right away, I knew that as a Party member he couldn't do anything without the Party's approval. To be in a country of selfless ideology, asking for leave from work for family affairs took courage and time.

Farewell, The Residency And Home

I returned, and found my home was in chaos after being searched by the order-keepers. Mother and DanXin were still not in, only DanHen the nine-year-old. Having gone through this catastrophe together, seeing him again sent a throb of excitement and pain to my heart pushing me to hug him. He, however, rejected my emotion with a nimble dodge. Hatefully he accused me, "It's all your fault! You tore my family into pieces!"

He carried his small schoolbag and strode out of the house.

"Where are you going?" I chased him as he went out the door and asked.

"It's none of your damn business! I don't know you."

Those were the last few words my little brother left me with. To speak to me again was many years later.

Although DanHen is not my son but a brother, and we never got along that well, watching his back fading away out of sight I suddenly felt a gust of distress, like a piece of flesh being sliced off my body.

Hu MeiMei told me my home was searched thoroughly soon after my mother was sent to the hospital. Although they didn't find the music scores they wanted, they *did* find several of my mother's old diaries. Reading them, they became suspicious that mom could have been a member of the Third Youth League at one time, during her high school years before the liberation. This was considered to be a political stain. (The Third Youth League is attached to the Chinese Kuomintang, in parallel to the Chinese Youth League attached to the Chinese Communist Party) For that suspicion Mom was sent directly to the Cadre's concentration camp for further investigation after being treated in the hospital for only two days.

My little brother DanHen was only kept in detention for one night. As it became a home without a family, the nine-year-old kept taking care of it all by himself. He borrowed Hu MeiMei's fire to cook one bowl of gruel and subsisted on it all day. Every day he went to visit Uncle Zhou at the hospital. He begged for mercy, kneeling before his sickbed. The little lion offered to sacrifice all eight of his incisors to trade for his brother DanXin's freedom.

The family baby also asked Hu MeiMei to pass his words to anyone and everyone in the family, that it was he *himself* who decided to go back to the Hunan acrobatics, therefore no need to try to find him.

For the sake of never being bullied and humiliated again he would train himself to be a Hercules. Until then he would not show his face to the public.

Hence, I was left alone at home. As a matter of fact I had never felt so lonely and so scared. If it were before, whenever alone it was my chance to practice my violin, but then, I was not at all in the mood to touch my beloved instrument.

I went to see the place where DanXin was being held, which was a detention area temporarily borrowed from Hunan Medical College's classrooms. I could only peep at the place from a distance as I was afraid of being caught.

I also visited Mother at the Cadre's Concentration Camp but the doorman barred me from going in since the rule was, "Cadres under investigation are not allowed to meet their families."

Later I found out that besides the rule, it was also the good hearted doorman who did not want a young boy's feelings to be hurt too badly, for my mom was locked up in a cow barn. The same as vast numbers of Chinese were treated during the Cultural Revolution.

No doubt, I went to Jiang's wooden hut but the new comer had no idea about the whole thing. To me, Uncle Feng's place remained the last hope for finding Chu XiaoLin and the truth behind the whole ordeal. Sadly, the result of my visit was, no result.

Now you see how pathetic it was that I, together with everyone around me, were experiencing such an awful occurrence without even knowing the real reason. I was turned into an ant in a hot pot, restlessly counting my minutes day and night.

Almost a long month later Father came back, finally. (I found out later he was on an errand for the Party so sent back to the city. That means he wasn't home *specifically* for the sake of the family but by coincidence. That was, however, quite understandable and common, as in that era the Party business was regarded as heavy as a mountain and family affairs as light as a feather.)

I, as a boy always distanced from his father, this time felt like throwing myself into his safe hands. I had never so strongly felt the great importance of having a family man at home. Nevertheless, his clay-colored face and cold mood functioned like the negative pole of a magnet keeping me away eternally, at a decided distance.

Father put his baggage down and went out right away. No need to ask, he surely went to rescue my mom and brother. I thought.

I started to make a coal fire and prepare supper, which I had stopped doing for about a month now. Seldom in my life, without Mom's consent, did I cut off a piece of meat from a moldy pig head that had hung on the wall for ages. I quickly fried up a dish of garlic and pig head meat. I dare say that was the most attractive and most delicious meal I had ever cooked in my entire short life.

Waiting for the clock to show suppertime, I set the table expecting Father to come back. If it were not that day but any other day in the preceding fourteen years, I would have replaced chopsticks with my fingers to peck little by little from the dish. But on *that* day, though revolution was going on madly in my stomach, my indomitable will stood strong.

Hour after hour Father did not show. I had to heat up my beautiful meal over and over again. Any footsteps or even a rustle of leaves in the wind, made me rush to the door. "Baba, the supper is ready." was a sentence I practiced countless times. But when Father really came back I had fallen asleep, bent over at the table.

Father's slap on the table woke me with a start. Vaguely, I saw my father's metal ashen face like a fearsome devil. Though the volume was not loud, the tone was extremely resolute and authoritative, "Bring all the books from the library here at once."

"I have no books from the library." I tried to play an edge ball.

"I will say it again and no more. Bring all the books from the library here, now." Father ordered with an increasing volume.

"Really, I took no *BOOKS* from the library." I quibbled again.

"I have no time for this." Father said as he started looking for something to beat me with in order to prevent his hands from being hurt.

"Music scores." I changed my words, "You want me to bring out books and of course I can't. I only have music scores, scores for my violin…"

"Again! That hand-lin? *I knew it!* I knew from the very beginning it would cause trouble!" Father burst into rage.

"It's not hand-lin. It is called a violin." I corrected him. Though I knew he said it on purpose, for the purpose of insulting the instrument and the boy who loves the instrument.

Seeing him continuously busy looking for something to beat me with, I started to be aware that there was no way to escape. Without any more ado I headed directly at him, "It wasn't me who took the music scores out of the library but even if you beat me to death I will not tell you who did it. I'll never sell out my friend!"

"Your friend? Ha, you don't have a friend. You will have a cabbage or a dead body. Haven't you heard Chu XiaoLin jumped down from the 4th floor?"

"Ai…" That was the first time I was told about XiaoLin's destiny.

Father ordered again, "Do as I say, bring your vio…*hand-lin,*to the table, now!" doing it again just to show his disdain towards the instrument, or more precisely towards me. If it were normal circumstances I would rather die than retrieve my violin. But on that day, I was in a state of shock over Chu XiaoLin's tragedy. In addition, I thought handing over the violin might do some good in extricating my brother from detention, so, I fetched my violin from underneath my bed and presented it on the table.

To Father, the violin was the root of all evil and it was time to dig the root out. Father tried to open the violin case but didn't know how. He gave me a glance, a signal to open it, and I did accordingly.

Father took my violin from the case and raised it above his head and then smashed it on the table, causing the dish I made to fall down and all over the ground. My violin screamed out terribly.

My father broke not only my violin but also my heart, into pieces as well as the term "Father". Perhaps all these I expected, I reacted considerably calm. I crawled on the ground to pick up the broken pieces of my violin that had jumped off the table and put them into my case.

Father's face looked longer and more bitter than ever, he uttered repentantly, "I am also to blame as I was too generous and didn't cut the evil root at its sprout state."

Father said that as he grabbed the head of my violin from my hand and slammed it on the ground again, "I regret, I regret…" He knocked on the table with his fist causing a "Don, Don" sound.

Again I crawled down on the ground to pick up my violin pieces. Each time my hand touched a piece it reminded me how I had made them with each stroke of the knife, chisel and file. My wounded hand during the violin making started to feel pain again.

Seeing me, Father attempted to take my violin pieces from the case. I held the case in my arms to protect them as if they were my babies. My mind was made. *This time*, even if he kills me, I won't let my children suffer from the trample again.

As Father showed no sign of giving up, I exclaimed with grievance, "What exactly did I do wrong? Who did I offend? I just want to play the violin and to be a violinist. What's wrong with that?" The more I yelled, the more I felt the injustice that made me lose my mind. I furiously threw the whole violin case down on the ground and hysterically shouted, "Are you satisfied now!?!"

Father paused, only for a second, he uttered in despair, *"You, roll out! Our family doesn't have such a son!"*

In actuality such announcement from my father was unnecessary as I had already been on my way out with my broken violin and heart. I didn't know where to go but what I did know was that that was a place, a place I used to call home and I would never want to return.

"What exactly did I do wrong? Who did I offend? I just want to play the violin and to be a violinist. What's wrong with that?" Those are questions that bothered me for decades, until recently when I came to realize that the real evil root was not the violin, but me being different, and my desire to be an individual human rather than a communist manufactured robot, a tool, "a nail in the socialist machine" as people were literally called in China during the era. THAT SIN offended the majority of the communist community.

Home, inside that nest I grew up in for nearly fifteen years, the place had been extraordinarily noisy with quarrel and joy. The zone used to be safe and secure, then became a hollow of emptiness, leaving only Father's inclining shadow from the dim light and a thick smoke out of his mouth to accompany.

13: FOUR-YEARS AS A CONSTRUCTION WORKER

A Mysterious Envelope

I left home, at the age of fifteen, all on my own, until today.

After leaving home, I headed straight to Uncle Feng's place. I had nowhere else to go, it was then I confirmed that the sack of musical scores Chu XiaoLin took out of the library was the cause of the whole series of tragedies.

Logically, I thought if I returned it to the library I could make a trade for my brother DanXin's freedom. No matter how hard I thought, I couldn't figure out why that sack of musical scores suddenly became so important when tons of the same were burnt during the Cultural Revolution?

As Uncle Feng had no idea at all what had happened to Chu, I decided to talk to him about it later when things became clearer.

According to Chu's words, Uncle Feng placed the sack in front of me. I opened the sack in order to pick out a few urgently needed violin scores. If there were any, I planned to return them after I hand-copied them.

During the process, a well-sealed solid brown envelope dropped out from a thick music score. Out of curiosity, I put it in my schoolbag thinking I would take a look after sorting out the sack.

I quickly went through all the scores and books. Excluding the couple of violin exercises I took previously, I found almost nothing was of urgent need, only a violin collection that might be useful later. I started to regret and doubt the value of Chu's doing such a thing for me.

I entrusted Uncle Feng to return the sack back to the library.

Hearing the news, Uncle Zhou jumped out of his sick bed and rushed to the library. Delightedly, he opened the sack secretly and soon found the thick music score. To his enormous disappointment, he found the envelope was no longer there. That turned his happiness into madness. His tact however, told him to conceal his anxiety behind a calm face. Uncle Zhou inquired with Uncle Feng as to my whereabouts. The simple minded Uncle Feng had no clue what all this was about and so led him to me.

At the same time, I was alone at Feng's place gazing at my heart broken violin parts which made me forgot about the envelope completely. Seeing Uncle Feng come in with Uncle Zhou, I jumped up to escape. Although the abandon place had no door, the exit was the same size as a door, or as wide as Uncle Zhou's body. With him standing there, I wished I could change myself into a string of wind to flee.

Uncle Zhou's eye looked much better though still a little blue. The first words out of his mouth were, "Did you see an envelope?"

Seeing him stand steady, I backed up a little to a comparatively safe distance and nodded my head meaning, "yes".

He promptly strode to approach me and eagerly requested, "Give it to me, quickly."

His action made me feel that that envelope might be very valuable, might *contain* something very valuable, or some kind of secret. Whatever it was, it must be something of great importance! I counter-questioned him, "Why should I give it to you? Give me a good reason."

"Because it is mine." Uncle Zhou moved a step towards me.

"If you move one more step, I swear to you that you will never see your envelope again."

Then Uncle Zhou took a completely unexpected action. He kneeled down on the ground in front of me and begged, "Please, please give it to me? I'll do anything you want."

Watching this, Uncle Feng was in total confusion. He felt he should do something to ease the situation so he tried to persuade me, "If it is his thing, why don't you give it back to him?"

The developing dramatic situation made me more and more confident that the mysterious envelope was a very powerful thing, which was in *my* hand, I mean in my schoolbag underneath my buttocks as I relaxed myself on it. I played the suspense, "It's at a secret place."

"OK, take me there. If you do, as I said, anything can be discussed."

"Anything?" I confirmed.

"Anything, as far as I can do, you name it."

"OK, release my brother, immediately." I tried it in an orderly tone.

"Alright, take me there first." he bargained.

"No way, let my brother go first." This time my tone was non-negotiable.

"Okay, okay, okay, I'll do it right away. You wait here, don't leave." he looked at Uncle Feng for his confirmation.

"Don't worry, he has nowhere else to go for a while." Uncle Feng reassured him.

When Uncle Zhou was away, I started to report about Chu XiaoLin, in a version no more than what I heard from my father. Hearing that, Uncle Feng looked very down and heavy. He uttered a few words, "How is the baby girl now?"

That was an unknown, I would like to know it very much myself. One thing for sure, she couldn't be very good.

Uncle Feng started to spread hay to make me a place to sleep. Suddenly, he stopped, and said to me, "I think that... what thing, an envelope isn't it? It may be better to keep it for a while, until things are more clear." He stopped there.

About two hours later, Uncle Zhou ran back and gasped out, "Your brother is home, now can we go get my stuff?"

With Uncle Feng's wink, I improvised a story, "It's not possible to go there today as the place is too far away."

"What?!" Uncle Zhou burst out in fury.

Uncle Feng tried to calm him down by saying, "Don't worry, the boy is okay. I promise you no one will see your thing."

Uncle Zhou started becoming like a ball leaking air. After being dazed for a moment he said to Uncle Feng, "If I can take your word? I mean if you, not the boy, can keep it for me and promise not to open it, it may be safer than in my hands for a while. Actually, I heard about you from my niece Chu XiaoLin."

"It's a promise. It won't get into anyone else's hands, and it will *not* be opened. As I said." Uncle Feng confirmed it again.

After haggling, the temporary result was that I would hand the envelope back to him when I was sure all my family members were safe. Uncle Zhou conceded, on my oath, that I would let Uncle Feng keep it for the time being and never open it nor let it get in anyone else's hands.

The irony was that his all-important envelope was only two meters away from him, in my schoolbag right underneath my buns.

As soon as Uncle Zhou left, I was all too eager to open the envelope, but was stopped by Uncle Feng, "You promised you wouldn't open it. It says 'Four horses can't chase up a gentleman's words.' Trustworthiness is a man's most important quality."

To show my trust to him and my trustworthy words to Uncle Zhou, I handed the envelope over to Uncle Feng. He hesitated for a second, then said, "On second thought, just put it in your schoolbag like that. It could be a big problem if you lost it somewhere. Besides, he insisted that I keep it for him."

Like that, I handed the envelope, together with four years of my life, over to Uncle Feng.

My Middle School Graduation

It was free to stay at Uncle Feng's place. But for every day's bread, more precisely, "for every day's rice", I had to start part-time grunt work for Feng's construction company. Being the new boy on the totem pole in a down to earth environment, it was very hard for me to balance myself as a spiritual noble in my artistic ivory tower.

It was okay during the daytime, but was miserable in the evening, for Uncle Feng's castle was as antique as the age before Edison who invented electricity. Though following the old tradition of candles could be romantic, they cost money. To Uncle Feng it wasn't much of a problem as he went straight to sleep, sawing logs as soon as it got dark, while I had to count numbers for hours before I could manage to get myself into dreamland.

Worse than the lack of electricity, was the lack of water at Uncle Feng's residence. This meant I had to do all my personal hygiene and grooming at the construction site. *Still*, that was not the worst. The biggest problem, above them all, was that I had no place or the time, to practice my violin.

Seeing me gaze at my broken violin, Uncle Feng suggested that he find me some sesame nails (very small nails) to put the pieces together. His good-hearted idea made my flesh crawl though I didn't forget to show my appreciation.

It was sometime later, Ma XiaoMao heard my story and gave me her violin with the head from the violin my aunt bought for me, the one I had repaired for her earlier. Just to mention it, from then on, every time I met Ma, Flute Chen was always there with her, like a full-time bodyguard. About Lu XiaoBing and Wang ShiYi, their relationship as a pair was made public. With help from Wang, Lu too, was busy preparing for the high school entrance exam.

I lost my interest in school completely even though it was close to graduation. My going to school was like a fisherman, three-days fishing alternating with two-days drying the net. Gradually, my life got into a new routine. I went to school (when I did) in the morning and sweated at the construction site in the afternoon.

As soon as I was off work I practiced my violin for a short while in wherever place was available to me, at the work place, at Feng's place or in a park. In the evening, I finally found the place for a pastime by taking part in the rehearsal of the Changsha Worker's Propaganda Team. Doing just as an old Chinese saying, "killing two birds with one stone".

Soon, I became the concertmaster of the amateur orchestra and was flattered to be the No. 1 violin player among the amateurs in town; even playing solo from time to time. Though all of this did put me in a good mood and gave a certain degree of satisfaction, I didn't forget my declaration, *"Not only number 1 amateur player of Changsha City but also the number 1 professional violinist in the entire Hunan province.*"

I, as a fifteen-year-old, was living a life mostly among adults. With a life like that a few months later, I said farewell to my middle school.

About the destiny of my other former Mao teammates, Captain Lee led quite a number of them to an army propaganda team, which was considered the best way out of school at that time. Although Mao XiaoMao so much wanted to follow Lee, she couldn't owing to her bad family social class origin, in addition to her withdrawing from the team before graduation. Above all, her persistent chasing of Lee resulted in unrequited love, making the "vast world" (country side) the only place for her to go.

On the other hand, Flute Chen's name was already on Lee's list yet he gave up the honor of his own free will. Hearing the people in XinJiang were good at singing and dancing, Flute Chen put some effort on going through back doors to keep Ma from going to the "vast world", mobilizing her going to the XinJiang Army Development Construction, together with him. Lu and Wang both passed the high school entrance exams and pursued their studies and love, at a higher level.

Since *"leaving"* home I had little contact with my family, all that I knew was Mom went back home after months of an inconclusive investigation into her political past, continuing her role as one of, "promoting production". Father was demoted for unknown reasons and where, what and how he was serving the Party was also unknown.

My little brother DanHen worked very diligently and enduringly with his training becoming a formal member of the provincial Acrobatics Troupe. My elder brother DanXin didn't manage to get into the high school. In order to not lose his urban residence status, (In China, urban residence registration and rural residence registration are social classes at opposite ends of the ladder. To change a rural residence registration to an urban residence registration may not be as difficult as a man flying to the moon, but certainly as difficult as a Chinese immigrating to the United States, if not more so) with the help of his teacher, DanXin went as a three-year volunteer to build railroads.

As for me, I was directly recommended by Uncle Feng and became a formal worker for the Changsha Construction Company.

Farewell To Teacher Li

Wang ShiYi told me that Teacher Li once visited wondering why I was no longer taking violin lessons from him. I guess I did so for fear of spreading my trouble so widely as to encompass him too.

Wang described the scene to me, that in front of my home, Teacher Li met not me, but my father. Father did not invite Teacher Li in, but tailed him to the church.

Father's original intention must have been to find Teacher Li's location in order to demolish the nest that poisons the youth. Surprisingly, Teacher Li wasn't afraid or angry about being followed. Instead, he led my father all the way and politely invited him into the church through the back door.

Facing Jesus, by conditioned-reflex of the everyday routine prayer during Father's university days, came a flash back in his heart, "Our Father who art in heaven..." That miraculous power stopped Father's intention of troubling Teacher Li. Instead expressing his hope with delicacy. Hoping that Teacher Li will stop doing things with good intentions resulting in bad outcomes, or to put it more clearly, "leading the youth astray". Teacher Li did not dispute but commented, "Who is astray? Time will tell for itself."

One day Wang came to see me during my evening rehearsal of the Workers Propaganda Team. He passed a message to me that Teacher Li wanted ten of his best students to perform violin unison, "XinJiang Spring", the only violin piece to survive during the Cultural Revolution.

I accepted the invitation right away for I knew there was a solo section in the middle of the piece and I, said to be the No. 1 amateur player in town, took it as, grounded upon conceit, that *I* would be the one to play the solo part. Nevertheless, it wasn't until the very moment before the performance that I learned Teacher Li had recommended a sheepish girl called Tang, supposedly the worst player in the group, to do the show-off job in order to infuse her with courage and self-confidence. On stage as the moment approached, seeing Tang shaking with hesitation, I exploited this excuse, stepping ahead to cut a smart figure.

After the performance when everyone had gone, Teacher Li asked me to his home. Though I had all the excuses prepared he didn't say a word about it, nor did he talk about the meeting with my father. Though he acted as if nothing had happened, and started to play a violin duo from "Hohmann" with me just like the old days, I couldn't help apologizing for my father's rudeness as a way to show my regret for the thoughtless action during the concert.

Teacher Li said with a smile, "Your father, just like the vast others today, is just a lamb who has lost his way. How could they be blamed for what they are doing when they don't even know what they are doing? Only the great love of our Lord could affect them, lighten up their heart. Someday they will reach their cognition of all the wrong doings in their past. I will never stop leading the youth to our Lord because of some accusations. Being God's servant, this is what I'm made for."

Comparing Teacher Li's treatment towards my wrongdoing with my father's, I was truly touched. But I became clearly aware that I was like some kind of poison or root of trouble in that society, and whoever was in touch with *me* would be in touch with trouble. I made myself an awkward excuse that his teaching method no longer fit me, and expressed my wish to end the teacher/student relationship. Again, he praised me for being much more thoughtful and sensible than before instead of being disappointed with me.

"But no excessive worry about me is needed. I'm safe with my Lord, as I always have been, and always will be." Teacher Li said.

On the way out of Teacher Li's room, he took me into the Church. Facing God, he prayed for me. He asked the Lord to light my heart and warm my body all my life. He also begged the Lord to send a brother or a sister to my side to lead and assist me wherever I might go. He even prayed for the forgiveness of my father.

I was speechless, not a "thank you", nor a "sorry". With an empty brain, I silently had my farewell with Teacher Li, the enlightenment of my music, as well as how to be a decent human being.

Encountering Teacher Yu

From the amateur orchestra I heard a rumor, that an excellent violinist named Yu BoPing was demoted from the National Army Singing & Dancing Troupe to the Hunan Provincial Beijing Opera as the concertmaster of the orchestra owing to a wrongdoing in his private life. As private scandal was thought to be the most shameful sin among our Chinese (*though we like it very much*), Yu's unpopularity at his workplace was not hard to imagine.

With a tiny hope, I recklessly went to see Teacher Yu all by myself. Unexpectedly, after hearing only one piece of my violin playing, he accepted me to be his student, "the only student in my life", he said. After the elated mood subsided, I finally got my feet back on the ground. I started to question whether it was *his* need to be needed in his time of adversity, or did I, the little Nine Brother, really have some talent, or perhaps was it both?

Teacher Yu gave me quite some homework at the first meeting. He lent me a violin method, "Rhoda" and asked me to hand-copy a few exercises for the next lesson. Finally, he made a bit of an embarrassing suggestion, that I take a shower and change my clothes, particularly my socks, before I come for the next lesson, as "My wife is slightly delicate and fussy." said with a tone full of love for his wife.

By then I noticed a photograph, a photograph of a very pretty woman with elegance, placed on the piano. Looking at the small, wizened and pale appearing Teacher Yu, I just didn't understand why he needed another woman when he possessed such a beautiful wife. The man's mania of having women other than one's wife, or as the Chinese say, "Occasionally, wild herbs taste more than the home meal", took me years to fully comprehend.

My Violin Stage On Construction Scaffold

Since I had formally become a worker of the Changsha construction company, I moved out of Uncle Feng's place and started a life on my own at the worker's dormitory.

The so-called dormitory was actually a shed with lots of bunk beds. There was no registration, no management and no charge. As far as there were beds available, anyone could occupy them.

That is to say, that all of my property had to be concentrated within the size of a bed. Good thing that wasn't much trouble for me as I had almost no property, not even a ragged suitcase like the little David Copperfield when he ran away from the blacking factory to seek his aunt. All that I possessed were two pairs of old shoes and a few tattered clothes. As for the violin, that was a part of my skin and I wore it wherever I went.

To practice my violin at the dormitory was unthinkable, therefore my work place, the construction site, remained the only available location. Every day when working hours were over and the others went home, I would hide myself in a half finished room to practice. Sometimes I got so inspired I would climb on the highest spot of the scaffolding. Facing the beautiful twilight and infinite space, with all my feeling and emotion I would enjoy my playing as much as I liked and the music pieces I loved. Recalling the scene, it was somewhat romantic. If it appeared in a movie, it would be a moving and touching moment.

Gradually, I discovered the number in my audience was growing, for as soon as I started playing, more and more windows would open, and people were standing by those windows. In the window closest to me stood the charming daughter of the army representative. (By that time army officers were sent to be in charge of all local working units. It was called the "military control period".)

Whenever the girl appeared, she always reminded me of Chu XiaoLin, which changed my happy violin music to melancholy. Just to mention, if I wanted, I could have found out about the situation with XiaoLin and LangSha through just a little effort, but I guess I chose not to as the result could be fearful.

In parallel to the growing number of fans, there were also an increasing number of enemies; an outstanding one was the foreman Peng. I was given a derogatory title, "Young Master Nine" by my workmates. No work group wanted me as I didn't fit in, "wearing gloves even on the hottest day in the summer" as people said and I truly did. In addition, from time to time I was out of sight, hiding somewhere hand-copying music scores, the homework Teacher Yu gave me.

One day I was caught doing my usual business, hand-copying music scores at my secret spot. The foreman Peng seized my music score and was about to tear it! I raised a spade over my head and shouted, "Dare you do it and I'll split your head in two!" That really scared foreman Peng, but being too full of shame to show his weakness, he very gingerly tore a small corner of the music score. I threw the spade away, stepped forward and gave him a punch on the face! My reckless action caused him to swallow two teeth; two decayed loose teeth.

That brought *big* trouble, big enough to hold a work unit accusation meeting. In the meeting, someone suggested that I should be fired at once. The suggestion was immediately supported by a thunder of applause. When the meeting chairman requested a vote by the raising of hands, Uncle Feng stood up.

He said, "There is no doubt that violence, no matter who does it, is crude and wrong and should be accused, criticized and even punished. But I'm the one who introduced the little Nine-Brother here. Therefore I should at least be held responsible for half of his wrongdoing.

However, to kick him out is equal to pushing him in a worse direction, that does not correspond with Chairman Mao's teaching, 'To cure illness and save life'. The little Nine-Brother is, after all, a boy below 16, he deserves a second chance. If we sack every young man who acts on his impulse of temper, how many would be left working for the socialist construction? And if the result is simply to fire him, why did we all bother to come here? My fellow workers, please, give him a second chance; this is the only thing I ask."

The meeting result was that I should compensate foreman Peng's medical fees and a sum equal to his ten days wage. I went to Uncle Feng wanting to say a few lines of gratitude but was mercilessly scolded by him, "I don't care about losing face, I don't have much face anyway. But you are young, you need to work and fight for your own face! May be someday you can eat with your violin, but you are a worker *now*, so look and act like one."

Though I kept my jaw moving, in my heart I knew I owed him a big one and felt what he said to me was right and honest. So I made up my mind to make a radical change from that day on.

About a year later, with a lot of effort, I did change and was gradually accepted and liked by more and more co-workers.

After all, construction work and violin performing are two totally incompatible fields. The fingers of a construction worker are as rough as steel files, how could they dance and flit sensitively on violin strings? If my life went on like that, how could I reach my dream of becoming a professional violinist, "The king of music"? No or yes, I must work out a way.

It was at *that* moment, while trying to think of some way out, I fell from a three-story scaffold, all the way down to the ground! That became my way out of the sweaty construction site. I was sent to a hospital. Though there was no major damage to my bones, the scratches and blood looked awful. I declared that I suffered from a fear of heights. Uncle Feng preferred to believe it, and requested the company transfer me to a cement product working unit, where more than half of the workers were women.

After that, the work I did was much more relaxed, lighter and stable and more importantly, there was no more laughing about hands covered with gloves. I at once felt happy and sort of satisfied. I worked harder than ever and a year later was even appointed the leader of a group of 6 workers. Slowly, I got used to the life and even started to think I was destined to be a worker. The passion to pursue the violin got weaker and weaker, in the end, taking violin lessons from Teacher Yu became more like a habit or formality.

About my music activities at the amateur orchestra, after being the concertmaster for quite a period of time, I felt somewhat fed up and that it was a waste of time. I quit it for good with no excuse.

Now, I sit in my house by a big bright window looking outside at my garden, flashing back on the first half of my life struggling.

Each time I reached a goal, I would start to feel bored and lost. Just like climbing a hill, it's a great challenge and fun to look at the top and climb, but as soon as you set foot on top of the hill, you discover the place you stand is tiny and sharp, and surrounded by bigger, higher rolling hills blocking your view to the other world.

In fact, the same applies to almost everything, for example, you hunt for a used car, all the fun is in the process of looking in the papers, internet, whatever source of information you might have, checking the make, year, kilometers, ABS, CD, MD, TV, Navi etc, but when you hand over your money, you also hand over all your fun and excitement at the same time.

One more example is that when we were little we all looked forward to becoming adults, but now we *are* adults, so what? This taught me that every time I reach a goal; I must look for a new goal. This is my understanding of, "life goes on," otherwise, I would feel my life had stopped, was terminated and see death lying ahead of me. Therefore I have lived my life, and will go on living my life of endless climbing.

When I write here I suddenly seem to understand why religion is so powerful. It's because it gives us consistent and continuous hope but never actually lets us reach that hope in our lifetime.

Chinese Teacher Liang And English Teacher Din

After quitting the amateur orchestra I had more time for myself. Besides practicing violin and reading books, I still had some surplus time and energy in the evenings. It was in that time I made myself a friend named Liang.

We soon got along with each other well. By talking to him, I learned his father was a Chinese teacher and mother an English teacher, both teaching at the Changsha No. 2 Middle School. As teachers, the only thing they wanted to do was *teach*, which was not a very popular thing to do in that era.

The parents organized their own private evening classes, free of charge for those who wanted to study (All education was free at that time). I immediately became an active member of both the Chinese and English classes, studying both languages very hard. In fact, at the time, I had no idea what my studies of Chinese and English were for. While today, when I write in both languages, I appreciate and value the foundation of both languages they laid and helped build. Thank you teacher's Liang and Din, wherever you might be now.

Farewell My Virginity

In the evening study group, I encountered Wu ZhangHua, a girl two years older than me. Everyone's eyes would meet her two full figured breasts before her not bad looking face or slender body.

Here is how she became my first sexually involved girlfriend. It was an afternoon in which she took me to her home. She asked me to turn my face away from her. When I was asked to turn my face back, she was completely nude. My mind went totally blank while my body was trembling. My little thing, wait, by that time might not be little anymore, was growing bigger. But the skin was still not peeled; therefore great pain, as always, occurred.

As I mentioned, ZhangHua was two years older and she worked in the medical field, therefore her knowing more about adult affairs was easy to understand. Seeing me have no reaction she felt a bit offended or disappointed. When I shamefully told her that I was in pain, she helped me lower my pants. When she saw my part she looked very happy. "You're a virgin." she said. Her following action really shocked me, as she was trying to put my thing in her mouth!

"This is the place I make water! How could you put such a dirty thing in your mouth? It's not healthy!" I said.

ZhangHua couldn't help laughing, but quickly adjusted her attitude with a sort of excitement and the kindness of love. She went away and was soon back with a big tea cup of warm water (at that time there were no bathrooms in almost all Chinese households, therefore we could not wash ourselves before). She put my thing into the cup, and gently washed it. Later I learned that that big tea cup was her father's. Next, she helped me peel my thing just like peeling a ripe banana, little by little. I was in great pain but excited at the same time. Once the banana was peeled, the pain was pretty much gone, remaining was the increase in pleasure. By that time I could not help but push her down on the bed, face down, as that was the only way and the only thing I knew about sex. I tried to push myself into her back hole but she turned over. She laughed this time for real, and remarked, "Surprise, surprise, you have such a fondness, but let's do it normally first.

She opened her legs... that was the first time I knew, I had an option! Seeing her front gate I started to feel fear. I was after all, an 18 year-old virgin, although much self-practice had been done, to fight in a real battlefield, that was my maiden voyage. Secondly, it was the inappropriate environment. You see, it was in her parents' home! What if one of her parents finished work early and popped in? We wouldn't be able to get my pants on in time. Therefore, in spite of the fact that she had her door open wide, welcoming me in, I didn't know how to accept the invitation.

When she realized she had to take me and lead me into her world, I heard the noise of footsteps. It ended up being someone else just passing in the corridor but resulted in me injecting right in front of her doorway. That was my first real experience, or the first rehearsal for many later. But for me, it was a farewell to my virginity.

Failure Of Farewell Hu MeiMei's Virginity

Although I had no contact with my family since I walked away from home, I knew well what was going on with my folks as Hu MeiMei came to see me at my work from time to time.

One day when my dormitory workmates were all absent, I boasted to MeiMei that my banana was ripe, the skin was peeled and ready for tasting. And above all, I knew the right place to taste the banana that wouldn't cause any pain.

MeiMei gave no resistance, not even an excuse of, "the rice will burn" this time, only closed her eyes as tightly as she could. When I was ready to break her gate defense she suddenly opened her eyes and asked me a question, a question so hard that it blocked me from penetrating anything further. She asked: "When are we going to get married?" She paused, and explained: "Because if we do this, we're going to have a child, you know?" That was it. We stopped there forever, and MeiMei's words, *"If we do this, we're going to have a child"* affected my life as an adult, for many, many years to come.

A Life Changing Phone Call

It was just another afternoon after having worked for the construction factory for four years; I received a unique phone call from the company head office telling me to report immediately to the office. "I don't think I can. You see, I have to work overtime today in order to finish the cement fences on time for the Hunan Provincial Zoo panda house. It's an important political task." I replied.

"It is more important that you come here at once." the phone said.

"If not, will you sack me?" I insisted.

"No need to sack you. You already no longer belong to our company. The details will be told when you are here. Come quickly, all the leaders are here waiting for you. Otherwise I'll send someone to get you."

"What? ......"

The phone call was cut off.

What on earth could be the problem? I worked hard and very well lately, the relationship with my co-workers had improved greatly. Everything was going well and smooth. *Why did the company want to kick me out?*

14: MY THIRD STAGE OF LEARNING THE VIOLIN

From An Amateur To A Professional

At the end of chapter thirteen, I mentioned a phone call from the head office of the construction company. The man on the phone ordered me to show up at the company head office immediately.

It was a long way from my work place to the head office of the company.

I peddled my bike as hard as I could all the way down, imagining every bad thing possible *and* my self-defense excuses. When I arrived at the gate of the head office out of breath, the always-arrogant doorman, abnormally polite, led me to a meeting room, where sat a group of company leaders around a meeting table. Seeing my face at the door, everyone stood up and welcomed me. That overwhelming atmosphere made me feel as though I was being mistakenly favored without rhyme or reason.

To make a long story short, the company informed me that all my papers were transferred away from the company, and from then on, I was a member of the Hunan Beijing Opera! My former working foreman Peng, was invited to give an opening speech. In the speech he stressed, "It is our company's pride that we raised such a talent." He went on to give quite a few examples of how hard I studied my violin and how much *he* understood me and supported me. He said this all very naturally, shamelessly and with great satisfaction. Thank God no one really paid attention to his hot air, as all were busy eating fish, skinned peanuts and drinking tea. When someone proposed that the celebration deserved a few bottles and dishes, the company leader ordered me to report to the Opera straight away.

Is this some kind of joke? I simply couldn't believe my ears! Thinking back from school to then, I had countless auditions just to get into a performing group, *any* group that might take me. Each time, after the family political record checkup, they all ended with the same result, "regrets" (Later I found it was all because I had an uncle living in the United States. At that time anyone having an overseas relation was at a huge political disadvantage).

After the same result again and again, I had gotten used to the failure, and accepted the possibility of never becoming a member of any professional music group. Yet the acceptance by the Hunan Beijing Opera, the highest level in the province, came to me so suddenly, especially, without an audition!

Looking at the dirty oily work uniform and smelly army shoes with holes that wrapped my body and feet, it occurred to me that I couldn't remember how many days since I last had a shower. I should be all right if it was within a week, for with such an appearance how could I go see Teacher Yu?

Nevertheless, an order is an order, as the Chinese say, "A military order is like a falling mountain, in no way to disobey." I ran to a washroom to clean up a little but it turned out to be in vain as there was no mirror and no water from the tap. I just wiped my face with toilet paper I had brought (there was no toilet supplying system in China at that time), shaped my hair a little with liquid from my mouth and then was on my bike again wildly headed to the Hunan Beijing Opera.

Wretched and breathless, I reached the front gate of the Opera. Even before I finished my self-introduction to the gateman, he pointed to a big rehearsal hall and said, "Just go. Everybody is there." That confirmed the unbelievable news, "I was made a member of the Opera." With extraordinarily high spirits, I flew to the rehearsal hall.

When I rushed into the rehearsal hall with a huge smile, I was more terrified than astonished to see what was going on inside.

There were eight portraits hung on the wall. In front of the portraits all the members of the Opera were sitting on the ground, crying, sobbing, weeping and sighing. The ones who made the most sound must be the family members of the dead, among them were Teacher Yu's pretty, elegant wife and their little boy. I looked up at the portraits again; the familiar face of my teacher Yu with a little cold smile appeared. Oh, my Go...d, my Chairman Mao!

An administrator came to me and took me out of the sea of tears to another office building.

"Everybody calls me secretary Deng." he introduced himself with a friendly smile. Then he turned to a very serious tone, briefly telling me how an unbelievable tragedy had happened to the Opera.

It happened during a trip in which the Opera went to the countryside to give some performances. When they took a boat across the DongTing Lake, the largest lake in Hunan province, the boat turned over in the middle. "We lost eight comrades; including your teacher Comrade Yu." Deng narrated with tears running out.

"But, but my teacher is very good at swimming, he even has a nick name, 'duck', how could a duck drown?" My question remained unanswered, as it was unanswerable.

Secretary Deng then told me it was Teacher Yu's wife who recommended me, for according to the policy, the families who lost their loved ones could have one from the family take over the position, as Teacher Yu's son was too small, I became the lucky one.

A teacher's life for a student's new life, even if it was God's will, isn't that will being a little *too cruel?*

It shouldn't be hard to imagine how complicated my feelings were, the sadness of my teacher's death; the sorrow for his family; the gratitude for the recommendation from his wife; and last but not least, the excitement in the change of my destiny!

The same day, after the gathering, I went to see his wife with great grief on my face. But his wife appeared rather calm. I expressed my compassion and gratitude, offering my help, any help that was within my ability since my teacher was gone.

"Since your teacher is gone," she followed my words, "it's meaningless for us to go on living here. Therefore we will soon move back to Beijing." The wife thanked me the same, then handed a few violin music scores that were prepared on the piano, to me, including Rhoda that the teacher once lent to me.

That was the last time I saw the pretty wife of my teacher.

On the second morning, after hesitation, I went to my workplace as usual, for beside the fact that I should say good-bye to my workmates, I needed to finish the cement fence for the panda house at the Zoo. It was urgent.

To my surprise, when I arrived, all my fellow workers were gathered waiting to give me a farewell party and the organizer was the long-time-no-see Uncle Feng. Everyone talked in turn about my kindness and the good things I had done for the company as well as to them. With most, I either didn't know or had forgotten, such as my taking over heavy jobs for the women and the old; I read newspapers for everyone during the political study hours. One old man narrated with tears, how I had walked an extra distance accompanying him to a bus stop on a rainy day with my umbrella. His moving tone made quite a few others run at their noses too.

Ah, people, I mean Chinese people, why do you have to wait until someone is leaving, or *dead* for all the good parts to be seen and mentioned?

After the party I accomplished those cement flower shaped balusters, thought of as my last "works", I outreached my attention and skills.

About thirty years later, I went to the zoo and saw my "works" still standing firmly between pandas and their viewers.

The year 1974, marked a milestone in my life. After four years working at the construction company, I stepped into a new world, the world of being a professional violinist of which I had dreamed for years.

When Come-True-Dreams Became Dull

Moved into the dormitory of the Opera, the twenty-year-old me, being called the "Nine Brother", for the first time in my life had a key to a room, and in the room a bed that belonged to me, to me *only*. More exciting, a professional violin, not the four hundred RMB level that DuGuo had at the City Opera, but an eight hundred RMB, the eighth grade, the highest grade violin made in the Shanghai violin factory.

Yet with the "eighth grade" I soon lost satisfaction as I remembered that my teacher Yu used to play on an old Italian violin, which was being repaired in Shanghai after having gotten wet. But there was something else, other than my teacher's Italian violin that I wanted even more badly, my teacher's position, the seat of concertmaster of the orchestra.

Not very long after I got into the Opera, my girlfriend ZhengHua's mother, forced her to break up with me, as I had turned myself from a "worker" (working class was the most respectable class at that time) into an "entertainer". With the heavy pressure of an "only daughter" and with her eyes closed, ZhengHua was married to some worker as arranged by her mother.

It was quite a period of time. I had no girlfriend as I had to concentrate all my energy and time on my violin studies. However, MeiMei, known as my sister, came to see me regularly. Somehow, as we both were growing more and more mature, we really behaved more and more like brother and sister. Both feeling more and more shameful about what we did when we were younger, never mentioning those things again.

Through the channel of MeiMei, I learned that my mother remained the same, living life like a clock, doing exactly the same circling every day. On the other hand, my father had been brought back from the May 7 Cadre School (countryside) to his original work unit (city).

As for my elder brother DanXin, after having done three-years hard labor building railways as one of thousands of "volunteers", he also came back home. Thanks to his special interest in photography, which had contributed a great deal to the regional newspaper during the three-year period, he was assigned to the photographic department of the Hunan Medical University (part of the old and present Yale University). From then till today, he is working in the same building where he was jailed for about a month. What a joke of, "not knowing whether to laugh or cry", fate is playing on him! But information regarding my youngest brother DanHen was inadequate.

I did meet DanHen once. It was at a political gathering of all performing units of the Hunan Province. The Acrobatic Unit was beside our Beijing Opera. I kept searching, head by head, finally finding my little brother who was no longer little but rather a muscled man.

The very moment I caught him with my eye, I discovered he was actually looking at me. When our four eyes met, he revealed a little excitement *and* uneasiness. I took the roll of breaking the ice by waving at him, while he seemed regretful; he immediately turned his face away from me, never turning back.

Because of my struggle for the seat of concertmaster, in addition to the piles of shortcomings and problems, such as my maternal genetic problem of, "never getting along with people" made me among the most unpleasant people at the Opera. Meetings of, "criticizing and helping" were frequently serviced for me. All the merit about me seemed to be only one, "great and extreme endeavor to practice the violin."

That was entirely true; I devoted almost all of myself to the violin. I was really, "keeping my nose to the grindstone" going mad practicing my violin. Every morning my violin sounded out, mixing with the young singers' "Yiyiyi, a-a-a", before the crack of dawn.

For my further study, the Opera arranged a violin teacher from the provincial music school, a small lady named Guo ShuMin, who was one of the very few fully-qualified professional violin teachers in the province.

If I am allowed to tell the truth, the period of studies with Teacher Guo was as dull and bitter for me as for her. As to me, to play the violin was no longer "for fun"; the purpose was not only to satisfy my feelings, but a serious and rational job. The violin was just a tool. The importance was not my affection but intonation, rhythm and technique. That kind of playing suppressed my musical enthusiasm and changed the flavor of my musical style. As for Teacher Guo, her headache was to reshape an amateur fancier into a professional performer. That was like training a wild horse to be a gentle pet.

"Teacher Guo, why do you only give me all these dull and tasteless etudes? It makes my feelings get stuck in the middle of my throat with no way out." I inquired dissatisfied.

"Ha ha ha," Teacher Guo laughed, in a way worse than crying. She explained, "That's exactly where your problem is, too much feeling and too little reason. To teach you how to play the violin is like a doctor curing a patient. Only strong and bitter medicine can help you get rid of your bad amateur habits."

As a violinist, even playing the violin became a dull business, what else could be worse? Would you imagine, not only my violin was a tool, but also I, the performer had to become a tool, "A tool of uniting the people and fighting the enemy." as our great leader Chairman Mao taught us. Every-day-work was to play those incomprehensible "Revolutionary Model Beijing Opera", and off work I was to practice all those boring etudes. Allow me to make a rather vulgar yet vivid parable. No matter how crazy one likes sex, when lovemaking becomes one's occupation, a job, and one couldn't make a living without "making love" for eight hours each day, how long could one keep going on liking sex?

Therefore, after a period of time with such a life, hand copying scores, rehearsals, performances... as soon as working hours were over, I threw the violin away, never wanting to touch it. I remember once, one of my brother DanXin's best friends got married. During the wedding someone suggested that I give a little entertainment by playing the violin. If that had been before, it would have been my favorite opportunity to show off, but on that particular day I responded coldly, "My working hours are over." Writing this reminds me of an article saying, "Anything you enjoy doing, stay an amateur."

Two years with the opera had passed, I felt unexplainably low and lost. Not only had I *still* not gotten the position as concertmaster that I so much wanted in the beginning, but more importantly, I had lost the goal or maybe even the meaning of life. I wrote in my dairy, "When a withered person in a desert discovered an oasis and used his last bit of strength to reach it, then found himself stuck in a marsh concealed by the oasis, in how much despair could he be?" This perhaps, is a vivid description of my frame of mind at that time. Hence, I was in real need to change my life and re-adjust myself mentally for a while.

It was at that moment an opportunity fell in my lap. In 1977 I did something my father had been doing for decades, watching the peasants at the countryside as one of the Communist Party representatives although I was no Party member, in fact, a planet far away from it. It was in this year that I experienced the rock-bottom life of Chinese society. I lived together with the peasants, and like the peasants, once literally starved to death, well almost to death. This later influenced my change of view on society tremendously and affected my attitude towards the poor throughout my entire life. My other novel titled, "Under a Banana Tree" has a detailed description of my experiences and observations from that year.

1978, with hand-made cotton shoes and a bamboo pack bag, I returned to my work place, the Hunan Beijing Opera. With suntanned skin and rough hands, I was given the old Italian violin which had belonged to my Teacher Yu, along with his position, concertmaster of the orchestra. The position I had fought for for two years but couldn't get, came to me like a cup of tea. It made me feel that the position was some kind of reward for my hard and outstanding work at the countryside, which gave me little pleasure or satisfaction of achievement.

Being seated on the first chair, I soon realized that I was inadequate for the position. First of all, I knew very little about Beijing Opera. Secondly, I was far lacking in orchestral experience. As a matter of fact my personality and violin playing style were *not at all* suitable for an orchestra, which was proved later in several western countries.

Re-Meeting Ma XiaoMao

One day, I was out having something to eat and happened to catch sight of a very familiar face by the bus stop. "Very familiar" might not be completely accurate, as the face was much darker than what I remembered. However, I wasn't wrong for that face greeted me.

"Ma XiaoMao, I thought you went to XinJiang. Why are you here?" I was truly surprised.

Ma gave a pale smile as an answer. During the interlude waiting for the bus, she told me that the life at XinJiang Construction Corps was much too hard for her and absolutely not a place she could survive. But Flute Chen insisted, "The more bitter the place the more revolutionary I will become." and it was unthinkable to be a deserter. In that case, Ma had to escape. She got back all by herself and was working at a candy factory.

"Poor Flute Chen, he gave up going in the army with all the others and chose XinJiang because of you. But now you left him alone…"

"Don't you worry. He said as soon as I leave him he would find a XinJiang girl and become rooted there." Ma uttered with a sour tone and lots of resentment.

To break the awkwardness she changed the subject to someone else, telling me that Wang ShiYi's father was liberated and returned to his old job as a professor at the Hunan Medical University and Wang ShiYi himself, was given a very good job after his high school graduation.

"How is Lu XiaoBing." I urgently asked.

"She went on to study at university, and after that…"

"No, no, no, I mean how are Lu and Wang?" I asked again very impatiently.

"You really don't know anything, do you?" Ma laughed. After stretching her suspense long enough, she told me that the two were about to get married.

"Re..ally?! congratula..tions." the bus was approaching.

"If there's something I can do to help, please come to me." I shouted at her back, with a feeling of superiority.

"What can you possibly do for me? You know I gave up the violin a long time ago." she said without turning her head, only raising her hand to wave, meaning "good-bye", if not meaning, "get out".

Ma XiaoMao, used to be a fragile and delicate flower in my memory, but now was much withered.

My Dream Of Becoming No. 1 Violinist Of Hunan Province Came True

Along with the down of the "gang of four", (Mao's hard lines with Mao's wife JiangQing in it, were crushed soon after Mao's death), the entire 8 models of Beijing operas vanished, together with their maker.

The Beijing Opera went back to the style of its old days. The western orchestra was no longer in need. Meaning we were all going to be out of a job. It was at that crucial moment, the composer of the province, Liu, created a symphonic Beijing Opera in praise of Premier Zhou, for which a full western orchestra was needed. For that, we had to combine the orchestra of the provincial Sing and Dance unit as well as the City Opera (where I used to go visiting DuGuo during my school years) and Conductor Xiao was appointed to be the conductor for the show.

As the show was Beijing Opera, our orchestra functioned as the backbone, and I, the concertmaster of our small orchestra, was naturally put in the position as concertmaster of the *whole* orchestra. Seeing all the violinists sitting behind me, especially DuGuo sitting far, far behind me, the vivid expression, "walking two feet off the ground" was not enough to describe my satisfaction and exultation.

When Conductor Xiao appeared in front of the orchestra, I was reminded of the letter I wrote to him in my school years, "I swear to you that someday I will become the No. 1 violinist …and you will have to lead your orchestra crawling and rolling to follow my rhythm", which I felt like shouting out once more in his face.

Xiao was the conductor of the city opera, a rank lower than the provincial orchestra, which became the reason for being looked down upon and teased by a few young musicians who would intentionally play wrong notes, or delay half a beat to see whether Xiao was able to determine the mistakes. This made the pearls on top of Xiao's head bigger and brighter than ever under the spotlight.

Seeing all of this, I was amused and happy with a sense that my resentment was being avenged, totally forgetting the seat upon which I was sitting in the orchestra. That is, until my feet were next to crippled after being trampled by my co-player next to me. I corrected my attitude, supporting the conductor and criticizing the naughty ones.

During intermission I went to Conductor Xiao to show my sympathy and warmth, but received a cold response in return. Later someone told me that Xiao was not at all happy with me on the seat, not because of my delay in stopping the naughty ones and supporting him in full, but rather due to my inadequacy to hold the position. "Even the concertmaster is a cripple in rhythm, how could my left hand be healthy."

I was outraged by hearing the rumor, thinking that such a "return of viciousness for favor" person must be punished! I had no chance to do so as he himself quit before that. Ironically, this time it was he who left a notice to me saying, "I'll pursue my study from now on and I promise you someday I will be the No. 1 conductor of the Hunan province."

That show was huge; in fact the biggest in the Hunan stages history. It took place at the Hunan Theater. The media, TV, newspapers, radio were *all* present.

I sent three tickets home hoping my father would come to see my glory on the stage. But only Mother, DanXin and MeiMei showed up and passed me the message that Father was not interested in Beijing Opera. In reality, he bought the cheapest black and white TV set he could find and took it home on his bicycle when I was on the stage playing. When Mother and DanXin went back home after the show, Father was still sweating, adjusting the antenna and the channel of the TV set.

"The show is already over." My brother said to my father.

"I'm not tuning in for the show. I want to see some news from CCTV. (Central China TV)" my father said impatiently. According to my observations, Father does not easily become impatient, *under normal circumstances.*

Teacher Gao Escalates Me To Higher Education

As I mentioned before, I had a new violin teacher Gao, who was supposed to be the best teacher in Hunan Province at the time. But I also explained how and why I didn't really enjoy my lessons with her, at least not as much as when I was with Teacher Li. Besides all of that, to take lessons from Teacher Gao I had to travel on my bike about an hour each way, this is one of the excuses I used to stop taking lessons from her, besides being deadly busy with the opera show.

One day after the rehearsal, Teacher Gao showed up. She asked me a question before I could even attempt to form some excuses for not taking lessons anymore: "What would you like to do in the future?"

"What future?" I didn't understand what she was talking about.

"Your future. You are a young man in your twenties, the prime of your life. I think you should pursue studies for a higher goal." she said.

"Oh, that. But I'm already goaled. You see, Teacher, I'm sitting on the first seat of the whole province. This is my utmost goal. I have no more goal." I answered honestly.

"Listen. How great is it to sit on the first chair of the province, the

Hunan province, and how big is the Hunan province, compared with Shanghai, compared with the *world*?"

"What do you mean Teacher? I mean, what do you want me to do? " I puzzled.

"People going up, water going down. Have you heard that? I know a teacher from Shanghai conservatory who would come to Changsha for new students. I think you should try. You should prepare yourself for the opportunity."

Seeing me silent, wondering, Teacher Gao added: "Come to me after the opera show season is over. I'll help you prepare for the entrance exam to study in Shanghai."

But, *Shanghai*? A vast city, far away. Is this a place for me, the little Nine Brother, a Hunan bumpkin? Teacher Gao left no room for negotiation. It felt a little strange, as I had never been a very good student of hers. Why did she suddenly became so serious about me, and, put so much pressure on me?

1978 was the first time the Chinese art and music academies openly recruited new students after the Cultural Revolution. The Shanghai music conservatory sent a famous professor, Sheng ZhongHua, (the sister of Sheng ZhongGuo who was supposed to be the No. 1 violinist in China, at least at that time) to Hunan to recruit new students.

Teacher Gao personally knew Teacher Sheng, so she went to meet her at the station with most of her students, including me, the little Nine Brother.

As soon as the train stopped, we saw Professor Sheng waving her hand, walking down from the carriage. The elegant appearance of the VIP left a deep impression. Off the train, the professor was surrounded by us. Teacher Gao introduced us one by one, and the professor shook hands with us one after another. Although the professor acted politely, she looked a little lost. When it came to my turn she suddenly uttered, "Did I forget something on the train?"

"Violin." Teacher Gao responded, "You can't come without your violin, can you?"

"Right, right, right, my violin." The Professor rushed back to the carriage and returned with her violin. When I stretched my hand out, waiting for my turn to shake hands, she thought I was offering my help to carry her violin.

"How nice and thoughtful of you." she praised me with her violin in my hand.

On the way to the hotel the professor still looked somewhat absent minded and all the questions asked her went in one ear and out the other. Gao stopped us and asked her again, "Calm down and think once more, is there something else left on the train?"

"Violin, suitcase, handbag, shoes, hat and no more." Sheng nodded her head rather firmly, but she added, "It should be everything and no more." with a tone obviously persuading no one but herself.

After we said good-bye at the front of the hotel and walked out, we were all simultaneously sharing our impressions of the professor. Just as I made my bold remark, "The professor acted like a fly without a head", the professor rushed out shouting, "I forgot...forgot!" she was out of breath.

"Calm down and take a deep breath, now tell us, forgot what?" Teacher Gao asked, with her hand petting the professor's shoulder.

"I forgot... Oh my God, I *left my daughter on the train!* She was sleeping, that's how I forgot."

What an artist and a mother! Ha ha ha!!!

The audition took place the next morning. One after another we played our violins on the stage while Professor Sheng, with her reading glasses on her nose, sat quietly, keeping her eyes down, focused on her lap. I wondered why, and had a peep. Oh my Go..d, no, Oh my Chairman Mao! She was reading a music score, the violin concerto "Butterfly Lovers", the *only* known Chinese violin concerto in all of Chinese violin music history.

Later I found out the whole thing was a formality, as that year and every year from then on, the Shanghai Conservatory of music took only a few violin students and the positions were filled before any auditions had even taken place. A place like Hunan, "a place even birds wouldn't shit" as people remarked, had no chance what-so-ever at the very beginning. That's why the professor wanted to make the most out of the trip by giving a recital in Hunan, the place her own mother was originally from.

And so, a chance landed in my lap. It happened when Sheng had her rehearsal with the orchestra. Her violin opened at the side, which occurs often when an instrument is brought from one place to another with different humidity levels.

The noise from the opening of the violin irritated her so badly that she had to stop in the middle of the rehearsal. I told the professor that it was a huge problem to her but a cup of tea to me as I had once made a violin from scratch.

After the concert, besides Teacher Gao, I was the only student asked to see the professor off to the station.

Waiting for the train to come, the professor complained that there were too few violin makers and repairers in the country. Then her eyes lit up, she said, "Oh yes, now I remember that the director of the conservatory, Professor Tang, is making a new course for violinmaking. He asked me to keep an eye out for talented students if I should meet. I could recommend you if you're interested?" Seeing me not so interested she added, "Of course the violin making students also learn to *play* the violin. As far as you are in Shanghai, with a small charge, you could also take private lessons, say, from me."

Teacher Gao made no obvious response, but from her face I knew that she at least did not oppose the idea. She waited for my response. Yet I gave no response. How could I respond? I made a white ugly violin at the age of 14 purely due to the lack of money. The purpose of making that violin was to *play* violin. But now I had an old Italian violin in my hand and the seat of the concertmaster, why on earth would I go back to learning how to make violins?

There was a gap of silence until the train was coming. I carried her luggage and Teacher Gao took her violin. The professor herself, held her daughter so tightly that the 8-year-old girl was screaming in pain.

Unexpectedly, later on Teacher Gao suggested that it may be a good idea and opportunity, my going to Shanghai as a violin making student. She said, "For sure this is a short cut for you to go to Shanghai. As far as you are there, you can learn anything you like and as much as you like. You can still be a great violinist after that."

I didn't give the teacher a concrete answer, as I didn't have one. Only puzzled, why did Teacher Gao so much want me to go to Shanghai? Why?

The End Of The Hunan Beijing Opera Orchestra And The Beginning Of The Hunan Radio & TV Orchestra

In 1978, the huge symphonic Beijing Opera in praising Premier Zhou, marked the "momentary recovery of consciousness just before the death" of our orchestra. Soon after the concert, not only us, but the western orchestras of all Beijing Operas nationwide were disbanded. Where to go was the question placed in front of every orchestra member.

Hence, as the old Chinese saying, "The eight immortals cross the sea, each applies one's own special skills" we each had to find a way out for ourselves. Some went to the orchestra belonging to the singing and dance troupe, and a few went to the Hunan Film Manufacture Studio, and some gave up a career in music and started something totally new.

In regard to me, besides escaping the challenge, I wanted to escape from the city in which I had lived most of my twenty-four-year-life as I started to get tired of it. I chose GuiLin, a little place of natural beauty known as the Xanadu. The local singing and dance orchestra accepted my application on the spot and with the offer of concertmaster. Yet, at the same time, all my personal papers had already been transferred to another unit without anyone consulting with the man to whom the papers belonged!

It so happened that at the same time the new Hunan Radio & TV Orchestra was established and the majority of the musicians from our Beijing Opera were transferred to it, including me.

It was Li, the head of the Hunan Radio and TV ("CEO" in the west) who received me when I went to inquire why. He used his official jargon in a rather soft tone, saying, "The rapid development of the radio and TV require us to establish an orchestra." He followed by making it known that the solid financial resource would provide the best quality musical instruments and training for the musicians, possibly all being sent to Beijing for a year.

He paused a little, drank some tea and announced, "For setting up the best orchestra in the province we need a *talented* violinist, such as you, to be the *concertmaster.*" He stressed the two words "talented" and "concertmaster", or perhaps the two words sounded specially stressed to me? Anyway, I went in discontented and came out with satisfaction and joy. That resulted in my trip, the first and last time to GuiLin, being an album of black and white sightseeing photographs.

New orchestra, new environment, new colleagues, everything was fresh and exciting! I felt happy and enjoyed myself every day, totally forgetting Teacher Gao's expectation of me to get out of Changsha and pursue my studies in Shanghai.

A couple of months later, the orchestra was to give its debut concert on the radio and TV, of course. We were all too excited to sleep. It was at midnight that something odd happened.

Search For My Brother DanXin

It was MeiMei along with a cute little round figured girl who came to see me. They told me with anxiety, "Something's wrong, your brother DanXin is missing." Then I remembered who that round girl was. She was the *so-called,* "Big Sister" with my father's clock on her wrist, the one I met at my father's place when I visited him some years ago at the countryside.

The story goes like this. With the help of my father, Big Sister managed to get away from the countryside and back to Changsha city where she found a job as an accountant at a department store. She got acquainted with my brother DanXin through my father and somehow the relationship went romantic. However, I vaguely knew that DanXin had always been interested in one of our neighbors named XiaoJuan. At the moment, XiaoJuan was a medical student at the Hunan Medical University, the same place DanXin was working, therefore it was natural that they bumped into each other often. It was my gut reaction to think that DanXin must be in a state of mental disorder caused by the whole love triangle business.

"Where could my brother be going?" I asked. "I don't know." Big Sister said, "I only heard he wanted to be left alone for a few days, possibly in the South Mountain?"

"South Mountain, the sacred site of Buddhism? That's far away!" I uttered with surprise.

"Suicide?" Immediately MeiMei regretted she said that, adding, "That's what everybody's worried about, isn't it? Otherwise we wouldn't turn to you, at this time of the day, I mean, night."

The *want-to-forgot* memory of Chu XiaoLin nose-diving from her window, stroked me hard. That kind of experience once is more than enough in a lifetime, how could I think of this happening again, with my own flesh and blood?

Left with no choice, I went back to the Dormitory, picked up a few things and with my yellow army bag, went out again. At the door I very briefly told my roommate that something had happened to my family and I had to go to the South Mountain right away.

"But, don't forget tomorrow's debut performance, the first time for us to be on the TV."

I rode my bike at violation speed all the way to the long distance bus station where I found the earliest bus for South Mountain would be at 6:00 am , meaning there were five long hours. I would count each minute.

I sat on a wooden bench, doubting whether those who were lying on the benches were actually waiting for buses, or just a free place to sleep for the night. Some old memories with my brother emerged...

I was pushed awake as I took too much space lying on the bench. I was in such an ill mood that I was about to call some bad names when the man who pushed me complained, "It's nearly six o'clock but you are still..."

"Six o'clock! Thank you, thank you my friend."

I checked my watch, it was three minutes to six, too late to go through the normal procedure of cueing for a ticket. I dashed out of the station and saw the bus with a sign in the front window, "Changsha to South Mountain". I chased the bus and hammered the door with my fist, but the bus refused to stop.

Yet my mind was made up, I *had* to be on that bus. It was a matter of the life and death of my bosom brother and I might just be the only one in the entire world who could save him! Watching the bus move away, "resourcefulness in an emergency" came to me.

I jumped on my bike again headed in the direction of the bus. Of course I had to run through all red lights, as they were my best opportunities. I can't say the speed, but I dare say the courage was far beyond a doubt qualified to participate in the Olympics.

About half an hour later, when I started to convince myself that manpower is in no way competition for a few thousand horsepower machine, I saw the bus stopped far away, vaguely within sight! I used the last of my strength peddling my bike up there and found that the bus had one of the tires stuck in a hole. When the bus started to move again, with me in it, I still couldn't breathe at a normal pace.

The bus arrived at the foot of the South Mountain just before noon. I got off the bus with sore feet from standing the whole way. Nevertheless, I felt more hungry than tired as I suddenly realized I had nothing to eat for breakfast.

I ate whatever I could get and headed to the mountain. The touring and pilgrimage season had just ended because the winter was coming. In the beginning I met people from time to time, but after getting half way to the top, I could see no one, not even a ghost.

The higher I climbed, the colder it was. I started to doubt whether it was the right decision to come here looking for my brother in such blindness. However, that blindness explains how at that moment it was more important to ease my mood and anxiety about finding my brother than actually to find him. Just like the year 1958, during the, "Great Leap Forward" when the whole nation was thrown into the movement of, "Exceeding the British and chasing up the Americans". The true meaning of that movement was to satisfy the mood and soothe anxieties rather than actually achieving the unachievable goal.

At the end of a "T" road, I chose the right direction, thinking it to be a short cut by intuition. I walked up and up, and the road became narrower and narrower. The ice frozen leaves were as sharp as thousands of knives.

Five hours had passed and it was getting darker and darker. I started to be more and more scared, scared of getting lost in the middle of nowhere, scared of bumping into some kind of wild beast, or being trapped in an unknown spot becoming a frozen mummy. There's no need to mention how extremely cold and hungry I was, yet I went on and on, climbing by the strong will to survive. It became completely dark and I was entwined by indescribable fear and despair.

I raised my head and looked upon the sky, praying for help, and that's when I saw two huge, high towers extending all the way to the moon. "Is this the way that leads to heaven? Oh my God! A few days from now it will be my brother's turn to look for me, or likely, my remains…" The sudden thought made my flesh creep and teeth chatter.

Next, I saw some indistinct lights flickering and vaguely, an electrical cable! Electricity, the symbol of human civilization, gave me, a helpless man in the grip of the power of nature, a glimmer of hope! Immediately I forgot the cold, hunger and fear, moving towards the light as fast as my legs and hands, could carry me.

Fate or not, those two huge high towers were a television transmission station belonging to the same TV station (the only TV station, the government TV station in Hunan) that my orchestra belonged to. Hearing I was from the central head station, the young comrade behaved very hospitably. He made me some hot water to wash my face and feet, and then something to eat.

Then, with excitement he told me, "There is an important mission tonight. The newly established Radio and TV Orchestra is going to give a debut concert tonight at nine o'clock!"

"I knew, I knew, I knew it a long time ago." I smiled with extreme bitterness and regret.

Through the TV monitor, I saw my orchestra appear on the stage, and the lady who used to sit next to me, took my seat. I realized, without me, the earth was still going around according to its course. When the conductor raised his hands, I too raised mine in violin playing position. However, soon my snore took part in the performance.

Early next morning, the very first thing I did was pay a visit to the South Mountain Police Station. After hearing the story about my brother, they said that no dead body had been found so far, but they would inform me immediately if they did.

I followed the main road all the way down, my mind occupied with the thought that, "shortcuts could be dangerous sometimes".

My South Mountain journey did not accomplish the goal of finding my brother, but the "wish" to find him.

The Secretary But My Shield Aunt Yu

Back to the orchestra from the South Mountain, the very first thing I considered was whether I should pack up my things and get ready to leave, for such a huge misdoing it wouldn't be unthinkable to get sacked.

As expected, a general meeting of the whole orchestra was arranged. I was asked to stand by the side of the dais, ready to be criticized.

My colleagues came in one after another looking at me with all kinds of facial expressions, be it worried or gloating. No need to describe just how serious the atmosphere was.

After ordering everyone to sit, the chief manager Liu, put his big cup with the words, "Dedicated to the Dearest Person" printed upon it (a sign of honor to those who participated in the Anti-US and Supporting Korean War movement in the early 50s) on the table and clenched his fist. But as soon as he opened his mouth to announce the meeting was starting, the secretary of CEO Li pushed the door open and called me out.

I was led to Li's office. After asking his secretary to wait outside, Li shook his head showing his meaning of, "hate the iron that is unable to become steel".

Seeing him look so troubled, my pride exploded. I immediately decided to give up all the excuses I was about to make. When I said to him firmly, "It's not my style to put others in difficulty. You do whatever is necessary with me. No mercy is asked." his wife Yu Hua walked into the office. Li stood up, giving his seat to his boss and went out to "wash his hands", at least that was what he *said*.

Let me give a few words to describe Yu Hua. She was average sized. With a well-maintained face, although over fifty, she didn't look her age. She talked with a sweet and milky voice, yet the connotation of her words was powerful and heavy. She used to be a singer with the Army Singing and Dance Unit with a nickname "Red Hetaera". If I'm allowed to make a guess, in the past decades, for sure Li was not the *only* revolutionary leader who was defeated under her skirt.

In short, Li leads the whole broadcast television, and Yu leads Li, though her public position was no more than the secretary of our orchestra, the secretary of manager Liu. While somehow Yu seemed to be a little in favor of me, calling me by my nickname, Nine Brother and asking me to call her, not secretary Yu but "Aunt Yu". That was *not* normal in a working relationship. Of course I knew nothing of what was in her mind, or in her sweet daughter's mind. But to make it absolutely clear, there was nothing beyond a friendly atmosphere between us, not even one private talk. That made our meeting alone, the first time.

"Hey, my little Nine Brother. Tell me what went wrong. Aunt Yu will help you out." She sounded like a savior.

I was overwhelmed by such an unexpected offer. After hearing my story about South Mountain and seeking my brother, she wiped tears from her face and said, "Alright, let's go back to the meeting room. I'll try to explain it to the comrades." She stood up, shaped my hair a little with her fingers, and remarked, "Why do boys nowadays like to have long hair?"

Back in the meeting room, seeing Yu, the boiling room suddenly became silent. Liu looked at his secretary, I mean his boss, nervously. Everyone must have been thinking that would be the end of me, the little Nine Brother. Even manager Liu had to "take it with him if he couldn't eat it all".

Liu immediately moved his ass to an audience seat. Yu moved from her chair to let me sit, while she herself stood in the middle of the dais. Liu offered her another chair right away but she rejected, probably because standing made her look taller.

Yu adjusted her throat a little, and then started to appraise the success of the debut concert, followed by her changing the topic to a story about her life with the Army Singing and Dance Unit when she was younger. Half an hour had passed, still not a single word about my misdeed from her mouth. When the story ended everyone gave her a big hand, yet she went on. She narrated a story that happened during the Anti-US and Supporting Korean War, "Once we were sent to give a performance at the front. On our way we met a few wounded soldiers. We made our own decision to move those soldiers to a safer place. Because of that, we were late for the performance. At that time we were all afraid of being criticized or even being punished. However, we were not criticized; instead we all received medals of honor for saving lives." (Her original story was much, much longer than this.)

When everybody started to doubt why this story was relevant to the meeting, the meeting meant to criticize and punish *me*, Yu finally brought the topic back to the point. She said, "The matter of little Nine Brother, I mean comrade Chen's absence from the debut concert, is no doubt a very serious mistake, but he did it to rescue his brother. It is always more important to save a life than a performance, no matter in war or in peace.

Yes, comrade Chen should be criticized, not for the absence from the concert, but for taking the decision on his own. What he should have done was report it to the leadership. This applies to all of you. From now on, no matter what happens, you should report to me, to manager Liu. The Great Party is what you all can and should rely upon. Otherwise you all would get lost, just like comrade Chen got lost in the South Mountain. Think how dangerous it was to be lost on such a big mountain. If it weren't for our comrades at the transmission station rescuing comrade Chen, perhaps we would not be here for, for the *congratulating meeting of the debut concert*, (she even changed the title of the meeting) but rather a memorial ceremony for the death of a comrade." She looked at me with pity, "Our poor little Nine Brother."

Laughter could be heard from the audience. "Is it funny? My dear comrades, did I say something funny? This is something serious, very serious; in no way should it be laughed about. (Laughter terminated immediately) However, there is a kind of, 'not afraid of bitterness and death' inside comrade Chen's psyche, which is worthy of us following."

Just a minute, how could a criticizing meeting turn out to be a *praising meeting*? This time, it was *me* who couldn't help but laugh out.

Very honestly, being sheltered by a leader, that was the first time in my little Nine Brother life.

With a big applause, from Liu too, the meeting ended like that. Manager Liu's smiling face looked relaxed, but not for very long, as he was wanted by Yu. I too, was caught by her at the door and received an order, "Come to have supper with my family tonight."

Meeting Aunt Yu's Daughter NiNi

In the evening, the naive me went Yu Hua's home, empty-handed.

Stepping into CEO Li's home, surprises came to me one after another. First of all, I found there was a toilet inside Li's home, unlike every comrade in the orchestra, including manager Liu who had to run from the dormitory to the office building, for just a pee. A story was told about a comrade who soiled his pants because he was unable to get into the building since forgetting to bring his ID. (Armed soldiers guarded the office building at all times.)

Secondly, I was amazed to see not only did the TV set have *color*, but when changing the channel there was no need to walk up to the TV and switch, instead simply push a button in a cigarette-pack sized box at a distance.

"Aunt Yu, what's that?" I ask curiously.

"Ha ha ha." she laughed with satisfaction. "This is called a remote control, my little Nine Brother."

This is a true story. It was genuinely the first time for me to hear such a high-tech colored term as, "remote control".

However, to compare with the next pleasant surprise the above surprises became nothing. The surprise was her daughter NiNi (not Li's daughter, but the daughter of Yu and her former).

She was so adorable, delicate, fresh and elegant; I associated her with, with what, kind of a fresh soft cream cake, perhaps? She was said to be the princess of the Hunan Radio and TV Bureau. Someone said she was a fairy, while others called her sprite. Nevertheless, I'd rather call her "beauty". With her outstanding appearance and social status, I mean her stepfather's social status, to be exact, her mother's status in her stepfather's heart, I heard someone made a bet, yet still no boy dared to look at her face, only turned heads to look at her back when her bike passed in the distance.

However, it was at that moment she not only walked towards me, but also sat by my side on the sofa! That made me immediately feel many thorns growing from the sofa.

"Nine Brother." she called me, with a voice even more sweet and creamy than her mother's.

"Yes." I stood up like a soldier being called by his superior.

NiNi smiled and pulled my hand to sit down. I felt an electric shock and collapsed on the sofa.

"You know it's very noisy for you to play the violin under my window every day?" From her mouth, even complaints sounded so pleasant.

"No doubt very noisy, that's why you insist on leaving the window wide open, not to mention you have it recorded and play it under your pillow over and over again." The mother laughed, and went on, "I'm sure my NiNi's appreciation of music very much came from me."

Knowing my violin had captured the heart of a young girl, a wave of joy and satisfaction welled up from my heart.

(Here skip ten minutes romantic conversation nonsense)

"Nine Brother." She called me again.

"Yes." This time I did not stand up, but crossed one leg over the other with my toe to the air.

"I heard you can speak English?" she asked.

"Of course. 'This is a pen'." I said in English, very proudly.

"Xixixi." NiNi 's laughter sounded like a gold bell.

"That's right, youngsters nowadays should study hard to catch up with the ever-lasting changeable situations." The mother made her very wise comment. While to me, at the moment felt not only NiNi, but even the old lady was also *very* charming.

Since then, NiNi came to see me at our dormitory quite often with the excuse of borrowing books or asking English questions. That made all the boys and girls in our orchestra, as well as all the young people in the Radio and TV Bureau change, having a totally different eye on me, the little Nine Brother.

Going To Shanghai

When the fever from the "great success of the debut concert" dropped back to normal, if not lower than normal, we all found that the new Radio and TV Orchestra was more of an amateur propaganda music group than a professional orchestra. The CEO Li too, started to realize this unpleasant fact.

With the solid economic power of the government mouthpiece, *"The throat and tongue of the Party"* as Mao decided was the roll of radio, TV and all press, Li made a remarkable decision to send the entire "troop" to Beijing for one-year of concentrated training.

"For the sake of the development of our orchestra, to be able to propagandize our Great Party and country better, we are not afraid of spending money. You all go to Beijing looking for the best teacher you can find and concentrate yourself on one-year of hard studies. A year later, we'll give a concert again. It will be a concert of high quality, high level, in a word, a concert of professionals..."

Li waved his hand in the air to end his speech. That stage presentation appeared much like all the heroes in Chinese movies, which gained the excitement of the entire meeting room and a warm applause. Unlike most of the time, our big hand was for real this time, for the favorable content of what he said rather than how great he waved his hand.

Hence, the whole orchestra was boiling, or as the Chinese say, "like the ants on a hot pot". Some said they would like to go to the Chinese Center Orchestra; others said it was better to go to the Center Conservatory of Music, while I was busy seeking a channel leading me to Sheng ZhongGuo, the No. 1 violin soloist, the crest of the Chinese violin world, the symbol of ...

For that I begged my violin Teacher Gau. Gau told me she didn't know Sheng ZhongGuo directly, but was willing to give a try through his sister Sheng ZhongHua, the lady violin professor from Shanghai who once came to Hunan to meet us. But my Teacher Gau strongly recommended I go to Shanghai instead of Beijing, for Shanghai was a better place for violin studies *and* because Teacher Gao knew many more people in Shanghai than in Beijing.

By that time, the friendship between NiNi and I was a little higher than normal friends, yet by no means that of boy-girl friends. We talked about ambitions from time to time. Once I asked her if she could choose where about she would want to live the most. Guess what she said? She said she would like to live in various *foreign* countries! That was certainly a shock to me, especially during that era, so I could only take it as a joke. I guess it's true now, as we have had no contact since then, I just wonder from time to time her whereabouts at the present.

About going to Beijing or Shanghai, I talked a little with NiNi too. And she replied: "Where is the best place and who will be the best teacher to study with, is the place you should go."

It was after that my mind was made: "Go to Shanghai." I went to see CEO Li at his home. Hearing I wanted to go to Shanghai all by myself instead of going to Beijing with our troop, Li was very upset. He talked official jargon like, "How could that be possible? This is a collective activity, to train our soldiers. How could I allow you to run wherever you like? I say you, little comrade Chen, have you forgotten your absence at the debut concert? I let you get away because you had a special circumstance, but this time my mind is set. No matter what you say, I'll never…"

"Please Head Li…"

Not waiting for me to finish, Li "pa" stood up, and angrily announced, "I said no means no! The decision is made, even if you beg my, my, I mean your, your Aunt Yu. I say to you comrade, you have no sense of leadership, no sense of collectivity, no sense of discipline, no sense of…"

Li wanted to go on, meanwhile his wife Yu Hua pushed the door open and walked in, followed by her lovely daughter NiNi.

"What are you two talking about? It sounds very serious." Yu asked, with a nothing-to-worry-about smile.

"Aunt Yu." I called her, in a charming earnest tone.

The matter of me going to Shanghai was set, just like that.

15: THE FOURTH STAGE OF MY VIOLIN STUDIES

Goodbye NiNi, And Go To Shanghai

The evening before my departure for Shanghai, I went to Li's home to show my gratitude to his wife Aunt Yu, but found they were both absent on a vacation. Sorry, a slip of the tongue. They were not on "vacation" but a "business errand". (In the communist period, it was common practice for officials taking private "vacation" or "combi" with the name of "business errand" so that all the costs could be reimbursed) NiNi was the only one left home.

Seeing me walking away, NiNi asked, "Wouldn't you sit with me for a while if I invite you to?

Two young people sit together, alone, what could they think, if not have happen?

NiNi's face flushed like a peach. She sat a meter away, beside me, asking me timidly, "Have you thought, if I say yes, will you take me?" She was moving toward me, little by little as she said that.

By then I realized that she was not just teasing me nor testing me, she could mean for real! I started to fear the consequence, "I, I, this is a rather serious matter that I'll have to ask your mother about before I say anything."

Hearing that, NiNi's mood changed suddenly. She stood up and spit out her words with disappointment, "Ask my mother first! I thought you were *different*." She paused, and went on, "I'm not my mother's *thing!* Why does everybody want to ask my mother?" She paused, and then sounding as if talking to herself she said: "I think I am going to marry the first man who asks me, only me, not my mother, to marry him."

I found such words from NiNi's mouth extremely seducing and encouraging. I wonder what kind of action you would take if you were in my situation? For me it was too much to endure. I embraced her. With certain gentleness, spontaneously I started to take off her clothes. She subconsciously resisted a little and then let me. Suddenly a voice came to my ears: *"When are we going to get married? Because if you do this, we're going to have a child..."* I stopped.

NiNi looked rather disappointed, she started to take off her clothes by herself, piece by piece, but at the last part and last moment she also stopped. Her flesh was white, transparent, elastic, delicate and juicy. I appreciated her beauty rather than sexual desire. Even today, I could still clearly remember her body, like a piece of art. Saying "gorgeous" would be inadequate. It was simply one word "beauty", a beauty that made my whole body stiff but my man part soft.

The power of a women's glamour is so magical and varies, some makes a man excited and rush forward like a mortar, while some makes a man nervous and withdraw one's part inside like a tortoise.

I was not ready to get married and have a family, *absolutely not.* I didn't know why, but I just felt something wasn't right. All I could do was make myself an excuse. Only myself knows that whenever it comes to a crucial moment, I'm actually quite serious, decent and traditional. I picked up her clothes to cover her breasts that I had already appreciated well enough and said, "I think, perhaps, we should wait, until we are mature enough."

NiNi was obviously not very pleased with my lie. She embraced me politely and said, "Now, at least I know what a real gentleman is like."

Being very honest, later I regretted a little, maybe a little more than a little, countless times. Until today, I still imagine how it could be if things didn't go that way. But the regret with NiNi was left there, forever.

The next morning early, MeiMei came to my dormitory and declared that she was, on behalf of my whole family, to see me off at the station. That again, sounded odd as how could she come on behalf of my family when she was by no means a member of my family? However, it was better than nobody seeing me off at the station. At least she could help me with some of my luggage. Later, during most times in my life, I have been alone, alone on departure, alone on arrival, in many places around the world.

After waving good-bye to MeiMei at the station, I hurried to the compartment, fighting for space on the luggage rack. As soon I swept my sweat and sat down by the window, I saw NiNi running into the station with great haste. A station personnel carried something following her closely. I quickly got off the train. NiNi looked relived when she saw me. She took the thing from the station personnel and handed it up to me, "I'm not good at cooking, but surely it's better than the meal on the train."

Holding the handmade lunch box, I suddenly felt extraordinarily touched and wondered whether I should leave my luggage on the train, forget the whole thing about Shanghai, and go back with NiNi immediately to live another life.

After the train whistled twice I was still staring at NiNi foolishly. If it hadn't been for that station personnel's push being strong enough, I would most probably have missed the train.

Now I recall the whole story, that station personnel's push was a push of historical importance, as my whole new life was started from *that* push.

I waved to NiNi, and promised I would come to see her the next time I came back to Changsha. In reality, that was our farewell. NiNi and me, we never saw each other again.

NiNi, as a friend, in fact a little more than a friend, I still miss her from time to time, not badly, but lightly, no matter where about or how about she is, she is always there in my mind. I believe she is the same too. What is that? HAZY LOVE? You tell me!

Like that, I said farewell to NiNi and that part of my life in my hometown, Changsha City, Hunan Province.

My Very First Days In Shanghai

It's not that I purposely draw a portrait of myself as a rube, or a country bumpkin in order to make you laugh, it's that I really *was* a country bumpkin when I was placed in a big city like Shanghai.

I remember the first time I went to Shanghai. I possessed no suitcase, therefore I had to wrap everything in a bed sheet. That was my main piece along with my yellow army bag, violin and other small items. Added together, the result was about equal to the weight of the main piece, hence I carried the two pieces on my shoulder with a bamboo pole. But when the train arrived in Shanghai, my carrying pole was no longer at the place that it used to be. It must have been taken by some comrade who needed it more badly than I. I had to wait for everybody to get off the train before I could move my stuff piece by piece from the train.

Luckily, if not by God's will, a rope that some countryman dropped solved my problem. I tied my main piece at one end of the rope and the others on the opposite end, one piece in front and the other on the back on my shoulder. My back arched, with that appearance, I stepped into Shanghai, one of the biggest and most luxurious cities in the world, then and still now.

As soon as getting out of the station I bumped into two pretty, young Shanghai ladies. I did have an excuse that I needed to ask the way, but what I wanted more was to hear a Shanghai girl's creamy coy voice. The voice was heard, yet not at all creamy nor coy, rather a mocking tone with a single word, *"alien"*. That voice of snootiness carved deep in my heart so that I still remember. It was at that very spot and moment I made up my mind, "One day, I will make Shanghai girls raise their heads, admiring me like a bright star in the sky."

Good people are always the majority, even in a city like Shanghai. With the help of some good-hearted people, I finally found my way to the Shanghai Conservatory of Music.

I stayed at the guesthouse of the Conservatory. It was a one-story house by the side of a football field. It had eight small rooms, overcrowded with 10 people just like me, coming from all over the country to be gold-plated.

I still have the aftertaste of that part of life, the different smell and taste from each person. The body odor, sweat and foot smell etc. that blended together to be the "Big Chinese National Harmonious Taste Symphony". No wonder *Uncle Big Head*, the Shanghai guy who was in charge of the guesthouse, disliked us as if we were a pile of dog shit.

The very first thing I did in Shanghai was visit Teacher Sheng ZhongHua. As soon as I was notified of the fees for the lessons (fees would be reimbursed by my orchestra back home) the lesson started. She gave me a lot of homework at the first lesson and then someone's phone number, asking me to purchase some blueprint reproduction copy music notes from him. (At that time, the majority of violin literature was still unavailable, and there were no copy machines then) But it turned out, most of the music sheets she asked me to buy, were never used. It was just a kind of business between the sheet music maker and the teachers.

I felt rapid progress in my violin performance during that period of time, ironically not due to Teacher Sheng's teaching efforts but the outstanding musical environment. In fact, Teacher Sheng was expecting her second husband's baby, and so far along that she couldn't even pull the bow straight across a violin. In the Shanghai Conservatory of Music, were gathered the most talented violinists. I could learn from practically anyone I saw. In addition, from time to time I received free tutoring from Sheng ZhongXiang, the younger brother of my Teacher Sheng ZhongHua, known as the king of technique among our fellow students.

Just when I was feeling great and thought my violin playing ability would leap to the national level, Teacher Sheng cut off my lessons due to giving birth. Hence, I found Teacher Yu LiNa, the one who recorded the only Chinese violin concerto, "Butterfly Lovers", one of the best violin teachers at that time and still today.

Tail up, I went into Teacher Yu's lesson room, tail down when I got out. She treated me like a beginner, a child, asking me to do all the very basic practices which I did a long time ago and had already forgotten. In addition, she was extremely strict on my playing. She would even count how many times I should vibrate on each note! I endured the hardship for less than one year, much harder and more bitter than the time I spent with Teacher

Guo back home. Many years later I started to understand that to learn from either Teacher Guo or Teacher Yu was just against my nature, for what they wanted to educate was a violin player good for any orchestra in the country, not a soloist with characters or features, which is what I wanted to be. As a person, I respect teacher's Guo and Yu much, much more than Teacher Sheng, as I could feel the love and passion when they were teaching and the strong sense of responsibility as a teacher, treating their students as works of art rather than customers.

Time flies. One year passed quickly. According to Teacher Guo's advice, I registered for the entrance examination at the Shanghai Conservatory of Music, behind the back of my Hunan Radio and TV Orchestra.

In that year, the conservatory had only 2 places for violin students, while the applicants numbered over 200 from all over the country. The first stage was not a live audition but a recorded tape. When the result was on the wall, I found my name was missing from the list. After my prompt inquiry with Teacher Yu, I learned it may be that my tape was mixed with someone else's. However, Teacher Yu comforted me by emphasizing that even if I was lucky enough to get to the second stage, there was absolutely *no chance* for me to get to the final. In this sense, getting to the second stage would only give me a little face when I went back to my home province. Teacher Yu's words really did give me a certain consolation; at least I could use it as the perfect excuse for Teacher Guo.

I immediately sent a telegram to Teacher Guo and then thought of packing my things and getting ready to return to Hunan, where I was from. I even imagined NiNi might be there waiting for me. But the next morning I received a very short long-distance call from Teacher Guo, "Do not move. Stay there. I'm leaving right away, and will be in Shanghai tomorrow."

The next several days I followed Teacher Guo to almost every single one of the Conservatory's that had something to do with the exam, and met every dean and vice dean of the department. In the end, we visited the home of the Conservatory director He LuDin, one of the most influential composers in New China, who was also originally from Hunan.

When his wife answered the door, Teacher Guo suddenly uttered a fluent Hunan dialect. (Teacher Guo was from the North part of China and her language was Mandarin.) That changed our status from students to *guests from home*. When she heard that her husband's conservatory never had a violin student from Hunan province, the home province they were from, she looked a little surprised. "Is that so?" she said. "I'll call the dean and ask if it's true that the tapes got mixed up."

Next morning, Dean Yuan rushed to the guesthouse to notify me, "Prepare yourself for the second stage exam."

I was so pleased that I took all my money out of my wallet, which was five yuan RMB, wanting to take Teacher Guo for a meal as celebration. Instead, I was scolded by Teacher Guo, "Things haven't even gotten started. Go back and practice your violin at once!"

"Are you seriously thinking that I have a chance?" I took the courage to talk back, "Teacher Yu already told me that I had little chance. To get to the second stage, is only to give me face to go back to Hunan."

"You think I came from so far away, and walked you door to door having done all this only for you to save face? Please listen to me very carefully; you have to do your best, more than best, absolutely, to get yourself into the Conservatory."

"Thank you so much for doing all this for me Teacher Guo." I said politely.

"You're welcome, and it's for me too." Teacher Guo replied.

"For you! Why?" I thought.

It took three days to go through all of the exams, including a live performance audition and a paper test of musical theory, etc.

As soon as the exams were all over, Teacher Guo started to get busy again. She went through all of her network and discovered good news for me. She told me excitedly, "You don't need to go back to Hunan anymore!" Immediately she asked me, "Where is the five yuan RMB that you wanted to take me out for a meal with?"

I rummaged through all my pockets; there was only three yuan and eighty-four fen left.

"There is still a week before your payday, how can you make ends meet with this small sum? Follow me, I'll take you to a relative of mine, we'll eat with them."

Teacher Guo took me to her "relatives", Aunt Zeng. That visit, later, became vitally important. Let me put it more concretely, to meet Aunt Zeng's daughter DongYa, a very serious and supercilious artist, was crucial for me in the days to come.

The day after, I saw Teacher Guo to the Shanghai train station. Looking at the clouds, Teacher Guo said something profound, "Look, all the people at the station start their journey at the same point, but once getting on the train they all go in different directions. Directions that lead them to entirely different worlds, where they will live different lives. You know what I mean? Once you get on the train of a university, it will take you to a totally different world."

I didn't pay as much attention as I should to her chatty words as I somehow I was suddenly reminded of NiNi. When Teacher Guo's train was approaching, Teacher Guo said to me very sincerely, "In the road of life I could only lead you to this spot, hereafter it is for you yourself to go forward."

I didn't really understand why Teacher Guo wanted to help me so much.

I was no more than one of her students, not even a favorite one. But later, from her husband I learned, Guo, as a teacher, treated her students as her own works results. Saying, a composer needs to have good musical works, artists need to have good works of art, novelists need to have good novels and a good teacher, needs to have good students. I, as an example, later become one of her works results of which she could be proud.

However, Teacher Guo's husband didn't tell me the *whole* truth. It was after a few decades, after Teacher Guo passed away, that I found out the real reason Teacher Guo wanted me to be successful so badly and the truth is very cruel, too cruel to tell at this point.

Thank you Teacher Guo. I have never been a good student of yours, but I respect and am grateful to you as much, if not more, than any of your students.

Freshman, Accommodation, And DongYa

On the new students' enrollment list, again my name could not be found. This time I went to see the Dean of the Enrollment Office immediately, by myself. The dean told me, "You have passed all of your exams, but we aren't able to have you this year due to a housing problem. You'll have to wait until next year. Of course, there will be no need for any exams."

"That's not possible, I mean it's impossible. I have to start *this* year!" my strong tone showing my firm determination.

"Unless?" he paused.

"Unless what? *Whatever.*" I asked eagerly.

"Unless you can provide accommodation for yourself, for the first year, just like the other local Shanghai students would." he said.

"No problem." I said very positively. However, the truth was not "No problem." In fact it was a problem, a huge problem as I had no relatives, no friends, absolutely no one in Shanghai to turn to for help. Where on earth could I find a place to stay in that vast city?

The contract for the bed I slept in for a year at the guesthouse was due to expire. I had to tie up my things and put them under the bed of a friendly former roommate. Carrying my violin and yellow army bag, I walked off the campus.

With no destination, I walked and walked. It must have been close to the middle of the night when I found myself under Aunt Zeng's window, (the relative of Teacher Guo where once she had taken me) the only window of someone's home in Shanghai that I had looked out through once.

When a young man in his 20s is cornered, how much is face worth? I ascended to the 5th floor, knocked on the door. When DongYa, the daughter of the family, opened the door, a devil glided into her home and later, into her life.

Hearing that I was too late to get into the conservatory campus, they let me stay on their living room sofa overnight. The next day, I told the truth, that I was temporarily out of a place to stay, (of course they had no idea that "temporarily" meant a year). DongYa said, without hesitation before her mother, "Stay in my room, I can stay with Mom for a few days."

There was a ray of light in DongYa's eyes, the ray of light when young boys and girls meet, which I had experienced a couple of times before. Several years later, DongYa told me that the moment she opened the door, such a sentence emerged in her mind, "A handsome young man with a violin in his arms, walked into my life."

Every day I would leave DongYa's home very early. After a long day of classes I would stay on campus late, trying to cause as little trouble as possible to DongYa's family. One week had passed and everyone seemed to get used to the new family style, until one day a shocking event took place.

It was a Sunday morning. As I was free from school I stayed in bed late. Meanwhile, DongYa was in the bathroom, thinking I was at school as usual, she entered her room (now the room I was using) without knocking, naked.

Her white delicate body reminded me of NiNi. The regret that I left at NiNi's place pushed me towards her. DongYa looked awkward, standing there like a statue. It was cold too. I held her back and led her to the bed. But to be frank I was not really ready for that. It was just the physical instinct for a young man to touch the body of a woman.

This time, nothing happened. DongYa was uneasy in the beginning, but gradually she got used to it, turning her face to me, she kissed me, on my eyes. Smiling, with joy and happiness. Suddenly, she jumped out of the bed, as she heard the sound of a key in the key hole opening the door. "Mom is back from food shopping. Quickly she ran to the door and then returned again, remembering what she was there for in the first place. She took a cloth from the clothes cupboard, gave me a quick smile again, and was out.

The next day after school I didn't stay on campus, instead I was waiting for DongYa to come back from work at a bus stop.

To make the most of my time I borrowed the very dim street lamp under the bus stop to do my harmonics homework. This grew to be a habit. Every time the bus drew near, DongYa would wave at me from inside and jump out of the bus and throw herself; I mean her hands, on me. We were young, we were in love, we were very happy. We were both aware that we were girlfriend and boyfriend, though the naked hugging business never had a chance to happen again.

However, this situation didn't last very long, as very serious and conservative natured DongYa made our relationship open to the whole family without consulting me.

It was a Sunday morning again. DongYa's elder brother XiaoMing and younger sister XiaoLi all came home. Everyone agreed that it was our free will to love each other and no one had the right to interfere. However, to stay in the same house before marriage would lead the neighbors to a wrong impression that the two are actually living together, therefore I was given two options: a.) Go on staying there but cut the boyfriend-girlfriend relationship or b.) Keep the relationship going but move out immediately.

Nevertheless, to me, I had only one way to go, go out immediately from their home, for the sake of saving face for DongYa, though to me, *staying* was of the utmost importance.

I wrapped up all my stuff in a bed sheet, leaving it temporarily there under DongYa's bed. Again, I carried my violin, walking out of DongYa's home and never in again, physically. On the street, this time not alone but accompanied by DongYa. Isn't it universal that when happy, people like to be together yet when sad, people want to be alone? At least I did.

We walked and walked without knowing where to go, until we both were exhausted and sat on an ice-cold street stone bench, trembling. DongYa's little romantic mood at the beginning was spent by then. We sat there, quietly, no conversation, no word, for a long, long time, until DongYa remembered that her art teacher, Huang, had a tiny small work studio. That night I slept on the work table of Teacher Huang's. Strange enough, I felt that hard cold table more comfortable than any of the five-star hotels I stayed at later in my life.

When the sun rose the next morning, I was happy again as I could forget all the problems, at least for more than twelve hours. I went to the conservatory with high spirits as usual.

At noon I saw a slender girl writing on a public blackboard post on campus. Her curved body reminded me of NiNi, again. I walked up involuntarily. I looked at her closely, I mean what she wrote on the blackboard closely. Guess what I found? Two misprinted words in the English she wrote.

"Excuse me, but…"I said in English.

"Do you understand English?" she turned her face around to look at me.

Oh my God! I mean my Chairman Mao, she did not look like NiNi, she was *more* than NiNi, not only the face, but also the voice and the way she talked. I wondered how she interpreted the look of my mouth half open. She flashed a captivating smile and said, "My practice room is 407 at the piano building, you, *spoony*."

She quickly corrected the two misprints, and walked away toward the piano building. I followed her without thinking. Room 407 was on the fourth floor of the piano building. Each room on the fourth floor was fixed for certain piano students to use, unlike our third floor in the orchestra building which was first come first serve. I followed her up. She turned her head to check if I was still with her. That encouraged me a great deal. I chased her up to the fourth floor and knocked on her door like a gentleman.

"The door is open." came her voice from inside.

I pushed the door open and hesitated whether or not I should close it as at that time if a boy and girl were together in a room with the door closed, it also led people to think, and in reality there most probably was, a boy-girl thing going on in there. She walked toward the door, slightly checked outside the doorway, and then lightly closed the door.

A few very simple sentences were exchanged, such as what's your name and where are you from, in English. She told me her name was YanHua, from Beijing and asked me if I could be her private English tutor. The trade was that I would be allowed to use her piano room freely, anytime when she was not practicing her piano, which included 10pm to 7am. A deal was made.

Everything went smooth, for the time being. The trouble was, my English wasn't very good, in fact not any better than YanHua's, maybe worse.

Now let's not forget DongYa. DongYa was no doubt the most important figure to me during my entire four years in Shanghai. In fact, the story between us alone could be worth writing another book. However, as this book is mainly telling the story of "Father, Son and Violin", DongYa's role is intentionally weakened.

Coming to reality, DongYa was an artist, working for the Shanghai Health Publicity Bureau. In that year, her painted poster won the first prize of the National Health Publicity Contest. Perhaps being influenced by me, she also decided to pursue her art studies at the Nanjing Fine Art Institute. That is to say, DongYa was away from me, at least physically, while YanHua was in my everyday life, literally every day.

As I described, she was slim, but not her breasts. She was from Beijing, a big city, pioneer of modern fashion competing with Shanghai. Her fashion style was very sexy, full sized breasts pushed the frock open between clasps, as well as her little round bottom bundled inside the very tight jeans, and especially her feet in her white high heels... That kind of appearance would be nothing today, yet it was the beginning of the 80s in China; Deng's movement of "Reform and Open" was just getting started. By that time corset trousers and high heels, particularly high-heels, were rather rare. Perhaps it was from that very moment that I became a captive of high heels.

Obviously, YanHua was from a good family, a rich family I mean. Otherwise she wouldn't be able to learn piano or invite me out for dinner so often. I can still recall clearly the first time she took me to a western food restaurant, which was also the first time for me to be in a western restaurant.

It was after school, I had to go out first, waiting for her outside of the school somewhere, as all boy-girl activities had to be kept underground. After we met, I followed her to the western restaurant. For the sake of my vanity, I stepped in front of her and led her into the restaurant. Holding the menu, I believed her when she said diet. Yet I said I wasn't really hungry which was an *absolute* a lie. No matter how carefully I chose from the menu I worried if my wallet was able to take the challenge. However, when the meal was over she didn't even give my wallet a chance.

Immediately my heart felt lighter, and heavier at the same time. In the evening we walked side by side along the WaiTan (the most popular spot in Shanghai) just like the other couples walking there. Facing the seawater, she hummed an English song "Love Me Tender". That was the first of a thousand times that I heard this song.

That overwhelmingly wonderful feeling, no words are enough to describe.

"I wish tonight could last forever." I uttered my poetic feeling.

"Why forever? Is there no tomorrow?" she yawned; not at all corresponding with my romantic mood.

That woke me up to the fact that we weren't exactly boy-girl friends, but English practice partners, plus perhaps, her companion of convenience.

"Of course, there will be a tomorrow. Tomorrow is Monday, my morning is early." That terminated the conversation, along with the romantic mood, as when we came out, we had to go back separately, in order that no schoolmates see us.

I said goodbye to her and was about to walk away, when she suddenly turned her face to me, held my head toward her and put her mouth against mine, drilling her tongue into my mouth. Not only did I not know what that was about, I was a little worried that this kind of *unhygienic behavior* might pass disease.

"What are you doing?" I said astonished.

"Kissing, that's the word in English. We should practice too." she laughed, as if she was playing with a pet.

Back to her piano room it was rather late. But I was too excited to fall sleep. Thinking of the taste of her tongue remaining in my mouth, her flexible sexy body, and the elegant fragrance of hers, I couldn't help my hand comforting my man's growing part. With her smell on her piano, her books, everything in the room, that night, I don't know how many times I made good use of the towel beside my pillow, not really a pillow but a pile of YanHua's piano scores.

The next morning, after our classes were over and before lunch, I had about twenty minutes together with her in the piano room. She acted as if nothing had happened the night before and sat in front of the piano playing emotionlessly. I was about to go out to avoid disturbing her when she stopped me and said: "Could you rub my shoulder? I feel so sore here." Of course, I was at her service. She seemed to enjoy it very much, acting as if she were drunk.

She stood up and asked me to sit on the piano bench and then she sat on me. She started again to play the piano. Her buttocks moved up and down, back and forth, side to side, on my man's part. After only a short moment I couldn't handle any more. She suddenly ordered me to speak English, as that would turn her on very much.

"This is a pen, this is a pen, this is, is, is a, a, hold, I got to go to the toilet." I used the last ability of controlling my body, with my legs tightly clamped, I got away...A bunch of laughter accompanied me all the way out.

That was one of the many little games YanHua liked to play with me. She knew I had a girlfriend. That didn't concern her, not at all. On the contrary, she felt safe. And to steal from someone's man gave her another kind of satisfaction. To her, I was no more than a pet, perhaps, but frankly speaking, I really felt very proud and satisfied to be with her too, particularly when we were walking on the street making people turn their heads.

I knew by then that if I wanted to keep my position, more importantly the right to use the piano room, the weapon was to keep her feeling mysterious about me and admiring my English. For that, I secretly started to study English very hard. When I say "very hard", I mean I put almost all my possible time and energy into it; I even took an extra English class at another university. As a result I had to ride my bicycle back and forth every day between two institutions.

I made very good use of my ear as a musician so I could remember things easily once I heard them. I used the tape recorder DongYa bought for me for studying music, to record the English I learned during the day and then listened to it over again and again all night. (Thanks to DongYa not being around, I had the time to do so) By this method, I could remember almost everything I had studied during the day.

Moreover, I even tried to learn the entire list of illustrative sentences in the Oxford Dictionary by heart. With such an attitude and effort, in Chinese we say, "The spirit of grinding an iron rod to be a needle" when YanHua asked me English questions, how could she not be surprised over and over again. I remember YanHua said to me, "If your knowledge were your semen, I would suck you as dry as a mummy." Thank God that was only words not action.

To be with YanHua was relaxed and safe, no matter if we were going to a movie, concert or restaurant, she would never let me touch my wallet. Not only that, but from time to time she even gave me some cash. Using

YanHua's cash to help DongYa with her economic emergencies happened occasionally. People are like that, anything could be shameful in the beginning, gradually they would get used to it. As we Chinese say, "When it becomes a habit it will be natural."

One year went very fast. One day YanHua took me to a hotel room, there for first time in my life I saw a strip tease dance, by YanHua. When I was seduced to the point of being out of control, she bit my ear, "This is your first and last chance. So, you do what you want, even if you want to know deep inside me! I'll accompany you days and nights without eating and drinking as far as you can. In one word, *I'm all yours.*" she said as she started to unzip my pants.

It was at that very moment, the image of DongYa appeared in my mind, so clearly and so strong. I held her hands, and put her hands around my waist. I hugged her, like a big brother. She wasn't really disappointed or hurt and said, "OK, you had your chance, I offered what I have for all you did for me for the whole year."

I see, it was just a thank you party for me being her pet for a year. Nothing really personal, I mean emotionally. I felt somehow relieved, I got what I needed, very badly and I had my fan too. Both win. Everybody is happy and nobody got hurt.

The party was over and YanHua started to get dressed. Then she said to me : "I've already got my visa to the USA."

"Ha, that explains everything. Now I know why you wanted to learn English so badly." I said.

She smiled, and added, "How about you? I mean when do you plan to go abroad?"

"Me, *go abroad?*" What a daydream question!

Life, sometimes is really like a game, you never know where your fate is going to take you. Like when I was in Hunan, I never thought I could go to Shanghai. When I was in Shanghai, I never thought I would go abroad. Now I am everywhere in the world, where else could I go? Outer space?

How to write about YanHua? I have been very hesitant, because what happened between us was very difficult to classify, as it was a little bit of everything… anyway, it was a kind of uncommon relationship, that could happen between any two young Chinese people at that time.

Later I asked YanHua, "There are so many young men out there. *Why me?* " Her answer was very simple and direct, "Because you look like my father." Through many conversations I figured out that her father was her first lover. They started to play love games when she was only fifteen. It developed into a habit that she couldn't live without.

I also found out that her father wasn't the only love game partner of hers. She has partners all the time, more than one at the same time and all of her father's age or older. That also explains why she was never in lack of money. Later a doctor told me that girls like her could be suffering from a kind of sexual related physical as well as mental problem. For girls like her, love games were needed as a kind of medical treatment...

After all, I'm grateful to YanHua, for the room, for building me a solid English foundation, which would be of great significance in my future life and now I live on this language, and all kinds of the little love games, and, and, and for everything.

After the farewell party, YanHua went back to Beijing and I remained in her piano room until the next year, I moved into the school dormitory.

About YanHua, around thirteen years later, we met again in Ohio briefly, only for fifteen minutes at a coffee shop at Oberlin College. She was married and divorced and re-married and re-divorced and so on. Not a single word was mentioned about those little love games we played during that year at school. Since then, I never heard anything from YanHua, not a single word. I just wish all the best for her, no matter where on earth she might be now.

Focus On Studies In The Second Year

I didn't gain much obvious progress in my violin studies during the first school year, apart from all the reasons in my previous story, my teacher, Sheng ZhongHua was also part of this. She had just given birth to her third child and in addition she was having constant domestic conflicts. Literally, physical conflicts. Her coming to school with Panda eyes was not unusual. When we had lessons, sometimes she played the violin more than I did (she was criticized by the school authority for practicing her violin rather than giving lessons to the students during school hours, far before I came). Nevertheless, Teacher Sheng had her good points, especially to me. We will have more details about her later.

I was very bad at student concerts. During the first one I was on stage playing Beethoven's "Romance" and I cut into the piano one bar too early; the second time was even worse, in which I played Bruch's Violin Concerto and withdrew from the stage in the middle of the third movement.

However, since moving into the student dormitory for the second year, I was able to concentrate all my energy, time and mind on practicing the violin. In addition, I took as many elective courses as I was allowed.

In that period, I was really like a piece of dry sponge thrown into an ocean of knowledge.

My great leap forward on my studies made my teachers happy and classmates envious.

Perhaps because of my rapid progress, my violin Teacher Sheng revealed her idle nature fully. She came to the lesson room without bringing her violin, instead, some nice left over dishes. After she had the door closed, she would open a lunch-box, "I made, try, see if you like it."

While I devoured voraciously, she would use my violin to play the piece of music I was studying, from beginning to end. You know how long a violin concerto lasts, about thirty minutes, while a lesson was about forty minutes. That means, by the time she finished the concerto, one lesson was almost over. Nevertheless, she always remembered to ask me in the end, "How did it taste?" Although not sure she meant the taste of the music she played, or the dishes she made, my answer was always, "It tasted great." Of course I meant her dishes, as I really felt, compared with her violin playing, her dishes certainly tasted better.

Teacher Sheng was not only idle but also somewhat slovenly, quite often forgetting things, this or that, absent minded as English says. I remember one time during a lesson; she eventually noticed that her socks were mismatched, one black and one white which amused me. Her explanation was, she came in a hurry and couldn't find both of either. When the lesson began, her black shoulder rest dropped off of her violin. When I hurried to pick it up and hand it to her, she was extremely embarrassed, "Here you are, my other black sock. Ha ha ha!" As a student I couldn't "ha ha ha", therefore I "hum hum hummed." "Ha!"

Occasionally Teacher Sheng came to the lesson room with her face colored and swollen or bandaged. No need to ask, last night she was again with her husband, "The victory or defeat was a common matter in a conflict."

Gradually, I started to like the way Teacher Sheng taught me, as her way of teaching, (if I may call it "her way of teaching") gave me much freedom which forced me to think and develop my own style of playing independently, unlike some of my schoolmates who followed their teachers so closely that they became copies of them, without the teacher, they didn't know how to walk.

The student concert that I participated in the second year, was *life-long* unforgettable. I played French composer Franck's Violin and Piano Sonata in A Major. When it was excellently over, I gained a long warm applause.

I too, like all artists, am a slave of applause. Since then, I could feel the obvious change of attitude from classmates' toward me.

Senior Year, Learning To Make Money

Regarding my violin study, I made big progress in the second year, the third year went okay, but in the fourth year it started to go downhill rapidly, the reason was that I had made an acquaintance, a man called Chai Ben.

Chai was the art editor of the school journal. It seemed to be all by accident getting to know him, but I still feel that it was kind of predestined. I even think that it was God's arrangement, for knowing him became very significant to my future.

The following is how I got to know him. One day I went to the School Journal Office to see another teacher and I happened to see Chai talking with a foreigner about a Chinese painting. Seeing them not use their mouths but hands, faces and whole bodies to communicate, I seized the opportunity to practice my English. By translating, I learned that Chai was trying to sell his own Chinese painting to the foreigner. In his rather humble and sincere tone, he used some quite proud language. As a result the foreigner opened his wallet with a satisfactory smile. Chai also smiled satisfactorily. I knew the painting had sold for a good price.

I didn't give much thought to this matter, yet unexpectedly, Chai waited for me at the doorway of the school dining hall.

"We eat out." he said to me.

On the table in a restaurant, Chai handed me some money, as much as ten RMB. I was in such ignorance at that time that I refused to take the money. You know, (maybe you don't know) ten RMB wasn't a small sum; it was equal to one-fifth of my monthly wage. I said to him, "It cost me nothing to help you, offering me a nice meal in such a restaurant is more than enough. How could I accept your money?"

Chai interrupted me and said, "Take it, we don't steal nor rob, we make money by our own skill. From now on, we are partners. Besides, I'm supposed to be your teacher, listening to teacher wouldn't be wrong."

My business sense initiated from that bill of ten RMB. From then on, not only would Chai come to me every time business opportunities with foreign guests arose, sometimes I actively helped him find sales targets. Every time, as soon as a painting was sold, I would immediately calculate how much my share should be. To sell paintings, from time to time I even played truant.

In addition to selling paintings, Chai also received a contract of two color photo calendars from the Shanghai Publishing House, one theme of, "Children and Musical Instruments"; the other theme of, "Beautiful Girls and Musical Instruments". For the sake of practicing the technique of photography, Chai lent me a Shanghai made Seagull brand, single lens reflex camera; which was supposed to be a top quality camera in China at that time, as well as helping me buy sufficient amounts of black and white film at an extra discount price from the Shanghai Film Production Studio.

I used the money from selling paintings to invest in a complete set of black and white dark room equipment. In my very small room I started an underground photography studio. My strategy was, "Small profit with many sales". Taking photos for schoolmates was free of charge, which is of great temptation to schoolmates but after the photos were processed, I charged ten fen RMB per photo. When my schoolmates saw their own photographs, few could resist opening their wallets. Several weeks later, I received more business than I could handle.

When my skill of taking photos reached a certain level I started to get into touch with beautiful girl models. That made some schoolmates badly envious. With the rumor spread, one day my violin teacher Sheng visited my little studio without informing me in advance, probably wanting to catch me on the spot doing photos, or girls.

"It's close to the final examination, you don't practice your violin. What the hell are you doing with your bloody camera?" Teacher scolded me in the corridor of my dormitory. Scolding, means someone is concerned about me and for that I was grateful.

But, Teacher Sheng's scolding was not strong enough to resist the temptation of money. I still used one hand to play Sibelius' Violin Concerto for the final examination and the other to take photos earning money and seeking beautiful female models. One thing here I have to make very clear, I was totally faithful to DongYa, and never had anything with the models more than modeling.

After the calendars were published, I haggled a little with Chai about how to divide the profits. But, friendship was more important, accurately speaking, the *next business* was more important. The next business was cooperating with the Shanghai Film Production Studio to make a pop song music tape. Disappointingly, that business consumed much of my time and energy but earned little money.

Perhaps to compensate for my time and effort, just before approaching my graduation examination Chai helped me get a small role as an actor in a movie. Consequently, I postponed my examination, going to the Stone Island in ShanDong Province with the film crew of the Shanghai Film Production Studio.

All these irresponsible behaviors made my Teacher Sheng very upset.

When I returned back to Shanghai from the film making, all my classmates had graduated leaving me alone for the make-up exam.

By then, my girlfriend DongYa had also come back to Shanghai from Nanjing. Under the heavy pressure from Teacher Sheng and the close watch of DongYa, I temporarily distanced myself from Chai and concentrated on practicing my violin. In that period, DongYa came to see me in my dorm very often. She always requested I play my examination, the Sibelius Violin Concerto, from the beginning to the end. Looking at DongYa, the way she looked at me with admiration, once again I was aware of my value as a violinist. I even had a little regret for the time that I had wasted. I decided to make every effort to remedy this.

In addition to the distraction, there was another problem holding my violin studies back, my violin and my bow, especially the bow. At that time I had no personal violin. I took the best, or more correctly, the *most expensive* violin from Hunan Radio and TV Orchestra. Yet the most expensive did not necessarily mean the best, depending on the individual. My bow was too heavy and too stiff. Every time I played, I had to lift the bow up so as not to kill the sound. We all know lifting up is always more difficult than dropping down.

After hours, weeks, months and years of this lifting-up-business, I grew a very bad pain in my back. Every time I played the violin, the pain just killed me and of course my body was in no way relaxed. My violin was also a violin out of which it was difficult to produce sound, especially the E string side that sounded as if it were muted. This demanded I use extra strength. Anyway, bad bow, bad violin plus bad combination, made me feel like I was wearing steel shoes to run a marathon. I think in this world, many violin students, if not most of them, are suffering more or less this kind of problem.

This was all until one day when my violin was open and I had to have it repaired so I borrowed a violin and bow, much cheaper, a much, much cheaper one, for practice. To my enormous surprise the violin and bow I borrowed were much easier for me to play! That's when I knew where my problem lay. I borrowed that violin and bow, initially for a week, but this stretched into months, until I completed my graduation examination.

Thinking back, I strongly feel that in the process of my growth, the people surrounding me, teachers, classmates, friends, and last but not least the girls close to me, had great influence on me in my life.

Just before the graduation examination, again, an "accident" occurred. My girlfriend DongYa was pregnant.

Please give me a minute to explain how the baby happened. Believe it or not, even though my girlfriend was pregnant, I was practically a virgin. *What a joke, how could that be?* Yes, nothing is impossible, in our great country with our great people. I have always been ashamed to talk about it, until recently; I thought it wouldn't hurt anyone anymore, why not to tell the truth to amuse our readers.

First of all, the idea to have a baby came from someone who told us I could stay in Shanghai instead of returning back to Hunan, where I was from, if we got married as soon as I graduated from the conservatory. They said that if we had a child, DongYa's working unit should provide a room for us to live together. It sounded great but the problem remained, how could we make that baby? I remember MeiMei told me that if I put mine inside her she could have a baby. That's simple and understandable, but where could we put the process into practice, as I couldn't go to DongYa's home, and my dormitory was shared by another schoolmate?

At that time in Shanghai, there were some very popular places for *making babies*, public parks, during the night. I wonder how many of Shanghai's population was produced there? We too, decided to follow the masses and give it a try.

One night, DongYa borrowed her sister's skirt (she herself never wore skirts), and I had on no underpants. Both of us got ourselves ready to *fight* for having a future together. But after we went to the park, we found we were just too late as almost all possible dark places were occupied by other couples. When we thought we were unlucky, the security guards came and the couple near us was captured on the spot. They refused to go with the guards as they had a marriage certificate in their hands.

I was very surprised and asked them why they don't do it at home as they are legal husband and wife. They told us, their working unit wouldn't give them a room to live together before they had a child. But without a room how could they make babies? All of us, the couple, the security guards and us, laughed with bitterness. We and the married couple were in the same boat.

After that incident, DongYa was too afraid to be caught and sent to her work unit, as that would be very shameful for a girl. Therefore the next solution was a test-tube baby. DongYa was working at a government Family Planning Propaganda Unit and I think it must have been from there that she got to know the test-tube-baby-making modern technology. One day she came to me with a big syringe and asked me to put my semen into the syringe and hand it back to her. That was my part of the business and was fairly easy as I had plenty of practice since being a teenager, the rest was hers. And *it worked.*

However, after we found out more about marriage related information we realized pregnancy, and even sex before marriage was considered a crime at that time in China. As the delay of my exam from school caused the delay of our marriage, we both knew how big a mistake the too-early-pregnancy was. *I was in deep, deep trouble.*

The rumor spread to my working unit, the Hunan Radio and TV Orchestra, secretary Yu, NiNi's mother, who used to be my protection umbrella, this time loudly roared her order at Chief Liu, "Immediately send a comrade to Shanghai to bring that criminal back to me."

Nowadays, pregnancy before marriage in China isn't a big deal, not at all a thing. But at that time, such a thing could ruin a man's whole life.

16: How, Step-By-Step, I Went Abroad

DongYa's Pregnancy And The Conservatory Graduation

With the order from secretary Yu, (the wife of the big boss Li and mother of NiNi, who used to be my shelter) vice Chief Zou of my orchestra came to Shanghai to fetch me.

Comrade Zou was originally from Shanghai, therefore to him, being sent to Shanghai was certainly a candy errand.

Hearing that I was wanted to return to Hunan without taking my final exam, I certainly refused to obey. To me, coming to study in Shanghai was like climbing the Himalayas, after going through all the obstacles and tribulations I finally got very close to the top, how could I possibly roll down to the bottom? Zou realized it was a waste of time to go on persuading me, in Chinese we say, "To play the tune to an ox.", he turned his effort to my girlfriend DongYa. After a long conversation in Shanghai dialect, DongYa changed her attitude and also suggested that I go back to Hunan for the time being.

She said, "Comrade Zou is your leader, he came from such a long distance (over a thousand kilometers) to take you back. If you refuse, what could he do with his face?"

"*His* face?" Meanwhile I was reminded of Teacher Guo, and all the effort she made to get me into the conservatory and me being not only me, but also her teaching achievement, her artwork. I lost my temper with DongYa. I yelled: "All my struggling and bitterness in the past and all my life in the future, have to be given up for *his face*, his, that yellow ugly face?!"

In the end, DongYa made a compromise that she would accompany me back to Hunan. She said she would tell the leaders in my orchestra that the pregnancy thing was all her fault and she would take all responsibility and consequence.

After two months back and forth persuading me, I started to give up as it looked like I had no choice but to go back to Hunan at once. Yet it was very close to my final graduation exam, which was postponed once already because of the film making. If I asked for another postponement from the conservatory, I would most likely never be able to graduate.

At exactly this crucial moment, a man appeared in front of me after having disappeared from my life for many years, that man was not anyone else but *my father.*

After being apart from each other for all these years, when my father saw me again he wasn't like the fathers you see in movies, excited. Instead I was greeted with no special facial expression at all, as if we had met each other a day ago. He very briefly told me that he was coming to Shanghai on his Party business and happened to stay at a small hotel very close to the conservatory. After having supper with me at the school dining hall, he went to see DongYa and comrade Zou alone. He went to see them both again the next morning. The second day he only met me at the school-dining hall during the meal. On the third day, before he went back to Hunan he said to me, "No need to go back to Hunan at this point. Finish whatever you need to finish in Shanghai. Concerning your working unit, I'll talk to your leaders as soon as I'm back in Hunan."

My father's few simple words razed the prejudice of him that I had built in my mind for many years. I instantly felt *warmth and love,* if it wasn't that our family had a no hugging and touching tradition, as well as his ice cold face, I would probably hurtle up to embrace him. Yet my father did not hug me, nor shake hands with me. He simply passed me two and a half RMB saying that it was for the two suppers I had paid for for him at the school dining hall.

As soon as my father went back to Hunan, comrade Zou came to see me, saying, "Although your father's opinion has his argument, my mission is to bring you back. How can I go back with nothing?"

"What do you want me to do?" I counter-questioned him.

"Unless, unless you punch me in my face, otherwise ……"

I didn't wait for him to finish his words and gave him what he asked for, *a big punch on his face*! In fact, I could have given him two punches if he would have liked.

Comrade Zou covered his loose incisors with his hand and returned back to Hunan. I'm sure he never expected such a favorable errand of coming to Shanghai would cost such a price.

Meanwhile, almost every day DongYa's mother worked on persuading her daughter to have an abortion. The mother even wrote a letter to my former Teacher Guo, asking her to talk to DongYa. However, I insisted

DongYa give birth to the baby, besides the baby would be *our* flesh and blood, he or she might bring me a favorable position to go on staying in Shanghai! (At that time, Chinese people had no right to stay wherever they wanted to stay. They had to stay where their folk registers were.)

After my father returned to Hunan, he went to negotiate with the leaders of my unit immediately and though his tone was very polite, his words were rather heavy. After all, Father was a Communist Party member, a government cadre who knew the rules of the officialdom game. In addition, it was the period in which the Chinese Communist Party launched the, "Strengthening the Legal System" movement for the first time after being in power for more than three decades; therefore my working unit couldn't ignore my father's opinion completely.

In order to solve my issue, both parties agreed to have an imitation lawsuit. My father found himself a lawyer and the unit also got a lawyer. With the case ongoing, it seemed that if I got married to DongYa immediately, it would favor my father's party. As for my punch on comrade Zou's face, as he was the one who asked for it, was not enough to be a criminal act, so I was only given a demerit punishment.

For this matter, Father came to Shanghai again. This time he didn't meet me, but went straight to see DongYa and her mother. His advice to them was, "As the matter is now, the best solution is to get married immediately."

Hence, DongYa and I registered for marriage right away at the Shanghai Xuhuiqu Government Office. Just like that, no pastor's orison, no church bells, no wedding dress, no photograph, no party and not even a dinner for family members and friends, I got married with my very first wife DongYa.

As soon as the marriage registration procedure was done, DongYa applied for an abortion permit certificate from her work unit. (At that time, hospitals wouldn't accept abortions without work unit's certificates; and the work units wouldn't write abortion permit certificates to unmarried couples.)

"What! The purpose you got married with me is to be able to get an abortion certificate?"

DongYa however, didn't argue with me about the abortion matter, but said something else to me, "To tell you the truth, the reason I decided to get married to you is not completely for the sake of love, nor following some senior's advice; it is more I feel sorry for you, for I realized that in the world, besides me, there isn't anyone else who truly loves and cares for you. So… alright, too many words could spoil the matter, the only thing I want to say to you is I would stay with you as long as you need me." She ended there, and took out a handkerchief, as if I had gotten cancer.

Regarding why she changed her mind and decided to go for an abortion, she was not willing to explain. After a long time of asking for the reason over and over, she reluctantly agreed to postpone the date of the abortion till after my graduation examination.

Through conversation with DongYa I could feel that her decision to get married to me had been influenced by my father. For that, I started to be grateful to him. After all, we were father and son.

Henceforth, I concentrated all of myself to practicing the violin and successfully passed the final graduation examination. To everyone's surprise, adding the points of all subject exams together, I was No. 1 in my whole class.

After all the hardship and madness for four years, eventually I graduated from the Shanghai Conservatory of Music.

What To Do After Graduation?

Like most people, I also thought that when I entered a university, it was a step leading to heaven. However, all university graduates would experience the same, "What do I do after graduation?"

All Chinese people would know that for outsiders to remain living in Shanghai, although it may not be as difficult as going to the moon, it certainly is more difficult than immigrating to the United States. Therefore, after a few attempts, I gave up. But, for the sake of having a life together with my newly married wife DongYa, I tried to look for a job with orchestras in the cities near Shanghai.

Both Suzhou and Wuxi expressed their willingness to accept me, particularly Wuxi which promised me the position of concertmaster of the orchestra. Once again, I deceived Hunan and packed up my stuff, ready to go to Wuxi.

Just one day before I had planned to go to Wuxi I went to say goodbye to Chai Ben, after all he was my best friend and more importantly my dependent in Shanghai.

"Why do you want to go to Wuxi?" to Chai, hearing this news was like hearing, "the sun rises from the west."

"Because Wuxi is close to Shanghai, I can't stay in Shanghai; Wuxi is the best place I can go. That's why." I explained with all my reasons.

"What's good about staying in Shanghai? Every one of your classmates are trying to go abroad and they don't even speak as much English as you do." He then told me that the majority of my schoolmates are planning to go to the USA, UK or Australia.

"That's because they're all rich as well as have relatives abroad." I said without much thought.

Chai didn't wait for me to finish, he interrupted and advised me that everything could be created with effort, including money and relatives. He strongly opposed me going to Wuxi, saying that if I go there, it was like putting a period on my life.

Then he took out a few letters, letters from the Eastman School of Music, Indiana University etc.

"Write the addresses down then go back and write letters to them. The Americans are trustworthy, if you write to them, they surely will answer. When you receive their answers, you make the next move according to what they require. Step-by-step just like that, one day you will find yourself walking on a street in the United States, or somewhere in a free world. Then, when you think back about today and that you wanted to go to Wuxi, how ridiculous it will seem." Chai went on and on.

The second day, I made a long-distance call to Wuxi saying that due to my wife being about to give a birth to our baby, I wasn't able to go there immediately. The same day I wrote two letters, one to the Eastman School of Music of NY, and the other to Indiana University. Very doubtful, I figured sending my letters might be just like throwing them into the ocean and never receive answers.

Surprisingly, *both* institutions wrote back to me and *both* said that they would be happy to accept me for my MA studies! In the letters were also enclosed materials concerning English proficiency TOEFL tests and Visa information.

That made Chai very satisfied and proud, he said, "Just as I told you, the road comes out by people's footsteps. Your next move is to go back to Hunan, take the TOEFL test, apply for a passport, find a financial sponsor, prepare money for the air-ticket..."

"But, my wife is expecting, how can I leave her alone here and go back to Hunan all by myself? It would be the same problem if someday I really could go abroad..." I didn't know how to finish my sentence.

"As this is your private business I shouldn't interrupt, but being a *real friend* I feel this is not the right time for you to have a child. Wait until the condition is mature, then you can have as many children as you like. I know there is no one-family-one-child policy in the United States."

With Chai's advice, I went straight to talk to my wife DongYa, "About our child and my second thoughts..."

DongYa didn't wait for me to finish my talk, she interrupted, "No need to persuade me anymore, I have also changed my mind, I'll do as you asked and have this baby." She said as she touched her full belly. "This small fellow recently likes to kick me. Look! He did it again, touch, and touch here quickly." DongYa held my hand against her belly tightly, "My little fellow, this is your father, can you call Father? Understand?"

The movement of DongYa's belly shocked me, making me aware more strongly than ever that that was already a life, life made by DongYa and me! There was in no way I could talk more about the matter of abortion.

A few days later when DongYa found out that I had changed my mind about giving birth to the child, she burst into tears. When she got out of the hospital after the abortion, she looked to be in great agony, she said grumbling, "I swear I'll never be pregnant again, *never!*"

"What did you say?" I pretended.

"Nothing." DongYa closed her eyes.

Later, we divorced exactly as my father planned, and as she had sworn, DongYa never got pregnant again...(More details will be given in following stories.)

Paving My Way Abroad

The very first thing I did after I went back to Hunan was go to see CEO Li, and more importantly his wife Auntie Yu. Knocking at their door I was so afraid the person who opened it would be NiNi. But my worry was unnecessary as NiNi was no longer living with her mother and stepfather. That was the biggest scandal in the history of the Hunan Radio and TV Bureau.

The rumor said that NiNi was pregnant and what's more, to everybody's shock, the one who made her pregnant was not the son of some big dignitary, or a well-educated gentleman with a social status, but a temporary part time worker at a low class factory. "A delicate fresh flower that no one dared to touch yet has been put with a heap of smelly bullshit", was what my colleagues gossiped and felt sorry about.

Of course no one was angrier than NiNi's mother, Aunt Yu, "How dare he, the boy didn't even ask me…" How could Aunt Yu know that the whole reason "*that* boy" could succeed was because he dared to be with her daughter without asking for the mother's permission. This to me alone seemed to be clear and understood.

The timing of NiNi's pregnancy was not long after the news of my wife DongYa's pregnancy had spread back to Hunan. If the timing was not a coincidence, I was probably, at least to a certain degree, responsible for NiNi's happiness or sadness, if her life was to be a sad one.

It was 1983 when I returned back to Hunan. The Chinese leader Deng Xiaoping launched a Nationwide Academy Diploma Campaign. All the government officials of a certain rank must have a college diploma. This caused our Chief Liu a great headache. At close to age sixty, he had to go to night school to study for a diploma. I remember one day Chief Liu was criticizing a comrade for being late to work, surprisingly the comrade talked back to him, "You dare to criticize me again and I won't help you with your……. with your studies anymore."

In order to have more time paving my way abroad, I took a Journalism Correspondence course at the Beijing Broadcasting Institute in Hunan. By doing so, I had a very good excuse not to take part in orchestra rehearsals often. That was naturally, not good for the orchestra.

One day, the orchestra leader KangKang told me, "OK, concentrate your time and mind on your study now. Come back to the orchestra again as soon as you finish." That is to say, only a few months in Hunan, after having been absent for four years in Shanghai, I was off work *again* studying full time, of course with full salary and school fees paid by the Hunan Radio and TV Bureau.

Who benefited the most from the Red China socialist system? I, the little Nine-Brother.

The journalism correspondence course had class only half a day a week. What should I do with the rest of my time?

When my story comes to this point, I need to again mention Hu MeiMei, the next-door-neighbor girl with whom I grew up. As I returned back to Hunan a married man, there was no way I could look for new girlfriends. In addition I was too busy preparing to go abroad to fool around with girls. Hence, MeiMei came to see me often, that killed part of my loneliness, of course, as my sister, like a real sister.

However, for that period MeiMei was also quite busy, busy with her university studies. The university she attended was not a well-known one, wasn't even considered to be a good one, for it was a poorly funded private institution named Hunan Science and Technology University. I could care less whether it was a well-established institution or not, as long as I could learn something, it was good enough for me.

Therefore, through the introduction of MeiMei, I got myself into the English class at the institution. After getting close to my English teacher, I used him as a bridge and got myself into an English class at the Changsha Railway Institute, the one known as the best English class in the city. By doing that, I ended up studying at *three* different universities at the same time. Thinking back on all of this, I really should say; "I owe you a great deal" to my Phoenix brand bicycle.

Here, I particularly want to mention a few words about the privately funded Hunan Science and Technology University, as what I learned, far more important than English, was the theory of system engineering of society, as well as the consciousness of the "Information Age" we were approaching. For that knowledge and consciousness proved to be very useful for my life then and in the future. For that, I would very much like to say to the founder of the institute, "Thank you so much, professor ZHANG QI REN."

TOEFL Test Of English As A Foreign Language

As I mentioned earlier, I studied Chinese and English with a husband and wife who taught at Changsha No. 2 Middle School at the age of sixteen. In addition, I studied English very hard during my violin study at the

Shanghai Conservatory of Music (thanks to YanYua too) so when I went to take the TOEFL test, I already had a good foundation of the language. Plus, I took some English lessons at two different universities and the result was my test score being over six hundred.

I sent the result to two American institutions for my post education, Eastman School of Music in New York and Indiana University. I was immediately accepted as a master's degree student, by both. Two formal letters of acceptance reached me.

Getting My Passport

I dare to say, no one in the whole country got one's passport as smoothly as I did during that time, unless somebody's uncle was a police boss.

I took the letter of acceptance from the Eastman School of Music to the Hunan police on Monday. The police officer gave me a paper form, asked me to finish all the requirements on the form and then to apply for my passport. The contents of that form included, working unit certificate; folk registration certificate; university entry notification letter; I-20 form; money guarantee certificate etc.

It was exactly at that time that the country's campaign of Reform & Open-Door went into effect. "Efficacy" was a very popular slogan. I quickly ran back to the Broadcast & Television Bureau where I worked.

From orchestra, library, folk register etc., I had my paper full of red stamps, until finally I went to see the number one boss, General Director Li. Li took a look at my papers and deeply sighed, saying, "It wants to rain and my daughter wants to marry, nothing I can say. You, go." Just like that, I got my last red stamp and the most important one. That is to say, I got all that I needed done from my working unit within *one day*.

The second day, in the early morning I went to Hunan police again. The police officer looked at my documents, obviously unable to read English very much, and asked me, "Which is the I-20 form and which is the letter of finance guarantee certificate?" I picked up the letter of acceptance from the school and told him that it was something similar to the I-20 form; as I had no economic guarantee certificate, I had picked up a school document that concerns economic guarantee and said, "This is a relevant document of economic guarantee." The officer used a pencil and marked the Chinese letters "I-20" and "Finance Guarantee Certificate".

"When can I get my passport?" I asked eagerly.

"Not very clear." The officer replied.

"You are the one in charge! If it isn't clear to you then who would it be clear to?" I was quite worried.

"The comrade in charge will be absent for some time. I'm only temporarily replacing his position. However, as far as I know, a passport application takes about two weeks generally, if not a bit longer." the police officer said.

"Two weeks? Oh my God, I mean my Chairman Mao! Efficacy is the slogan today. You see, our Broadcast & Television Bureau took only one working day to finish all procedures. Our leader would like to see how effective the police could be." I challenged him.

"OK, I will do it at once. But there are a lot of procedures. So it's impossible to do it in one day, say, as quick as three days, I can try. That should be ready by Friday." the police man said with confidence.

My few words about "efficiency" worked, perhaps. I got my passport on Thursday, which was only two days after I handed over all my papers. About the fees, it was several ten RMB (not much money), that included the cost of the copies and the fee for the passport itself. I even forgot to bring a few packages of cigarettes to the police.

Making Money To Go Abroad

Once I had my passport, which was very rare for a Chinese at that time, my comrades in orchestra started to ask testing questions about when I leave for abroad. Even my personal belongings such as furniture, bicycle etc., were settled by other people.

Although I always answered "very soon", in my mind it was very clear, to go to the United States was still very elusive because I had no economic sponsor and no money to pay for the expensive tuition. Under such circumstances, it was *completely impossible* to get a visa from the US Embassy.

Whatever, I had no choice except to find a way, working hard, to earn money. The know-how to make money from selling paintings that I learned from Teacher Chai in Shanghai was the only money making skill I knew. So, I moved the whole thing to Hunan. I went to see many artists in Hunan, paying about ten to twenty RMB a piece for their Chinese paintings. Then, I would take the paintings to an expert to have them mounted, and sell them for one or two hundred RMB a piece to foreigners. My customers included foreign English teachers, tourists and sometimes even foreign individuals whom I met on the street.

There was an event by chance, or by *destiny*, that changed my life. One day I was invited by a TV reporter from Hunan TV to act as an interpreter in order to interview a "Chinese Cultural Study Group" from Australia. During the interview I got to know an artist named Lawrence. After a few outings together we kind of became friends. That changed my life.

One day, I brought about thirty Chinese paintings to Lawrence's room hopeful that he would like some and pay for them. As I introduced him before, Lawrence himself was an artist. He used his very critical eyes to appreciate some of my paintings and then commented that my paintings were pretty good, at least they were original art, not like those commercial copies selling at the so called Friendship Stores (used to be shops only selling things to foreigners) that tourist guides took them to. Next, he made a call to another guest. About ten minutes later, there was a queue outside Lawrence's room!

Lawrence let everyone in and I gave a brief speech about Chinese paintings. In fact, I was no artist myself so only told them something very shallow that I had learned during the business, but everybody looked very interested and serious. The atmosphere was somewhat like a classroom.

As soon as my talk finished, one person asked me, "How much?"

"How much what?" I asked.

"How much money? For this painting?" She pointed to a silk painting with very easy to understand English.

"Oh, this, this is a small painting, eighty RMB." I explained.

Someone else asked, "How about that one?"

"That one, en, that one is bigger, should cost two hundred RMB. I'd say."

The group of Australians were all amused by the fact that Chinese paintings were priced by size just like tablecloths.

Someone again asked me if I took only RMB or Australian dollars as well. I told them it didn't matter very much, even how much they paid didn't matter very much, as long as they pay.

While I was talking to Lawrence, everyone was busy looking for paintings they might like. In the end, I sold every single painting I brought there! My ragged army bag was filled with Australian dollars and Chinese renminbi!

That was the richest day in my life up till then. In fact, I had never seen so much money at one time before that day! That was a day I will never forget for as long as I live.

It seems everyone bought paintings from me, except one man, Lawrence. After, I explained to him that I was making money in order to study abroad and that I also needed a financial sponsor. Lawrence obviously didn't know the real meaning of "sponsor" and told me that if I was going to Australia, I wouldn't need a sponsor if I brought some paintings with me that were real art.

Australia? I never thought about Australia, up to then I only thought about the USA and the USA only.

Go To Australia

One year passed very quickly. That was the time I visited my wife DongYa in Shanghai. (In China by that time, people could not move freely from place to place. One had to stay in one's birth place, even if people from two different cities married, they could only live together in the smaller city which one spouse had lived, but not in the bigger one that the other came from. I was from Hunan, a much smaller city than Shanghai, but DongYa is from Shanghai, so we had to live separately even though we were supposed to be married.)

Certainly I went to see my old friend, the one who taught me the painting business, Teacher Chai Ben.

When Chai heard my story about Lawrence, he said "Why *not* Australia? Why must it be the United States? Now it's not where you choose to go, but where you *can* go, except Tanzania or Zambia."

Then he handed me a brochure of La Trobe University in Melbourne.

"Your English is good; going there to study English Literature should be the quickest way to get yourself abroad." That changed my life's course from the USA to Australia.

Following Chai's advice, I applied for English studies at La Trobe University in Melbourne. I wrote a letter to Lawrence about my coming to Melbourne. Lawrence was really a worthy friend; he called the University straight away. Less than three months later, I received a letter of acceptance from La Trobe University.

The next task was applying for a visa.

Although up to then I still didn't believe I could really get myself abroad, I started to believe Chai's saying, "There was no road, man walked on it, step-by-step, the road became."

Obtain A Visa

Every Chinese abroad or trying to go abroad would know, no visa, no going abroad. In order to get a visa, one must have money or a financial sponsor. I, at that time, just like many others who were trying to get out of the country, had gotten everything but. Though I was so sure my hope was elusive, still I decided to go to Beijing to have a try. Even if in the end I could not go as I wished; I would have an explanation, an excuse, an answer for DongYa, Chai Ben and for every one of my friends and fellow orchestra members and most importantly for myself. Just like that, holding my passport, I went to Beijing.

Very early the next morning after my arrival in Beijing, I went to the Australian Embassy. Before I could even get close to the front gate, I saw an announcement written in Chinese, "Overseas student visa section please go this way", then the address with a map. Luckily the place wasn't too far away. I quickly walked towards the address. Still a fair distance from the building, I saw a huge crowd in front of a big mansion.

Strange, applying for a visa in China was like buying a train ticket, no proper line? When I got close to the building, it was not strange anymore because now I was one of the crowd, trying very hard to go forward. Of course I was not pushing others away to get myself in for a visa, but to read another notice as there were just too many people.

There was no way I could read what was on the notice, only overhear people asking the same questions to which no one could give an answer, "Why did they close visa issuing temporarily?" "When will they start again?"

Meantime, inside, a Chinese staff member made an announcement, "Due to various reasons, we've stopped issuing student visas. Wait for further notice." was said in a one hundred percent Chinese bureaucratic tone. I understood that there was no reason at all to stay and sweat with the crowd. I pushed my way out, sat by the street, thinking.

"Should I just go back home like that?" I was reminded of Chai's saying, "There was no road. People walked on it, step-by-step, a road became. Just keep walking; one will get to ones destination in the end." I decided, I shouldn't go back, but forward. I must find another way that leads to my destination.

Right then, a young man about my age came to chat with me. He introduced himself as Zhu-Zhong.

"We haven't met before. How many times have you been here?" he asked me.

"First time." I answered honestly.

"This is my 11th time." he said with a superior tone. He started to show off his rich experience and tell me all about how he did everything up to here. In the end, he asked me, "How is your financial guarantee? Is it a bank deposit certificate, or just a letter from a sponsor? If it's a bank deposit certificate it would be much better, but if just a letter it will be difficult..." Before my answer, he was about to continue saying something else. I knew he wasn't really interested in my situation but in finding someone to talk with so that he would have some relief from his loneliness and pity.

I have neither." I told him the truth, in order to end the meaningless conversation.

"*What?* You have neither money *nor* letter and you dare to come all the way from Hunan to here for a visa? What an international joke! I swear to you if you can get a visa, I will put my first name last, and last name first." (Which is considered a kind of insult in China.)

Such a conversation brings no useful information nor good feelings but is a pure waste of a lot of time. I excused myself with something I needed to go do and left Zhu-Zhong.

I went back to the Australian Embassy, walking around looking for opportunities. An opportunity came right to me. I saw two Aussies, one female and one male walk out of the embassy. I went up to them pretending that I just arrived, knowing nothing about the visa situation. I asked them for the direction of the visa section, where I just came from. They stopped for me and seriously listened to my question, then very kindly pointed in the direction of the visa section.

Seeing I looked a little puzzled, they said, "We are just about to go there too. If you like, we can go together."

I didn't mind, not at all. On the contrary, I was so delighted I could walk together with them, which meant we had more time to chat. In the conversation, I got to know that they were not staff of the embassy, but managers of some schools in Australia, in Beijing to recruit students. For them, students were business.

Through the exchange I got to know the reason that visa issuing had stopped temporarily was because the Australian government was adjusting their overseas' student policy. The people in charge of the visa section were in Australia for a meeting. They would come back in a week.

What an important bit of information this was! At least I didn't have to go there every day waiting to find out which day was the right day.

I made good use of that week by visiting Tianjin, the neighboring city to Beijing. Unexpectedly, during this trip I had found my key to the door of Australia.

The story goes like this. After the Chinese reform & Open-Door Policy, the Chinese Musicians Association established an "American Music Research Association" which was located in the Tianjin Conservatory of Music. I, with my thesis of "The American Jazz", became the youngest member of the association. As I was already in Tianjin, I certainly took the opportunity to visit with the general secretary of the association.

Hearing that I would study abroad very soon, (which was rare and difficult then) the general secretary appeared to be very warm and invited me home for dinner. I remember nothing from the meal, but I do remember he gave me a list of names and addresses of association members. On the list were some very famous and important leading musicians, included the country's leading soprano Zhang-Quan.

Back to Beijing. I paid a visit to the members on the list one by one. When I visited Zhang-Quan, the old professor seemed to be very happy to see me. (After a long persecution during the Cultural Revolution) She even thought of me as one of her school progeny. (Professor Zhang was a graduate from the Eastman School of Music in New York) From her I gained an even more important name, the one in charge of Chinese Central Broadcasting Station's Foreign Music Program.

I went to see the head of the Music Section of the Chinese Central Broadcasting Station straight away. I was warmly received because I was introduced by Professor Zhang. When hearing that I was about to go to Australia for my music studies soon, he asked me for a favor. He said, "If you have a chance to meet the Australian Embassy people, please pass my message to them. That is, when they provide us the music program; please give us stereo instead of mono. The person from the music program in the Australian Embassy was here a few times but we couldn't talk much due to the language barrier." Then he found a business card for the person in charge of the music program at the Australian Embassy. I took a look. That gentleman was the Cultural Secretary of the Australian Embassy.

That business card became my *key to Australia.*

The next day I went to the Australian Embassy in the early morning. I showed my working ID as staff from the Hunan Broadcasting & TV bureau, but presented myself as sent by the Chinese Central Broadcasting Station coming to see…, I showed the doorman the business card of the Culture secretary of the Australian Embassy. A few minutes later I met the gentleman on the business card! I was respectfully invited to his office. We started to talk about music. To me, music is what? Music is *my everything,* my love, my job, my cup of tea… Of course I *did* pass along the message from the Central Broadcasting Station that their stereo music programs were appreciated and I added, the music could be closer to the Chinese people's taste.

The cultural secretary was obviously getting excited by my words. He picked up the telephone and said to me, "If you don't mind, I would like you to meet someone, the director of the Radio Australia Chinese section. His name is John Crone. He happens to be in Beijing."

"I don't mind, not at all." I replied. How could I *mind,* I simply couldn't afford to mind! It was so much more than I expected!

A few minutes later, Mr. John Crone shook hands with me at the Cultural Secretary's office. The three of us were talking in a very good mood. When the topic came to some problems about their music program and their communication difficulties with the Chinese, the secretary suddenly asked Mr. Crone, "Why don't you ask Mr. Chen to see if he would like to help us?"

Mr. Crone catered to his superior, saying "You know what? I thought the same. In fact I have been looking for a person who is mainland Chinese and understands English, western culture as well as music and radio broadcasting."

I was more than delighted; my English was simply not good enough to describe how excited I was at that very moment yet my words came out like this, "I would love to help you, but…"

"But what?" They asked the same question at the same time.

"But I'm on my way to Eastman School of Music in New York."

I didn't wait for too long to tell them that I could postpone going to the USA and instead HELP them at Radio Australia located in Melbourne, for a short period of time.

"Do you have a passport?" the secretary asked.

"Yes I do." answered me.

"Have you got your passport with you now?" the secretary asked again.

"Yes I do." answered me again.

"Do you have any friends in Australia?" he kept asking.

"Yes I do." I kept answering positively.

"How is your financial situation? I mean do you have a bank account in Australia?" He looked at my eyes with the last but maybe the most important question.

"Yes I do…I mean I will have as soon as I am in Australia."

"When can you depart for Australia?" This question was asked by Mr. Crone.

"At once, immediately, right away!" I couldn't help standing up from my chair.

"OK, everything sounds great. Could you leave your passport here?" That was the real final question of the secretary.

"Yes I would be very happy to leave my passport here. But for how long?" I asked.

"Until tomorrow morning ten o'clock. Okay?" The secretary raised his hand to shake mine, which meant bye-bye.

Mr. Crone walked me out of the office. We talked about a plan for making a series of radio programs introducing Australian music to Chinese people. But Mr. Crone made it very clear and repeatedly, that it would only be a part time job, not enough to make a living. I told him not to worry as I had other means to make my living.

The next morning at ten o'clock sharp, I received my passport, *with a visa to Australia*. I felt my body was floating in the air and could not remember whether I walked out or flew out of the Embassy!

I went to the visa section again on purpose, looking at the crowd with a satisfactory smile of victory. In the crowd, I discovered that man again. What was his name again, Zhu-Zhong? If you replaced his last name with his first name, it would be Zhong-Zhu, which sounds like "boar" in the Chinese language. I was so amused I burst into laughter. I waved at him. He noticed me and walked towards me.

I couldn't wait until he got closer, because that would simply be too cruel. I only waved my passport and kept my voice down enough so that he couldn't hear, "See you in Australia."

Leaving My Motherland For A Foreign Land

After I had my visa, the very first person I must see was certainly my wife DongYa. I went from Beijing directly to Shanghai. DongYa arranged for me to stay at a guest house of the Shanghai Public Health Bureau where she used to work.

After a simple meal at a cheap place, she asked me, "Do you come for the procedure?"

"All procedures going abroad are set. What else?" I asked.

"No need to pretend. You are here for divorce procedure, right?" DongYa said it very clearly with a calm demeanor.

"Divorce?!" Although I felt the day of divorce would come sometime, it wasn't true that I was there for divorce, at least not that time.

"It's okay to tell the truth; the truth is, since the day we got married I *knew* today would come. Only I didn't expect it to come so soon." DongYa proceeded to tell me a shocking story that I had not known until that day.

DongYa told me that when my father came to Shanghai from Hunan, to ask DongYa to get married with me, she felt very envious; envious that I had a father who would ask a girl to marry his son so that his son wouldn't get in trouble in his working unit because of the girl's pregnancy.

Yet my father's explanation shocked DongYa. My father said, "If you still don't understand the real meaning of the marriage I will have to make it more clear to you. I do this, not for the sake of *him* (he wouldn't call me "my son"), but completely for the sake of you, in fact for the sake of anyone I would do the same, because only I understand him the most. Saying one's own son isn't a good person, is something very painful. As a father, I'm not able to change him, but should at least work hard to prevent him causing trouble for the society. In other words, to keep his damage at the minimum level to the society, please believe me, this time I'm ask you to get married with THAT PERSON completely for *your* sake, for the sake of your reputation in society. If you are married, the relationship between you and him would be legal. Marriage and divorce is a normal phenomenon, not a scandal, no one would say anything about it…"

DongYa was shocked by the words coming out from my father's mouth and asked, "Divorce? What about the little baby inside me?"

"That is why you should not give birth to the child. Because I'm sure he won't be with you for very long. As I told you, no one knows him better than me."

Seeing DongYa in a state of confusion, Father added:" We don't want a criminal in the family, and you are the one who can prevent him from that. For him, for us and mostly for yourself, if you really love him, you should marry him and divorce him."

Hearing that, DongYa had nothing further to say.

My father continued his persuasion, "About this matter, I have exchanged thoughts with your mother. I think, as long as you don't give birth to the child, she wouldn't be against your marriage as much as before."

Finally, Father ended his brainwash like this, "This time, I came to

Shanghai especially for you, therefore I have no intention to see *him* (me, his son). There is no need for you to tell him either. Let's promise, to keep this as a secret between us, until the day you two divorce."

"*Secret*", what a powerful word! It was that word which captured half the heart of DongYa.

"No wonder as soon as we got our marriage certificate you asked me to accompany you to the hospital for an abortion. So it was that old man's setting." I suddenly realized the truth, and felt a bit shocked.

"Now you know what happened." DongYa went on, "Remember what I said to you when we got out of the hospital after the abortion?"

"Yes I do, oh no, remember what? I mean I only remember you said something to me, but not what you had said." I was reminded of her saying, "I swore I would never have a baby again in my life."

"I said…" DongYa stopped, perhaps having no strength, or realizing that is wasn't necessary to say again.

No quarrel, no intermediation, no law court, we divorced, very peacefully and calmly.

The very last words DongYa left me with were, "Do you know what was the real and most important reason I decided to go for the abortion? It was because I was frightened that my child would have a father who treats him just like your father treats you."

My father's image came into my mind, I had felt a little closer and that he was worthy of respect just a short while ago, now again, it had all gone back!

Oh God…

Like that, I left my wife, the very first wife of mine, never having contact again, until today.

Leaving My Working Unit And Fellow Colleagues

Returning to my working unit, the Hunan Broadcasting & TV Orchestra, I started sorting out things, cleaning, throwing garbage (each time it comes to moving to another place I always have no idea where so many useless things come from) burning documents and personal letters as well as photographs, the rest of my property that had any value I sold, or simply gave away. Seeing all this, my colleagues no longer asked testing questions such as, "When will you go?" On the contrary, all of them became overly friendly.

Leaving My Family

I used almost all the money I had gotten from selling Chinese paintings to the Australian Cultural Group for an air-ticket to Melbourne.

The last day before leaving for Australia, my elder brother asked me to have a meal at his place. I went there to see a full table of dishes waiting for me. In addition to the dishes were other members of my family, my parents, elder brother and his wife and of course MeiMei was there too. But my younger brother still did not show up.

The dishes on the table were made by my elder brother's wife, the so-called *Big Sister*.

Let me borrow this opportunity to talk a little about my sister-in-law. I had always opposed them as a couple. I once even wanted to threaten Big-Sister that I would tell my brother about the "she-and-our-father-thing" at the farm. But, they got married after all, while I was studying in Shanghai. Facts are facts. Does it make any sense to mention those past matters anymore? For the sake of my elder brother, I had to cover all the facts inside me. But inside my heart I cursed my father, seeing him as no more than a monster covered with human skin and the *appearance* of always-doing-the-right-thing.

Perhaps to keep their dignity, my parents showed neither happiness nor celebration on their faces. They didn't even mention my going abroad. Seeing me saying nothing, only eating, my mother couldn't hold it any longer. She said "We don't exactly support your going abroad, but if you insist on going; we will not object either." She took out an envelope, the inside full of small bills and explained, "I have counted; there are a total of two hundred RMB in it…"

Two hundred Chinese RMB, was the sum total of support I received from my parents from my university education up to the point of going overseas for further education.

I looked at the envelope in my hand, suddenly all of the dishes tasted the same, "bitter".

Thinking back, so many thunders and storms, winds and frosts through all the years, thinking forward, unknown difficulties and obstacles I would go on to encounter, my heart cries with no tears.

Just before I was about to leave, I wanted to say something exciting, "Please don't worry about me, I would…"

I wasn't quite finished when my father cut in, "Worry? No worries anymore. At least you won't make more damage to our Chinese society." After a light laugh, Father's facial expression became very serious, as if he was worried I would expand the damage to more people but this time, all over the world.

Like always, it was MeiMei acting as the family representative. Just as she saw me off to Shanghai, she accompanied me to Guangzhou to see me board the flight to Melbourne.

In Guangzhou, to save money, MeiMei and I shared a hotel room as brother and sister (then an unmarried couple couldn't share a room in a hotel). We were in the same room but not the same bed as there were two beds in the room. Nothing happened until the middle of night when I woke up for the toilet and found MeiMei was not sleeping at all.

We turned on the light and started to chat. She tried to ask me how my married life was with DongYa. Once I realize she was actually referring more to our private life I stopped, as I felt somehow uneasy talking about my life with my wife to her, as a sister, especially the test-tube business. I turned off the light, and went back to sleep. MeiMei lost her temper... only once in our lives in my memory had she behaved like that. The next morning, everything was back to normal. MeiMei too, behaved normal, as if nothing had happened during the night.

Just before I boarded my aircraft, I passed her that envelope, the envelope of two hundred RMB, which my parents gave me as their support for my education overseas and said to her, "Buy some candy that you like."

The flight of Cathay Pacific took off down the runway, carrying me with my dream, leaving my motherland for a completely unknown world.

17: THE FIFTH STAGE OF MY VIOLIN LIFE

How Australians Value My Violin Playing

On the aircraft headed for Melbourne, I recalled the last twenty years of my personal history. A history of struggle: from falling in love with the violin at first sight during primary school, so much so that often after school I walked a few kilometers to the music store just to stare at it, my nose flattened against the glass cabinet; with help from Master Zhou, making my first white violin at age fourteen; during my middle school time competing with my big rival Ma XiaoMao in the Mao Propaganda Team; overhearing western violin pieces played by my first violin teacher Li from a church window; then becoming the concertmaster of the Changsha Amateur Orchestra; a conflict with Conductor Xiao at the Changsha Opera; fighting with foreman Peng at the construction company for the right to play violin; an ignorant and shameless struggle for the position as concertmaster at the Hunan Beijing-Opera; the hardship and bitterness of education at the Shanghai Conservatory of Music; followed by money making, the TOEFL test, a passport application, visa etc. etc., walking such a long way until the day I was *finally* flying on a plane!

If all of these facts couldn't prove that "a man fighting for a better life" is the correct way, to prove that I won, I'm a violinist and I had been doing the right thing, what else can?

In front of this hard fact, I think anyone would agree. *So why am I not satisfied with myself?*

After much thought, I realized that for me to feel my success, even if I were recognized by the whole world, it still wouldn't be enough because there was one man who didn't recognize me and for me, *that* one man was more important than all the people in the whole world put together. That man was my FATHER. Yes, my father and his attitude towards me, dismissive towards my success, was the wall standing between me and feeling satisfied, proud and fulfilled. Therefore, I must go on working harder to beat him, in any and all aspects. I must become a more respectable and richer person. I must speak better English than him and girlfriends; they must all be prettier than his wife.

In short, emotionally speaking, as long as I could convince *him* and somehow make *him* appreciate and admire me, I would do anything.

On the plane, excitement with anxiety; satisfaction with disappointment; hope with frustration, was a true reflection of my frame of mind at the time.

I believe the majority of overseas' students like me, who knew no one, had no family, no friends, no background, would have to go through a long and bitter process before they could gain legal immigration status and economic success.

I must be luckier, or there must be a God who specially looks after me. I was totally financially safe after only three months in Australia and six months later I started to feel rich (of course not that "rich", rich only to compare with my life in China); in less than one year I bought my own car, a house and there was an Australian citizen waiting to change my identity from an overseas student to an Australian citizen.

Indeed I loved Australia, and still love it now. But there was one thing that made me very sad. That was how Australians valued my violin playing. I mean, my violin playing wasn't recognized nor appreciated by Australians. I had a considerably good income as a manager at a private institution, but could not give up my identity or value as a "violinist."

Though I took part in some rehearsals and concerts with several orchestras in Melbourne; none invited me or accepted me to be their full time, regular member. This made me truly melancholy until one day when someone told me the reason. The reason was, though my violin playing techniques were okay, the style was quite different from the westerners. To put it concretely, my violin sounded too harsh, too noisy, apart from the factory made violin and extremely cheap steel strings I used, the way of playing I had learned from the Shanghai Conservatory of Music was too energetic, in addition to some "rebel" from the Cultural Revolution left in my blood.

Nevertheless, I, "the little Nine-brother" at that time, of course, was not able to realize my own problems, instead accusing the Australians of having rather low taste.

How Norwegians Valued My Violin Playing

Except violin, life was wonderful in Australia. Work, friends, barbecue parties or beach walking on weekends, when everything went well, I started to doubt if I really needed to make an effort to study in the USA. Or, why not get married with the Australian woman who was truly in love with me and settle myself down there? At exactly this time, I met Marianne, a Norwegian scholar who happened to be in Melbourne doing her research. We were pure friends, only meeting a couple of times and going to a movie together once.

One night I woke up in a nightmare and in the nightmare something about my father and my violin ... I made a mid-night call to my new friend Marianne. On the phone I said, "Somehow I feel uneasy here in Australia." Marianne replied, *"Come to Norway."* That became the reason for a ticket to Norway.

Norway should be a high class westerner's world, yet unfortunately, my violin playing was received the same as in Australia. First, I was rejected by two professional orchestras in Oslo. I only had a small position at a semi-professional orchestra far away from Oslo.

"If you don't have anything else to do, why don't you get some education at the Norwegian State Academy of Music?" Marianne suggested. Being married to Marianne, a Norwegian citizen, everyday life and expenses were covered. I couldn't accept *more* so I said:

"Of course, I would love to. And this is part of what I'm here for. But..." I was thinking of finance, as I had no income here like I did in Australia, as I was jobless.

"Education is free in Norway." Marianne figured out what was on my mind.

"Free? You mean free, *FREE!?*" I followed her advice and went to the Norwegian State Academy of Music for violin lessons.

My teacher was Professor Boyhansen. I remember in the first lesson, he turned on a tape recorder and said, "Play something for me, whatever you'd like to play is fine."

In order to show off my technique, I played Wieniawski's "Tarantella", an extremely fast, difficult piece of music that I had spent more than ten years practicing. After playing, I was quite proud of myself for not stopping in the middle and making no mistakes.

But Professor Boyhansen looked somewhat amused. What hurt my feelings most was his comment, "Music is not sports, it's not to see how fast your fingers can run."

Professor Boyhansen's teaching method was totally different from any of my former Chinese teachers. Unlike all other teachers who during the first lesson always asked me to change my way of holding the violin or the bow, Professor Boyhansen gave me some very simple, easy melodies. Besides that, he asked me to listen to him giving lessons to others, Norwegian students, as if my profession was listening. In addition, he lent me some tapes and CDs, advising me to listen to more tapes and CDs at the academy library.

After a period of time, Professor Boyhansen handed me a tape, saying to me, "This is what I recorded at your first class. Take it home and listen to it carefully to see if there are some differences between the other tapes and CDs you have been listening to."

After listening to my tape at home, I felt nothing was more convincing. I found that my recording was indeed *very different* from all of the other tapes and CDs. To put it concretely, my recording sounded more like the Chinese ballet, "The Red Women Army" full of gunpowder, just like the great leader Chairman Mao's teaching, it was like, "A weapon that unites and educates the people against the enemy." While those western recordings, such as the ballet "Swan Lake", sounded soft and sweet, like someone once said, "The art that has influence on and is appreciated by the human soul."

Apart from my way of playing, the instrument itself that I played was very different from the violins Europeans were playing. They all used very fine, old Italian masters violins and fine expensive gut strings on them, while I, although updated to a handmade violin by a young master from Guangzhou instead of the factory made violin I played in Australia, I was still playing on some very cheap China made steel strings.

Sheng ZhongHua Comes To Norway

No one knows the name Sheng ZhongHua outside of China. But *in* China, many people still remember this name, even though she has disappeared from China for a few decades now. She is the second daughter of the most well-known violin family in China. Her elder brother, Sheng ZhongGuo, is the symbol of a Chinese violinist. She was my teacher when I studied at the Shanghai Conservatory of Music, the absent minded one.

All of my violin experiences in the west made me very upset, so much so that I began to doubt that the Shanghai Conservatory of Music from which I graduated, was *really* "World Class". I decided to write a letter to my former teacher Sheng ZhongHua.

Sheng wrote back to me immediately, with well written handwriting and very nicely chosen words. She said, "Couldn't be that bad, could it? Next time you take a lesson from Professor Boyhansen, please also send my regards, and don't forget to tell him that if there is an opportunity, I would very much like to see how he teaches."

I honestly passed Teacher Sheng's message to Professor Boyhansen. Boyhansen heard that and thought it would be a great idea. For if he not only teaches me, but also teaches my teacher Sheng, afterwards Teacher Sheng could bring his method back to China and influence more Chinese people. In other words, Professor Boyhansen would become the teacher of another nation.

After some letters back and forth, I met my teacher Sheng at Oslo airport. Just like the first time I went to Australia, she brought with her a violin, or should I say, "a wooden box that looked like a violin" of mass production from a Chinese factory.

The first time I took Teacher Sheng to meet my professor, she asked me to give Boyhansen a tape of her solo performance. To my surprise, when I opened it there was no tape in the case. What confused my professor and I even more was that it was not a mistake. Teacher Sheng took the tape out and gave him an empty case on purpose. I have no idea even to this day what purpose that could possibly have been.

What made Professor Boyhansen even more upset was upon their meeting for the first time, Teacher Sheng didn't mention exchange of teaching methods and ideas, or learning from him, but *instead* asked for the names and addresses of orchestras in Oslo, expressing her willingness to work for one of the professional orchestras there.

The orchestra that Teacher Sheng applied for was the same one I had once applied for but only got to the second stage of auditions, not the final. As for Teacher Sheng, according to violin performing ability, being accepted as a member shouldn't be any problem, or so I thought. I was waiting for good news from my teacher, waiting for her to get into the orchestra. As a former student, I would be proud too (having more face, as the Chinese say), and also proof that the Shanghai Conservatory of Music was indeed, *World Class*. It was only I, who was not good enough.

However, after a few days, an astonishing result came. Among the seven applicants, only one couldn't get into the second stage (being eliminated in the first stage). That applicant was the greatest, most famous violinist in my motherland, a professor from the best music institution in China and the one I used to worship, my former teacher Sheng ZhongHua!

I had no idea what this strike meant to Teacher Sheng. To me, it was vital, critical even. To me, Norway, as a high class western country rejecting Teacher Sheng's way of violin playing was a negation of my twenty years hard work and arduous struggle, *a negation of my life!*

However, Teacher Sheng is a person not easily admitting defeat. At Teacher Sheng's strong request, Professor Boyhansen helped arrange a violin recital for her. My heart was consumed entirely with good wishes, supporting her, hoping she could put all of her abilities to good use and obtain recognition from the Norwegians. I counted on her success to gain a little face back for my country, China, for the face of our education.

To put all my hope into action, I gave (not lent) her as a present, my own violin, made by a Guangzhou master special for me. I prayed to God, to Buddha, to any Gods existing in the universe, for my teacher Sheng's successful recital. I expected the concert would be sensational, *outstanding*. I even imagined the newspapers, radio and TV people interviewing Sheng, and myself giving a cool translation.

Teacher Sheng's violin recital took place at the small hall of the Norwegian State Academy of Music.

I went to the concert hall on the recital day very early. Waiting until the time was near, almost no one came into the hall, only the few who were already there. I felt rather abnormal and quickly ran to the door to tell the doorman to let people in. To my astonishment, there was no doorman, for there were no people to let in. I hurried back to the hall, carefully counting head by head, a total of less than ten people if I remember correctly. All the people inside the hall were black haired but for one blonde, the one playing piano accompanying Teacher Sheng.

Nevertheless, I still hoped that among the ten, someone had come from the media, carrying a tape recorder or a video camera. If they put Teacher Sheng's recital in the papers, or on the radio or TV, it would also have some influence. However, sadly, Teacher Sheng's performance, how could I, a former student, put it into words?

In a nutshell, when the show was over, I was glad that there were just a few people and felt lucky there were no media people there who might leave some recording as evidence. Teacher Sheng did have many excuses for not having played as well as expected, just like in many of her previous performing experiences, such as one when she was young, she played an unsatisfactory solo because she took a medicine, which made her sleepy.

Teacher Sheng's three month visa as a visiting scholar passed quickly, like the blink of an eye, and I was busy thinking of something besides the violin that I could give her as a "going back to the motherland" gift.

Three months quiet and unknown in Norway, Teacher Sheng was suddenly in the newspapers, on TV *and* radio! The pity was, her face on the media wasn't because of her outstanding violin playing, but rather for her procedure of applying as a refugee. The justification for Teacher Sheng to be a refugee was OUTSTANDING, because if she goes back to China, her husband would beat her to death.

The news of Sheng ZhongHua's refugee application spread to the ears of Professor Boyhansen. He wasn't happy, not happy at all. He told me, "I invited your former teacher as a visiting scholar to Norway to learn my violin teaching technique and understand more about western music, so that when she goes back she could benefit students in China. Since she intends to stay, it will be meaningless to go on with our project."

This, Professor Boyhansen found it a difficult-to-understand phenomenon, namely, "Chinese intellectuals once out of the country don't want to go back". I dare say it's a perplexing phenomenon to most people in western developed countries throughout the world. I will explain, for after the establishment of New China, Chinese intellectuals with the title of the "Stinking ninth category", were among the lowest in social status. Throughout the endless, *countless* political campaigns, the intellectuals were always among the targets of ridicule. As one slogan proclaimed, "The more knowledge, the more reactionary (to the society)". How could the westerners possibly understand the inhuman suffering and ill-treatment Chinese intellectuals experienced? In addition, being extremely narrow minded, selfish and shortsighted are general characteristics of the Chinese nation. Therefore, we, people from a "mind one's own business and care for nobody" nation, will rarely go back to the motherland once our feet are on other soil. (This was the situation in the 80s. Nowadays, I have no idea how much has changed.)

I am Chinese too, I possess all the Chinese characteristics, I am also a person who "cares for nobody". However, I must care for Teacher Sheng, because after all, she was not only my former teacher, but also because I was the one who caused her to be in Norway in the first place.

Hearing Sheng had applied for refugee status, my first reaction was that she had cut off her back road (a road she can use to escape when she is cornered. The "back road" was her motherland).

I immediately went to see Sheng and blamed her for not discussing with me before she made such a big decision. I, although having been her violin student, *did* have more years in foreign countries, spoke more languages and knew a little more about local policies and legal systems.

Sheng smiled at me and silenced all of my complaints with one sentence, "I could do anything for love. For love, I would give up everything, such as fame, social status, face…everything."

Love? Love, L O V E ! ! ! ?

No wonder she said if she goes back her husband would beat her to death! It reminded me of some rumor saying that after Sheng gave birth to a child with her second husband, she started to see someone else, a tall young photographer. The young man somehow came to Norway first and that became the true, secret reason Sheng wrote to me so nicely about coming to study with my Professor Boyhansen. Evidently, the rumor was true. Indeed, Sheng was giving up her family, her career, her value as a violin professor and even her future life in China.

After hearing the word "love", I really wondered if I should be happy for her or sorry for her, because I knew so clearly that although Norway, to the majority of people, may be the world's richest, safest, most free and leisurely paradise, it was definitely not the ideal place for Teacher Sheng to stay long term, as Sheng was a kind of person who constantly needs to be appreciated. To people like her, Norway would be the most monotonous, desolate, lonely, boring hell because the value of Teacher Sheng, or her name, was limited to those only in the Chinese community. Therefore I thought, one day, someday, she would realize that and go back to where she belongs, the Chinese circle. Even if unable to return to the mainland, she would try to go to Hong Kong, Taiwan, or even Singapore or Malaysia.

Thinking about all of this, I grew a kind of feeling that my helping Sheng come to Norway was, "good will ending with a bad result". A sense of guilt came to my mind spontaneously.

Meeting Sheng ZhongGuo

I think it was in the early 90s that I went back to China once and took that opportunity to visit Teacher Sheng's mother in Beijing. Sheng's mother is a super mother who raised eleven musically talented children, among them the eldest son Sheng ZhongGuo, is a great violinist, the idol and symbol of the New China violin soloist. The mother was staying with the eldest son which gave me the chance to meet the greatest violinist, the one I couldn't possibly have *dreamed* to meet when I was a young boy.

I went to see them with a heavy heart as what I did for my teacher didn't really give her a very good result.

Sheng's mother was originally from Changsha, the same city I'm from. Therefore, I felt very close when we met.

Sheng ZhongGuo said, "You are my sister's student, but also a half hometown fellow of my family. We don't need to take all the trouble to go out, just stay home and have an everyday family meal."

After the meal, inevitably, Sheng ZhongGuo and I went to talk about violins. Sheng ZhongGuo showed me his violin, a pretty good old Italian violin. The reason I say that violin was "pretty good", meaning not extremely good, is because it wasn't a violin that should be in the hands of someone at *his* level.

In short, the meeting with Sheng ZhongGuo, the absolute top in my country up to that time, made me realize very clearly that within violin as a branch of art, regardless of software (way of performing) or hardware (instruments, the violins themselves), China was a great distance behind western developed countries.

I'd rather stop here and omit the details, as it might hurt the feelings of many. Moreover, some information may be considered private or confidential within the industry circle.

After saying goodbye to Sheng's mother and her son, the great Sheng ZhongGuo, I walked alone in the street for a long time feeling a total loss, and defeat. Just imagine someone finding out that his master is not an invincible man, as he had always believed, and now starts to doubt what he has learned from his master and the value of so many years of effort and hard training. How would you feel?

Self-Renewal From Scratch

The harsh reality forced me to realize that if I really wanted to be a violin performing artist and make a living in the west, as the saying goes, "When in Rome, do as the Romans." I must adapt myself to the European way of violin playing. Thinking that way, I was glad I wasn't a professor or famous and had no face to lose. As long as I work hard, I can learn and renew, becoming a completely new person.

Back to Norway, I completely gave up my *peacockery* and self-respect as a violinist. I honestly, seriously and solidly, took violin lessons from Professor Boyhansen.

As a human, one need to not only be aware of his deficiencies, but also to acknowledge them. It is indeed a painful experience. However, I also came to understand that to realize I'm not a very good violinist, at least not as good as I think, is just like realizing I'm not a very good person, at least not as good as I think I am, and is a life milestone that marks a higher level of maturity and new stage in life.

Now that my mind was clear and thinking corrected, everything was on track quickly. After a period of learning and practice, not only my style of violin playing, (software), but also my violin itself (hardware) had a fundamental change. I bought an old Italian masters violin for the price of fifty thousand US dollars in Sweden, which I loved so much that I would *die* for it.

I still remember the last lesson Professor Boyhansen gave me. He let me listen to the recording of my very first lesson. Hearing that revolutionary, Red Guard-like energetic harsh flavor, I couldn't help laughing with shame. I must have looked very awkward. It was embarrassing. He then changed to another recording. The cream flavored sound was very sweet, charming and elegant. In the end he told me that this was my playing too, that he had recorded in the previous class. I was so surprised I found it hard to believe that with effort one could make such a transformation, beyond recognition.

Then, Professor Boyhansen solemnly announced, "Basically, you should be able to work for European professional orchestras." Immediately, he invited me to take part in his own chamber orchestra.

The very first concert in which I participated was a contemporary Italian work. Unfortunately at the time and until now, I only remember the piece was very difficult, but not anything else, not even one phrase of the melody.

Soon after that, I finally got a position with a *professional orchestra* in Oslo. That meant I had a stable job, or to convert it into a Chinese saying, "To hold the iron rice-bowl of capitalism". Following, Marianne and I bought a big new condo (with a bank loan) and soon after, I bought a used BMW. Like that, Marianne worked for the Oslo University, I worked for the orchestra, our life finally settled down.

What is the dream for most Chinese? To fight their way abroad. To live in one's own house, drive one's own car, live together with a western woman, this should be considered the dream and *my dream had come true*.

I took some photos of what I owned, house, car, blonde woman, and had them sent to my elder brother DanXin back in Hunan, hoping he would show the photos to the whole family especially to our father. Imagine my father and my family looking at the pictures with wonder and envy! I was immersed in a self-righteous mood, a mood of great satisfaction.

My body shape, meanwhile, was unconsciously getting rounder and rounder in that mood, a mood of comfort and contentment.

Violin-Sound At The Karl Johans Gate

Anyone who has been to Oslo must know the street named Karl Johans Gate.

Norway is a small country. Oslo is the very small capital of the small country and at the very center of the small capital, Karl Johans Gate is located. It is the most popular and crowded zone in the whole country.

It's a narrow walking street leading from the railway station to the royal palace, with a total length of say... about two kilometers. By the two sides of the street there are variety shops, cafes... in the evening, people like to gather here for street performers as spectators, or for nothing but hanging out. They walk up and down, up and down along the street. When they see something interesting they stop, if not interested they keep going.

In the very first days of arriving in Norway, this was a place where I often killed my valuable young time doing nothing. Since I had gotten a job in the orchestra, my life was on track and I had less and less time to waste there.

It was a long time since I had passed the Karl Johans Gate when one night after rehearsal one of the orchestra members asked me to go through Karl Johans Gate with him. THAT became another turning point in my life.

When my orchestra colleague Per and I walked on Karl Johans Gate, in the distance I saw a Chinese man with a camera hanging on his chest, standing in the middle of the road. He asked pedestrians passing by whether they would like their pictures taken.

That reminded me of when I was at the Shanghai Conservatory of Music and had the same side business of photography service for my fellow students. A sort of sympathy and understanding grew. With a bit of worry, I said to Per, "Nowadays who has no camera? How could he have business?"

"Wrong. Who every day would carry a camera around? People just take pictures for fun in a good mood, in addition he is taking black and white, that old thing has become new today. You know many young people today don't have black and white photos of themselves. I for instance, have had quite a few taken by him. In fact, some turned out, not bad…" Per said.

Sure enough, there were a few people in a queue waiting for their pictures to be taken. Influenced by the atmosphere, I was about to queue by the end, in part to show a little support to the compatriot but then I heard the sound of a violin tuning and then violin music. This shocked me because the style of playing that piece of music sounded so familiar, too familiar! I looked toward the direction of the sound and immediately regretted having done so.

If I had worn a hat, that hat would have been blown away from my head, not by wind, but by my hair which stood on end! Because the lady who played the violin didn't just have a playing style similar to my former teacher, she even looked *exactly* the same as her. The reason I put it this way, is because even today, I still do not wish to admit this cruel fact. The fact was, the lady playing violin in the street was no one else but my teacher, a professor of the Shanghai Conservatory of Music, our great Sheng ZhongHua!

Sheng avoided showing her face to the audience, totally different from what I used to see on the stage. She occasionally looked up to exchange a look of love with the camera man. The camera man, who looked much younger than my teacher, returned her look with encouragement.

Then I figured everything out. That was the man with whom my teacher Sheng fell in love. It is for this *street photographer* that professor Sheng had left her second husband, their child, all her students in China and her honor as a teacher with the title of professor at the Shanghai Conservatory of Music. All to come here, and play violin at Karl Johans Gate in the cold wind at night.

Afraid of being seen by Sheng, I quickly hide myself among the crowd. Listening to that familiar sound of her violin, looking at the familiar figure; I was badly hit by an emotional storm.

First of all, I felt extremely sorry for a famous violinist, a violin professor, falling to be a street player. Particularly, the professor who was my idol, whom I *worshiped*, my ideal which I had hoped to reach during my years in China. This was precisely the same person I would feel lucky to meet, honored to shake hands with, proud to be her student, and now, she was actually sort of begging on the street in front of my eyes! No one could say the impact was not colossal.

However, this "falling to be a street player" might after all, be the general view of ordinary people; Teacher Sheng might not at all think the same. Perhaps she was enjoying the flavor of a totally new life, experiencing a new meaning and value of being alive, appreciating human rights and freedom that she couldn't possibly have in her home country.

The brain was busy thinking, emotions were also restless and my heart was touched completely. Imagine, a woman, at her age (close to 50), giving up everything *for love*, what kind of courage that would take! Could anyone not be moved by that? If that was not reality but in a novel or movie, a pair of lovers, away from home, one taking pictures and the other playing violin to make a happy living together, what a brilliant touching and romantic story that would be.

Unfortunately, in front of my eyes was neither a novel nor a movie, it was simply a plain fact, reality. Especially since I had the distinct impression that it wouldn't be a question of *if* this romance was a great movement in her life-long love symphony, but one of *how long* this great movement could last.

Therefore I analyzed my feelings toward the whole thing; I found a quiet part of me being touched by sadness. However, do I really need to be sad? Haven't we heard the saying, "I would rather take a short true love and happiness, instead of life-long-together suffering"?

In fact, again, the way Teacher Sheng chose to live was her right and freedom. Who am I? Her FATHER? No. I was no more than a student, a former student to be exact. Why should I worry so much about her? I had provided a bridge to get her to Norway. I had already completed my historical mission. Teacher Sheng was at least not like many Chinese students, making loud complaints to those who had made huge efforts to bring them abroad, saying things like, "How can you not to take care of me after you got me out of the country? You should be good to me until the end!"

My thoughts were awakened by a push from my impatient orchestra colleague, Per. He was puzzled and asked me, "Do you know that Asian woman playing the violin?"

"Ah…" I stammered.

To personally know the great Sheng ZhongHua, used to sound like hot air, Chinese people say, "blowing a cow skin", meaning to show off by knowing some great person. But this time, I hesitated to admit and just took a fifty kroner note, stuffed it in Per's hand and said, "Please help me, put it into the violin case." I emphasized "put" not "throw" it into the violin case.

"Why so much, usually a ten kroner coin is considered more than enough…"

I didn't let Per finish, pushing his back forward. I walked on, looking back at me, once, twice, with an incredible expression; he gently and carefully PUT the fifty Kroner bill into Teacher Sheng's violin case. I had no courage to witness my teacher Sheng's reaction to the money and rushed home.

Self-Questioning Of My Own Life

Coming back from Karl Johans Gate, I still couldn't get my mind off Sheng's playing on the street. I slept not one minute the whole night.

Sheng's brave action of giving up everything for love inspired me greatly, making me re-think the fundamental meaning of life. I seriously questioned myself, "Do I really feel satisfied with this current lifestyle? Is this truly my goal in life?"

My mind became clearer after I analyzed my violin life calmly and rationally. It brought me to this kind of conclusion: Me, being an individual with strong personality and not sociable by nature, basically am not suited to play in an orchestra in the first place. Besides, I found I never really liked those classical masterworks I played in the orchestra. I felt a distance between me and western classical music, especially music written for the noble class. On the contrary, I felt much more connected to music with personality and passion, such as ethnic ballads, pop songs, local tunes, country folk music or even some jazz. In other words, compared with complex symphony, I preferred the simple, passionate, beautiful melodies.

In addition, one minor problem with me was that I couldn't really get along well with my orchestra colleagues. Violinists all over the world seem to share this same characteristic, _arrogance_. For instance me, as one of the world's violinists, I feel good and very special about myself, not an ordinary "feeling good" about myself, but "feeling extraordinarily good" about myself, far superior to anyone and anything. To me, the whole world is made of four strings, nothing else.

If that was the case, why should I torture myself every day with the same group of people I wasn't good with, to play the same kind of music repeatedly that I wasn't really in love with? Was that really my original intention or dream when learning to play the violin? Is this my purpose in life? We all know life is limited, short.

Should I spend my time and life on things I don't like in order to go on living? If so, what's the meaning of being alive?

The greatest psychological crises for a human being is no more than doubting the ideology and meaning of life that one has struggled and fought for, or to deny one's meaning of life. Imagine, my Communist Party member father has to face the fact that that the communist ideology as a social theory, _does not work in reality_. All that my father struggled and worked for was meaningless and in vain. What a cruel and broken-hearted picture that would be to my father.

Then, I started to recall how I got myself into this violin "pirate ship". At the very beginning, I just purely liked the violin sound, the look of the violin and how people played it, for the music too of course and a little bit of limelight in front of others, perhaps. Gradually, the violin became a problem standing between my father and I. It became my *weapon* to fight my father. The purpose was to gain Father's recognition. Later, violin turned to be more utilitarian, my means of making a living as well as a way to gain social status.

Anyone who wants to be a serious musician needs to have the sense of dedicating all of oneself to classical music. Yet am I really willing to dedicate myself to *classical music*, to use all my time and life, to go through the numerous great historical violin works? No, no, no, I'm a different kind of person. I need to look for the music, or to make music that I really like, that would touch my heart and express my feelings.

Hearing that I wanted to quit my orchestra job, a secure income and social status that I worked very hard to get, a dream job that many people would admire including my teacher Sheng, most would think that I must be crazy, out of my mind, but Marianne didn't think that way. She said, "Someone with dreams is far better than someone without dreams. I like you because you are a man of dreams."

Searching For A New Way Of Life

It's a universal and eternal truth, that no matter how great one's ideal or how beautiful one's dream, it can't replace everyday rice or bread for westerners. I, as a person, (in the Norwegian society, the equality between men and women is absolute, therefore, I cannot address myself as a "man" but rather a "person") cannot always rely upon the woman with me to feed me, especially when she was wearing two hats, working for the university and continuing her academic papers at the same time.

At this time, a man showed up that changed my life's destination. The senior man is called Crow, a violin shop owner in Oslo. When he got to know I could not only play violin, but also make and repair them, he immediately asked me if I would like to have some kind of co-operation with him. We soon became business partners. Later I learned that Crow was at the age of looking for a suitable successor.

Based on my past experience with buying-and-selling Chinese paintings, I knew business would generate economic benefits. Yet I still didn't expect a comfortable life would come so *soon* after getting myself into the violin business. Not but a few months later I gave up my old BMW, replacing it with a used Mercedes Benz.

However, the economic emancipation did not make me forget that I was a musician, an artist, not just a craftsman or a salesman; I must find my own artistic way of life. For that, first I changed my post graduate study at the Music Academy from "violin performance" to "violin acoustics". This study consisted of three parts: violin acoustics theory, violin playing and violin making. I began to adjust violin sound and make small repairs for other musicians. Thanks to my violin playing ability, combined with theoretical studies in addition to my intelligence and the ingenuity of my hands, I soon won some fame among local musicians.

Unexpectedly, my walking away from classical music did not make my Professor Boyhansen angry, on the contrary he encouraged me to do so by saying, "There are various types of music in the world, classical music is just a part of them. To find music that one truly loves, can really expresses one's feelings and have the passion to share with others, is everyone's freedom and right. I think this way, and teach this way. That is why I use different methods to teach different students. I do not wish my students to copy me. One Boyhansen in the world is enough. My task is to find the characteristics of each student and push them towards their own direction. Of course, this doesn't apply to those who are to be professional orchestra players."

Professor Boyhansen ended up telling me that though he could continue teaching me some violin playing technique and skills, he couldn't help much about the music I might like. So he suggested I go see other professors in other academies in other counties.

Following Professor Boyhansen's advice, I spent several summers at some music academies in other countries, starting first with all the Scandinavian countries, working through to Germany, Hungary, Czechoslovakia, Poland, Romania, the Soviet Union, Austria, UK, France, Switzerland, south to Italy and Spain, as well as the United States, looking for music that I might like and experts of violin acoustics that I could study with.

To my disappointment, almost all teachers and professors in the world were more focused on violin playing basic techniques and skill rather than the music itself. In order to catch original flavor of local or folk music, I decide to find my own way.

I tried to get myself into some folk music group. I even spent a few nights with a Gypsy band. Through that, I got to know a lot of musicians and music that was new to me. Among the musicians and music, some touched me and moved me very much. Those were perplexing days of my life, until I meet a lady, a lady known all over the world.

Kyung Wha-Chung Point In A Direction For Me

The known name is Kyung Wha-Chung, a world leading violinist. The opportunity to know her came when she gave a recital in Norway; she had a minor problem with her violin. We two Asians in a northern European country soon got along well. Once after rehearsal, we sat together in a restaurant having some very hot Chinese food. When she learned that I was like a little lamb who had lost my way in the violin world, she suggested that it might give me some inspiration listening to the French jazz violinist Stephane Grappelli. "That's the sound coming from the soul." she said.

In addition, she strongly recommended that I go on doing my research of violin acoustics. She also openly told the orchestra that I was a genius when it comes to sound adjustment. That certainly had a great influence on my later career as a violin maker.

Stephane Grappelli's performance opened a window to me, and through the window I found a totally different music world. In pursuit of my violin dream and career, as well as in search of my style of playing and my kind of violin music, I decided to go to Indiana University for further study. The school had accepted me as an MA student before I got out of China.

At the same time, my business partner Master Crow set forth his decision of retirement. He made his hope clearly and concretely that I inherit the shop, all tools, materials, instruments, customers of the shop, and work independently. This was truly a once in a lifetime opportunity for anyone. But my decision of going to the United States was made. Therefore I showed my appreciation but did not accept the proposal.

Of course, nobody in the world would understand my stupid action. Master Crow was so upset that he said, "You want me to go on working until I hit God?" Who could not be hesitant facing such a good man as Master Crow; and all the good things he was offering? But with my undeniable passion and the strong support from Marianne, we became busy preparing to go to the United States. As soon as we received the letter from Indiana University that they would allow me to re-enter the school, we sold all our property, furniture and car. Marianne resigned from her university job and said good bye to all her colleagues, friends and family.

Just at the time we had put all of our property into our wallets and were checking the price of one way tickets to Indianapolis from different travel agencies, I received a letter. *A letter from my family.*

That letter, again, changed my life course.

PS:

To avoid misunderstanding, please allow me to explain that many Chinese violinists who went to the west in the 80s were outstanding. Some of them were very successful in the world. But rarely were the successful ones in their Chinese "original package", they were mostly re-educated in western countries.

My former teacher Sheng ZhongHua too, after some years of re-study, became a violin professor teaching at a well-known Norwegian music institution until her retirement.

18: THE FIRST RETURN HOME IN THE EARLY 90S

Being Checked For ID Card And Temporary Residence Permit In Beijing

I opened the letter. It said, "On behalf of your family, I inform you that your father is suffering from cancer…"

The one who was "on behalf" of my family was not exactly a member of my family, but the girl who always "on behalf of my family" wrote to me or called me, saw me off or met me at stations when I traveled out or was coming back. That girl was no one else but MeiMei, the next-door neighbor girl whom I grew up with.

There was some sadness; after all, he was my father. It must be something biological, I guess. In addition, maybe just a part, a small part of me thought that this might be my last opportunity to show my success in front of my life-long rival. I decided to go back home to see him before going to the USA. I hadn't been home since I got out of the country. Like it or not, just like my father was my father, China *was* my home country after all.

I tried to dress myself to match the image of what most overseas-Chinese would look like according to most Chinese people at that time, in other words, the standard overseas-Chinese image appearing in the movies and TV at the time. I got myself into a white suit with a black bow tie. Looking in the mirror for some self-appreciation, to my disappointment, I looked somehow, like the old gentleman always standing in front of KFC.

Meanwhile Marianne came home. She opened the door and saw me dressed up like that, "Who died?" she asked, thinking I just came back from a funeral.

Knowing that I was preparing my return to China, Marianne gave a sigh of, "I see", and then couldn't help laughing. However, after laughter she solemnly reminded me, "Dressed up like that going to China, you're not afraid of catching a cold?"

"What do you mean?" I asked.

"Being robbed." Marianne said, and then told me a story about how a Taiwanese went to the mainland and was robbed and stripped to his underwear so that he caught a bad cold. Marianne continued, "So nowadays for safety it's wise for returning overseas Chinese to deliberately dress and appear to be just like mainland Chinese. You're of mainland origin, why make yourself look like a western antique? That is equal to deliberately making yourself a target!"

Although I said I wasn't afraid, inside, I felt what Marianne said could be right. Talking about disguising myself as mainland Chinese to go to China in order not to be robbed, I had no need to be disguised, as I WAS from mainland China. I only need to put on those old clothes I brought from China! Those were the most fashionable and the most avant-garde, black shoes with white silk socks, corduroy bell-bottom trousers, white zipper jacket and black artificial leather bucket bag. I thought with *those clothes*, not only would I not be cheated or robbed, but I could also bring those cloths back home and give them to relatives. Really, none of those clothes were patched and I had little chance to use them in Norway anyway. It would be a pity to waste them! The only trouble was, most of my pants had become too small for me as I grew fat.

Since it took time for Marianne to resign her job at the University, she couldn't go on the same flight to China with me. I took Finnair from Oslo to Helsinki then on to Beijing.

When I arrived in Beijing it was already dark, therefore impossible to catch another flight from Beijing to Hunan. Worried I would be recognized as coming back from overseas, I carried my violin (a fifty thousand dollar old Italian violin) in a cheap old violin case. Walking from the international arrival hall to the domestic arrival hall, from time to time I turned my head around to see if I was being followed.

When I got to the domestic arrival hall, I found my supposedly typical Chinese way of dress was very different from others, because apart from me, *no one* was wearing black shoes with white silk socks, corduroy bell-bottom trousers, white zipper jacket, not to mention, a black artificial leather bucket bag.

At the hall gate I ran into a young woman with a small child. I said hello to her in order to ask her if she knew of a reasonable guest house to stay overnight. Learning she was the wife of an overseas Chinese man and had come to Beijing from the countryside to apply for a visa to reunite with her husband, I was relieved. From her information, there was a small guest house not far from the airport. I immediately suggested going there by taxi together. The lady thought a little, perhaps calculated two sharing the taxi fees would be as much as a bus fee, and accepted my proposal. As the lady had a lot of baggage, I naturally had to help her. A man and a woman with a child, it was easy to be mistaken as a family.

In the taxi, I saw the meter showing an initial fee of ten RMB. I clearly remembered it was only two RMB the year I left China. I couldn't help asking, "Hey, I say comrade; your meter (I didn't know what the meter was called in Chinese) might be out of order, as the initial fee should be two RMB." The driver didn't answer my question but laughed a little. I laughed too to cover my embarrassment. I started to think that I had been away from the country for some years; it was understandable the price had gone up. But how much, I wasn't sure. Then I asked him, "Comrade, I mean mister, how much do you earn a month?"

"How about you *Sir*? How much can *you* get a month?" he kicked the ball back to me.

I remembered that at the time I went abroad, my monthly wage was sixty-eight RMB. Therefore, I took a chance saying, "two hundred RMB, plus ... ." I couldn't think of what to plus.

The driver smiled and said: "I say sir, you got to be joking, ah? One month two hundred? That's not poor, but *abject*." Then he looked at me conjecturing in an absolute, non-offensive tone, "Mister, listening to your accent it sounds like our great leader... (Mao and I come from the same province). You must have been in there for about ten years ... at least!"

"What do you mean?" I didn't get him.

"As a taxi driver, I've seen sooo many, all kinds of people. When I see someone as somebody, I can't be too wrong."

After I repeatedly said I wouldn't be angry, he proudly started his analysis, "*First of all*, you look very pale, it shows you have had a lack of sunshine for a long time; *secondly*, your clothes, all of them are about a "decade-ago" fashion, yet they still look very new. I assume they were looked after by the prison all the years you were in; the *third* is the way you're talking, just like about a decade ago..." Then he kindly advised me: "Just got out, listen more, talk less, so that you don't reveal your secret so easily. For example, nowadays, who uses the title '*Comrades*'? Instead, we say Miss, Boss, Mister..."

Before the conversation ended, we arrived at the guest house. The woman who shared the taxi with me asked how much the half fee would be. Seeing I was paying for the whole thing, she took her baby as quickly as she could and got out of the taxi, running toward the doorman to ask for help with her luggage.

I knew she was terrified thinking that I was a newly released criminal! I stopped her, showed her my old working certificate of Hunan Radio and

Television. I made up a story saying I was a TV actor and for the sake of playing a role I deliberately practice outside. The woman looked at my work certificate; in addition she couldn't forget that I had just paid for her part of the taxi, she reluctantly said, "I thought you didn't look like a bad person." Although she repeatedly said, "no thank you", still, I helped her with her luggage which she could not possibly carry into the guest house by herself.

I said to the young lady by the front desk "Comrade, oh no, Miss, please check in."

"Identity card." The lady didn't even raise her head, instead keeping her eyes on a fashion magazine. I quickly handed her my working certificate from Hunan Radio and Television. The lady gave me an evil eye, "No time for playing games, show me your ID card."

I turned around and saw the woman with me holding a credit card sized thing in her hand, I immediately said to her, "After you."

That front lady took a look at the woman's identity card and confirmed, "Two adults and a baby?"

"Oh no, we're not husband and wife ..." the woman quickly explained.

"Without a marriage certificate you two can't stay in the same room." Before the woman tried to say something, the front lady added, "Nowadays too many have kids without being married. Who cares?" "It's okay to have separate rooms, I snore badly, please get us two." I cut in.

"Two rooms deposit is one hundred RMB, two rooms cost two hundred, total, three hundred RMB. Do you need a receipt? Hey, where's the receipt book?" That front lady was pretending to look for receipts. (Without giving customers receipts, they can cheat the owner of the hotel and state tax.)

"Oh no, we are not ..." the woman was eager to explain, but stopped when she saw three hundred RMB in my hand. "We don't need a receipt." I added.

"Even with no receipt I can't give a discount, it's the same price, three hundred RMB." The front lady took the money from my hand, counted twice, then repeated to check the authenticity of the bills and then threw two keys on the table in front of us. From beginning to end, she didn't bother taking a good look at us.

I took the woman with her baby to room 203, found the heat was out of order and changed them to room 204. After I settled them down, she tried to comfort me by saying she believed I was not a bad man, otherwise I wouldn't have helped her and paid for the taxi and room. I had no need to explain to her that my paying for her room was neither trying to be Jesus nor a rich man, but to reward her for covering my foreign identity.

After I said "good night" like a real gentleman, she smiled with confidence, "I thought I ran into a lady-killer." I turned around; caught the sight of her stuffing her big dark nipple into the baby's mouth.

Embarrassed, I felt that to use the words "lady-killer" was too much flattery of herself. Watching me walk out the door, she suddenly asked me if I was a corrupted official fugitive? Before I could deny, she comforted me, "Don't worry, I won't betray you, now there are just too many corrupted officials on the run. In fact, my husband could be counted as half such an official."

After saying good night to the woman, I got myself into room 203. Without heat the room was dreadfully cold, I had to talk to the front lady, "Miss, could I have an extra blanket." The lady again gave me a cold eye and then ignored me. I was somewhat offended, raising my voice, "I said Miss..."

Before I went on, the lady shouted at me "How dare you call me Miss, and ask ME to give you a *blanket*? You got the wrong person!"

Of course, at the time, I had no idea that in China, "Miss", also meant prostitute and, "add an extra blanket", could also mean "to get a prostitute."

This time I got really angry, shouting back at her, "Yes, I called you Miss and asked *YOU* to give me a blanket. Is there something wrong with it? You need money, I give you, how much you say! If you can't do the job, ask someone else!"

My voice was so loud that it caught the attention of the doorman. He ran towards me and asked, "What's wrong?" I was a little afraid of getting myself in trouble so I quickly explained, "I was just asking for an extra blanket, but this Miss..."

Before I could even finish what I was saying, the front lady jumped up and roared "Who is *Miss*? Your mother is *Miss*!"

I was shocked by the extreme rudeness of the front lady. The doorman said to me with a mysterious voice, "There is no Miss here. Guest, please go back to your room and rest."

"But I need an extra blanket." I still didn't want to give up my reasonable request.

"An extra blanket!" That doorman put his voice even lower, "You go back to your room and rest for a while." He winked at me.

"But..."

The doorman patted my shoulder and softly whispered "Don't make such a big fuss. We don't offer blanket service here. You go back to your room and wait, but keep quiet."

"Oh, I got him. He must be afraid my yelling would be heard by others. If everyone asked for extra blankets..." I thought to myself. So, I winked back at him, although awkward, it was the only way I could express, "I understand".

I went back to my room and waited. Soon, someone knocked on the door.

"Who is it?" I asked absentmindedly.

"A quilt." a woman's voice replied.

I was so pleased that I jumped out of the ice cold bed, feeling grateful to the doorman for what he did for me. But when I opened the door, there was just a young woman with NO blanket.

"Where's the blanket?" I said what I was thinking.

"Quickly let me in, others will see me." The young woman pushed the door in. "Yo, your room is so cold ah!" spoken with a Sichuan accent, the young woman was now sitting on my bed. She went straight to the point, "A hundred RMB for me and fifty for the front. If you want me to stay overnight, another fifty, total two hundred RMB. We don't bargain here."

"What do you mean?" Although I understood exactly what she meant, I still pretended.

"Yi? Was you who wanted a Miss, wasn't you? It's safe here, don't worry." The young lady began to take off her coat.

At that time in China, prostitution was supposed to be illegal. It still is today but could never be stopped.

I just got back to my home country after so many years; I certainly didn't want to get myself in trouble. Therefore I continued with my performance, "What? You want to use this room overnight and you're asking me to pay you two hundred RMB? Why?"

"Dare you play games with your big sister? Just wait and see." The young lady got very angry, put on her coat that she just took off and rushed away.

Soon after that, the friendly doorman became very unfriendly; he came with two other people wearing red armbands and intruded into my room. Shouting at me: "Security Check, Security Check. Show your ID card and temporary residence permit!" (At that time, today too perhaps, people coming to big cities, needed to apply for a "temporary residence permit" with fees.)

That situation left me no choice but to show my passport. As soon as they saw my passport, everything ended very smoothly and quietly. I wasn't only given a better room with good heating, but also a thick blanket. It was the front lady who brought the blanket to me, with a nice friendly, respectable smile.

Less than twenty-four hours back in my motherland, I strongly felt hit by a fact, the fact that no matter how hard I was trying to be an ordinary Chinese, I had become very *foreign*. In addition to the change in myself from living overseas for years, more significantly, my country had changed radically. So radically that it became hard to recognize. In other words, it certainly was *not* the homeland I had remembered.

My Father In A Hospital Corridor

Arriving in my hometown Changsha; it was GuoXiong, a life-long friend of my elder brother DanXin, who came to pick me up in his private car at the airport. Besides him there was another person, the person who was not exactly my family member, yet had always been "on behalf" of my family to see me off and pick up at the stations. That person was of course, MeiMei.

According to MeiMei, both my brother and his wife were in the hospital taking care of my father, therefore they couldn't come pick me up. I recalled back to a time during the Cultural Revolution when one of our uncles paid a visit from the United States to his homeland. He was received with a very warm welcome from the local government and the entire family, I felt a little isolated.

Not seeing each other for some years, MeiMei had turned into a woman. But the feeling of her change in appearance was only at first sight, once she talked; all went back to the past.

On the way to the hospital, as I chatted with MeiMei, I learned that after the death of her father she took her father's job doing the same work her father and my mother did, in the same place (PanJiaPin) where we grew up together. She took care of her step-mother as her younger sister, the daughter of her father and step-mother, went to study somewhere in the USA. After my mother's retirement MeiMei naturally became the link between my mother and her former working unit.

Did I mention GuoXiong came to pick me up with his own car? Yes, he came with a Volkswagen Santana, the car that had disappeared years ago in Europe became the bestselling car in China during the 90s.

At that time someone owning a private car; that was really something, not to mention, a foreign car. Imagine, it was in the same country, the same generation in which possessing private property was thought to be a kind of crime! Even growing some vegetables outside under one's window was considered to be a wrong doing!

Since Deng's Open-door policy and the slogan, "To let a small portion of people get rich first", China had changed dramatically. GuoXiong had been working for the foreign trade company; that should explain everything. He was one of the "small portion of people" allowed to be rich first.

GuoXiong drove us directly to the hospital, saying, "MeiMei will take you to the sickroom, all your family is there. Your stuff, (my luggage) I'll take to the guest house for you."

"Thank you so much. You can take everything for me, except the violin." I said, embracing my violin, about to get out of his car.

"What are you bringing a violin to the hospital for? Can't you trust me? I've been the closest friend of your brother for more than thirty years."

GuoXiong said.

"It's not that I don't trust you, my brother Guo. It's that this is a very precious violin, worth *fifty thousand dollars*!" I deliberately put stress on the words, "Fifty thousand dollars", slowly, loudly and clearly.

Carrying my violin, following MeiMei, we went to the hospital's warded building. One floor after another, the aisles were filled with temporary steel-wire beds and folding chairs, looking very disorganized. When we reached the fourth floor, it looked as bad as the other three floors we had just passed. The corridor was choked. I was about to make a complaint, something like, "blocking traffic", when MeiMei pressed her index finger to her mouth indicating me to be quiet, and then pointed to a steel-wire bed in front of us, saying, "Your father."

My father's face was covered by a blanket so I couldn't see him. Beside the steel-wire bed a woman sat on a small stool. The woman looked up and called my name, "DanJiu". This woman, of course, could only be my brother's wife, the Big Sister. Thinking back to the past at the May 7 cadre's school and how I had witnessed the disgusting affair between she and my father, I didn't want to say more than one sentence, "Where is my family?" By saying those words with *that* tone, I was telling her that I still refused to accept her as one of "my family."

"Mom went out to buy food, and brother (her husband) went to talk to someone at the hospital to try and get a bed for Father." the Big Sister answered.

"How about one more person?" I didn't want to say the words "younger brother", for the sake of saving face after having no dialogue between us for many years.

"Well, my son is going ..."

"Oh no, not your son, I mean..." I interrupted her.

"Oh, you mean younger brother DanHen. He's preparing for acrobatic shows abroad, very busy lately."

In fact, I wasn't really paying much attention to what she was saying, as I was shocked by the sight before me. I couldn't possibly believe what I was seeing, *my father, my great and proud father*, after all those years of revolutionary struggle, ending up shrunken, in a steel-wire bed by the corridor of a sick house. The scene brought me back to the Cultural Revolution, when my father's superior Minister Wang threw himself into a pond killing himself. I really started to wonder about the significance of what my father's entire generation had been fighting for all their lives.

Hearing our conversation, a little movement occurred in the steel-wire bed. Big Sister quickly helped Father remove the blanket from his head exposing half of his face. I heard a very vague, husky voice from Father, *"You are here."*

I replied with a very low voice, "En." Fortunately, it was rather dim, so I couldn't see Father's face clearly, only feel his emaciated body lying there like a dry skeleton. Seeing no action from me, MeiMei pushed my back moving me closer.

I reluctantly moved half a step forward, about to squat down when a nurse came over and yelled out, "There is only one person from each family allowed to be here at a time! So many people here, how can I walk?!" This time I was the one who was really in the way. Though I complained of rudeness with my words, inside my heart I was grateful to the nurse, for saving me from this hardship, which was being face to face with my father.

"Take DanJiu home and rest first, here, leave to me.", Big Sister said as she handed the house keys to MeiMei. Now I had really become a family guest. MeiMei brought me to an old dormitory building, skillfully opened the door lock, smiled and said, "Please come in." The tone seemed to be, "on behalf of my family."

My brother's family was living on the ground floor, two rooms with a small kitchen, no sanitation, meaning neither bathroom nor toilet and outside a small yard with two hens for the purpose of laying eggs. There was a decent bed in the inner room of the two. That is, of course, the main bedroom. Supposedly the outer room was a living room, but it also had a sofa bed. Looking at the things on the bed, it was obviously Mother's bed. My eyes swept a circle of the room, seeing many familiar items that I preferred to forget. I was trying to find a place to sit, but felt full of thorns everywhere.

"What would you like to drink? Tea, cola or 7-happiness...?" MeiMei asked as she opened the refrigerator.

"What is *7-happiness*?" I never heard of such a drink. I looked towards the fridge, "Oh, that's seven-up. In fact this is not even 7-up, this is called SPRITE. Okay, I'll take Sprite, what you call 7-happiness." MeiMei passed me a can of Sprite. To my astonishment, the can was warm.

MeiMei explained: "This refrigerator of your brother's has been out of order a long time. Now it functions like a cupboard. Just drink it. It doesn't concern." MeiMei poured the Sprite into a glass for me.

"It doesn't concern", is a saying widely and most frequently used in Chinese communities all over the world. But warm Sprite? It might not concern MeiMei but certainly concerned me, very much.

"If you don't want 7-happiness, what did you call it, S-pri-ge? We can have tea instead." MeiMei was about to make tea.

"Don't bother. I can have my drink at the hotel." I said in a snobby tone.

"Hotel? Why? Brother has already arranged a room in his working unit guest house for you." MeiMei explained.

"No guest house, I'm going to stay in the *Hunan Hotel*." I emphasized.

"Hunan Hotel! That's expensive. Why must you stay there?"

"Yes, it must be Hunan Hotel.", I said it again.

MeiMei, of course did not know the story in our family history. The story from when I was little and my father and Mother took my brother DanXin to Hunan Hotel for a New Year Celebration event and left me all alone, at home, cold and hungry... It was at that time, I took a vow, "When I grow up, I must stay at the Hunan Hotel once, all by myself."

"If you insist on staying in a hotel instead of a guest house, the new HuaTian Hotel is a better one." As MeiMei went on speaking, I was already out the door of my brother's, because regardless of where I stayed, anyplace would be better than the home of my brother. After MeiMei worked to convince me repeatedly, I agreed to stay at the guest house, "For one night and *one night only.*"

Following MeiMei, we arrived at the guest house of my brother's working unit. As soon as I settled down and finished my rest-room affairs, MeiMei said, "If there is nothing else, I will go."

"Go where?" I asked.

"I don't know. Maybe to the hospital to replace your sister-in-law, or back to your brother's place to help your mother cook." MeiMei replied.

"Aren't you working?" I asked.

"I'm working, but took the day off today. Your sister-in-law is no longer working, she had an early retirement." MeiMei told me.

"Retirement? Only in her early forties, *retire*?" That was unbelievable to me. "The business of her working unit wasn't very good; in addition she was always taking long-term leave to look after your father, so she was persuaded to retire early from her working position. But "retirement" was a good way to put it. In fact, it was equal to an off-working-position." MeiMei explained.

"What is off-working-position?" I asked.

"When one has lost one's job, unemployment. Oh, yes, do you have children, yet?" MeiMei asked me jokingly.

"Oh no, I mean we can't." I answered.

MeiMei, "Why not? Don't you want children?"

I said, "Marianne can't have a child, a physical difficulty. Why did you suddenly ask me this?"

"Nothing particular, just chatting casually." MeiMei smiled with some meaning behind it, as if Marianne's physical problem could do her any good.

I was a little tired, so I flattened myself on the bed, but for courtesy's sake I kept the conversation going by asking her back, "Now let me casually ask you, do you have children yet?"

"No, but I hope someday I will have one." MeiMei smiled. I continued, "How about a man, have you got yourself a man?"

"No, I don't think I can have him, but maybe a child from him."

MeiMei said and slowly she sat down on the bed beside me.

"Remember?" she said.

"What?" I asked.

She smiled again, with a little shame on her face, she went on, "Remember when we were kids, we went to steal a raw banana? The owner punished me by squeezing the raw banana into my nose..."

"Oh, that!" I laughed, a little unnaturally, as we were quite adults by then, that's just kids' stuff, so what? I didn't know how to explain. But, of course I remembered that, I also remembered that after a few days, the wife of the owner gave us a ripe banana, and told us, to eat a banana we had to wait until it was ripe and we needed to peel the skin and eat it by mouth, not nose...

"The banana should be ripe by now." MeiMei said, with her face down to the floor.

"How about you? Have you had a ripe banana yet?" I didn't remember how the conversation went on exactly; I only remembered it went on uneasy. And the result was I found out MeiMei was still a virgin, had never sat on anyone's bed, except this one, at the guest house.

Only a few minutes later, I fell asleep. Meaning, nothing happened between me and MeiMei, nothing up till that day, and nothing the day after or after, till now.

Chen Family's Last Reunion Dinner

When I woke up I was surprised that the person in the room was not MeiMei but my brother DanXin. After all these years he looked very much the same, with an honest and kind smile, still healthy and strong, not like me, becoming rather full figured. My very first question was, "How could you throw him, I mean, you know who I mean (Father) in *the corridor*?"

DanXin sighed deeply; and then told me helplessly that it was arranged by my old schoolmate Wang ShiYi's father.

Hearing this I felt insulted and furious, thinking how could this Wang ShiYi be so cold as to do such a thing? But after my brother's explanation I was grateful for having such an old friend as Wang ShiYi.

In China, the government cadres are divided into very distinct ranks, though communism's ideology is equality. From a certain class to another class, is classified as high rank, or middle rank, or general rank. My father's class was just one grade away from high rank; therefore he didn't qualify for the privilege of staying in a Senior Cadre's Ward. The General sickrooms had always been overcrowded, simply no beds were available. The people in the corridor have to wait for someone to die to make a vacancy. That is to say, some family's joy comes from another family's tears. To even be able to stay in the corridor (waiting list), the patient needs to have some kind of relation, a very popular phrase was, "back door".

My father's back door was Wang ShiYi's father, as he was one of the authorities with influence at the hospital. It was he who claimed that my father's disease had scientific research value and therefore needed to be observed every day, closely. With great effort Dr. Wang managed to get my father on the corridor "waiting list", waiting for a young man inside the room to die and get his bed.

Seeing I was rather shocked and puzzled, my brother chose a relaxed tone and with a sense of humor said, "This is China. Not Australia, or No, Noway (Norway)." he paused, "Let's eat first."

"Okay, okay, where do we eat? I don't really like Huo GongGian (a well-known restaurant in town)." I intentionally talked haughty.

"Today we eat at home, because of your coming back, Mother started to prepare a week ago. She began cooking yesterday, making many dishes you like, rice powder steam pork, fried liver etc. You will see with your own eyes, a whole table."

"*What?* Taking me for someone who just got out of prison?" I laughed, with complicated feelings.

Carrying my violin, with my brother DanXin, we went to his home. Just at the entrance we ran into our younger brother DanHen paddling a tricycle used for food shopping at the unit dining hall. There were two people sitting on the tricycle, my father and DanXin's wife, Big Sister.

After so many years, my younger brother DanHen was no longer a small pile of bones covered by a sheet of thin skin. Instead, he had turned into a bruiser. Yet our formerly strong father, to the contrary, had become a small pile of bones with thin skin.

Under such circumstances, I concentrated my attention too much on my younger brother DanHen's facial expression, just in case, so as not to lose the opportunity to say hello to him after so many years of non-diplomatic relations. Thinking of how great the natural power was to reverse things and humans, sadly, DanHen pretended to be too busy to greet me. Obviously it was not time for our diplomatic relations to be normalized. Therefore I pretended nothing had happened and went into DanXin's home in front of them.

Seeing Big Sister and DanHen were going to sit our father on the sofa, I immediately removed my violin from it, purposely murmuring, "Don't sit on my precious violin." I searched for some better place to put it but failed.

"How about you put it on the cupboard, together with your old broken white violin." DanXin suggested.

Mentioning my... THAT *"broken white violin"*, my heart was startled. It brought me straight back to the old days when I had made it and my father smashed it during the Cultural Revolution. But the atmosphere there didn't allow my thoughts to go any deeper and I was really so eager to show off my precious expensive violin to the whole family, to make them proud of me, or regret what they had done to me, or envy my success. For this purpose, I pretended to be angry with DanXin for what he said, "How could you think the same of this violin and *that* violin? This is an old expensive Italian violin, worth *fifty thousand dollars*. It's US dollars I'm talking about." Again I stressed "fifty thousand dollars" slowly, loudly and clearly. However, the pity was, there was no one in the family impressed by the sum of money except the pretty wife of younger brother DanHen's. What a disappointment!

Mother and Big Sister were busy in the narrow kitchen and MeiMei was busy transporting dishes from the kitchen to the table. A rare family reunion dinner was about to begin. Three brothers plus DanHen's wife, sat down around a table. DanXin gave an opening speech, "Now DanJiu (my name) is back. We come to discuss what we can do and how we can help our father."

Honestly, I wasn't prepared for DanXin's proposal. As MeiMei wrote in the letter that Father was dying, I thought I was called back for farewell business. By the way DanXin looked at me, I had no way to escape but by saying something, "What and how can we brothers help with Father's disease? What about the hospital and the doctors? Besides, when we were small, Father always said that we brothers were all unreliable and if he was to be sick he could rely on his Communist Party and the socialist system."

Hearing that DanHen, "dong", stood up, looking at not me, but the ceiling, as if he was going to take some action. His wife pulled his arm, "What are you doing? Stupid."

"WC, I have to go." Brother left the table and went out.

DanXin was obviously let down by my words, but he kept himself calm and added softly, "It's alright to *SAY* depend on the Party and the system, but when reality comes, it's a different story. Nowadays the government is working on healthcare reform, who knows what kind of changes they're going to make?"

"No matter what changes they're going to make, it will only be better for the government and worse for the people. Many work units have, in fact, abolished the free medical care system. Though in principle all of Baba (father)'s health fees should be covered, *in reality*, only some basic cost can be reimbursed. Any slightly better medicine or something with nutrition, have to come out of our own expenses." Guess who made such a comment? It was my mother. She said that when she was carrying the last dish to the table. What she said, and the way she made the speech, literally surprised me, making me wonder... "My mother, the most revolutionary woman in new China; how and when did she change to be one who held what the Chinese call, "society disaffection"?

All the dishes were on the table. Mother, Big Sister and MeiMei were all also on the table. After hearing the topic of healthcare reform, MeiMei inserted a sentence, "I heard that soon, the whole nation will implement a 'private health insurance policy'."

Father made a bitter laugh, removed the dentures from his mouth and indistinctly said something no one understood. Big Sister quickly stopped him by saying, "No more about that."

"What did Baba say?" DanHen's wife asked.

"Baba said we do not have to worry about his health insurance. For when the time comes, he will have completed his mission of human contribution and should have already met Mr. Karl Marx." Big Sister interpreted, but also added a sentence, "Don't listen to what he says. Nonsense!" Big Sister put one piece of meat into her mouth, chewing it softer and then put it back on a spoon and fed Father. She said to Father, "We wouldn't let you go. You should co-operate, trying to eat more nutritious food. Don't worry about money, especially now DanJiu is back."

The scene in front of my eyes brought me back to May 7 Cadre's School, looking at this disgusting, "love-affair woman and man", now actually together, openly, at home in front of everyone! If this can be tolerated, what couldn't? I intentionally made a throat clearing sound and said to MeiMei, "Where's that two hundred RMB I threw to you before I went abroad? Did you use all of it to buy lollipops?"

"How could I use your money? I kept it all for you. Besides, I never eat lollipops." I knew that MeiMei was a good girl. I didn't have to mention two hundred RMB, even if I left my life to her, I knew she could be trusted.

"You still kept them for me, how great! Please pass ALL *two hundred yuan* to my brother, to use it all as my father's nourishment fee." I deliberately stressed "two hundred yuan" and "all".

"Baba is ill and you give two hundred yuan, ONLY?" DanHen's wife said to me as she held her husband down.

"Two hundred yuan isn't enough? It's a lot! It filled a large envelope when received. I counted, three bills of one yuan, twenty-one bills of fifty fens, and the rest were all small notes and coins. That's all I got from our parents to support me in my university education and further education abroad. Now I give it ALL back to him to pay for whatever is needed. Isn't it fair?"

"Do you think to save two hundred yuan was easy for us?" Mother clipped out a piece of fat meat from a dish, (she could use chopsticks to catch meat, it meant Mother had recovered quite well from her stroke during the Cultural Revolution) and angrily said to me, "That two hundred yuan was saved out of one cigarette after another from your Baba's mouth, for many years. Remember picking up cigarette ends for Baba when you were little? Baba saved all the money for your education since then."

Hearing Mother say that also reminded me that I had no memory of

Father ever *buying* cigarettes. No matter if he had come back from the countryside or some kind of political campaign, he would always bring back tobacco leaves. He dried the leaves, spraying some alcohol on them and heating them in a pot and then rolled up tightly, finally slicing them and putting it all inside a small rectangular iron box, ready for use. I had always wondered why Father didn't take the easy way and just buy a package of cigarettes instead.

Suddenly it was all clear. He was trying to save every single fen of money, for our education.

So that's it! Such a touching story, how could I not have thought about it before? Instead, I looked down on that envelope, disregarding it, not knowing that, not only was it filled with small money but also great hardship and affection for many years from Father. I had even thrown it to MeiMei just before boarding my airplane and asked her to buy herself some lollipops... I now understood how valuable that two hundred yuan really was. The real significance was not the amount itself, but my father's feelings and wish to support our education and pass the message to me that he did his best. Thinking of that, my mouthful of food tasted of nothing.

I was busy with what was in my mind; Mother went on with what was in her mind, "The doctor said your Baba's cancer resulted from long-term cheap, bad smoking." She clipped the big fat piece of meat, making a circle in the air, not knowing if it was to strengthen her point or to draw my attention, that piece of fat meat came down into my bowl. I lowered my head to hide my shyness and made a complaint to hide my embarrassment, "When we were growing our bodies needed fat meat, you gave us vegetables and now we want to lose weight and need vegetables, you give us fat meat."

DanHen's wife quickly agreed with what I said, "The fat meat is really too oily, you see, you see. Oil is dripping off. Using all this oil could make another side dish. From now on, no need to use so much oil."

DanXin laughed and sighed, saying to his young sister-in-law, "Think of the 1960s, we were all dying from starvation, one can understand why people our age are so hungry for oil."

Talking about oil, I took the hard-to-get opportunity to make the family history joke about DanHen frying oil beans without fire when he was three or four years old. The friendly approach received no response from DanHen. That made the very funny story, not funny at all.

Father seemed to understand my effort; he made an ugly smile and a gesture. Big Sister immediately interpreted, "Baba says, 'We all help ourselves, no need to pass food to each other.'"

Seeing this fat woman acting as Father's spokesman grew my anger again and I said, "How come *this woman* turned into our old man's stomach worm? The old man makes a gesture and she knows what kind of gas he wants to punch out!"

"How could you talk like that? It's all thanks to PanJie's (Big Sister) help that the family is still in shape."

It seemed Mother had for a long time wanted to praise PanJie, that was a golden opportunity. Of course she wanted to say more, "I'm not well myself, like a mud-made Buddha crossing a river unsure of the safety of myself. Eldest son has to work; second son is abroad, couldn't do any good; the youngest one lives far away. Our family depends on PanJie to glue us together."

DanXin smiled modestly and said, "All of this, is what a wife is for in a family, for it was *she* who wanted to ask for all the trouble and be one of our family members. The real person we appreciate and should thank is MeiMei. Although she is not our family member, over all these years has been acting like one, or more like one, in our family."

The youngest of the family, DanHen, couldn't help talking after all the silence, "Who said MeiMei is not our family member? To me she has always been my sister and we never treated her as politely as others outside of the family."

"What do you mean exactly? Just spit it out, Stupid!" DanHen's wife said impatiently.

"What I mean is, we should be grateful to MeiMei, grateful to PanJie…" He stopped, paused, and then looked at his wife.

The wife was certainly not a fool. She, of course, understood every single word that her husband was trying to say. She talked back, "You're namely talking about MeiMei and PanJie, but what was the under meaning? Spit it out."

DanHen waited for his wife to finish all she wanted to say, took a careful look at his wife and gingerly said, "It's good someone can read the under meaning. To compare, one knows the difference. Come everybody, I propose a toast. To PanJie and MeiMei." He stood up, raised his glass in the air and then put it close to his mouth about to drink. While at exactly that moment, his wife pushed the glass a little; half spilt out of the glass and went into DanHen's nose. This time, he *really* needed a water closet.

In my impression, DanHen had only a serious face, like a sheet of iron. It wasn't until that day, I realized he could be quite funny, on the right occasion.

Being praised by the family, Big Sister was of course very pleased. But she didn't show much on her face, rather brought the conversation back to our father's situation. That made it look as if she was the one worried about Father's disease the most. She said, "It's useless to thank me at this moment. Someone has to find a back door to move Father into a Senior Cadres' Ward. If we wait for the young man to die in order to get his bed, I wonder when that would be."

After saying that, Big Sister chewed some beans in her mouth and then again, put it back on the spoon to feed Father. I noticed her mouth was really busy, in all functions.

Father smiled, but his mouth didn't receive the soybeans from the spoon, instead muttering something. Big Sister stopped him before he finished, saying, "Not again, 'Communist Party member not afraid of death, what else could one be afraid of'; 'to give my body to the hospital for medical testing in order to contribute to the country's medical research...' I have been listening to these quotations so often and so frequently that I can recite them by heart."

DanXin bit my ear in a very low voice, explaining to me that it was because the cancer expert, Wang ShiYi's father, once said Father's disease had some kind of characteristics and therefore had research value. But that was purely fiction, used as an excuse to get Father on a waiting list, waiting in the corridor, however, Father took it seriously and repeated with great solemnity, "As long as I can contribute to the medical research of my motherland, my life has meaning to go on. For that, I would rather give up a quick death and live in pain." What was more, Father wrote in his will, "After my death, I donate my body to the country's medical research. As I am a Communist Party member, I live, as the Party's human, when I die, I will be the Party's ghost." and so on.

Big Sister took her husband's topic and said to Father, I say comrade Chen, please get realistic. Who cares so much for your Party or country anymore? You have devoted almost all your life to the revolution. Now is the time to think of *yourself*. Eat more and have your disease cured. When you go back to your work unit, try to get promoted to one higher class so that next time, you can stay in a Senior Cadres' Ward, not a corridor in a general sick house like now."

Big Sister's speech sounded rather sarcastic to me. My anger pushed me to grab this chance to attack her hard. I said loudly, "Who caused that mess at the May 7 Cadre's School? If it wasn't because of that, our old man would have been promoted to a high rank Senior Cadre years ago."

DanHen, "PON", smashed his chopsticks on the table, "Say it more clearly, what does that mean?"

"Why does *that girl* care for our old man so much? What do you think, she learned from Lei Feng? (Lei Feng was a Mao-made-figure who only did good things, never bad things to people)." I didn't want to show my weakness so easily.

DanHen *"dong"*, once again stood up. DanXin was quickly trying to put out the fire by saying, "Come on brothers, we family cannot meet so easily, now finally we meet..."

Not waiting until DanXin finished, DanHen roared, "Who wanted to meet *him*? Remember that year?! Who broke our family into pieces? 'Doing nothing good but spoiling everything!' All that Baba said about him couldn't be more right. After this *thing* disappeared, we finally became more like a family again. Why ask this *thing* to come back and spoil us again?"

"Sit down. How could you say things like that?" DanXin was doing his best by saying that to DanHen.

DanHen sat half down, but it didn't stop his anger. "Wasn't I telling the truth? Doing nothing but giving sarcastic comments. I said there was no need to tell him anything about the family, just think as if we don't have such a thing in our family, so that we could live much more peacefully."

As the elder brother, being talked about like that by the younger brother, I felt much loss of face. But looking at him, all the huge muscles, I understood that if we exchanged fire I was in no way a worthy opponent. Remembering how I used to bully him so much, I had to take care not to be foolish enough to give him a chance at revenge. Moreover, I just came back from the west. I had to show some elegance and class. Therefore I could do nothing but laugh dryly to cover my embarrassment.

Perhaps trying to keep the balance, DanXin argued with DanHen by saying, "How could you say that DanJiu is doing nothing? He *did* come back to discuss things with us."

I finally seized an opportunity to save my face a little, I said, "I didn't come back to discuss things with you guys... I was..." I couldn't go on because if I went on to say, "I thought I was wanted for the funeral" it would be equal to lighting the fuse to DanHen's fire. Therefore, I quickly changed to, "What could we possibly do to help Father away from his disease? In reality, isn't it enough for *that woman* (PanJie) to take care of him?"

"Do you think it's easy to take care of a sick person?" All of a sudden Mother went back to her natural bad temper, "Every meal has to be fed spoon by spoon, change diapers several times a day, when stool couldn't get out, fingers had to be used to dig, going up or down stairs he has to be carried on the shoulder..." The more words the more Mother got agitated.

In such a matter of principle, I simply could not give up fighting. I also, went back to my original rude feature, shouting at Mother, "Does this man (Father) deserve respect from you and the whole family? All of what he did with that woman (Big Sister with the nickname PanJie) at the May 7 Cadre's School, that ugly shameful disgusting scandal, God knows, ghosts know!"

DanHen jumped up again, this time a physical fight was unavoidable. DanXin quickly stepped forward to stop his youngest brother, who was about to hurt his younger brother, his many efforts seemed to be in vain. DanXin had to leave this arduous task to the youngest brother's wife. That made things much easier. Only an eye stare of the wife and the husband had to obey, reluctantly though.

By then, Big Sister cried out, saying, "Taking this chance while everyone is here, let's make the whole matter clear, otherwise Baba has to carry this unjust blame all his life."

Unexpectedly, the truth is, actually a very touching story.

The Touching Story Of Father And The Big Sister PanJie

The truth was, PanJie and Father did have a kind of special relationship, but the relationship was not something between "man and woman" as I, and other people thought, rather a pledged relationship as "father and daughter".

The story went like this. Not long after PanJie went to the countryside as one of the millions of re-educated youths, her father passed away. The countryside where she went was the same place Father's May 7 Cadre's School was. At that time another Cadre named Shen, of higher rank than Father, had a special interest in PanJie. Of course, Cadre Shen was not only interested in PanJie, but many other young girls of PanJie's age.

When PanJie turned to Father for help, Father figured out a way to stop Cadre Shen. He asked PanJie to wear his watch and eat dinner with him often. That gave people an impression, that PanJie already had a *protector*. That would keep Cadre Shen from temptation. The rumor went to the top, which resulted in Father receiving a disciplinary act from his superior, delaying his return to the city, missing an opportunity of getting promoted a rank higher.

Extremely grateful to Father, PanJie proposed a willing father-daughter relationship and vowed to take care of Father all her life. PanJie's proposal was like a dream to Father, as he always wanted a daughter, but we all came out as sons. Therefore, having a daughter like PanJie, to my father, nothing could be more exciting and satisfactory. In order to avoid jealousy among the family, the "father and daughter" thing was kept confidential from all our brothers.

For the sake of becoming a legal and real permanent member of our family and having an everyday life with Father, as soon as PanJie returned to the city she started looking for a target among our brothers. I was said to be a bad boy and the younger one was too little. The elder brother DanXin, was the only choice.

By chance, DanXin was just going through a heart broken critical period of time. He had just parted from his girlfriend. It was a question of, "To be or not to be" to my brother. At this time, PanJie appeared. Of course in the beginning there wasn't much about love between them. PanJie had her purpose; DanXin has always been a very good hearted boy and could never reject anyone.

Gradually, DanXin started to realize PanJie was a good girl, at least far better than he expected. Although it wasn't a hot love story like all the movies, as good friends or even life companions it was not entirely impossible. Yet there was one question that worried DanXin a lot, "Am I good enough for that kind of lovely girl?"

Later, it was the rumor about PanJie and Father that pushed DanXin to make his final decision. Of course rumor was ugly, rumor hurts, and once, DanXin was pushed to the edge of collapse. What's worse was he couldn't even ask Father if the rumor was true.

After going to the Southern Mountain alone, through quiet thinking, DanXin was brought to the following conclusion, "If that rumor was true, as a son he should take the responsibility to accept the girl with a bad reputation because of one's own father. If the rumor was false, he was also willing to take the unjust blame *for* Father. As a son who lost love, it would be better to do something good for the family than just disappear from life.

Like that, DanXin married PanJie. Just before they got married, PanJie insisted on taking a physical medical examination. This proposal was quite beyond DanXin's expectation. Of course he didn't know that having a physical medical examination was something PanJie really wanted to do. For hundreds of explanations or statements of their innocence wouldn't be as good as one word from the doctor. That word was, "virgin".

However, the best part of the story was not all listed above, but my brother DanXin was wrong about one thing. That was, he thought the love in his heart had died. With the marriage, DanXin started to be in love with PanJie and believed his life could never be better or happier than to be with his wife PanJie. PanJie of course felt the same, not only to become a member of the happy family, but also, she got the best husband in the world.

Someone calls our family a "happy family"?! If that was the case, am I not a guy of, "lucky but not aware"?

After hearing this story, I paid a respectable look to our thin and shrunken father on the sofa, suddenly feeling him become greater.

Perhaps this story was too emotional, as afterwards everyone was dead quiet, each eating one's own food and chewing one's own feelings. Everyone except the pretty young wife of DanHen, who from time to time asked me, "Do foreign countries have this, or that?"

Although I had no idea of her intention, at least it lubricated the atmosphere.

The dinner was about to end but the discussion of Father's problem ended nowhere. Therefore, DanXin had to make an accent to his closing speech, "About our father's situation, there is no one we can rely upon, except the brothers of ourselves."

This dinner, became the last reunion dinner of our Chen family.

Just before I walked out of DanXin's home, my pretty sister-in-law reminded me suddenly, "Don't forget your expensive violin." I realized how lost I was. It seemed this time that I came back to see my father, the violin was brought in vain. Watching me carrying my violin carefully, the young wife confirmed, "Are you sure the violin in that ragged case is worth 50,000 US Dollars? Boasting it, aren't you?" This question would be meaningful if it was coming out from my father's mouth.

Something Has To Be Taken Seriously

I expected MeiMei to walk me back to the guest house, but DanXin took her place. Back to the guest house, DanXin said to me gravely, "There is one more thing I wanted to talk to you about for a long time, which is the relationship between you and MeiMei. We are all grown-ups now. No one needs to listen to another; therefore I could only express my hope, hope that you could think of MeiMei a little, though I know you have Marianne there in Norway."

"The relationship between MeiMei and me? We have no relationship, I mean, not as a man and woman." All those things happened in our childhood, though we joked and teased each other from time to time, but to me, that wasn't a relationship. MeiMei to me, is just a sister, no more, no less.

"But, why does MeiMei never see a boyfriend? I think she has you in her mind." DanXin paused, sighing. "I also knew little about women, until I married PanJie."

Honestly, at that time, I really had little thought about MeiMei. I was in a state of emptiness.

"Well, you look tired, plus you might still have some jet-lag, take a good rest first." DanXin brought the conversation to an end.

I had too many things in my mind. I was lying in bed staring at the ceiling, recalling what had happened the whole day.

Through the day, there were a couple of things I had to admit. First of all, the story of two hundred RMB saved from Father's tobacco was indeed touching. Thinking about that, the monthly wages of our parents wasn't that much. Besides, our parents had a long-term separated life that required two sets of living expenses; in addition they had to raise four children. Where and how could they afford big money for my education? So, to pass that many-years-saved money from tobacco to me, was a message from Father saying, "Sorry, son, I have done my best." Therefore I really shouldn't measure the value by the number of two hundred.

Secondly, PanJie's story was even more impressive. That showed Father wasn't at all a bad man, in fact a very good man, just not a very good father, to be more precise, not a very good father to me, to me *only*. Or, should I turn my way of thinking around, that it wasn't that he who wasn't a good father, but I, who wasn't a very good son?

"Am I not a very good son?" No, that couldn't be the case, for if so, how could one explain my father's quotation, "I don't like DanJiu by nature."? That was the phrase which hurt me so badly and made me so sad, causing my heart to live in darkness for so many years... since I first over heard that conversation when I was little.

In short, the story of two hundred tobacco money, and the real relationship between Father and PanJie, made the image of Father much better in my mind. But still, it was *not* enough to change my opposition mode and emotions towards him.

However, as the matter stands, I thought it would be better to find ways of helping Father move to a Senior Cadres' Ward, on one hand to express my gratitude for that two hundred RMB and the other, to show off my ability to the whole family.

Nevertheless, there was one thing I was not aware of much at that time, which was, my deciding to do that, beyond doubt, was mostly coming from the power and affection of the blood relationship of being *Father and Son.*

19: THE FIRST RETURN HOME IN THE EARLY 90S (2)

High Rank Cadres' Ward

My elder brother DanXin arranged a room for me at a guest house in his working unit. I stayed there only one night and the next day I moved to the Hunan Hotel, (the one that has elevators, which my father took my brother to once when we were little but not me, hurting my feelings) to keep my word, that I would one day stay in the hotel as a guest. I moved again after that to HuaTian Hotel, the newest hotel in the city, as MeiMei suggested.

In those couple of days, my mind was filled (stacked) up with complicated emotions and thoughts. I locked myself in the hotel, seeing no one except for MeiMei, as a channel to my family. In addition, if I did go out, I might get lost in the streets because of the enormous changes in Changsha city which was now completely different from my memories.

In those quiet two days, memories of my father were like a movie flashing back repeatedly in my mind, making it more and more clear that the existence of my father was profoundly important to me; or to put it in other words, *to win the battle with him*, was fatally important to me. If he were gone, to whom could I show off my success resulting from my very hard work and struggle? How boring that life would be! Now, finally, the chance has come. If I could get my father into a High Rank Cadres' Ward, (a special building in the hospital only for officials ranking higher than fifteen cadres while my father was one rank lower, so he is called a middle class cadre) that would be a very good retort to what he used to call me, "useless thing". Like a resounding slap on his face. At the same time, I could make him understand that the real "useless thing" was his Party, the Chinese

227

Communist Party that he used to believe he could rely upon.

Yet only one man can he rely upon, that is one of his sons, the biggest headache and the "one too many", the most "useless thing" in the family. Now that son has become the most "useful thing" and is regarded highly by the whole family. The battle between father and son, would of course, conclude with the father's failure and the son's *victory*.

The plan sounds wonderful; however the problem remains of how to find a back-door leading to a High Rank Cadres' Ward and to get my father in?

The reality was, I didn't really know anyone who was in power. In fact, with my not very sociable personality, I didn't even have many friends, plus I'd been away from my city, living abroad for so many years. How could I suddenly find someone to "open a back door" for me? I decided to try, try anyone I knew in town.

The very first man in my mind was my old schoolmate Wang ShiYi, as his father was a professor at the Hospital he was the one who helped my father get into the hospital corridor. They must know *someone* who could open a back door for me. Though I couldn't say there was a deep friendship between Wang and I, at least I had helped him to get the most beautiful girl, the school flower, Lu XiaoBing, to be his wife. If only for that, he owes me.

I got Wang's address from my brother DanXin. However, the address was too old. Wang had moved away from there to a much better, new, apartment building. The apartment building was so gorgeous that I found it quite easily.

A new luxury building appeared in front of me. I walked into a marble lobby and then a Made-in-Japan elevator that lifted me to the eighteenth floor, walked out of the elevator and turned right to the end. Wang ShiYi's name was on the door. A middle school aged, pretty little girl, answered my door bell. She called out "Baba (Dad) ..." but stopped her voice with disappointment when she saw my face. Her smiling face suddenly turned cold, saying, "We do not accept home sales."

"Wait," I explained, "I'm not your Baba, but your Baba's friend."

Hearing that I was not a salesman, but a friend of her father's, she didn't change her face much, perhaps meaning that either salesman or a friend of her father's, to her, there wasn't any difference. She turned her face away from me and shouted, "Mama, Baba's friend, AGAIN!"

Then, I heard a familiar voice, "Just a second, I'm in the middle of shampooing my hair. I'll finish soon. Please let the guest in."

I was not let in, but waited in front of a large, iron barred double door, like a prison. A few minutes later, before I could finish my imagining of how Lu would look now after all these years, Lu came out from the bathroom to the door with a large towel on her head. When she recognized me, she was initially surprised, then blushed with embarrassment and waved her hands, saying: "Oh my God, I'm wearing no make-up."

Quickly she ran back to the bathroom. I had no chance to see her face, but saw the back. Yes, that was the back I remembered from when she danced, "The White-Haired Woman" at the middle school, but twice as much.

"Can't you let me in first?" I asked with a sour smile.

The pretty daughter reluctantly opened the door for me complaining to her mother, "Your guest, why ask me to open the door?"

I had a quick day-dream, that this young girl dressed in today's fashion, could be my own daughter!

Wang ShiYi's "palace", could be described as magnificent ... large living room, complete western-style furniture, large ultra-thin TV, central air conditioning etc. In short, many times more gorgeous than the hotel I was staying in. If I were to compare it with my brother' small, old rooms ... Silly me, how could they be compared?

When again, Lu showed her face, her made-up face to me, I looked at her, looked at her and couldn't help saying, "If walking down the street, I would hardly recognize you, when wearing this make-up."

"Don't be so cruel. Look at yourself, maybe more than twice as much as you used to be." She was amused by her witty words and burst into laughter. I recognized the laughter, as it sounded the same as before.

After a talk of nostalgia, Lu did not lead the conversation to her husband. I wasn't there only to renew old friendship, but to look for a back-door into a High Rank Cadres' Ward in a hospital (As I mentioned before, Wang's father used to be a professor of the Medical University and a well-known doctor of the Hunan Hospital. He once saved Lu's father's life during the Cultural Revolution, with my help. That was how Wang got close to Lu).

Hearing me mention Wang ShiYi, Lu's facial expression cooled as she said, "You're looking for him, me too. He's a busy man, especially recently. I heard he is opening a new company with somebody, again. He hardly comes back, perhaps once a month, which is mostly thanks to our daughter."

Then, she started telling me that she didn't like her husband's partners very much, particularly one person. The person we both knew and the person who caused Lu to quit the Mao Team during our middle school years. That person was Chuang, formerly the worker's representative Chuang, the one in charge of our Mao Team. According to Lu, Chuang turned himself into a real estate investor, while after his graduation from university, Wang worked as an architect. Somehow, Chuang and Wang became business partners.

How ironic, Chuang as a very successful real estate investor! His owning mistresses, not only one but five, proved it. Rumor said that he made a promise to have sex at least three times a week, with each one of them. No wonder Lu and Wang's daughter had such a cold attitude towards her "Daddy's friends"! As cold as to "visiting salesmen."

However, Lu quickly added, "I believe he's not like those men." But what I heard her saying was more like, "I HOPE he's not like those men who take mistresses."

After she heard that my father was still lying in the hospital corridor, she immediately showed her willingness to take me to see her daughter's grandfather. After all, I once helped to save her father's life.

At Wang's parents' home, although Wang's father looked much older than in my memory, his spirit was much higher and younger. The grandpa answered the English questions to his granddaughter, at the same time answering Lu's question as to where about his son might be. I had no chance to raise the issue of my father, until the last minute when we were about to leave.

"With your power and my status, now," (emphasizing "my status as a foreigner"), if we talk to the hospital leader, is it possible to get my father from the hospital corridor into a room?" I mentioned this because I remembered, in the early 80s there was a family relative from the United States visiting us. The local government was extremely busy looking after not only the US relatives, but also the whole family. Because of that history, I made my proposal.

Wang's father smiled, though not saying NO, *"impossible"* was obvious. However, he said, that although he would retire completely soon, he would try to get the chance to do the surgery for my father.

On our way back, Lu answered my question or rather misconception, regarding "foreigner". She said, "Who cares about foreigners anymore? Nowadays people are only interested in your money. Even if you were a *real* foreigner, immediately people would ask how much you intend to invest, what kind of project would you engage…" Pausing, Lu said with a heavy voice, "What a society it is today. As long as you have money, anything can be done, corruption, prostitution … a living being can be dead and a dead could live again…"

My mind had no room for the emotion of the great changes to my motherland, as my mind was filled with the sorrow of my father being one rank away from the high cadre's class, therefore not having the privilege of being in a High Rank Cadres' Ward. Instead, I had to beg Wang's father to exploit his power to get my father from the corridor into a general hospital room.

Every patient can be cured in a hospital room. It was what the Chinese Communist Party fought for in the first place, or what any enemy country in the west, say, the USA, Japan…

"Nowadays, two things speak. Power and money." Lu added,

interrupting my thoughts." You don't seem to understand the situation from this point of view. You really *are* becoming more and more a foreigner."

By then, maintaining my face, the most precious "Chinese face", was no longer fatal. I had to honestly admit, "I'm just a violinist, how would I come to have big money or power? Talk about friends, after being out of the country for so many years, I have no one, except you, and Wang ShiYi."

"Let's go, I'll take you to see someone." Lu said.

"Who?" I asked.

"Soon you will know."

Once out of Wang's parents' home, I suddenly realized that Lu just brought me there as an excuse to inquire as to her husband's whereabouts, as she knew seeing Wang's father was useless for my father's issue. She had the idea of taking me to see another person in mind from the start.

"Do you need an excuse to go to your husband's parent's home?" I thought but did not ask. Maybe women's faces are thinner, or did it apply to the whole Chinese nation?

Before I asked, unable to wait, she told me to whom we were going to see. Our middle schoolmate, Ma XiaoMao. Lu briefly explained that the father of Ma's husband is the Premier Liu of a High Rank Cadres Hospital. But Ma's husband just died, therefore she wasn't too sure whether it was the right time to see her and talk about my father's problem.

"Ma XiaoMao married? Her husband died? How?" I just had too many questions and didn't know where to start!

Following Lu, we arrived at the Library of Hunan Medical University, the same place my brother was working, in the photography department. The real surprise when I saw Ma, wasn't that she was working at the same place as my brother, nor that she had gained no weight after so many years, but that she looked almost the same as during our school days, not much older, apart from becoming a little nobler.

Seeing me, Ma didn't expose much joy, at least not on her face. She only made a comment that life is just like movies, classmates or friends after a long time will meet again. Then, briefly she asked me how well my life has been, and how well my life would be. Before I finished answering, she started to tell us that she was very satisfied with her life, at least up til now. "I like to work in the library because I like reading. I've had this habit since childhood. In the future if you write a book, I'll read it too." But I think, if her explanation wasn't trying to cover up her unhappiness, she must not be living in the real society. I mean, she must be living in the virtual societies of the books she has been reading.

Lu cut our conversation off, telling the real truth, which was of course, to ask for Ma's help in finding a back-door for my father to get into the room of a High Rank Cadres Ward. I, even as a half foreigner, felt Lu's honesty and straightforwardness was somewhat too blunt or abrupt. I quickly made up a clumsy lie, "No, no, I mainly wanted to see my old classmates."

To talk about getting help from the father of Ma's dead husband, we will have to talk about him; and to talk about him; we will have to talk about his death. However, my worry about the embarrassment seemed to be unnecessary, for Ma didn't show much sorrow on her face, softly commenting: "This is my fate. Is there anything I can do?" But her tone showed that she would never succumb to any fate that she did not like. Thinking about it, how could Ma, a person extremely eager to excel, easily show her inner pain to outsiders?

Ma clearly expressed that to find a back-door into the high rank cadres ward was almost impossible and at the same time gave us some basic information about Premier Liu, the father of her dead husband, being an iron-hard, inflexible man.

"Begging you to bring some gifts to your father-in-law, is also impossible?" I was surprised such unfamiliar words could come out from my mouth.

Ma smiled with disdain. It's most probably for the sake of old schoolmates, she started to tell us some truth. The truth was, there were just too many people trying to pay off her father-in-law by all means. Among those, a wife of a middle ranked cadre, through all kinds of channels, was sending different gifts. But Premier Liu still adhered to his principle not to let the middle ranked cadre into his Hospital.

Liu said: "High rank cadre's ward is for high ranked cadres. Ordinary people should stay in ordinary hospital. If ordinary patients stay in the high rank cadres' ward, how can we call it the *High Rank Cadres Ward*? No matter how bad or widely corruption spread, I, named Liu, am going to uphold the principle, in no way making one more bad example."

In a word, Premier Liu was untouchable, a man who can hardly be paid-off. He was a man always doing the right thing and the right thing *only*.

Later I learned that the wife of the middle ranked cadre, who had been trying hard to send Liu gifts, was my own dear mother. My mother, always proud to be an honest, straight forward person, never learning the bad habits of society such as going through back-doors, had now adopted it so well as to send gifts to someone in power who she didn't even know. It was like a bird learning to swim or a fish learning to fly. Incredible Ah!

Looks like my mother was also following with the change in society very closely, "Gone with the times".

My poor face must have been full of disappointment and sorrow, but Ma's eyes brightened suddenly with an idea, she said: "If I propose to my father-in-law that I want to go abroad in order to achieve my husband's last wish and you tell him you can help me with that, we might have a chance.

It's at least worth trying."

To help Ma go abroad is to achieve her ex-husband's last wish? What do these words mean? Lu later explained.

The story goes like this. Stories of my success returned to my hometown through various channels. Ma's husband Liu KangKang was much influenced by my fantastic stories, under strong pressure and supported by his wife, Liu's dream of being successful abroad was also aroused. In order to go abroad as an overseas' student, Liu followed my footsteps, learning English, taking the TOEFL exam and earning money for the school fees.

All went pretty smooth, until the last step when he went to the Bank of China to transfer fees to a school in Australia. The bank machine found in his dollars, two fake one hundred US dollar bills which he had paid a high price for from the black market. (At that time, Chinese RMB was not an internationally exchanged currency.) Perhaps after long-term overwork and mental stress leading to the ultimate collapse, Liu heard the word "counterfeit," and smiled. Then, like a piece of wood falling on the ground, he never got up again...

Liu's story made me feel very sad. Yet in order to get a back-door, I had to accept Ma' proposal. I went to see Premier Liu, Liu Kang-Kang's father. Claiming myself one of his son's close friends. I revealed my willingness and ability to achieve his son's last wish, which was, to help her daughter-in-law, Ma, go abroad. Of course, I couldn't forget mentioning a little about my father's present situation.

Premier Liu said nothing on the spot, but the next day, he asked Ma to tell me, "Give me a week or so to find a way. I will go talk to Minister Wu and try to work on him to see whether we can let him go home for a while?" In fact, Premier Liu and Minister Wu were best friends and old comrades for many years. Their relationship was more like brothers. For the sake of his daughter-in-law going abroad, Premier Liu had to sacrifice his iron principle temporarily, to ask his friend for the bed.

Ma was truly crafty, able to make iron hard Premier Liu become flexible!

Through this matter, I had seen a new face of the Chinese nation after the "reform and open door" campaign, the interpersonal relations were finally on track with the world and had become no longer just about friendship, but also about the interests of each side.

There's no such thing as a free lunch in this world. I had to quickly find a way to get Ma abroad.

In fact, I wasn't really worried about, "how to get her abroad," but rather *"what after she's abroad?"*

Re-Encounter Jiang LangSha, Chu XiaoLin, And Uncle Feng

Waiting for Premier Liu to get a bed for my father at his High Rank

Cadres' Ward, I was alone in the streets to re-familiarize myself with a city that I was once very familiar with. All the main streets of Changsha had been reformed (rebuilt) beyond recognition. Only some small alley's preserved the old "flavor".

I casually walked into a small alley, surprised to find that almost all the shops around were book wholesalers. I ventured to talk to a woman in a store. She told me this street was *THE* well-known, might even be the largest, "copy books wholesale market." (Saying "black book" wouldn't sound very pleasant) In other words, any best seller books, as long as they were on the state publishing house's book shelf, here it was available at wholesale price, several times lower than the state's price. The books from this market went throughout the whole country, meeting the needs of hunger of spirit for those who were still poor in materials.

I took a strong interest and walked along the alley, shop by shop. My steps stopped in front of a small bookstore, not because there was something special about the store, but because in front of the shop was a small book stall, a few words were written, "Retail World Classic Literature Works." That stall was arrayed full of books that I loved in my childhood during the Cultural Revolution, western literature masterworks, such as, "Red and Black", "War and Peace", "Third Reich", "Les Miserables ", "Notre Dame de Paris ", "David Copperfield ", and so on. When I saw Romain Rolland, "Jean Christophe", I couldn't help but squat down.

An enthusiastic feeling when reading those books in my youth was aroused. I spontaneously picked up the book John Christopher, and opened the familiar first page.

"This is the dearest of all the books I would recommend; it was my guide in life." a familiar voice, a voice I had heard before. I looked up, oh my God! Not that many years ago, wasn't this man telling me the same words? Yes, this was the same man, Jiang LangSha.

After so many years, he had aged a lot and lost a lot of weight. This is the man who greatly influenced my way of thinking and thoughts when I was young and unformed. In addition, how could a boy forget the man who was the first and last that tried putting himself (part of himself) into a young boy's life?

Suddenly re-encountered so many years later, I was confused. I smiled at him awkwardly. He obviously didn't recognize me, but went on selling his quotations that he must have been selling for many years. With lack of psychological preparation, I took the opportunity before his recognition and quickly bowed away.

Back to the hotel, after hours, my mind still couldn't calm down. My formative years, all those things, like a movie playing in my mind: violin playing at the railroad track; Jiang's little wooden hut near the railway; falling asleep on a railroad track in the rain; I was taken by Jiang to his bed;

under his bed a box of books; assuming I stole large stacks of sheet music from the library hidden at Uncle Feng's… *How did all those end?* They all ended by Chu XiaoLin jumping from the fourth floor window of her home … and finally, the sight of Jiang LangSha being captured and taken away…

What then? I don't even know whether Chu XiaoLin is "to be or not to be" (I mean dead or alive).

More and more bothered by those questions, I decided to go back to the book market. I went straight to the spot where I had met Jiang last time but Jiang wasn't there. Instead, a fairly good looking country girl was, cleaning the ground in front of the bookstore, (the spot Jiang was borrowing to sell his books). The young girl told me she didn't really know Jiang well, that she was told by the wife of the bookstore owner to let Jiang sell books in front of their bookstore, for Jiang could attract more customers to the store, (they were selling completely different books) and also because Jiang is poor but a good man. To use the wife's original words, "Jiang sells books in order to support his long-term sick wife; and I never heard of him seducing any other women, an honest, good man."

Jiang was married? How could that be possible! Stripping the skin of Jiang's man's body, he is indeed simply not a man. This fact I knew the best. Just to think of it, a sudden pain came to my back again.

The fact that Jiang got married made my curiosity increase. After walking up and down in the book market a few times, I couldn't find Jiang. I returned again to the bookstore, asking the pretty country girl for a favor. I told her that I was an old friend of Jiang's, just returning from abroad and would like very much to meet him. I wrote my hotel phone number and along with another paper of value, passed them to her together, asking her to make sure to call me when Jiang shows up.

The next morning, I received a call from the country girl. In addition to the information that Jiang was there, she asked me, "Boss, how long are you going to stay in Changsha? If you need a full time companion (a girl to be with the guest all the time as a private service), I have a pretty good looking sister…"

I quickly went to the front of the bookstore. I squatted down picking up the book, of course "John Christopher", pretending to turn the pages. Jiang started his sales quotation like a tape recorder, "This is the dearest of all the books I would recommend; it was my guide in life."

"You said it to me before, many years ago, *remember*?" I looked up, ready to see his expression of surprise. Jiang looked at me, not surprised but puzzled. After a short while his facial expression turned to astonished.

"It's you, *little nine-bother*, you grew fat, hard to recognize!"

We started to chat.

"Hey, how much is this book?" a customer asked.

"Twenty RMB, forty percent off." Jiang answered, and turned to me continuing our talk.

"Hey, can't I get it a little bit cheaper?" The book buyer started bargaining.

"Fifty percent off." Jiang quickly responded and immediately turned back to me again.

"How about sixty percent off? Do you do business or not?" the book buyer looked a little offended for being taken too lightly.

"Take it, and go away." Jiang looked a little annoyed.

"I would also like a copy if it's sixty percent off.", said another customer.

Jiang looked really troubled; he answered nothing, started to pack up his bookstall and said, "We'll find a place to talk."

"How about your place?" I suggested, of course to find out more facts about his life.

"En…" Jiang hesitated, then nodded, "Might as well, but my place isn't a very nice place. However, there is a person, I mean *used to be* a person, but not really a person anymore, you should meet, perhaps."

No doubt, the person, "used to be a person, but not really a person anymore", must be his wife. We will meet first then I will think about whether I should claim compensation from her for my bottom pain.

Jiang skillfully sorted his books into two large boxes, and then loaded them on a bicycle. I followed him, into a very narrow alley, walking to the end. We stopped at a very old brick house. He opened the iron gate and pushed his bike in. I followed him; hardly able get my body through the narrow pass. I found myself in a book warehouse.

"I know the owner of the place. We stay on the second floor. He lets us stay for free, we look after the warehouse for him in return." Jiang explained.

Following Jiang through the warehouse and up the narrow staircase, we arrived on the second floor. All the way I smelled unpleasant mold, up to the second floor where the smell changed from mold into that of an awful toilet. No need to look, a toilet stool was right in front of us.

Jiang made no sign of apology as he opened the door to let me in. A familiar sight appeared before my eyes. The layout of the room was almost exactly the same as the wooden railway hut all those many years ago. A single bed, a wooden chair with just the addition of a table, a computer and some books.

This is entirely a bachelor's place; there wasn't the slightest smell of a wife, a woman, a family. I couldn't suppress my curiosity and asked, "Where's your wife?"

"There." Jiang nodded.

"Where?" I couldn't see.

"Sleeping right in the bed."

Then I found someone really *was* in the neat quilt on the bed. I remembered what the country girl in the bookstore had said, that Jiang had a long-term sick wife.

I extended my tongue out, lowered my voice and said, "I'm sorry, I didn't know…"

"Never mind, she can't hear nothing." said Jiang.

"When will she wake up?" I asked.

"Good question. She's been sleeping for many years." said Jiang.

"What!?"

Jiang started to tell me the story.

Chu XiaoLin's Story

That year (during the Chinese Cultural Revolution), Chu XiaoLin jumped out of her window from the fourth floor onto the canvas roof of a van. She was taken to a hospital immediately. After emergency treatment, though not dead, the brain damage turned her from a *"person"* into a *"vegetable"*. No wonder Jiang mentioned, *"technically* used to be a person but not a person anymore."

After Jiang was taken out of his wooden railway hut he wasn't put into jail, but returned to his adopted father, the real father of Chu. The father kept his word, "My daughter alive is your wife, and dead is your ghost." Jiang was forced to marry his adopted sister, then a *"cabbage"*, as his life-long wife.

After the marriage was done, the father's health deteriorated day by day and he was literally paralyzed after a stroke. On the contrary, the mother, who used to be in the wheelchair, since watching her daughter climb up in the window, had suddenly stood up from her wheelchair and actually started to re-learn how to walk! When the father became paralyzed, the couple had a role reversal.

Then the mother helped the father get in the wheelchair that she used to sit in and pushed her husband around.

Just like that, Jiang took care of the XiaoLin, a *"cabbage"* that would never wake up.

I took a quick look at the bed. I don't know if I should describe her as "fat and white" or "bloated"? (She looked completely different from my memory) I felt a tremendous psychological shock and in it a strong sense of remorse.

When Jiang was busy feeding milk to Chu, I had his permission to take a look at his computer. I found on his desktop a Word file called, "My Father".

"Is it the book you once told me you wanted to write?" I asked.

"Not complete yet. I plan to continue it after I pass the TOEFL test

(Test of English as a Foreign Language)." said Jiang.

"You're taking the TOEFL too?" I was really surprised.

When I learned that he had been thinking about going abroad, I started talking about my experiences living abroad. I ended by telling him that not only does a high score on the TOEFL count, but more important is money…"

Jiang told me both TOEFL and MONEY shouldn't be major problems, as his English was already quite good and after many years of saving, plus profits gained from the stock exchange, his only problem was his wife.

"If someday my Lin sister (he still called her sister, not wife) could wake up, or become a real plant, a flower or a tree, I could carry her and leave the country so that I could learn more English, read more classics in the original language. By that time, I want to use English to write my own story. For I have the will and passion to let my story be heard all over the world. To let people see the real life of ordinary Chinese people in the *New China*." Jiang said with fantasy glittering in his eyes, small narrow eyes with luster inside.

Watching him, it was as if I were seeing myself in the time before I went abroad. I dare say, at that moment no one knew Jiang's feeling better than I.

Who made the life of Jiang and his sister Chu so miserable? Was that all my fault? The society and the age were nothing to blame? However, the society and the age don't have to take any responsibility. What about me, should I take no responsibility either? Even if I didn't want to take any responsibility, couldn't I find a way that both parties, or even all three parties, could win?

I asked for Jiang's e-mail address, took a look again at Chu XiaoLin and made a promise that we would meet again. I was out of Jiang's home (if that can be considered a home).

I didn't return to my hotel, but went straight to the Changsha Construction Company, the unit I used to work at from age 15. To save time, I've deleted all the details. Let's just say, through all the difficulties; I found Uncle Feng. He was, by that time retired from work. Since he couldn't receive a full retirement pension, he went to a suburb, renting a small vegetable garden from a distant relative, and after many years of picking up building material from construction sites, he built himself a small shed. He was making a living by repairing people's houses.

I didn't tell Uncle Feng much about myself, especially not mentioning anything about abroad. I only talked about helping Jiang study abroad, to let him bring his dream to reality. By looking after Chu XiaoLin, Uncle Feng's life would also become richer. Of course, I didn't forget to mention Jiang's promise that he would send money regularly.

Uncle Feng heard what I was saying; no words, nothing, only silence. He started to prepare space for a bed.

I knew I did a good thing, for myself, for Jiang, for Chu, even for Uncle Feng. I assume Uncle Feng's life in the future, of being needed by another human being, or a plant, would be of great significance to being a human.

Before I left, Uncle Feng took a cloth bag out from under his bed. He opened the bag layer after layer, until an envelope appeared in front of my eyes. Many years ago, it was *this envelope* that caused all the tragedy to Jiang and Chu that lasted to that day and the tragedy had to go on. I touched the envelope, with great fear. Fear that in it there could be too much of a secret. Finally, I couldn't gather courage enough to open it, only saying to Uncle Feng "The time is not right yet. Let it stay in your place for a little longer. I'll come to take it when the time is right."

Two days later, Jiang transported his sister, his wife, his only family in the world, to Uncle Feng. After a long talk about how to look after XiaoLin, Jiang passed a notebook to Uncle Feng, in it, all the details about XiaoLin's records and hospitalization.

After many thanks, Jiang finally promised Uncle Feng, "I will come to see you both often."

20: The First Return To My Homeland In The Early 90s (3)

Farewell Concert In My Hometown Changsha

After having settled down the matter of Chu XiaoLin, I felt my heart become much lighter. At the same time, Marianne completed her job-handover to her successor at the University and came to Changsha to visit my father. I asked DanXin to pass the message to Father that a Norwegian guest named Marianne was waiting for his interview.

Father answered immediately that to receive a foreign guest in a hospital corridor would cause international confusion and give a bad impression. The Party was working on ways to get him into a Senior Cadres' Ward, therefore, until then, Miss Marianne could take a good rest for a few days or go around taking a good look at the enormous change to our great socialist country after the great, glorious, and always correct Chinese Party's open-door and reform policy.

Honestly, I myself didn't think it would be a great idea to let Marianne see my father in a hospital corridor either. It was, after all, not a great, glorious, nor correct thing to do.

So, I asked Marianne where about she would like to go and what she would like to do. Marianne answered that there was, "Nowhere and nothing in particular. If Father is unable to see me for a while, why don't we pay some visits to the places where you grew up?"

I thought that was a great idea too, especially to take a beautiful western girl around, letting people know the blonde was my woman. *How much honorable face I could gain!* So I took Marianne, starting from my kindergarten, elementary school, middle school, then to Changsha Construction

Company, Hunan Beijing Opera, up to the Hunan Radio and Television Orchestra. Sure enough, wherever we went, we received warm receptions. Of course, I understood that ninety percent of all the warm receptions were for the "foreign guest" Marianne.

The visiting ended within two days. Then there was nothing more to do. By chance, at that time some old violin friends and former colleagues made a request. They would like to listen to me play that old precious Italian violin that I brought with me everywhere in China. That made me particularly excited! Having taken all the trouble to bring such an expensive Italian violin to my hometown; it would be a waste if I didn't show off a bit. So I found my old partner pianist DanDan (not blood related but a sworn sister) and the two of us hastily rehearsed a little.

Next, we rented a rather luxurious nightclub. When I went to inspect the site I felt that the place might be too big for a private party. I was afraid too few people in that vast space would make the atmosphere of the party a little too lonely. However, in Changsha, a city not that big, the news of my giving a private concert party spread very quickly. More and more people sent me messages saying that they would like to come. The day before the party it was in the Hunan provincial major newspaper!

When the time came, I went into the nightclub and Oh my God! Never mind seats, the whole place was packed with people everywhere; it wasn't even easy to stand! I was particularly touched as my violin teacher Li, the one who first taught me violin in the church, led dozens of children forming a string orchestra, playing for the opening. Evidently, Teacher Li no longer needed to keep teaching violin secretly.

I borrowed the opportunity while the children were playing, to take a look at the audience. Besides neighbors I grew up with, my former schoolmates, working colleagues from various units, and their spouses and children were all there. The rest, at least half of the people, I didn't know.

Of all those among the crowd, my eyes fixed on my former teacher Guo. When she noticed I was looking at her, she waved dismissively meaning, don't bother to come forward and greet her, just prepare for the concert. I was bursting, elated by thinking about how if I had not met Teacher Guo, I wouldn't have gone to study in Shanghai and I *definitely* wouldn't be here tonight. To put it in another way, I would have to come to places like this every night to play the violin for money, in nightclubs. So I decided, after the concert, I would talk to my teacher to show my nostalgia and gratitude for all she had done for me.

But after the show, in front of piles of flowers left for me by different people and a queue waiting for my autograph and to have photos taken with me, I felt my bones were so light that I could float. I was just too distracted with the excitement to remember, "I should talk to Teacher Guo after the show".

I had no idea what kind of impression I left on people, my expensive Italian violin, my dressed up (white dress shirt and black bow tie) like the old gentleman in front of KFC and my western re-educated way of playing. Yet I knew that my personal feelings and satisfaction had reached the highest climax. Unfortunately that mood didn't last long, as DanXin found a small note on a flower. In the note was Teacher Guo's handwriting, "Not bad, but I expected you to be much better..." I got very upset reading this. I crumpled it in frustration. My dear teacher, *what more do you expect*, an Oscar, Nobel Prize, or Olympic Medal?

There was something that puzzled me very much from time to time, as I mentioned before, I just didn't understand why Teacher Guo expected so much from me. We all knew she had a very talented son, a genius violinist. That was the reason she resigned from the position as concertmaster of the Hunan Orchestra and concentrated on teaching her son to be a world class violinist.

Nevertheless, I was strongly stimulated by Teacher Gao and I again made up my mind. Next concert, I would make it bigger; make an enormous concert, great enough to impress Teacher Guo!

However, I never imagined that this very casual, rushed private party would be my farewell concert, if not life-long, at least for the next 10 years.

Father's Farewell To The Hospital Corridor At Last

After my party/concert, Father was moved into an individual room of a High-Rank Cadres' Ward, specially arranged by Ma XiaoMao's father-in-law, the Premier Liu. I took Marianne to see Father there.

Seeing Marianne, a foreign guest, but his daughter-in-law, Father made an effort to sit up in the bed, revealing a diplomatic kind of smile from his iron face. He put in his dentures and official like, said a few not-so-fluent words in English to express his welcome and then asked Marianne whether she was used to Changsha food. Learning that Marianne did not eat meat, Father immediately turned from an official into a parent, quickly ordering PanJie, in Chinese, the Big Sister (from now on I also call her PanJie) to find a good vegetarian restaurant in town for Marianne. That explains the Chinese old culture, "for the masses, food is above all." However something Father didn't know was, the most frightening word for Marianne in China was, *"eat"*.

In order to show off my English, I deliberately talked a lot with Marianne in front of Father. Father, as a former university student of English literature, seemed indeed impressed which made me feel truly great and satisfied for quite a while.

Marianne said almost nothing, keeping very quiet, listening to the father and son, until the "interview" was about over. Marianne suddenly said to

Father in Chinese, "hao hao xiu xi, bu yao rang ni er zi wei nin dan xin (Take good care of yourself; please don't make your son worry about you)".

Not only Father, but also all of the people present, PanJie and nurses, were shocked. Naturally, who would expect a blonde western girl's pronunciation of Mandarin Chinese to be as good, if not better, than *all* of the Chinese people present!

"You don't need to worry about me." said Father removing his dentures, (I suppose he wasn't so comfortable) and then stammered something. Hastily, PanJie walked us out of the room. I asked, "PanJie, what did he say?" This time, I intentionally addressed "PanJie" loudly and clearly, indicating my change of attitude towards her.

She was of course, very pleased to hear that. But to my question, she only smiled bitterly and said, "What else can Baba say? All the same old stuff, such as no need to worry about him, he can always rely upon his Communist Party and the Chinese government."

Right after that, PanJie made a funny face behind Marianne and in order not to let Marianne understand, she said to me in Changsha dialect, "Rely upon Party and government, all words and words only. When it comes to reality, for instance, often I went to Father's unit for help but couldn't even find the one who was in charge."

After my continued questioning, PanJie had to tell me the truth. The truth was, DanXin simply didn't tell Father that it was *ME* who found a back-door to get him out from the corridor of a general sick house into a room of the High-Rank Cadres' Ward. Instead, he told Father that it was *his Party* and government that gave him "special care." That touched my father very much, saying that he had worked for the Party and government all his life and finally received such an honorable result. That proved the Party's warmth and the superiority of the socialist system.

"If he didn't know it was my hard work and ability to cause all these things to happen, didn't I do all this for nothing?" I said using a half-joking tone, although my feeling was sincere.

"We will tell him later. This is a promise. But meanwhile the most important thing is to let him rest well." PanJie patted me on the shoulder to comfort me, and to show her closeness to me at the same time.

Alright now, I have proven my ability and resolved the room problem for Father, flaunted my good English in front of him; helped Jiang LangSha escape his life-long burden while at the same time adding new content and meaning to Uncle Feng's life; taken my western woman Marianne around, from my kindergarten to my last work unit; and last but not least, (or should I say most importantly) I showed off my expensive old Italian violin to a lot of people in my hometown. I could claim the first trip back to China was a brilliant, almost perfect victory.

Following Father's order, DanXin found a very decent vegetarian restaurant in town and booked an individual room with a full table of dishes. When it was time to go, Marianne suddenly said, "I don't feel so well today. You go alone, but don't forget to bring me a loaf of bread, please."

"How could that be tolerated? The whole table of dishes is specifically ordered for you by my father, *our father*, I mean! In order to make everybody happy, *you have to go* regardless of how you feel." I dragged Marianne out, almost by force and went on with my comments, "You foreigners! Yeah, really selfish, only thinking of your own feelings and not the others."

My comments about foreigners upset Marianne, she said angrily, "You Chinese people are the ones only thinking of your own interest and pleasure, never caring for how others feel. Selfish!"

DanXin and his wife had put all of their effort into carefully selecting a whole table of the best vegetarian dishes (at least the best they could think of), in the end to be called "selfish", what would people think about it? This kind of difficult-to-explain conflict occurred quite often in everyday life between us, I got used to it, but how could I explain it to Father?

After being persuaded in every way possible, Marianne finally agreed to go with me under one condition, "Never force me to eat anything at the table." How could guests *NOT* be forced to eat in front of a Chinese table? In reality, Marianne was with tears, crying for mercy at the table, begging I not force her to eat any more. As Marianne didn't eat more anyway, the vegetarian food had lost its original meaning; the rest of the people simply put a hot pot on the table, in it, a big leg of dog meat. When Marianne saw that she was so horrified she threw out everything from her stomach that had just been forced in with so much effort.

Back at the Hotel, Marianne was lying on the bed discussing what we should do next. What she *meant* was going to the United States. But I thought she was asking me about the next day. I said "Tomorrow we could take a walk along the streets, get some small gifts that you like."

"How about the day after tomorrow?" she asked.

"Let's wait for tomorrow to think of something about the day after tomorrow, alright?" I was a little too tired to go on with the discussion.

Marianne said, with a very quiet voice, as if talking to herself, "That's a pure waste of time. If you want to spend more time with your family, I understand. If that's the case, I could probably use this chance to take a research trip to Yunnan to see the Moso minority people."

"What! Go there *again*? Didn't I accompany you there once before? You already know the people there look almost the same as the rest of the Chinese, only not as good looking. The lake is pretty but not worth seeing twice, I mean going such a long distance." I yawned. The following of what Marianne said was all gibberish to me.

"Wake up." Marianne pushed me.

"Can't you talk about the matriarchal social system of Moso people tomorrow...?" I rolled over and went on with my dream.

"No, it's a phone call, from your family." Marianne pushed me harder to wake me up.

The phone call was from my younger brother DanHen's wife. She asked me to go to DanXin's home immediately, as everyone in the family was there waiting to have an urgent discussion with me.

"What could be so urgent?" I said impatiently.

"Father wants to move out from the High-Rank Cadres' Ward." my pretty sister-in-law said.

"Who would dare move Father out?" hearing that, I was completely awake and asked anxiously.

"No one, it's Baba *himself* who wants to move out." sister-in-law explained again.

That's odd. I'd gone through so much trouble to get the old man out of a dirty, noisy, dark, crowded corridor and into a nice clean quiet single room of a high rank hospital! Why the hell does he want to move out? I apologized to Marianne and asked her to go to bed if she likes and not to wait for me. Hastily I went to DanXin's home.

An Old Revolutionary Encounters A New Problem

On my way rushing to DanXin's home, I couldn't figure out why it was my little sister-in-law who called me, when usually, if not DanXin, it would be MeiMei. However, the most puzzling question was why Father wanted to move out of the High-Rank Cadres' Ward. I certainly couldn't imagine that before the phone call from my little sister-in-law, there had been a hot discussion between all the family members.

The topic of course, revolved around Father's *new problem*. This time the problem was not that we couldn't get Father *into* a room at a hospital, but to the contrary. Father insisted on moving out of the room where he already was, in the hospital!

The trouble started when Father noticed that the name tag hanging on his bed remained, "Minister Wu". What bothered him more was that all the nurses kept calling him Minister Wu, even after Father repeatedly corrected them by telling them his correct title should be, "Deputy Commissioner Chen." Under pressure, PanJie had to tell Father the truth, that the bed actually belonged to Minister Wu. It was his second son who conquered all the obstacles and finally found the back-door to manage his lying in Minister Wu's bed. Therefore, all the nurses had received orders from Premier Liu that, "In order not to reveal the secret, no matter who is in that bed, keep calling him Minister Wu." Of course, PanJie told the truth partly to keep her promise of letting Father know that it was my effort and achievement that got him in a room and out of the corridor.

When Father learned the truth, particularly the fact that "it was his second son who found the back-door", he insisted on moving out. Saying that to accept a back-door contradicted his beliefs and principles as a revolutionary, Father stressed, "If a person gives up his beliefs and principles before death, it would be a negation of what he has been fighting for all his life. Being alive like that would be meaningless. As a revolutionary, a meaningless life is the same as being dead."

Seeing PanJie with a long face, which she rarely showed, Father explained patiently, "Everyone is going to die anyway, the only difference is how and when. My hope was to let the hospital use my body for scientific research so that I could make good use of my flesh and blood as a final contribution to the country's medical project. I thought to move me here was arranged by the Party and organization in order to receive better tests, that's why I was so pleased. In a word: I'm a Party member. I'll follow the Party's arrangement regardless if it's in a room of a High-Rank Cadres' Ward or in the corridor of a general hospital. I will obey with no complaint."

Everyone was upset, puzzled and troubled by Father's attitude in this matter, except PanJie.

However, I think even I understood more about Father than PanJie. I knew, that besides his "adhering to revolutionary principle" in not accepting a back-door, the more important factor was that he was not willing to accept a mercy from his second son, or let my conspiracy of "showing off my ability" succeed. In other words, he would rather *die* than be a loser in the hands of his opponent, which was me, his second son. This was why, when he said, "It's HIM again, doing all those things. My pure and innocent life was almost stained at the last moment." he was particularly emotional.

Under Father's strong will and insistence, the family had no choice but to move him out of the High-Rank Cadres' Ward.

To move out of a room was easy. The problem was move where, as once out of the corridor, he couldn't get back in. That was why everyone was at DanXin's home and couldn't figure out a way to deal with this new situation.

Financial Situation Of My Brother DanXin's

Finally out of that nice room at the High-Rank Cadres' Ward, Father had nowhere to go. Therefore PanJie proposed taking Father home for the time being. As I described before, DanXin's home had only two rooms, one for the host couple and one for our mother and her grandson (grandma slept on the sofa, and grandson on the floor). The small, two room home was already overcrowded. If Father moved in, where could he be put? It would only work if DanXin and his wife slept outside on the open veranda.

DanHen said with an indication, "If we could buy a commercial flat nearby, that would be the best solution."

My unsophisticated brother DanXin, didn't get his youngest brother's hint and that the words were for the pretty young wife. Smiling with bitterness, DanXin said, "Talking about nearby, right behind our building there are new apartments for sale. I could even use my working years to get a favorable discount."

The pretty young wife, who also apparently failed to understand what her husband really meant, immediately encouraged DanXin, "Why wait, buy one. What is saving money in the bank for?"

"Saving money? Where do we have money to be saved?" PanJie couldn't hold it in, "I'll count every single RMB for you. DanXin's month's salary altogether is two thousand RMB, that's twenty-four thousand RMB a year. The sum total wouldn't be enough for our son's education." Talking as she got herself a pen and piece of paper, she wrote (no wonder a former accountant). "The annual tuition is thirteen thousand RMB, board living costs at least seven hundred RMB per month, eighty-four hundred RMB a year. To put tuition and living expenses together would be twenty-one thousand RMB, plus all kinds of unexpected school fees from time to time. In addition, stationery, books, pc, etc. You count if it's enough or not!" PanJie finished writing and put the paper in front of her young sister-in-law. Probably feeling it wasn't enough, she complained, "That's what your 'Education Industry' had done for us. When you say "industrialization of education", all the oil has to be scraped from every single student, *student's parents* to be more accurate."

My pretty sister-in-law was working for the City Education Bureau. Holding a position as a middle rank leader, she, of course, immediately stood up to defend the "Education Industry" claiming, "Nowadays, every working unit is working hard for the economy. Education has always been a blank sheet, but with the high-speed development of our country's economy and consumption, people in the education field are also forced to make money. Now, if not from the students, from where will that fat oil come?"

"How could you survive with such an unbalanced income?" DanHen asked his big brother, rather worried. Brother answered helplessly, "Not dead, proves able to be kept alive."

After DanXin's landmark quotation, PanJie went on with some details, "How do we make our living? We live on my one hundred and fifty RMB monthly pension, plus six hundred RMB income from a temporary job. But recently even that six hundred are not a guarantee as I must use so much time taking care of Father." PanJie changed to a joking tone, "So I say, my brother and sister, I return what you said to me, back to you, "What's the use of saving all the money in the bank? Might as well lend it to us to buy a flat."

DanXin immediately stopped his wife, "That's something you shouldn't joke about. They have their own lives. They also need to move and pay school fees for their child. Not to mention they have already paid for most of Baba's nutrition costs..."

"And every time Mother needs presents to give for making connections, the money has also been from DanHen's pocket." The young wife bitterly knocked the head of her husband.

DanHen thought it was the time to spill it; he gathered the courage to face his wife who was in charge of the family finances and said, "In fact, what PanJie said was not entirely inconsiderable. Our flat truly is not very luxurious but rather, livable, for the time being. We could think of lending our deposit to DanXin to buy a flat first in order to solve Father's problem. We can wait for better chances later..."

Before DanHen finished, his head received a *slap* like a volleyball from his wife, "You must be out of your mind! You have two brothers in front of you, why do you need to come out for the roll of the protagonist?"

"How could you call it protagonist? This is our family's affair..." This time DanHen's mouth was blocked by the fist of his wife! The wife said to him, "You have no right to open your mouth now, wait until your earning is half as much as mine!" Said by his wife in this way, DanHen could really only shut-up. As acrobatics didn't offer a good income, all together DanHen's monthly income was just about a thousand RMB; however thanks to the "education industry" policy, the young wife received quite a good salary. In addition to her versatile abilities such as giving private lessons and writing teaching method books, she could receive a considerable additional income, "gray income" as the Chinese put it, so when we say "women's liberation", the key is turning their economic status around, in which women can make the same or more than men. This was the reason the young and little wife could hold her huge husband under her control, *completely*.

"So you tell us, what should we do with Father? Throw him in front of the hospital, outside?" DanHen said helplessly.

Silence, quiet, deadly... nobody had anything to say, even the sound of breathing could be heard. Again, DanHen's wife broke the ice, "I say... you Chen brothers, why don't you all ask your "second son" of the family? Hearing people often say so and so's relative is from abroad and brought back many presents for the family, only the second brother of your family brought nothing for me. That made my colleagues laugh at me saying, 'It's useless to have a brother-in-law in a foreign country.'"

To my young and pretty sister-in-law, I, the "brother" was only a matter of "useful" or "useless". After listening to the complaints from the sister-in-law, DanXin tried to defend me, his brother, "Please don't think that there is gold to pick up everywhere in foreign countries and that anyone can get rich as long as they get out of the country. The people abroad may have their own hardships. For instance, our DanJiu, we don't really know his financial situation. If he's strong financially, seeing the family situation, he wouldn't sit and do nothing about it. On the contrary, he has said nothing so far, it could mean that his economic situation may not be very good. Therefore, we shouldn't make difficulties for him, but try to understand."

DanXin's speech certainly didn't convince the young sister-in-law. Therefore she argued again, "No money? No money, how can he bring a fifty thousand dollar violin back home? Ask him to sell that violin. The money should be enough to buy a flat. Or is he bragging and that old ragged *thing* isn't worth much money at all?"

Not waiting for his wife to finish, DanHen said heavily, "I'd rather die than beg him for money."

The young wife dug at her husband, "No good at earning money, no good at begging for money. What a useless thing you are!" Then she turned her face to PanJie, complaining, "You see how unlucky I am, really the worst luck, couldn't stand the temptation of all his sweet words and unconsciously got in his bed, sorry, I mean got on his boat. Now I can only blame myself for being young and naive." Seeing nobody seemed to want to call me, she sighed again and said, "If you all sit there doing nothing, *I'll call.* Let me be the wicked one. What's the phone number of second brother?"

The above was the dramatic scene that occurred at my brother DanXin's home before I went there.

When I reached DanXin's home, a full table of dishes was waiting for me. I wondered how the Chinese people could eat all around the clock, regardless if it was day or night. Before I started my question, my young sister-in-law told me, "The old revolutionary of your family is facing a *new* revolution."

After DanXin narrated all the trouble, I asked him, "As our family has such a special, difficult situation, couldn't you have a good talk with your work unit, to see if they can help solve your housing problem?"

DanXin smiled bitterly, shook his head meaning my question was totally out of question, therefore unanswerable. DanHen looked up at the ceiling exposing some sturdy nose hair. PanJie was about to make some comments as young sister-in-law stepped forward, "My dear brother, abroad for all those years, how could you talk like an ancient man? At the present time in China, who would expect to get a flat from their working unit? The real estate has long been reformed and today everybody has to buy commercial housing with loans or without."

PanJie followed, repeating her family financial balance in front of me, bringing the conclusion, it's absolutely impossible for DanXin to buy a property with their financial ability, or lack thereof. Therefore, to buy a property all is left to me.

"Like a mud Buddha across the river can't ensure their own safety, in addition they very often must help that little girl called HuanHuan." DanHen added.

"HuanHuan? Who's that?" I immediately took DanHen's conversation, looking at him; hoping this question to be the start of the first dialogue after so many years. But I didn't succeed; as DanHen stood up and went out to wash his hands, he excused himself.

The following is the HuanHuan story as told by PanJie.

Story Of A Little Girl Called HuanHuan

HuanHuan was a 6th grade elementary school girl, who happened to be DanXin's neighbor. Her parents had a big fight after losing their jobs at the same time and both walked away from the home, leaving HuanHuan alone with her sick seventy-year-old grandmother.

For more than a year, part of her tuition fees were donated by her classmates and many of her clothes too. The following is a description of what a day was like for HuanHuan:

She gets up early in the morning making breakfast and lunch for grandmother as well as her own lunch box for school. In the afternoon, after school, she goes to the market picking up vegetable leaves from the ground, sometimes, if lucky, she might get a little leftover pork skin, bone or something from good hearted meat sellers.

After she finishes eating dinner with grandmother, she goes out to help some wealthy classmates do their homework (which becomes her major source of income). Sometimes she gets some small jobs from neighbors, but that she can only do during her sleep time.

Hearing that, DanHen made a painful comment, "Children from poor families grow fast. What a cruel and ironic pride of society, particularly so many years after the liberation took place in our great country."

But his young wife argued, "Yes, some are poor, but also many are rich. Like a school I know, each class five to ten out of forty are coming and going in the private cars of their parents. Kids like HuanHuan, picking up vegetable leaves for a living, is after all, a minority. Among those who can afford to go to school, picking up vegetable leaves for ones living, are of course, a minority."

Hearing that, I lamented that, "To be able to pick up vegetable leaves and make a living today, what a *'great leap forward'* that has taken place in our great country, a progress worthy of intoxication!" I said that remembering the year 1960, never mind picking up the leaves of vegetables, even the leaves of trees, bark and grasses were not easy to get, and that indomitable struggle for survival we fought with that little fat brother, the son of Minister Lee, for the right to cut wild grass for food in a public zone…

However, a person or a nation making a vertical comparison with oneself could always result in satisfaction and intoxication. Thinking back to the Stone Age, the Beijing Man lived in caves, shouldn't we be fiercely proud and intoxicated? Yet, if making a horizontal comparison with other people or nations, it might not always be the case of pride and satisfaction. For instance, to compare my house in Norway, with DanXin's home, that 14-inch "color" TV (it should be said to be "gray and yellow" TV), the refrigerator that could only be used as a cupboard and the washing machine that could cause an earthquake when used… I felt pressure or rather a sense of responsibility, perhaps it should be called, "a sense of being needed." But on the other hand, I have my *own life*, I have my dream to pursue! How could I give up my dream for others, sorry, I mean for the other people in my family, and not go to the United States to pursue my musical studies?

Seeing me abstaining from the discussion of buying a new flat, my young sister-in-law got desperate, sarcastically saying, "I always thought the Chen brothers were something, now I'm in the Chen's family and I finally got the truth. The truth is, all three brothers put together, can't compete with a small wife like me."

"Who said that?" Her remark made me furious! How could a big man, three BIG *MANS*, I mean, be pushed against a wall by a little woman?

I suddenly felt that to prove to my family I wasn't an ordinary man, but a man with special ability, ability not only in playing the violin but also with the capability of making big money, in one word, to prove that I was the "strongest" son in Chen's family, was more important than *anything else*, at least at that very moment.

Therefore, evaluating little sister-in-law's prodding tactic, I saw it as an opportunity, an opportunity that I had been searching for, for many years. An opportunity had finally come to me with the room in the High-Rank Cadres' Ward but it didn't last long enough, yet this time, an opportunity came that could put me in the role of the strongest and most remarkable son in the family for a long time, if not forever.

I immediately asked DanXin to get the bag that I had asked him to take care of for me. *I took ALL the traveler's checks, a total of fifty thousand USD and "PA", threw them on the table.* That feeling… no need to mention how "cool" it was!

It was after midnight when I went back to the hotel. In order not to disturb Marianne, I tiptoed into the room, but found she was still reading a book about the matriarchal Moso people. Seeing me come back, she asked a question that she had been waiting to ask me the whole time, "What happened?"

"Nothing, nothing important that you would understand." I tried to stall, and passed.

"Nothing, or *nothing important*, which? If you don't tell me, how can you know I won't understand? Try me." Marianne held fast.

It appeared that it wasn't automatic to pass; I had to make a simplified version of what had happened at DanXin's home, as simple as possible, *especially that fifty thousand USD part.*

I told her my version in a very relaxed tone. After hearing the story Marianne said nothing but her facial expression showed one word, "unbelievable". She put her book under the pillow, covered her head with the quilt and went to sleep.

I knew she was mad at me, but still made an effort to ease the atmosphere. I pulled the quilt up and asked. "No comments?"

"Don't bother me please; I have to get up early in the morning for Yunnan." Marianne didn't show her face but covered her head even tighter.

"What did you say? We go to Yunnan tomorrow? How could you make such a big decision without consulting with me?"

Marianne, "Wow!" removed the quilt, shouting at me, "Consult? Do you really find such a word existing in your dictionary? Do you realize what you threw to your family was not just our money, but also *our dreams*!?" Marianne got more and more agitated when she started to talk; she simply got up and started packing her bags.

"Alright, It's okay to go to Yunnan, but at least give me one day to prepare, please?" I knew nothing more I could argue, only make a concession.

"Who invited you to go to Yunnan with me?" Marianne turned off all the lights. Suddenly the conversation ended, leaving only pure darkness between us.

I knew I had no choice but to accompany Marianne to Yunnan, therefore before dreaming I thought about what I should bring with me for the trip, but after coming from my dreams back to reality, Marianne was gone.

A Winter Fire

Needing someone to talk to I made a phone call to MeiMei asking her if she could come see me at once. But she told me I had to wait until she was off work. I hung up the phone, not knowing what to do. I was restless when the phone rang again. "I knew that MeiMei would change her mind", I thought, deliberately picking up the receiver slowly, I said, "MeiMei..."

"Sister? (MeiMei in Chinese sounds the same as sister) When did I become your sister?" I recognized that voice, it was Ma XiaoMao's.

When one is lonely and isolated, they're not too fussy about whom they talk with. Ma soon came to see me at the hotel. After I narrated the whole story of the night before, the never-care-much-for-others Ma, expressed her unusual interest and sympathy.

"How much does this room cost a day?" Ma said raising a completely different issue.

"What do you mean?" I asked.

"You can stay in my place if you like. I mean, your wife's gone, you're only one man. At my place you can cook and have internet access too."

Ma, seeing I winked at her, immediately explained, "Don't get me wrong. You know me... What I meant was, you stay at my place; I stay with my husband's family as I have been doing. So that you can save some money."

I didn't realize that Ma's invitation to stay at her place was because she was afraid I wouldn't honor my promise to help her get out of the country since my father moved out from the High-Rank Cadres' Ward.

Saving money, with internet access and cooking facilities, it was indeed very tempting. In addition, staying in someone else' home, to pry at others way of living is also some people's interest. I accepted the invitation, sorted my things, checked-out of the hotel and went to Ma's home.

Although Ma's home was much better than my brother DanXin's, it was a far cry from our schoolmates Wang ShiYi and Lu XiaoBing's. The room looked a bit messy, books everywhere, but with an atmosphere of a kind of elegance. In fact, I felt quite at home. In a glass cabinet I noticed a violin and next to the violin was a framed picture of Ma and a handsome young man. No need to ask, that man must be Ma's husband, Mr. Liu KangKang. I moved half a step forward in order to take a closer look. Hey! Her husband looked a lot like a man... who? I couldn't recall at that very moment.

Ma thought I was looking at the violin in the glass cabinet and smiled shamefully, "It's put there more like a decoration. Not a very good violin, certainly in no way compares with your old expensive Italian."

That language took me straight back to the middle school year when I fought with her over who was the better violin player. After all these years the opportunity came to me. I fiercely opened my Italian violin, touched the strings to make some sound and asked, "Would you like to try?"

"Give me a break. I haven't touched a violin for years."

Seeing me taking the violin out of the case, Ma made a gesture, "Xu, neighbors are having a nap." What a huge disappointment! But that also reminded me in China how important it was to take a nap and that foreigners would find it hard to understand, except the people in Spain.

I opened the refrigerator looking for something to drink, but found almost nothing inside. Ma explained, "As a matter of fact, since KangKang passed away, I seldom stay here." When someone has lost her loved one, the loneliness was not difficult to imagine. But before I could find the most suitable language to comfort her, Ma actually added, "I'm too lazy to cook. To stay with his parents I need not do any housework." I shivered, not knowing if it was because of the cold weather or her cold, bold confession.

Ma briefly gave me instructions for the computer power supply and kitchen facilities, such as how to use the gas. When she explained the use of electric blankets on the bed, she said, "When you get up from bed you must turn it off. Nowadays lots of counterfeit products often cause fires." She walked towards the door and added, "Here's the key. About lunch, you can make your own or eat out, as you please. When you go out please lock the door. When I finish work I'll bring some food back. You can make dinner, or we can do it together." After that, the door was closed, from outside.

Since Ma was so relaxed and casual, I really started to make myself at home. I boiled some hot water and made a bowl of instant noodles for lunch. After that I found nothing else to do. After having lived so many years in a foreign country I thought I had gotten rid of the habit of napping, but I was wrong, as not long after lunch I started to feel sleepy.

I made myself at home again by sleeping in the bed. It was very cold, so I turned on the electric blanket. The bed began to warm up. I had a dream, a daydream, actually a nap dream. In the dream I met Ma's dead husband Liu KangKang. To my surprise he was the same person as one of my colleagues at the Hunan Radio and Television Orchestra.

I woke up from the dream, looked at the photo again and felt a little uneasy. Then I decided to go out for a walk.

There was a small book stall on the roadside, I stopped, took a look of some odd magazines. Not sure how much time had passed; I heard a fire engine's siren from far to near and nearer, passing me in the direction of Ma's house, one after another. I was a little curious, but still couldn't get my eyes away from a journalist report in a magazine titled, "An odd case of virgin prostitution".

I took my time returning to Ma's residence, Oh my Chairman... God! Heavy smoke hanging in the sky, and fire trucks piled up. I rushed closer. The two-story dormitory building of Ma's that was here a moment ago, was gone...

Looking at the miserable fire scene, my first reaction was, *"My violin!"*

Then I saw TV reporters interviewing the head of the fire department. The head replied, "Because the rescue was quick and efficient, so basically nobody's dead."

"Is it 'nobody's dead', or 'basically nobody dead?'", a reporter asked.

"Nobody's dead, basically." The head of the fire department said again.

"What was the cause of the fire?" another reporter asked.

"The cause of the fire is under investigation. From the current situation, we do not exclude the improper use of electrical appliances..."

No need to mention, that my fifty thousand dollar antique Italian violin, as well as all my baggage, in which were some items that had been with me for years, together with all the property of Ma and memories of the first half of her life, regardless old or new, high class or low class, east or west, expensive or cheap, had been equal materials for the fire and all were gone in that short period of time. All that was left were our two lives and what those two lives were wearing on their bodies.

When my head cooled down, I realized I must go to tell Ma as quickly as I could. Rushing on the road calling for a taxi, I found I didn't have enough money for a taxi; I rushed to a bus station. When I arrived at Ma's working unit, The Library of Hunan Medical University, she had left work early. One of her colleagues told me, "She went to a food market. She must have some very important guest coming, for normally she doesn't go to places like food markets.

I was shocked, exhausted and couldn't walk any further. I went to see DanXin. However, my dear brother had no idea why I needed his help to find a room at the most reasonable price, when I rejected a nice room at the guest house of his working unit when I first came. Perhaps he thought I regretted giving him the traveler's checks for the fifty thousand USD. However, he asked me only one question, as he already read from my face that something big must have happened, "Where's your luggage?"

"Hey, never mention that again!" I almost cried.

Not long after I got into a cheap room at the guest house, MeiMei came to see me. She told me she first went to the hotel and was told I checked out.

After I told her what had happened that day, she kept very quiet, only at the end remarking, "If I had known I would have taken a day off."

"Don't ever say that again!" I roared.

MeiMei wasn't scared; on the contrary she knew it wasn't the best time to be present, quietly she disappeared.

I was in bed, alone, what had happened in the afternoon, like a movie repeatedly showed on the ceiling. More and more I felt it was time, I had to go looking for Ma XiaoMao, but where? I had to go find her. I got up, just about to go, someone knocked at the door. Believe it or not, it was MeiMei, together with Ma XiaoMao and my brother DanXin. From their faces there was no doubt they had heard everything about the fire. *Silence, nothing but silence.* DanXin knew there was nothing he could do to help, he gave a hint to MeiMei and left Ma and I alone.

I was waiting for Ma to burst out, crying or even threaten to hang herself, but beyond my expectation she didn't cry nor say any extreme words. Instead, she opened a food box, said "Italian Pizza, you must not have had anything for supper yet."

Hearing the word "Italian", reminded me of my violin. I lost control, tears flowing down my nose spraying out. Ma was immediately infected, also consuming a stack of tissue.

In order to help my dear readers understand my feelings more, I give the following explanation. For that Italian violin was absolutely not easy to get, for anyone. In fact, it took me many years, traveling to many countries in Europe to find it. To lose this violin meant that the world would never ever hear the unique and extremely beautiful sound of that violin again; the sound not another fifty thousand dollars could buy. Really, it was not about the money, *at least not only*.

Let me put it in this way. There are millions of people in the world, but only one out of the millions is your taste and style that you would love with all your heart, and could never be replaced. If you lost this person, how would you feel?

When we both calmed down a bit, Ma sighed and said, "Something gone is gone, nothing we can do to bring them back, like, like my husband... those old photos and diaries..." She looked at the other bed in the room, and went on, "I have no idea how to tell his old Baba (her husband's father). Hey, anyway, I too am homeless and have nowhere to go; have to stay here for the night." Hearing her comments I was a little disappointed for she didn't mention a single word about my violin!

We went to bed, separately, leaving only a very faint light on, for we could easily be terrified if the room was too bright or too dark.

After a while Ma called me, "Hello", to see if I went to sleep.

"What?" I immediately responded.

Ma said, "How come you always bring me bad luck?"

I asked back, "How could you say that?"

Ma argued, "Forget? Who made all the trouble for me in middle school, finally causing my being sent to XinJiang after graduation? And this time, we meet only a few days, you see what happened..." Ma made every effort to control her emotions, she changed to a softer tone, "Now I'm cornered and have nowhere to go. You will *have* to keep your promise to get me out of the country. The sooner the better."

"To get you out won't be a problem; the problem is what to do with you after you're out?"

"I only need your help getting out, the rest you don't need to worry about. This is an agreement and promise." she said firmly.

In the room next door, someone was playing a tape recording. It was a very popular song by an American (half Chinese, half French) pop star. The song went something like this, *"Winter fire, winter fire, you are so cold and I am so hot, so my love for you is like a fire in the winter. Winter fire, winter fire..."*

Hearing the word "fire", I couldn't help jumping up and punching the wall, "Shut-up!" The response was a louder, "Winter fire, winter fire..."

Seeing me restless in my bed, Ma got up from her bed. She turned off the last light and sat by my side on the bed. She put her hand into the quilt, first touching my chest. As there was no response, she stopped. No one was in a romantic mood, or to her, it may have meant something else. Who knows?

Ma slowly moved her hand down, and down... and said, or ordered, or begged: "Bring me out, just get me out." Next door, the pop song, "Winter fire, winter fire..." went on. I nodded. Her hand stopped there; perhaps she reckoned she had reached her goal.

Under extremely abnormal circumstances, "sex" could function as a kind of effective anesthetic, at least for me at that moment. Yet why did she take the initiative of doing that? To stimulate, comfort, seduce, or to express her determination that she would do anything to go abroad? Or maybe something else much more profound? Hey, as a girl, then a woman like Ma, who never reveals her true feelings, how could I figure out what really was in her mind. Only in reality, after that fire disaster, our relationship had unprecedented variation.

After the fire, I was literately penniless, or should I say cent less. A veritable pauper, not even having money to pay for the cheapest room at the cheap guest house, or everyday food, much less a plane ticket to Beijing. To ask brother for money I just gave to the family, I would lose face, to borrow from my rich little sister-in-law would be unthinkable. What should I do, and what *could* I do?

But, nothing to worry about, as the old Chinese saying goes, "When a boat reaches a bridge, naturally it would have a pass for the boat to go on." At this critical moment, MeiMei handed me three thousand RMB. I knew that sum wasn't easy for her to save, and felt somewhat embarrassed. But she said she wasn't going to marry somebody soon, therefore was in no need of the money for the wedding and if I feel bad about it, I could just borrow it, giving it back to her later, with interest. "I'm responsible for the whole thing too. For if I had taken a day off that morning..." MeiMei joked a little. This time I dared not be mad at her, but smiled a little. Yet I knew that smile must look awful, worse than crying.

MeiMei's offer was like the old Chinese saying, "To send carbon to the people in snow", in English it should be, "A friend in need, is a friend indeed." Yet MeiMei, was certainly more than a friend.

On my way back to Norway, I had completely empty hands, but on my shoulder a tattered violin case, inside, that broken white violin I made when I was little, smashed by Father during the Cultural Revolution.

Why did I bring that violins' remains to Norway? I could think of all the reasons, reasons like, "It took too much space in DanXin's home"; or "To take a violin with me everywhere had been my habit"; or "Nothing else belongs to me that I could bring except that violin"; but all the reasons were excuses. The real meaning behind taking that broken white violin with me to Norway was probably to take my last remaining memory out of the country.

Empty handed, the most painful question at the airport, or immigration was, "Where's your baggage?" But that wasn't the worst, as before going to China, Marianne and I were about to go to the USA, and had both quit our jobs and sold our apartment. All the money we had saved for years was given to my family. Like this, after going back to Oslo and before Marianne came back from Yunnan, where should I stay? And what could I eat?

21: A TURNING POINT IN MY LIFE COURSE

Arriving at Oslo Airport, I was with no luggage, no money and no idea of what to do or where to go, and of course, no woman.

At the restroom I ran into a slim, nice gentleman. Later, I followed him for a coffee. I pretended to "happen" to pass there. After passing twice he didn't notice me and I had to say hello to him. I made up a story that I was here with my girlfriend to see some friends off. But after our friends were gone we had a little quarrel, my girlfriend simply took the car and went away, and left me here at the airport alone.

The gentleman laughed and said that was his exact same story, except his girlfriend didn't take the car. So after he looked around for a while and couldn't find his girlfriend, naturally he invited me to his car.

"Where will you go?" he asked.

Where would I go? That was a really good question. I hesitated a while, then asked him to go to the Oslo center first. When I arrived at the center, I got out of that nice man's car and realized, that although I had lived in Oslo for several years, I really had no friends and no place to go, except the violin shop, Master Crow's place.

Crow's violin shop was a two-story wooden house. The shop was on the first floor and the second floor, a living area. The loft was used as a store room for violin making materials and laundry was in the basement. Hearing that Marianne and I got lost during the trip and I lost my key to our home (he didn't know we had no home anymore), Master Crow couldn't help laughing. One thing without doubt, I had to stay in his house for a few days, until Marianne came back to Oslo, *if* she came back.

Master Crow saw my broken white violin and again couldn't help laughing. But his facial expression changed when I told him that it was made by my hands when I was a little boy. Carefully he covered my violin, jokingly he expressed his hope, "If you stay here, you will have to be my apprentice, to learn how to make violins."

Enter The Gate Of Violin Making

Staying there and eating there, naturally I had to work for Master Crow. On the other hand, I knew according to my father's condition and family situation, the money I had given, would definitely not be the last. From then on I had to send money home for sure. The question was only how much and how often?

Master Crow naturally took it as an excellent opportunity to train a successor to keep the shop going on. He not only taught me how to repair violins, but also deliberately let me receive customers. But I had a problem, a huge problem; a problem that has not been solved completely, even today. The problem was, no matter if the customer was young or old; I would never miss the chance to show off my violin playing ability.

Master Crow of course, didn't know, I did that also for another reason. That reason was, after I lost my Italian violin in the fire, I really felt like I had lost my soul and had no peace in my mind ever. So under that "show off" business, I was taking every opportunity to try more violins, hoping to find a violin that I could use, temporarily. Until one day, the most well-known Norwegian violinist visited us. I still didn't give up the opportunity to show off my violin playing. Master Crow had enough.

After the guest was gone, he very seriously said to me, "If you want get into the violin business, the very first quality you need is to *forget that you are a violinist*. You have to change your position from the front stage starring role, to the back stage supporting role. Therefore, you have to become hospitable and humble in front of customers, regardless of the customers' age, gender or playing ability."

Being hospitable and humble were qualities I lacked in my bones. However, in order not to freeze to death in the 20 degree below zero temperature, I must pretend to be hospitable and humble, at least temporarily, until Marianne came back.

Marianne came back to Oslo at last, but without a job or house what could Marianne do? Of course we all know Norway is a social welfare country and we could always go to the government's "Social Office" getting help with a place to live and food to eat, but our pride didn't allow us to do so.

We both had good education and high self-esteem, how could we put ourselves together with those losers? After discussion, we agreed that I would go on staying at Master Crow's place and Marianne would stay with her sister for the time being.

One more important reason I wanted to stay at Master Crow's place was, I couldn't find a violin to replace mine after having tried so many violins at his shop, so I was growing an idea, to make a violin by myself, for myself, again, after a few decades. If I could make a violin when I was a kid, why not now?

I formally accepted Master Crow's offer to be his apprentice. I told Master Crow that in order to learn better, I'd rather continue staying in the small room at his house instead going back to my comfortable home.

Master Crow was of course very pleased to hear that, though he guessed I must have had a quarrel with my woman. His attitude towards me suddenly hardened, saying that if I really wanted to learn, I had to listen to everything he told me. For the sake of making a violin for myself, as well as that small bed and food every day, I promised positively.

Early next morning, Master Crow woke me up; he took me to the loft selecting wood from piles of materials. He was very careful and serious, which made me a little impatient, saying "They all look to same to me." Master Crow told me, "Every piece of wood is different from the other, just like humans. First we must find the best top and back materials and then we need to make a good match of them. For just like humans, to put a good man and a good woman together does not guarantee a good couple. Therefore to choose good material and make a good match is the first step, the very basic and most vitally important step for making a good violin. For this reason, there is never too much time spent on it." He turned his back to me, got himself in the piles of wood, knocked each piece of the wood, made some marks on each piece, doing that repeatedly over and over again.

I thought what he said was reasonable and convincing, so I pretended to be patient with my face. When I started to do the looking and knocking on the wood... Hey! I started to notice some differences in the sound pitch, tone color and vibration of each piece. In this way, I unconsciously got myself into the, "selecting wood" business, seriously, curiously and energetically. Looking at me being fascinated by what I was doing, Master Crow seemed to be impressed and said, "That is more likely going to make good violins."

I took five sets of materials that Master Crow had chosen for me, to the violin making workshop. My violin making career started from there, professionally.

When I tried to make the first violin, I sawed the wood in a violin shape too harshly, so that too much wood had been taken. That meant the top, which could have been a beautiful violin a few minutes ago, was now just a pile of firewood. On my second try I was very careful, but again made a mistake on cutting the f-holes, the top wood simply cracked. That was a waste of one top wood and two weeks' effort.

The failure of two told me I must not be anxious, I must be very careful and patient with every single sawing and cutting. On my third try, I worked as carefully as I could. Three weeks passed, a nice looking white violin was born. I was extremely excited when I looked at the white violin hanging on the wall with the memory of making my first violin when I was a little kid under the instruction of Master Zhou. I could feel the pain of my injured hand years ago.

The same problem with my quick-tempered nature arose when putting on the varnish. I didn't wait for the first layer to dry. I put on the second layer, resulting in the varnish wrinkling, so that I had to wash both layers of varnish away with alcohol and start over.

At last, when the varnish was done, again being impatient, I didn't wait long enough for the varnish to dry thoroughly and rushed to put the parts on for a sound test. This left a few finger prints on the violin, permanently.

The series of failures all told me a simple fact; everything had to be done step-by-step, carefully, with skill, following its natural course. A single careless move of the knife or brush could spoil the whole thing.

My pride did not allow me to fail at what I was trying to achieve. I worked much harder and much more carefully. In the end, I reached my goal successfully, with the fifth violin. I confirmed that the varnish had dried thoroughly, nervously I put on strings. When my bow touched the strings it made the first cry, I was extremely excited, the feeling very much like the first time being a father.

About a week later a chance came to me. In Norway we had a very young and talented violinist named Yoachin, his violin broke just before his big concert with the Oslo Philharmonic. When he brought his violin visiting our shop, he saw my new violin on the table. He played it and liked it, borrowing it for a few days, then longer than a few days, then he played my violin at the concert instead of his own. And then he came with his Mama to our shop asking, "How much?"

Before I even had a chance to say, "It's negotiable." Master Crow answered, "Thirty-six thousand kronor plus consumption tax." That number was far beyond my expectation. Thirty-six thousand kroner equals six thousand US dollars! Was my violin really worth that much money? But Master Crow was serious.

When the payment was due, Master Crow took a ten percent materials fee and thirty percent for tools, parts, working space and a small profit, the rest, sixty percent, was mine! Like that, I tasted the sweetness of violin making and concretely touched the charm of money.

Sometime later, Yoachin played Paganini's Concerto with the Norwegian National Symphony Orchestra in Oslo Concert Hall live on NRK, the state television station. Following that, my name as a "violin-making master" was also in the Oslo newspaper and it looked like I was on track to be "rich and famous".

As time went by, I was more and more recognized and talked about as a violin maker, while on the other hand, I, Daniel Chen, as a violinist, was gradually forgotten. For me, it was a hard process, to transfer my self-identity from *player to maker*. But one thing was really true, during the process I found violin making more and more interesting and more and more aspects and things to learn or study. In addition, violin-making helped me a lot with my academic studies of "violin acoustics".

By the way, I never forgot my promise of getting Ma XiaoMao out of China. As a matter of fact, as soon as I got back on my feet, I put some ads in the Oslo local newspaper looking for a spouse for her. In less than a week I received a dozen letters. I removed all the too-old and too-young, too-handsome and too-ugly, too-capable and disabled, leaving two gentlemen, one fat and the other skinny. I sent the photos of the two candidates to Ma. It was up to her to take meat or bone.

Master Crow's Story

Although Marianne and I met often, we didn't live together. That didn't cause much of a husband and wife crisis as we didn't have much intimacy when we *were* together. One night, as often happened, I had what the Chinese call a "spring dream" (to have sex with someone in a dream). It was just at a very good moment when suddenly I was awakened by shouting! It was Master Crow's voice from the next room.

Not knowing what happened, I quickly ran out and pushed his door to open. I turned on the light to find Master Crow, on the floor, breathing heavily. Before I tried to help him he got up and apologized, "I'm sorry to wake you up, I just had a bad dream."

"It's alright. I was having a dream too." I said but couldn't tell him that I was in the middle of a very good moment!

Once awake, I couldn't get back to sleep so easily, so I went to the kitchen and got myself a cup of hot milk with cocoa. Again, in the middle of my enjoyment, Master Crow came and also sat at the dining table, having a cup of heavy black coffee.

Nothing to do, he started to talk about what happened in his nightmare. In the nightmare, his adopted son and daughter in Hong Kong were in danger; he was trying to rescue them desperately. But no matter how hard he hit the accelerator pedal of his Mercedes Benz the car simply would not move. Then he had to get out of the car and run, but his legs couldn't move, then he fell off the bed...That's about the story.

Master Crow finished his story, spontaneously, he asked me about my family. Not only would my family story be too complicated to tell and to understand, but also I didn't feel like talking about my private affairs, for it really hurt. Therefore I told him a made-up story, saying that I was adopted when I was very little from China to Australia.

After having heard my story and thinking I was an orphan, Master Crow probably felt it was God who had brought us together. He looked to be deeply moved and started to tell me his family history.

Master Crow was a German, born to a violinmaking family in East Germany. When he was about 10 years old World War II started. One day he came home with his dog, and found his home razed to the ground after an air raid. He lost everyone in his family except Mary, the dog. Then the little boy Crow, together with his dog, followed a neighbor, Hans, escaping to Norway. A few years later, after they had settled down in Norway, Hans returned to his homeland.

Soon Hans sent Master Crow a letter. In the letter Hans said he went to see Master Crow's old house site. The new house owner told Hans that they had found a lot of violins, bows and violin making tools as well as materials in the cellar. The new house owner thought someday the old house owner might come back for those things; therefore he kept everything as carefully as possible for all those years.

Hearing that news, young Crow, for the first time and the last time too, returned home to collect all the violin property that his family had inherited from their ancestors for generations. Back to Norway, Master Crow followed in the family's footsteps and opened a violin workshop in Oslo.

Here I need to insert a side story, the story of Master Crow's only family member Mary, the dog. After the air raid, Mary was the only family member who survived. They had been together since and never parted. But just before Master Crow was about to go back to his homeland Germany, Mary went out by herself for some time every day, and when she came back, her feet were always dirty with mud.

Master Crow thought Mary was out looking for a boyfriend; therefore he was happy and didn't pay much attention. But one day, out of curiosity, Master Crow followed the dog to a hillside area. Crow discovered that Mary was digging a small cave with her paws.

Master Crow thought that it must be some kind of dog game, so didn't care much. On the day he went back to his motherland (or should I say fatherland), Mary, for the first time in her life, refused to follow her master, even when dragged by force. Master Crow thought it was only a matter of three or four days, so he left the dog home. Crow left enough food and water for Mary. Of course Crow never expected that this time apart from Mary was to be forever.

When Crow returned back to Oslo from Germany, Mary wasn't at home. Looking everywhere possible, he couldn't find her. Finally, Crow went to that little hill and found the dying Mary in that self-made, small cave. When Crow cried for Mary, she responded with a very weak and small, snail move. Crow suddenly realized, Mary was over 15 years of age and it was her time to go to heaven. But what made Crow feel even more sad, was that when Mary knew she was going to die; she dug herself a small cave to end her life there, quietly, in order to save her master from the sadness of seeing her body.

Crow took some soil and with both hands, mixed the soil with tears, blocking the last little air hole of the cave, so Mary could have less pain before going to meet God.

Alone back home, Master Crow immediately wrote a letter to his girlfriend Margaret. In the letter he again and again begged Margaret for forgiveness, as in less than twenty years of his life he had twice lost his loved ones. Therefore, in order not to lose any family, the only way was not to make family.

Just like that, Master Crow, with all the violins, tools and materials inherited from his family and photos of Mary hanging on the walls, lived all by himself for a few decades, until the time he met me and he was just over sixty-five, a time to think of retirement.

"Until this age, I began to regret from time to time. I sometimes think, to have a family, have people to love and to worry about, is the true happiness of life!" It was because of that kind of loneliness and the need to be needed, through the Norwegian Church he got in touch with a Church in Hong Kong, adopting two orphans, a brother and sister there and financially supported them.

After his life story, Master Crow finally suggested I make peace with Marianne and move back with her as soon as possible, to have some children, the sooner the better.

In The West, Family Above All

As Master Crow said not once, "Although you are smart, get started very quickly. If you really want to take the violin shop, your skill and ability is far away from enough. So I think you'd better talk to your wife and go learn some hard skills in other European countries before I am too old to look after the shop."

Although I wasn't too sure I wanted to take Crow's violin shop, with the thought that it might help my violin playing and violin acoustic studies and in addition, as Master Crow suggested, I should move back with Marianne, (he didn't know we had no place to stay) I decided to go to some other European countries to learn some skills and knowledge of violin making.

I first went to Hungary's Liszt Academy of Music, taking part in the stringed instrument making section. During my study period at the Liszt Academy of Music in Budapest, Hungary, my instructor of violin making was Irog from the former Soviet Union and my instructor of bow making was Etzler from Germany.

Although they were from completely different countries and cultures, they shared the same quality, which was that they both loved their families above all else. Master Iroq had obviously moved from the former Soviet Union to Hungary to escape the poverty. As his wife and children were still back home, Iroq was making every effort to bring his family to Hungary. Therefore at work, other than violins, I heard the most from him about his family.

Master Etzler too, was talking about his pregnant wife very often, sometimes when he received a phone call from his wife, he would put down all his work and run back home. I remember once, a customer was about to buy his bow after trying it for two hours, but Master Etzler was constantly checking his watch. As soon as it reached 7pm, Master Etzler stopped the customer from trying more and said he must go back to see his wife. That left the customer and I dreadfully puzzled.

The next day I asked him why he did that, he answered, "Yesterday, I made an appointment with my wife at a restaurant at 7:30 pm." That answer made me even more puzzled. Then he explained, "I work for money to make my wife happy. If my wife is unhappy, money is useless and work is meaningless."

In western culture, family is regarded as the smallest component of society; therefore the stability of a society has to be based on the stability of the families. Because of this, the social system, whether cultural, legal or religious, all regard family as the most sacred. For example, if someone immigrates to Europe or America, his family would legally immigrate with him after a certain period of time. Even for overseas students, their spouses and children could automatically go where the father or mother is later.

In the West, even insurance companies offer discounts to those who have a stable family. In the United States and other western movies, all are filled with the, "family above all" value. In the western church, people address each other as brothers and sisters, filled with a family-like atmosphere and love.

In fact, family above all may not only be a common social value in western culture, but also among *all human beings*, even among most of the animals.

Yet that was not true in China from the 1950s to 1980s, for in this period, Chairman Mao and the Communist Party were above anything and everything. Next to Mao and the Party, would be the so called "people" and "work". Family was at the lowest status in Chinese society during that period of time.

According to my personal experiences, my first wife DongYa was from Shanghai and I was from Hunan. We met in Shanghai during my time at university and married in Shanghai, but after I graduated from school I had to go back to where I originally came from. Therefore we never actually lived together as husband and wife right up until our divorce. In other words, we were just a paper couple. In China, a separated couple is called the mandarin duck and DongYa and I were among the millions.

Speaking of family being the basic unit and foundation of social stability, I know of many stories that would explain China's instability at that time. It was in the 90s that I went to Guangzhou; there I met a seventeen-year-old prostitute. I asked her why she didn't want to go home. She told me that she simply had no home to go to. She was the eldest daughter of the family, with Father and a remote mother seldom at home.

After her father's death, the three kids never heard from their remote mother again. She first wanted to work as a prostitute to help her younger sister and brother. But after being caught by the police for a week, she went back home and found her sister and brother were gone. Without family members, the home was no longer a home. I thought at that time, if more families are like this, how could the society be stable?

Why was my mind so unstable? Because I was away from my family!

After Hungary, I went to more countries and met more violin making masters, Cremona in Italy, Mittenwald in Germany, as well as Paris, Moscow and short courses at two universities in the United States. It was at the violin repair and restoration course at Oberlin College that I restored the white violin I had made when I was a kid, which my father had smashed to pieces during the Chinese Cultural Revolution.

When my classmates asked me, "How come this naked thing (they didn't even bother to call it a violin) is broken like this? How could it happen?" I hesitated to tell and could only put my pharynx to the bottom of my stomach. The story of that ragged violin was beyond human imagination and only people who had gone through that period of history in China would understand.

After one month of hard work, I finally put all the pieces back in shape, the shape of a violin again. When I made some sound out of my dear "naked" violin after so many years, I found that it was the most beautiful and exciting violin sound in the world, though most of my classmates were making gestures to cover their ears and scoffing at me. I was very happy. At the moment, the happiest man in the world.

Through the violin making process I became acquainted with many violin making colleagues (now I can call them my colleagues). By working together with them, I noticed very different qualities from myself as a player. Unlike the players, snobby, show-offs, pretentious; they were simple, humble, down to earth and most of them valued their family more than anything else. They also helped me discover the interest, charm and challenge of the violin as an instrument itself and more and more I got myself into the profound art of violin making.

267

Part From Marianne

After I was re-educated by western values, "family above all", I felt I should do something for my family that I had formed with Marianne in Norway.

After returning back to Oslo from a studying trip in other parts of the world, I began to look for a house and talk to banks about loans. I wanted to give Marianne a surprise. Yet Marianne was quite upset when she found out what I was trying to do, "How many times do I have to tell you that when you do things you should consult with me?"

"I wanted to give you a surprise." I explained.

"Surprise? Indeed! I am surprised, congratulations. But I'd rather you tell me the date we go to Indiana University than having been surprised by *this*." Marianne said.

"About Indiana University, I think I won't go there for some time, or never, because I grew up quite much recently. Being realistic, we're at the age to plan our lives, to settle down, have children. I mean, just like everybody else, to be normal people having a normal life." I explained.

"*Normal?* If you're normal, why should I waste my life on you? I thought you were something special, because you have your dream..." Marianne reasoned.

"But my dream may be too far away from me and I might never reach it in our lifetime." I took the speech over.

"A man with a dream that can't be achieved is far better than a man without. I don't have as much talent as you do, so I can only be a scholar to study and research the achievements of others. But you have a gift and you should pursue and create your own art. If I were you, I would rather die in the middle of pursuing my goal, than become an aimlessness mediocre." maybe not Marianne's original words, but it's what she meant.

"What, did you say? I'm... mediocre?" I felt greatly insulted.

"What else do you expect me to call you? If you don't play violin, you aren't *YOU* anymore. Look at you, degenerated into a mercenary small business, I don't know such a person, or I really don't *want* to know such a person, not anymore." That's about it, the last words from Marianne to me that I can remember, and would never forget.

I knew it was useless to argue with her any further, because it wouldn't have any result. There was only one thing I didn't want to admit, *I am not mediocre*. Or as Marianne said, I had become "mediocre", which really meant, my mind was changing to be more pure and noble.

Marianne really wasn't the kind of woman who would be satisfied with a peaceful, stable, ordinary life. She needed to continue looking for what God was asking her to do in life. She needed to find more truth of life, of the relationship between body and soul.

About our relationship, Marianne described it like this: "We were fated to meet each other, as it was originally arranged by God, for that I have nothing to regret. But after we met, we didn't go parallel; therefore I have no choice but to go on towards a different direction. It's like two lines from different directions meeting together, but then part again, each for its' own course."

With my strong will, we bought a new apartment. Although we lived together under the same roof for a while we felt far apart from each other. Not to mention having children, as we didn't even bother doing things to make children. In reality, husband and wife remained only a formality. Therefore, from sometimes to very often, I still stayed at Master Crow's place.

The relationship crisis with Marianne made me think that without her I would be alone, helpless in Norway. That made Master Crow closer and more important to me. In order to please my master, I purposely wrote to my friend in Hong Kong, asking him to take care of the two adopted children of Crow's. My friend wasn't really happy to do so, but on my face, he reluctantly went to see the two children.

The result was ugly, as the brother and sister in the photo I gave to my HK friend were *not orphans*, but children of a social worker for a charity organization. What made things even worse was that the two kids didn't even know about the existence of their Norwegian Papa, Master Crow, who had been sending money to them every month for more than 10 years.

I hesitated for some time, wondering if it was right to tell him the truth, as I was so afraid the truth would shock my master, to death. But he didn't, in fact, he had guessed because the letters he received from the children were all too good to truly be written by children of their age. But Master Crow would rather believe everything was true than investigate. To put it this way, he was doing it more for his own need, than that of others. Besides, after so many years, the photos of the children-growing-up had gradually become a part of his life, if not the only part of his life.

Again, a good intention had led to a bad result. I meant to help him but resulted in hurting him. Although Master Crow didn't blame me in words, the atmosphere and mood between us was never the same.

That was one of the reasons I was forced to re-think my life in the future. Master Crow's personal life, again, taught me that family was vitally important, more so than anything else. Therefore I started to think, if by going to Indiana University I could save my relationship with Marianne, I should do it. Not for the sake of my life's dream and pursuing my music education after the Shanghai Conservatory of Music, but this time, for the sake of keeping our family going, the only family I had in Norway.

Although by going to the United States I most probably wouldn't be able to support my sick father back home, wasn't it true that I had my own life? Could I really let him control my life, especially after his saying, "I dislike DanJiu by nature."? (Why didn't Father like me? By nature?) Why should I change my life for such a father? Was he really worth my effort and the sacrifices I was making? On top of it all, I had already done my best, once and for all.

Master Crow learned that I had changed my mind about taking over his shop, instead going to the US. He said nothing. With a gloomy face he silently gazed at the photos of Mary on the wall, for a long, long time.

While I was busy preparing for the United States, Master Crow was also busy with something. He appeared to be taking things out of his bedroom to his car and driving somewhere, repeatedly. Since both of us were busy, we simply closed the shop for a week.

One night, I was awoken by some noise. It sounded as if he were moving things out again. The next morning, at the breakfast table, he suddenly asked me how much money I had saved for the United States. I told him about twenty thousand USD. Master Crow smiled a little, mysteriously.

After breakfast, he told me that he was going somewhere for a while and asked me not to worry about him. It sounded rather casual, so I didn't think too much about it. Soon after, he went outside to his car, waved his hat towards his shop and me, and was gone.

That was the last sight I had of Master Crow. The same day, Master Crow's accountant came to see me. He passed me a letter from Crow. *In the letter there were three things written:*

1. He sold all his property to me, his house, violin shop and everything inside, violins, bows, tools, materials, all things and everything, for the price of twenty thousand US dollars, requiring a cash payment, immediately.

2. To keep it a secret between the three of us as long as he was alive.

3. He has chosen a good place to spend the rest of his life. He appreciated our respecting his choice and we promise him never to try to look for him.

Master Crow's accountant said he had no idea why ol' Crow would sell his millions of krone worth of property to me for the ridiculous price of twenty thousand US dollars. He only knew that by doing so, it would ease the procedure and save all the trouble of non-relative inheritance legal issues and problems. What puzzled the accountant more, was why Master Crow would need twenty thousand US dollars in cash immediately, as in Norway, a high welfare country, the elderly people have an absolute guarantee for their living expenses.

Being extremely honest, the temptation of paying twenty thousand US Dollars cash to get a property worth millions, right then and there, was tremendously high and hard to resist. After a few days hesitation, I decided to leave this matter to my Marianne. I passed the money to her and said,

"For the sake of our family, it's all up to you to decide."

Marianne didn't take the money, instead she kissed me, (after a considerably long period of time she did that, I couldn't even remember when the last one was) and said, "Do as we planned. You go first, I'll stay and find someone to rent our apartment to pay for the loan and come after you."

So, the thing was set. I told Master Crow's accountant our decision and handed the keys of Crow's house to him. Of course, to this poor, poor accountant, these were the oddest things he had witnessed in his entire life and he could never understand.

Just when I was about to order my plane ticket to Indiana, a family letter from China reached me, again.

This letter was written by my brother DanXin. In the letter, besides some family affairs, he mainly told me that our younger brother DanHen had gotten divorced. After the divorce, DanHen decided to quit his job in acrobatics and work as a cook in a Chinese restaurant as he had always wanted. (Later he became a very good chef in a nice restaurant in London) That meant that for quite some time, DanHen was unable to give Father sufficient financial support.

Suddenly the scene of Father lying in a steel-wire-net bed in the corridor of a hospital came to my eyes. That tragic image was so strong and so impactful that all my resentment of Father was temporarily blurred.

On the surface, it was such a simple family letter that changed my entire direction in life. However, from the inside, it was a very complex and difficult process. Think about it, the world leading violinist Kyung-Wha Chung's heartfelt advice didn't change me from pursuing a violin playing career; Master Crow's life hope and property didn't change me from pursuing a violin playing career; but finally, it was the image of Father lying in a steel-wire-net bed in the corridor of a hospital that changed me from pursuing a violin playing career and woke me up from the dream of becoming a world class violinist, to live in a realistic world of making everyday money.

I went back to Master Crow's accountant; put the twenty thousand dollars cash on the table and asked for the keys in exchange. Of course I did it all by myself, alone, without consulting Marianne. I thought if she wanted her kiss back, I had to kiss her.

The next day, my shop, Daniel Violins, was open for business. All my American dreams, my career as a violin soloist, *became history.*

Four years with Marianne also ended there. She left me, for a reason not difficult to understand, especially since it was not at the time when I was poor, but on the contrary, when I started to make money. But Marianne certainly didn't think the same way most people would. To her, she left me because I had become poorer and poorer in spirit. There were of course, other crises in our relationship apart from that.

I was far away from the country I came from, alone in a foreign land, living a solitary life like an ascetic monk, for as long as another four years.

From A Violin Player To A Violin Maker

I have the kind of character, or quality that is... no matter what I do, I take it very seriously and professionally. I also apply this to my violin making of course. Since I took over the violin shop, gradually and continuously, one by one, I had made over a hundred violins. Under the encouragement of one telephone call from Master Crow, I sent two violins and a viola for the 1993 International Violin Making Competition. The results were promising. Both of the violins went to the final and the viola had gained a certificate of diploma.

From then, I began to be in the newspapers from time to time, on the radio or television. The strange thing was, all that didn't make me feel fulfilled. It was probably due to two reasons. First of all, this "good" was my violin making, rather than violin *playing* that I had struggled to achieve for many years. The second reason may be far more important than the first reason. That was, the "violin making" made me walk out on the world of four strings, from the art of violin playing, the small micro-world in the ivory tower, to see and live in the immense, vast world outside.

For instance, the word "make", let's take a look what others have been making. Throughout history people have made the Grand Canal at Babylon, the Pyramids, the Great Wall... today, people make cars running on the road, or vehicles flying in the sky, or even out into the universe. All modern civilizations have made cities; in the cities we have various buildings, gardens, computers etc. In short, just take a look around us. Is there anything that is not made by people, by people other than me? But what have I made? A violin, which is precisely a wooden box that can make a musical sound. What is a violin to the society as a whole? To put it nicely I'm a violin making artist, speaking in reality, I'm no more than a small carpenter or a craftsman!

To make it simpler, after my identity shift to violin maker, I started to realize my real position and weight in society. Moreover, because the heavy burden as a "violinist" had been lifted, I gradually lost my desire to show off in front of others, becoming simpler, humbler. With a broader view of the world, I gradually became aware that the whole vast music world I had been intoxicated within for the last twenty years, itself, was just a very small part of human society. The sacred and noble music was after all, entertainment.

The more I learned, the more I realized, that apart from my four violin strings, I really knew very little about the outside world. Since being yanked out of that fantasy art world, I needed to learn how to live in the real world, from scratch. I had to learn many basic skills and a lot more about *real life*.

Gradually, I had a new vision of life: I should not, like in the past, "take the violin as the purpose of my life", but take "learning violin making as a means of learning other things", to go on seeking and finding some new life content and lifestyles, to enjoy life in its various flavors.

In short, the violin business brought me to another world. I had the chance to meet many different people and see new things. With no woman around me, and especially no longer needing to practice the violin for hours each day, I suddenly felt I had a lot of free time. To pass the time, I read a lot of books, rented many videos and participated in social activities as much as I could.

For example, on Sunday morning I would surely go to church. By that, little by little, I came to believe in the existence of God. That rationale change, made me start to think about the true meaning of life. Gradually I became aware of how ignorant and selfish I was. At the same time, I more and more appreciated the importance of family and realized I was lacking the most important qualities of human nature, "love, forgiveness, tolerance, humility, virtue" and so on.

I started to dislike myself and felt obliged to re-learn how to behave in society. Through a cycle of self-criticism and re-education, I had the feeling that it was God who sent my father to block my way on a continuing slide down towards the abyss of the narrow violin world.

One thing I must make clear, is that when I said I don't play violin anymore, I didn't mean I no longer touch the violin at all. I only gave up my life's goal of being a professional violin virtuoso. In reality, when I had time, I would always play for enjoyment.

There is one more side story worth mentioning before I end the chapter. One day, an elderly lady named Christiana Olsen came to my shop with an old violin. She passed the violin over to me, which had been with her all her life, together with her touching life story.

Lady Christiana's violin and her life story aroused my interest in "re-playing" the violin. (Ms. Christiana Olsen's story, I wrote a book about. "The Violin Lady", written in Chinese, was published in Taiwan. Later, I spent three months at the film school of USC (Hollywood) writing a movie script in English, titled, "The Christiana's Violin"). Of course, this time, the so-called "re-playing" of the violin was not to be used as a profession, but as a hobby, so I didn't have much psychological stress and burden. I felt relaxed and happy, as playing the violin was no longer for fame, but simply the expression of music and the love of life.

I invited my old partner, pianist Miss DanDan, to Norway; together we made a CD of my favorite classical violin pieces. Following that, I worked with a Norwegian pop violinist, Leslie Egerer and made a CD of some popular songs. We have been music partners since and eighteen years later, Leslie became a Hollywood music star and I share the honor with him.

I could feel that I had changed; become cheerful, humble and even began actively contacting my family in China, especially after I lost my own Norwegian family with Marianne. The family in China was the only one I had.

Finally, I would like to mention Master Crow. In the beginning he made calls to me, as he never told me his number. Gradually, the phone calls became less and less frequent, until there were none. I quite often imagined how my Master Crow would end his life, like his beloved Mary in an unknown cave?

22: THE SECOND RETURN HOME

Back To China Again

After my violin shop in Oslo was on track for some time, I received a letter from MeiMei. It said, "Your father is dying, this time it's for real."

I made an international call to my brother DanXin and learned that Father was again, needing an urgent surgery. Right away, I decided to betray the Norway's May Music Festival (May Music Festival is the best season of the year for business) and return to China.

This time I didn't bring an expensive old Italian violin, instead I brought the violin I made when I was young, which had been smashed by my father during the Cultural Revolution. I had restored it by myself again in a US college, with the idea of taking her back to where she was originally born, the place she belonged and along with her, of course, quite a bit money and the determination of overcoming the difficulties with my family.

When I heard the sound of the aircraft engine on my way back to China, it reminded me of my first time abroad many years ago. That was the time I heard the engine and had the thought in my mind, "Now I'm a violinist, I'm a fine person, I won!" This time I had to change the sentence however, "Now I'm not a violinist anymore, I'm not a very nice person, I lost!"

But thinking about it twice, I decided I should never call myself a "loser". For instance, in this case, it was true I had lost as a violinist, but by doing that, I had lost handcuffs at the same time. I became free. Free to do whatever I wanted, read, write, travel, make friends, learn to abandon vanity and build relationships and enjoy life. Indeed, if I thought of it this way I was a big winner.

Hey, come on, one can say whatever one wants to say and however they want to say it, as long as it feels good, right? Sometimes, the spirit of AQ is very great and useful. (AQ is a Chinese figure who loses all the time but later always finds a good way to comfort and satisfy himself. In China it's called the Spiritual Winning method.)

After the meal on the plane, I yawned, wanting to take a nap, but just couldn't. My entire mind was obsessed with one word, "loser". Little by little, I started to realize that for all those years, I only fought with Father on the surface but inside, what I really needed to win was his respect. Maybe not only respect, more perhaps, LOVE. A word we were not used to, nor was it familiar among Chinese society, at least in my family.

The First Thing I Did When I Arrived In My Hometown Changsha

As soon as I landed at the Changsha airport, I ran out to meet MeiMei and DanXin's best friend Guo, just like the first time I returned to China. My brother DanXin was too busy in the hospital taking care of Father to meet me at the airport.

"Go straight to the High-Rank Cadres' Ward." I ordered Guo as if he were driving a taxi.

"How do you know your father is staying at the High-Rank Cadres' Ward? Someone told you?" MeiMei asked, with a tone of jealousy.

"What? My father's already staying at the High-Rank Cadres' Ward? How did he get in?" I was surprised.

"If you don't know, why did you say 'Straight to the High-Rank Cadres' Ward?' " MeiMei laughed a little, but couldn't cover her jealousy.

"I wanted to go there because I thought I must talk to Premier Liu to get a back-door. This time I had made up my mind, no matter what my Baba says, I would keep him there, if I could get him in." I told the truth.

"I thought you knew everything." MeiMei said. "You don't need to talk to Premier Liu. In fact, after you left us last time, Premier Liu made phone calls from time to time asking about your father's situation. This time, it was Premier Liu who actively took your father into his High-Rank Cadres' Ward, with your father's name."

Then MeiMei explained that it was Premier Liu who told Mother to talk to Father's work unit and have them ask Premier Liu for a special favor for Father. Then the hospital, based on the work unit's request, gave Father the special offer of a bed in a single room at the High-Rank Cadres Ward. He even persuaded Father that it was all arranged by the Party and had nothing to do with him. Besides that, Father's body was already too weak to make decisions and do things by himself.

"That's very strange. Premier Liu used to be known as a leader who adheres to his principles. How come this time..."

Before I finished, MeiMei stopped me with a jealous tone, "Because you got his daughter-in-law to Japan."

"What? Ma XiaoMao went to Japan?" I was even more surprised with this piece of information.

"Not went to Japan, but is going to Japan soon. Everyone knows you arranged that, so no need to cover up anymore." MeiMei said.

Followed Guo adding, "You and Premier Liu 'Help each other' (a very much used saying within the Chinese community). Besides, as the popular proverb goes, 'man in power, who doesn't use it in time, will find it useless when the time is over.' "

Since Father was already in the High-Rank Cadres' Ward, I didn't need to go see Premier Liu immediately, but rather go see Ma XiaoMao first. Therefore I said to Guo Xiong in a conversational tone, "Then how about we not go to the hospital, perhaps I should go where I'm going to stay first?"

"Wherever you want to go, it's entirely up to you. Which hotel, name it?" Guo Xiong asked.

"Perhaps I should go to my brother DanXin's place first, to see his arrangement." I said.

"Your brother's arrangement? Ask me, I know better, to his work unit guest house, before. No doubt about it." Guo Xiong said.

"Why guest house again, my brother bought a new apartment, didn't he?" I said remembering I had left money for him to buy a new apartment last time.

When I mentioned the new apartment, Guo suddenly switched his power off, no more response. MeiMei took over, "I thought that too, that's why I got the key from PanJie."

When Guo's car entered DanXin's working unit, the Hunan Medical University, he asked, "Where first, I mean to your mother's place, or your brother's place?"

"What? How come my mother and my brother don't live together?" I suddenly had a sense of being cheated. Didn't I leave the money to buy an apartment so that they could live *together*?

"Your brother's new apartment is on the fourth floor. It wasn't that he wanted to buy an apartment on the fourth floor, but got it by drawing-straws. Even after offering money, people wouldn't exchange it for the first floor, for the simple fact that there are just too many benefits to living on the first floor. For instance, people can run a business by just opening a window, or raising some chickens to lay eggs or planting some vegetables. Some people even dig a basement and use it as a store room." Guo Xiong explained.

MeiMei added, "Fourth floor, how could your parents climb every day? Fortunately, the working unit let DanXin continue renting the old house he used to live in, so that your parents, now only your mother, could go on living there."

So that was the story. It sounded okay. I hesitated as to whether I should first go see Mother or DanXin's new home. To be honest, I wouldn't really like to go see my mother alone. For if I had, what could we have talked about when I really had nothing much to say to her? But if I didn't go see her first, it just wouldn't sound right, especially when outsiders had already initiated the issue. By accident, or perhaps MeiMei guessing what was on my mind, she suggested, "I think it's better to go to DanXin's new home first, as his mother is most likely visiting his father at the hospital."

Thanks, MeiMei!

The New Chinese Homes, Palaces Surrounded By Garbage

Before I say anymore, I must make it clear that what I wrote happened in the 90s. Nowadays, China has improved *very* much.

On the way to DanXin's new building, some private cars were parked haphazardly along the road. In front of the building, each unit had a huge iron gate. MeiMei opened the iron gate with keys.

The passageway was filled with bicycles. Walking side-ways to the stairs, I was given a warm welcome by all kinds of garbage, cigarette butts, sputum etc. With a scene like this, I thought to use the Chinese word, "new building", was somewhat a distortion of the language. At each dwelling there was a trash can in front of the door, as if standing guard. After seeing 8 guards, we finally made it to the fourth floor. MeiMei opened the door for me but didn't let me in, because, "Change shoes first." I was stunned by the sight inside DanXin's home.

DanXin's home had indeed changed, "from a bird gun to a cannon" (a Chinese expression). A huge living room paved with smooth, shiny marble like an ice rink, a massive genuine leather sofa, new furniture and luxurious chandeliers…

"Ah, he spent my money like that!" I blurted out.

However, MeiMei explained that nowadays all new Chinese homes are like this; my brother's new home was actually below average. Today, most middle class Chinese family homes, (after stepping across the garbage on the stairs), are of an exaggerated luxury.

As soon as I put my things down, I suggested we go see Father. Though MeiMei said it might be a bit too late, she immediately called the hospital. Of course it was PanJie who received the call. Just as MeiMei guessed, PanJie said, "Today is a little too late, as Father is resting. Come tomorrow morning, not too early, not too late. DanJiu must be tired too. Just take a break; I'll come back soon to cook."

Since I didn't need to go see my father right away, I could use the time to go see Ma XiaoMao, to ask her about my father's room, how long he could stay and whether she had some new demands. Of course I wouldn't forget to mention the two Norwegian gentlemen I had introduced to her.

I took a look at MeiMei, looked at her clothes, very ordinary clothes, but I commented, "Nice clothes, uh, you have very good taste."

That very common compliment to women surprised MeiMei. She stared at me, "What's the matter with you today, is the sun coming out from the west?" MeiMei said, looking as if tears would fall.

Frankly speaking, I didn't expect a simple compliment would make MeiMei so emotional. I quickly tried to change the subject and escaped alone for Ma XiaoMao's.

Ma XiaoMao Did Not Forget Our Schoolmate Flute Chan

When I met Ma, the first thing she told me was, that in fact, she had been long preparing her way to Japan. Going to Norway was only a backup, just in case she failed to go to Japan. Therefore when she got her visa and was ready to go to Japan, naturally the rumor was that I had caused it. She felt no need to explain and just let the rumor be.

"I appreciate so much your helping my father. I don't know how to thank you?" I asked for her demand.

"That's not the problem; the thing is, I'm not so sure how long the hospital can keep your father." Ma said.

"What do you mean?" I got nervous, afraid, wondering if I could meet Ma's new conditions.

"Your brother didn't tell you? Your father's work unit didn't pay the full medical fees in time, with the argument that your father isn't actually a high rank cadre, so only the fees of an ordinary hospital level can be reimbursed."

"What? The government has its policy." I didn't have more to say. As the Communist Party's policy states, all cadres who took part in the revolution before 1949 will have full Medicare covered.

"That's right, the government has its policy, but the local government has their ways of playing around that. (A very popular and vivid description in Chinese society.) This isn't only your father's problem; it has become a phenomenon for many retired senior cadres. You just got back, have no idea about the country's domestic problems. Staying longer you would find out a lot of things." By end of the conversation she hadn't put it into words, but her facial expression said, *"You owe me."*

"How could I repay you?" I didn't want to owe people.

"Repay me, oh no, I'm alright. But if you have the chance, and ability, I would appreciate your giving our old schoolmate Flute Chan a little help." Ma revealed her true hope.

"Flute Chan, wasn't he happily rooted in XinJiang?" I remembered that once Ma had told me.

"Don't make fun of him, that's too cruel. You don't think he's poor enough, both in money and in life?"

After an explanation from Ma, I learned Flute Chan's health broke down and he returned to Changsha. As XinJiang Construction Troupes were supposed to be part of the Chinese army, the retired people should have social benefits, which includes Medicare. As he couldn't get any, he went to Beijing together with other petitioners asking the top government for Medicare and other benefits they were entitled to, yet every time, he was caught and sent back. He was now making a living selling roast mutton by the road side.

Stocks And Family

Back to my brother DanXin's home, MeiMei and PanJie had already prepared dinner, but DanXin wasn't back yet. I of course, asked about Father's situation. PanJie shook her head with no words. MeiMei explained to me, "The doctor said your Baba would find it difficult to recover, he can only be maintained."

MeiMei's letter had said the same thing, but not until then did I know what she wrote, "Your father is dying, this time for real", *was for real*. Father's illness, cancer, no hope, hopeless, what the doctor had said, "maintain", meant we were actually counting the days towards death. As the situation was clear, what more could be asked?

PanJie wanted to change the heavy atmosphere; she turned on the TV set, a 28-inch full color TV. The TV was showing a very popular Japanese program, the same program I watched from time to time. The strange thing was that the Japanese host in the program I saw outside of China was quite old, while on China's TV he was still a young fellow. I noticed what the audience wore in the program and then understood, that was a program made decades earlier. The odd thing was that the Chinese would easily take what appeared in the TV program, which was out of fashion in the west, as current fashion and imitate.

My brother DanXin came back. Greeted me briefly and put the television remote control into his command. He changed the channel to see the stock exchange information. "How could it drop again?!" DanXin's face turned pale.

Although I knew almost nothing about stocks, still, I had read some articles on the Internet, saying that China's stock market is a man-controlled business, in which means and tools are used by a small group of people to take money from a vast number of people. China's investors were doomed to suffer from the start. Simply imagine that China's stock market is a golden trap, into which the people *want* to jump.

The more I talked, the worse DanXin's face became. I wasn't paying any attention to how my brother looked; as I had no idea stocks had anything to do with him. I only wondered why I was talking about stocks while MeiMei was constantly interrupting me and PanJie too, kept asking me to eat more. What surprised me was that as soon as dinner was over, the always midnight man DanXin, suddenly said he was tired and wanted to go to bed early. That was a great disappointment to me when I was right in the middle of my chatter, in a very good mood.

"OK then, you go to bed first, we'll go on enjoying our talking." I said to my brother.

"How can your brother sleep if we talk here?" PanJie said.

That made me pay closer attention and look around DanXin's new home. A large living room with two bedrooms, a kitchen and bathroom. One bedroom for brother and his wife and one for their son. There was obviously, no place for me.

"If that's the case, I could, could stay at the guesthouse where I used to stay." PanJie quickly replied, "How could that be? Before we had no place, you had to stay in the guest house, but now we have a place, especially, especially…" PanJie stopped there.

In fact, I originally thought to stay with my brother's family because I wanted to show my brother how greatly I had changed, changed to care for the family. I looked around again, made up my mind and announced, "I will stay in my nephew's room."

"Where does your nephew sleep?" MeiMei laughed. "He can sleep in the living room. He's just a kid, nothing to worry about." As soon as my voice ended, PanJie disagreed, "No, no, son is very busy with his studies during the day at school and in the evening he has piles of homework. Therefore he absolutely needs his place. So just listen to my arrangement: DanJiu, sleep in the master bedroom, DanXin and I will sleep in the living room."

After going back-and-forth and my repeatedly stressing that the living room was closer to the restroom and how important that was to me, the final decision for me to stay in the living room, was reached.

DanXin went to bed early. Listening to my bragging, my nephew with his mouth half open, was dragged to bed by his mother. MeiMei made an excuse and left. In the living room, only PanJie and I were left. I didn't feel like boasting in front of just one woman and said, "You may go to bed too. I'll just watch a little TV." Strangely she didn't go to bed, instead, muttering something about my brother and a huge loss in the stock market.

The story goes like this. DanXin didn't use the money I left to him to buy the new apartment. For he had guessed my money didn't come easy and thought I might need it someday urgently, especially after the fire. He had a talk with DanHen.

DanHen had a long negotiation with his wife, even promising to quit his job with the Acrobatic troupe straight away and go to work as a cook in order to make more money. The young wife agreed to lend money to DanXin for a certain period of time so that he could buy a new apartment.

After I returned to Norway, I wrote to DanXin that I had given up violin playing and inherited a huge property from Master Crow. DanXin started thinking of using the money I left him to return what he owed to DanHen's wife.

But things didn't go as planned.

Just before DanXin was about to return the money to DanHen's wife, he heard some very attractive news from his best friend Guo Xiong, that he had gained a lot of money from the stock market. With that kind of charming story of easy money, it was just too attractive to resist.

After repeated ideological struggle, my brother decided to give it a try. Just like millions of other Chinese, he thought "gain" was the only word when it came to the stock exchange business. He made a very nice plan, to use my money to gain and then to save my money, and only use the profit to re-invest.

My brother was careful and conservative; he started with a small amount of about a thousand US dollars and within a very short period of time had gained a two hundred dollar profit. DanXin got very excited and put the rest of the fifty thousand dollars into stocks all at once. Then, the Chinese stocks suddenly fell... down, down, down, down, every day down, always down, including the day I was there. My brother had lost half of what he invested, not knowing when he could get out.

Sleeping on the sofa bed in the living room, I felt full of thorns, unable to sleep, wondering why and how my brother could get himself into the stock exchange business. Thinking of the money lost, the money I had worked very hard for, giving up my life plan of studying in the United States, the money I gave instead to solve the family's crisis. Doing so altered my life course and my brother; he simply took it and gambled. The stock exchange business *is* gambling, isn't it, especially China's?

The deeper I questioned, the more pain I felt. The more I thought, the quicker my blood circled. With the quilt I felt hot, without, I felt cold. No matter what I did, I just couldn't get comfortable enough to sleep. Unable to sleep meant more thinking, from heartache to anger. Imagine, my brother, the world's closest blood relation, my dearest person, the highest trust, how could he do such a big thing without asking me?!

I was so upset, distressed, disillusioned; suddenly I felt that in this whole world, no one is reliable. On second thought, that might not be completely true. How about MeiMei? Is she not reliable either? That can't be... why has she not gotten married to someone, anyone? Is she, I mean, come on... me? That couldn't be...

Gradually, I was in an old-fashioned black and white film, in an old European town. I walked to an intersection and made a right turn. An old wooden house appeared in front of me. In my real life, that wooden house was not any house I had owned or had been in, yet in the dream I was so familiar with the house, I knew it all, exactly, the front gate, the wooden stairs leading to the second floor. On the second floor were my parents and several brothers and sisters.

Those people were not people I knew or had met in real life, but I recognized them well as my family in my dream. They all had European faces. I looked in the mirror and found I also had a European face. "That's strange, how did my face become like this?" I asked my family in the dream. But everyone in my family looked at me, surprised, saying, "How did your face suddenly turn Asian?"

Could anyone explain this phenomenon to me? As I said, everything appeared in the dream, that European town, that wooden house, those members of the family; I had never seen or met in my real life. The question being, how was all that information stored in my brain?

While I thought about it, I was still in my dream. It was true that while in a dream I could tell myself that what happened before was just a dream. My dream continued. In the dream at that time, Marianne appeared and told me: "All you have seen in your dream was your previous life, to be precise, the soul of your previous life. The human body can only live once, but the human soul never dies. When someone dies, the soul attached to the body leaves the dying body, waiting for the next human body to attach to. The Chinese belief is, "soul reincarnated", the birth of every life, every family formation, are acts of God, fate, or destiny. So, fate is not a coincidence, but God's will. If we don't treasure it, we will be punished by God. When we die, our soul must go to Hell. God would lock up our souls, probably just like we humans are locked up in prison for crimes...." When my dream came to this point, I felt my body falling very quickly, "pop" I was down to the seventh level of the hell, extremely cold, scared and in pain!

I woke up and found myself rolling from the sofa bed to the marble floor. No doubt cold and painful. Before I continue my story, I would like to ask my readers: Have you ever had such dreams of meeting people or being in places or witnessing events that you have never seen in your real life? If so, how do you explain where this information came from in your brain? In addition, have you also had a dream to dream experience? So-called, "dream in dream" is while dreaming, you could tell yourself that was not true, you could force yourself to wake up from one dream and continue with another dream?

I turned on the living room light; to exploit the nearness, I went to the bathroom. Sat on the toilet, recalling the dream I just had. Yes, a birth of every life, every family formation, are God's arrangement, a fate or destiny, therefore we should appreciate it. Compared with fate, what are stocks about? Some kind of paper, nowadays not even papers that we can hold, touch and feel, but some numbers on a computer screen. When the PC is off, everything is gone.

I habitually consumed some toilet paper though nothing came out of my stomach. Out from the bathroom, I found DanXin sitting in the living room. I apologized that I had occupied the toilet for too long a time.

"I'm not waiting for the toilet." DanXin said.

"But why did you get up in the middle of night? Are you afraid that I would fall into the toilet?" I tried to show my sense of humor.

Yet DanXin certainly was not in the mood to appreciate my humor. After a stalemate for a moment, I felt the time and air begin to solidify. I knew the atmosphere was no good, I told myself that I had to find a better joke. "You know...I mean...I say..."

DanXin immediately responded, "Anything you say, I will listen. You'll feel better when you pour everything out."

"I just want to say... what was that? I forgot. Or you say first." I declined too.

"OK.", DanXin took a deep breath, gathering the courage, "About the stock thing, I know...But don't worry; I won't use any of your money, in time all your money will be returned to you. This is a promise."

"You think I care for the money?" I blurted out; my voice filled with heartache and anger, revealing that I actually cared about the sum of money very much. I said it again, "You think I ONLY care for that money?" As soon as I said that, I realized that I should actively show a "family first" attitude and immediately changed my tune, "Money is of course important, but our brotherhood is more important." I felt a little uneasy after saying that. In real life, often, for we Chinese, emotional language or affection is not easy, though it's from ones true feelings and heart.

"Forget it, forget it, not only have you lost my money, but also disturbed my sleep. Go back to your bed, never mention those, stock...things, again." I hit my head to the pillow, adding, "Turn off the lights, please." Lights were turned off. I heard the sound of my brother shutting the bedroom door.

Having just turned my body to a more comfortable position, I heard the sound of DanXin's bedroom door open again and then the very unfamiliar, small but sincere voice of my brother, *"I'm sorry."* I hastened to snore loudly like a huge pig. Suddenly, I felt very warm, from my heart and throughout my whole body.

After that, we never talked about the stock thing again, as if nothing had happened, though from time to time I've felt some grievance. It's not fair, not fair at all, that my brother played stocks and I paid for it.

The next morning, DanXin and his wife got up early, but I still pretended to sleep late to show them that I was comfortable, though the truth was, I was not, not at all comfortable.

At the breakfast table, I put the money I brought for Father on the table, saying: "I've heard Father's work unit failed to pay the full medical fees to the hospital. We can use part of this to pay for it." After saying that, I pushed the money on the table towards DanXin's direction. I did that, of course, to show my respect to DanXin as the leader of the family, and also, that despite the stock trouble, I hadn't changed my full-trust attitude towards him. DanXin of course, didn't want to be in charge of the money; instead suggesting I hand it to Father directly. I understood his position and feelings, besides, it was an opportunity for me to show my feelings in front of Father, maybe the last opportunity.

"So, let's go to the hospital immediately." I proposed. "Every one of us needs to work in the morning, so let's go together in the afternoon." said PanJie.

"Then who's in the hospital taking care of Father?" I asked.

"Mama." PanJie answered. By the way and tone she spoke, I felt PanJie's warmth towards Father had cooled down to a certain degree. However, even if that was true, it wasn't difficult to understand as, "chronic illness loses the best child."

PanJie, as a young woman, had spent so much time and energy, over so many years on my father, a physically destined to disappear old body, how strange it was!

PanJie didn't notice I was thinking, she went on making arrangements, "In the afternoon DanHen will come. The hospital bed is too hard. I borrowed a three-wheel canteen vehicle. DanHen and I will go buy a sponge mattress for Father first. After that I will call you, then you can come to the hospital.

MeiMei, Silly?

DanXin and his wife had gone to work and I was left home alone. I was bored for I had nothing to do. I switched the PC on. Talking of computers, it really is a very good way to soak up time. As soon as connecting to the internet, we get into a vast world, or fixing a minor problem with your computer could also take up hours.

When the computer was on; the QQ (the most used Chinese communication network system, similar to Messenger) showed MeiMei was online.

"Hey, it's DanJiu, is that you, MeiMei?" I wrote.

"4d4d." The other side replied, meaning "yes yes" in Chinese.

"What're you doing? If nothing, we'll go out, okay?"

"!!!???" MeiMei replied.

"How about going out for a movie?" As soon as I sent those words, I felt that these words, that I had used to ask young girls for a date, were quite, out of date.

"hhh, 886." MeiMei off-line.

I could guess 886 was Hunan dialect meaning "bye-bye luo", but what was that "hhh"? Was it laughing "ha ha ha" or Chinese initials for "good good good", or Japanese HHH, meaning to "have sex"?

When we met I asked MeiMei what she meant by "hhh"? She said she meant "hum hum hum", to express her surprise or that it was beyond her expectation. She said years ago she had asked me out for movies, but my reply was always, "Movie, why? That's the best way to waste time."

To show my sincerity, I insisted on taking her out. I brought enough RMB, plus a credit card. Together we went to a Japanese owned shop in the center of Changsha city called "PingHeTang." When we saw cosmetics, I asked her if she wanted any. When we saw jewelry, watches, shoes, even discounted Japanese washing powder, I asked her if she wanted. MeiMei looked very happy but wanted nothing.

Every time I asked her, she used her hand to touch my forehead. I thought something must be wrong with my forehead. I found a mirror by the side of a photo place. I looked at myself in the mirror, nothing seemed to be wrong about my forehead, no dirt, no hair, sorry, some hair. She laughed and laughed. Eventually I had to ask her why she was touching my forehead all the time. Her answer was, "I touch your forehead to see how high a fever you have, because you must be very sick, or abnormal today!"

We spent about an hour there without buying anything. I felt very bad for I had spent no money, so I suggested: "Let's find a good place to have lunch."

"I rent a place, we can cook there." MeiMei's tone left no room for negotiation.

When I raised my hand calling for a taxi, she told the driver it was a misunderstanding, as I was calling for a friend on the other side of the road. She dragged me to the other side of the road, a bus stopped just in front of us. Following her, we got on the bus and she paid the bus fare.

When we arrived at her place, it was a small flat in an old building. She told me it was her relative's place. As the relative bought a new place and moved out, they left some old furniture to give people the impression they were still living there, so when developers came for demolition they could demand a good price. MeiMei volunteered to stay there looking after the place for her relative, free of charge. Little by little, MeiMei brought her things into the flat, gradually the small flat became kind of her own castle.

MeiMei very quickly and skillfully made a few dishes, in which the fish soup was extremely fresh and tasty, more delicious than anything I could remember. After the meal, MeiMei only put the dishes away, not cleaning them immediately.

She took a small bench and sat in front of me, as if waiting for some action. Seeing me look a little uneasy she asked me the question, a question that she probably wanted to ask for a long time, "Why don't you have a child?" I spit out something hidden deep in my heart. I didn't have a child, because of the bad relationship between my father and I. I was so afraid if I had a child, the relationship between my child and I would be as bad. Of course, that was only part of the excuse. The truth was, I wasn't ready to have a child at that time, mentally or economically.... recalling that conservation, I really don't remember much. I only remember the impression she gave me, which was that *she could help me with that if I wished.*

That offer was really beyond my expectation. I looked at MeiMei, she used to be the small girl living next door who shared the kitchen with us, the girl we grew up together with and who we might grow old together with too. I never felt she was not one of the family. I thought it was time to say something, "MeiMei, thank you, for all these years."

Those words came so sudden MeiMei didn't know how to react. She looked at me, as if she saw something stronger.

I wanted to say more, but found no words were good enough to praise her, for so many years. "MeiMei, I say, you are really, really a little, a little bit silly. I mean…"

"No need to explain, I know I'm silly, not only silly, but very silly, a silly fool, not only a silly fool, but also ugly." MeiMei said as she made a silly grimace and then playfully, "You remember the Lei Feng Diary? 'As long as we can serve you, I am willing to be a silly fool'."

All Chinese people born in the 50s, 60s or even 70s, would know Lei Feng's quotation, "Serving the people, willing to be the people's fool." If the Lei Feng story was true, that he was willing to be a fool to serve the people, he must have a deep and true love for the people. But when MeiMei says she would like to be my fool, what kind of feeling towards me was inside her? I stared at her, "the silly ugly fool". I felt she was rather pretty…

"I wonder how is the banana?" MeiMei suddenly started to talk, in an ambiguous tone. She went on: "It should be ripe enough by now…and…and the skin should be peeled off, and ready for…?" MeiMei stopped there, timidly she lowered her head.

It reminded me during our childhood steeling a raw banana and MeiMei was forced to have it in her nose without peeling the skin… and later we were taught, we had to wait until the banana was ripe enough and peel the skin before eating. This has been an inside joke between MeiMei and me. I mentioned it from time to time to embarrass MeiMei and I always got what I wanted. But that day, MeiMei mentioned it again, certainly this had a profound meaning in it, which made me flush, and feel a little nervous and uneasy. After all we were adults then, we both knew what she was talking about. Yet I wasn't ready for that, I mean with her, as MeiMei to me, had never been a female figure, but a member of the family, in fact the closest family to me next to DanXin, but never more than that... It was from that moment I realized, to her, I might not be just a family member, but also a man, maybe more a man than anything else to her.

I wondered if we had had enough time, say, another hour or so, what would have happened. But we didn't. We had to go see my father.

About MeiMei and me, I thought we would be like family all our lives. By that point, she may have the idea in her mind that marriage with me was not possible nor important, but for a child with me, she was desperate. Yet the reality was, MeiMei remained unmarried all her life and we parted from each other not long after that, forever.

23: THE JOURNEY OF THE NEW CHINA (ANTI–COMMUNISM VERSION)

"Sending Carbon To Snow" To Father

At the entrance of DanXin's building, I met my younger brother DanHen and PanJie with a rickshaw. I was going to take the initiative and say hello to him when his cell phone rang. He exploited the opportunity to avoid making eye contact, instead speaking into the phone. Perhaps feeling it was too rude, he glanced at me and then nodded his head. That ambiguous nod could've been meant for the person on the phone or for me.

Afraid of missing the opportunity, the opportunity to re-establish diplomatic or domestic relations between two brothers after no contact for so many years, I imitated his head-nodding continuously. After the phone call ended, DanHen glanced at me again, but quickly turned to PanJie. With a friendly joking tone he said, "Something wrong with that man's neck?" In this way, the relationship between us two brothers returned to normal.

"PanJie, sorry. What could I do? My daughter has an emergency, needs me back immediately." Though DanHen was still talking to PanJie, the content was actually for me to hear.

"What can I do? You want me to drag this dreadfully heavy rickshaw all alone?" PanJie worried. "How come alone? What about me?" I captured a good moment to show the new me.

"How could we let our honorable foreign guest drag a rickshaw? That simply shouldn't happen." PanJie said and laughed. Even more cheerful was that my younger brother DanHen also laughed.

"Let's go. Go." I went up to take the rickshaw from DanHen.

"Then I leave it to you." DanHen was still facing PanJie, but the words were obviously for me. After that, he turned his body in my direction, bowed a little, walked away for a few steps, turned his head to me again, smiled and ran away.

The change of attitude towards me from DanHen made me feel high. I dragged the rickshaw running as quickly as I could, which made PanJie run after me complaining of pain in her stomach. After we bought a comparatively expensive sponge mattress, again I dragged the rickshaw running like crazy towards Father's hospital. This time, maybe a bit worried to be seen by acquaintances.

"DanJiu, the foreign VIP guest of the family, sleeping in the living room and dragging a rickshaw." The outstanding deed quickly spread to the whole family, making my parents, Father in particular, very surprised.

Having arrived at the hospital, regardless of PanJie offering her help, I took the sponge mattress by myself and went upstairs to Father's room.

When I got into Father's room, our eyes met. He made a very friendly facial expression lying in bed. His mouth moved a little, with no need for PanJie to interpret as I knew he was trying to say, "You came back." Frankly, my father's face looked rather bad, truly ugly, but I can't re-call when he had ever shown such a nice and good looking face *to me*. Obviously, Father was showing me the change in his attitude towards me. I think it was because I made a move first.

Facing such an unfamiliar atmosphere, I didn't know what to do. Just when I was trying to find a way to break the deadlock, a small nurse walked in. Although the nurse looked at PanJie when she spoke, clearly she was saying things to me, "Please go pay your room fees immediately, as our Premier Liu is in real difficulty."

As soon as the nurse went out, I asked PanJie, "Our father is a retired cadre. In the past I only knew that part of the nutrient fees, or some expensive imported medicine had been cut, how could his room fees also be...?"

"Nowadays, nothing is impossible." PanJie went on, "Father's work unit never denied payment, but couldn't pay in time due to the bad economy. The hospital has not only once wanted Father to be out. It has been all thanks to Premier Liu's face and Premier Liu knew you were coming back soon."

It was the fact that I was playing a heroic role of, "sending carbon to snow" as the Chinese saying goes. I quickly took out a package of US dollars, which I had made from violins, exchanged from Norwegian Kroner to USD. I handed it to Father.

Father took a quick look at the package, asking, "What?"

"Profit on your investment." I answered with a sense of humor.

"What investment?"

Either Father didn't get me or didn't buy my sense of humor. I had to explain, "Your investment in me. Now I earn US dollars, enemy's money, to pay for your medical fees, just like the old days when the red army used enemy weapons to kill enemies."

Father smiled, apparently to cover his embarrassment and bitterness. Anyone, if thinking a little, would feel the sort of taste my father had. A member of the Communist Party which created renminbi, must be helped by US dollars before he dies...

Father moved his body a little, hesitating if he should take that package of "sugar-coated bullets" or not. At exactly that key moment, my "long-time-no-see" Aunt came in. Seeing I was present, my aunt was very excited, maybe more excited than seeing her brother (my father). I was of course very happy to see her too. As I wrote early on, my first few years in memory were spent with Aunt. For me, in many ways she was closer to me than my mother. It had been many years since we last met. She looked at me, looked at my father and didn't seem to know who to talk to first.

Father also looked very happy. I knew I shouldn't interrupt the brother and sister, or at least it wasn't the right time to hand over the money. I told Aunt that I would wait for her outside. Aunt showed her understanding. She sat by Father's side, holding his hand saying she had come on behalf of the whole family (family in Xinhua, the old hometown) to see him. Father made some, "ah, ah" sound to answer her.

After a while, when it was a little quiet, Aunt took out a letter for Father and said, "My elder brother and your younger brother, the Second, asked me to hand it to you. I don't know what he wrote in the letter?" Her facial expression and tone when she said that showed it to be true, that she had no idea what was written in the letter, but perhaps she had guessed a little. Guessed there was not something very pleasant in the letter.

Father used his skinny hand, trembling, and took the letter to show his respect, but soon handed it back to Aunt, saying, "You read for me."

"What?" Aunt didn't understand what Father said and looked a little embarrassed.

"Baba asked you to read the letter for him." it was PanJie again, doing the interpreting.

"Shall I read?" Aunt hesitated a little, maybe she didn't want to get involved with the family boys' affairs. So as not to embarrass her eldest brother, she pretended to open the letter, but stopped and said, "Oh, I forgot my reading glasses. I think PanJie better read it. Yes, PanJie, you're the best one to read it." Aunt passed the letter onto PanJie. Not waiting for Father to say anything, she stood up and said she would like to see me outside.

PanJie took the letter and opened it, ready to read. Aunt started to walk out and said, "This is something between you two boys. I'll go see DanJiu outside."

I was waiting for my aunt outside the room. Aunt saw me and said, "Let's go. We'll find a quiet place." indicating something big might happen inside the room.

Meanwhile, PanJie already began to read the letter from my Uncle Ding.

Uncle Ding's Letter To Father

Hey Elder,

Knowing that you are ill, we entrust our sister to come see you. This shows that the family has never abandoned you, although you have abandoned the family. I wrote to you to also express our forgiveness for your mistake of joining the Party but not for the crimes your Party committed.

Before the liberation, by Father working as a medical doctor plus a small land rental, our family was okay; the family sending you to university proved that. However, after the liberation, the family land was taken by your Communist Party. Fortunately our father had only a small piece of land and therefore was not classified a landlord. Landlords were objects of dictatorship, many of them were annihilated, disappeared, killed, slaughtered, in extreme cases in some areas even eaten, literally eaten, by revolutionaries.

After that, our entire family had to be dependent on Father's medical practice. Father was a very soft hearted man. Very often he reduced his fees or charged very little sometimes for poor people. That made our life more and more difficult. You, as the eldest son, the only one in the family who works for the government, not only brought nothing home to support the family, but also threw your burden, leaving your son for us to raise.

Our poor father was over worked, to death. Except for sending and picking up your son, you were back home twice, not even coming back for our father's funeral.

You say, "The Communist Party is made of special material". I have no idea what kind of material that could be, but for sure, not human. How could your communists be working for the happiness of the masses, as it always declares, when you don't even care for your own family? In reality, after the rule of the Communists, the life of many families was getting worse. The people around us were like this and so was the whole country. It was because of your change that I started to be suspicious and oppose your Party.

Was I wrong to oppose the Communist Party? Decades of Communist China's brutal dictatorship demonstrated that the New China's history is a history of deception. The Communist Party has never, will never, stop its deception.

Let's take a quick recap: First your Party cheated all the farmers. Before 1949 under the slogan, "Down the local tyrants and divide the land to everyone", using the peasants to get the political power and government. As soon as the power was in the hands of the Communist Party, using the name of the People's Commune, it took all the land away from farmers.

Right after that, your Party carried out the policy of price scissors with urban and rural areas. That made the majority of the farmers become state-owned slaves.

Following, your Party cheated the intellectuals. In the year 1957, your Party launched a political campaign called, "Hundred Flowers Blossom", first inviting the intellectuals to criticize the Party and give comments, then putting a "Right Wing" hat on the intellectuals who believed the Party and truly tried to help it. Shamelessly, your Party called it an "overt conspiracy."

From the year 1958, your Party started a new campaign, "Great Leap Forward". The failure of that campaign led to China's economic collapsed, and millions of people starved to death in the year 1960. To escape from the responsibility, your Party called that man-made tragedy, "The Natural Disaster" to cheat all the people.

After a few years, in 1966, when the Chinese people were just recovering from hunger, Chairman Mao deceived young people by writing a letter calling them the, "Revolution Teenagers" and using the title of, "Cultural Revolution", destroying the whole country's system of government. As soon as Mao got all the power in his hands, he "burned the bridge" by exiling all the young people to the country-side as "educated youth", to have them "re-educated by farmers". Eventually, Mao passed away and the "ten years of chaos" ended.

Your Party started to cheat the factory workers and under the flag of "Reform and Open-Door", millions of the workers have lost their jobs. Next, your Party deceived the Chinese people with "Medical Reform", "Education Reform", "Housing Reform", "Stock Market", and a variety of other means. Every campaign, or movement, or new policy of your Party, has resulted in part of the people being exploited and suppressed.

Like that, one group after another. In the end, all Chinese people, every family, in turn, has suffered, before, now or later.

This is the Party you have fought for all your life, lacking humanity, just as your Party always says, "The Party is above all". To put a party's political ideology and interest above humanity, what is that? You look it up in your dictionary, for what I found was fascism. Yes, your Party is practically a true party of fascism. Do I need to give a few examples to remind you?

During the Cultural Revolution, class struggle extended into the families causing family members to fight with each other. Son fought with parents, husbands and wives became enemies. Countless happy families, destroyed. We all know the family is the basis of the society. When many families were destroyed, how could the society be stable?

Under the rule of your Party for forty years, the Party that implements cruel, merciless struggle and violent revolutionary philosophy, China has become a lawless society. When I say "lawless", I mean your Party takes emotions above the law. So called, "No kill can't appease the resentment of the people". To kill a man is not a punishment based on his crime, but rather to appease the resentment of people, the anger stirred up by the Party itself. As long as there is anger, the Party could ignore the dignity of the law, men were killed without proper legal process. Just shouting slogans, "No kill can't appease the resentment of the people" a man can be pulled out to be slaughtered, to be cut into pieces, or even to be cooked and eaten.

In China, the citizens' right and freedom can easily be arbitrarily deprived in various ways. If the Party doesn't like someone; someone could be taken to be labor-educated, or sent to detention, to be in a concentrated-course etc. Those people, even after being released and sent home, would be monitored all the time by the neighbors, no rights and no freedom.

Another of your Party's major crimes was, "anti-law of nature" ignoring the law of nature, not knowing that our human beings are no more than a part, a tiny part, of nature itself, instead wanting to override, going above nature. With the ignorant and arrogant slogan, "Man must conquer nature", no fear and no concern for nothing and anything. Thus, a lot of forests were cut down, a lot of water sources were polluted or ruined and the ecological system was damaged greatly. As a result, we have been repeatedly punished by the merciless nature and our children and grandchildren have to continuously pay for what our generation has done to nature.

The Chinese Communist Party is such a party, a party of ignorance, arrogance, lack of human feeling and an irrational evil party. It is also your Party that has completely destroyed traditional Chinese culture, moral and ethical value, brainwashed the whole nation and made them thoughtless tools of the Party.

You kept saying, "for the benefit of the masses". Your Party ended up unable to give you, a retired old revolutionary, the very basic benefit of paying the full fees of the hospital. Why can't you see the fact that everyone else can?

I admit I am an anti-revolutionary. For our country, for our people, for our future generations and for my own interests, I have to go on anti to your communism.

I hope you can make a comprehensive summary to your life, as well as to your Party, for our future generations, as well as the history of China.

Finally, I sincerely hope that whom I am going to lose is not my brother, but the evil Party my brother served all his life, and in the end, abandoned him.

Your Younger One at Xinhua home

After PanJie finished reading the letter, she found Father had no response. She thought Father went to sleep and felt a little pity that she did all that work in vain. When she was about to cover Father with a blanket she heard Father say, "Read it again, no need from the beginning, just from, 'Was I wrong to oppose the Communist Party?'"

While PanJie was reading Uncle Ding's letter to Father again and again, I was pouring out what was hidden deep in my heart for years, to my aunt (as I said before, her existence to me, in many aspects, was more than my mother). I told her all about the bad relationship between Father and I, or should I say, my trouble of never getting Father to recognize my true value. (How could I admit that I needed his love as a son? Sour, isn't it?)

To show Aunt my true feelings toward Father, I handed the package of money to my aunt that I had failed to give to Father and asked her to pass it to Father. It was that very moment my tears couldn't help falling, although it wasn't easy money, I was so emotional mainly because I felt very aggrieved. To analyze the feeling "aggrieved", it should actually be "love"! No matter how Father treated me, I realized that I actually *needed* his love as a father, especially when I knew I was going to lose him, quickly, that feeling grew even stronger.

However, I'm not the kind of person to be satisfied by all giving, no receiving. I'm not that high or stupid, or not that detached. In short, I love my father and need him to love me back. Over all the years, I took Father as my rival, until that day when I figured it all out. *What I really wanted to win, above all, was his love.* However, how to win his love remains a question.

"There is one thing haunting me all these years that I could never figure out by myself." I finally couldn't resist asking my aunt.

"What's that?" Aunt asked.

"Why doesn't Father like me by nature? Am I really his son?" I spit out the root of my entire problem that had been in my heart for years, suddenly afraid of getting a reply like a novel or legend, such as I'm the son of a martyr, or my mother was with someone extraordinary…

"Ha ha ha, what's the matter with you?" Aunt laughed as if I just made a joke. Her attitude toward my most serious matter provoked me and made me mad, very. I said again: "Yes, I overheard it with my own ears as he said that to Mother when I was little." I stood up, waving my fist to add tension to my words.

Seeing me in such an emotional state, half sad and half angry, Aunt regretted that she had answered my question too lightly. She stopped laughing, switched to a rather serious expression saying, "You are my brother's biological son and there is no doubt about it, not to mention how much you resemble your father. Just let me tell you how much your father loves you. After the liberation, for a few decades, my brother only came back home twice, for bringing you there and taking you back. Even when our father, your grandpa passed away, your father didn't go back to see him."

Looking at me with a desperate face caused by the answer, Aunt suggested, "If this question troubles you so much, why don't you ask your father directly, yourself?"

Yes, why did I never think of that, to ask my father directly, myself?

Different Political Views Between Father And Son

Aunt went back to Father's room. Once again she sat by his bedside and put her hand on her brother's shoulder speaking some words of comfort. Father didn't respond to her greeting but asked her a question, "Have you read the letter the Second wrote to me?"

"I...did...not really..." This sudden question made Aunt not know how to answer, "I mean, I guessed a little, though."

"Then read it carefully again." Father indicated PanJie pass the letter to Aunt.

By then, she knew there was no way to escape. She stopped PanJie and said to her brother, "Well, okay, I'll read it. If you have something to say, say it. I'm a good listener."

Father made a huge effort to half-sit up, put on his glasses, as well as his dentures and then clearing his voice a little, very seriously he said, "I see the Second (my Uncle Ding) hasn't changed a bit, speaks as extreme as always. It is true that in the past few decades our Party made some mistakes, some of them even serious, but that could not necessarily prove wrong the ideology and theory of communism. Communism as a new human society system needs a testing period. Therefore its unsuccessful temporary period could be caused by operational errors. In history, nothing in the world can be guaranteed success the first time. Any success is a result of many experiments."

After hearing that, I couldn't stand it any longer. In order to gain Father's love, I could make all kinds of concessions, but I couldn't give up my political position. This was a matter of principle. And it was the absolute bottom line. I couldn't help state, "How many times does your Party need to experiment and fail? How many innocent people need to be killed? And how many nations need to be destroyed before you prove the correctness of your communist ideology?"

Father, hearing that, used all his strength, trembling his body towards me and made his voice as loud and clear as he could, declaring with great solemnity, "The ideologue of Communism is to liberate the whole of human kind, to contribute to the happiness of all the people..."

Father's body was shaking. To me, he suddenly became the symbol of the Chinese Communist Party. A sense of vindictiveness aroused spontaneously, I deliberately raised my voice, "To contribute to the world? How nice it is! To show the misfortune of the Chinese people for decades, to show mankind how terrible the true face of communism is, should be the greatest contribution of your Party to the world!"

Father raised his right hand just about to say something but was interrupted by a severe cough. I knew that by then, Father was no longer my opponent, physically. Aunt, with surprised big eyes, smiled to stop me and then patted Father's back and gently said, "I say my big brother, before you save the whole of human kind, I think it's better to save yourself first. And then your family, your neighbors, colleagues, the people around them, and gradually..."

Listening to my aunt supporting me, I felt somehow comforted, but also doubted why the communists had no tears, even in front of their coffins. Look at my communist father. He kept saying, "to save all mankind", after he spent his entire life struggling, ended up not even able to save himself, but relying on his son to bring money back from the *capitalist society* to save him! Even facing such a cruel reality, Father wouldn't give up his high words for communism. Sad, isn't it?

Father stopped coughing. He gave up fighting with me, didn't bother to look at me again, and only waved his hand weakly toward the door meaning, "get lost."

I felt a sudden regret, regret that my "little-bear spoiled the big plan." Looking at my spirit go from high to low, Aunt got up and pushed me out the door. Gently she said, "You see the way you talk to your father, the stubbornness is from exactly the same mold as your father. Just as the saying goes, like father like son..." And then she went back to the ward.

From the window I saw Aunt help Father lie down, and go on talking to him, "Hey brother, I don't want to argue with you about what's between you and the Second (my Uncle Ding). I only know that since communism can't be achieved in a few days, can you, in your lifetime, restore your human nature by showing your love to your son *as a father*?"

"You have seen everything. That's his attitude towards me. How could I show my anything to him?" After Father said that he breathed heavily.

"My dear big brother, there is something that you obviously don't know." Aunt said as she placed the package of money I had asked her to pass to Father, gently on Father's body. And then she told Father, for to win his love, how I was consciously trying to change all the problems with myself... selfishness, vanity, arrogance and so on, and trying very hard to be a good person.

Moreover, in order to earn money for his medical treatment, I changed my life, stopped pursuit of my dream to become the "king of music", giving up the plan of going to the United States for my future studies to be a famous violinist, instead learning to make and repair violins for others. In a word, the son had chosen to be a loser in his fight with the father.

Finally, Aunt very sincerely said, "Yeah, It might be about the time to think about things..."

Father didn't respond to what his sister said to him, nor did he take the package of money she had placed on his body. When Aunt stood up about to leave, Father turned his body causing the package of money to fall on the ground. Hearing the sound, she immediately bent down to pick it up and put it back on Father's body. It was at that moment Father opened his eyes; very seriously to Aunt he said, "Yes, ah, some historical traces have marked on our generation."

Father's face, was by then not at all good looking, but still to him, it was profoundly important not to lose face.

24: THE JOURNEY OF THE NEW CHINA (COMMUNIST VERSION)

Stay At MeiMei's Place With Aunt

About my sleeping in brother's living-room, though DanXin repeatedly expressed his "sorry"; I also repeatedly said "no problem", but in reality there was some problem. After all, that was a living room, a room for everybody, no privacy and not convenient, for me or anyone in the family. Of course, a large portion of the "inconvenience" was an excuse because I wanted to stay with Aunt, as MeiMei had offered her place for Aunt to stay. Just as she said: "It's not a great place, both of you are welcome as long as you like, until the owner wants it back." I packed up my things and got a taxi to MeiMei's place, staying with Aunt.

As soon as I brought my things into MeiMei's place she said to me, "Make yourself at home. Meaning she wouldn't treat us as guests." I thought to "Make oneself at home" were just some usual words of courtesy, but MeiMei wasn't just words, she meant it. So from then I had to worry about the everyday living for Aunt and I, for instance going to an open market to buy food, relying on my own judgment to decide if the meat was water injected or not, that vegetables were not covered with pesticide...etc. The result was always negative; the difference was only in the quantity or level of how much poison we took into our bodies.

I would have to cook for Aunt too, as well as wash her clothes, since she was extremely busy with her big brother, my father, and endless other things. Every simple thing in the west could be very complicated in China, things as basic as buying a bottle of good medicine or a naturally raised chicken. Somehow it felt good, as I believed it was my turn to repay, not completely but partly, what Aunt did for me when I was little, really little.

MeiMei went to work every day and Aunt was seldom home, I felt that was home, when with Aunt.

Sometimes I got really bored and thought about going out to visit some of my former colleagues and friends in the music field. But every time, just before I was about to go out I felt embarrassed, so afraid of what they would think of me if they found out that I, who used to be the concertmaster, supposedly the best violinist in town, now, not only was I in no symphony orchestra, not to mention having an Oscar or Nobel Prize, on the contrary, turned out to be a self-employed, small shop owner and craftsman.

However, what I didn't know was that the whole world had changed. What I worried about was just my outdated prejudice. In reality, people had all become more and more realistic and practical. Making money had become the priority. Very different from the past, my colleagues weren't staying at home practicing, but out at work, teaching, running from place to place for performances. If they had known the scale of my income, they might be very much envious!

Knowing I wasn't the only one who had changed my life course due to unforeseen reasons, might have been the best psychological comfort and balance for me.

A Significant Dialogue Between Aunt And Father

My aunt was there on behalf of Father's family and having come from so far away, naturally she visited the hospital every day. When the sister and brother were together, what could they talk about? Of course family trifles, such as things concerning Uncle Din but most likely things about me the most.

Father said to Aunt, "I've known for a long time that my disease has no hope. I endured all the pain of staying alive because I thought my body could contribute to scientific research for the country and people. But not until recently did I realized that it seems science does not really value my body much. As this is the case, I have done all that I could for my Party, my country and people, I don't really need to suffer so much just to stay alive, perhaps to end the earlier the better..."

Aunt cut off her brother and said, "My big brother, apart from your Party, your country and your people, have you ever thought about doing something, may be just a little, for *your own family* while you are still alive? A quick death, that's easy and happy for you perhaps, but a bit selfish. Don't you think so?"

Father looked a little surprised. He added, "I thought if I die, not only don't I suffer any longer, but I also reduce the burden on the family and save all the trouble for everyone. How could you call it selfish?"

To bring her point out Aunt explained, "You only see things from your own view point. (Is that the way all Party members do?) But the whole truth is, your family members are willing to pay for the cost and willing to take all the trouble, so long as you can be with the family, a day longer the better. For you to live a day longer we all pray to Buddha, to God. If you could see what we are thinking, you would bear the pain and live longer."

After she finished talking, Father opened his mouth but no words came out. Aunt saw her words had made her point, she talked a little more, "Also, as a father, have you ever thought to leave something to your children?"

This time Father responded very quickly, "What are you thinking your brother is? A corrupted official? I worked for the Party, had a very honest simple life, what could I leave to them?" Father paused, raised his hand indicating Aunt not to interrupt and went on, "Besides, now the kids have everything, especially DanJiu, needs nothing, nothing from me at all."

Aunt seized the opportunity to quickly interrupt, "Brother, you're right, now DanJiu may have everything he needs *except one thing* and for that one thing, you are the only one in this world who can give it to him." she stopped there.

"What's this one thing you're talking about?" my father got impatient and couldn't help asking.

"Hahaha" Aunt laughed and explained, "*Fatherly love.* You tell me, who else can give your children fatherly love except you?" Seeing Father not giving an immediate argument she went on, "Suppose you are right, that your body is useless for your Party and country, but have you thought to use your useless body to do something useful for your son?"

Father laughed a bit, with sadness he said helplessly, "Don't be so sarcastic. You see I have to be in bed all the time, nothing can I do for myself, not even go to the toilet. What can I do for my children?"

"Nothing, you don't need to do anything, just stay alive." Aunt explained, "One more day you live is one more day DanJiu can feel the importance of his existence to you. I mean, to make him feel how important he is to his father. In a way, this is what you can do for your son. This is also what I meant, 'to die may be easy and happy, but selfish'. Therefore my dear brother, I'm afraid you might have to go on suffering from pain and keep yourself alive, for as long as you can."

Father smiled wordlessly. After a pause of meditation he said, "If only to make DanJiu feel like a hero and to meet his satisfaction or vanity of being successful and important, I guess I could put up with the pain. But if it will let him use the shortcomings of the current health care system as proof to negate our whole socialist system, that would be tantamount to abandoning my political beliefs which I have fought for my whole life. It would be equal to negating the value of my whole life. That, I simply cannot do."

Aunt sighed deeply and almost desperately she pursued, "For you, DanJiu has given up his life dream of becoming a world leading violinist. How come you, as a Communist Party member, can't do things a small bourgeois can?"

Hearing that, Father's eyes were wide open, staring at his sister while she intentionally avoided making eye contact. Both were aware that such a discussion could only go to extremes that would hurt brain and heart; therefore they both adopted the Deng XiaoPing's "no debate" strategy.

However, just before Aunt was about to leave, she asked Father a question, the question that I had wanted to ask, for a few decades, "Oh yes, why don't you like your son DanJiu by nature? DanJiu said when he was a boy, he overheard you say that to your wife. Is it true that you said that? And why?"

Father closed his eyes, giving no reply, instead going into a deep, deep meditation...

Two weeks had passed. One day, PanJie phoned me to go to the hospital to see Father, repeatedly explaining it was at Father's request. Recalling the last meeting, during which a huge argument between us, due to different political views, had worsened the relationship restored only recently with huge effort from my side, I was sincerely determined, this time, no matter what happens I must control myself, as there wouldn't be more chances to show my maturity in front of Father. A real warrior shouldn't go on fighting his opponent when he is already down on the ground.

Together with PanJie, I went into Father's ward. I had no chance to show my friendly attitude as Father had taken the position away. He asked me to sit down. That was my greatest hesitation. Not because there were thorns on the small stool in front of his bed, but something worse, for when I sat down, I would be very close to my father, actually too close to feel comfortable and when I sat down, I would be embarrassed to leave the small stool after a short period of time.

"PanJie, you sit down." I tried to get away.

"Father specifically asked YOU to sit down, not me." PanJie said as she pushed me down on the small stool. Then I understood that me sitting there was planned. As if rehearsed, as soon as I sat down, Father nodded to PanJie. She quickly and skillfully took a letter from Father's pillow and handed it to me.

"Read it, loudly." Father ordered. I looked at PanJie for help as she walked toward the door. That left me no choice but to pull a thick letter out of the envelope. When I looked at PanJie again, she had closed the door, from outside.

A True Communist View Point Towards The New China
(Father's Letter To Uncle Din)

Hi Younger Din,

To have received your letter was beyond my expectation, a pleasant surprise. Just recently I have also been thinking of those things you mentioned in your letter. I wrote it down partly to answer you to exchange ideas and do some rethinking, and also partly to show my respect to you.

Indeed, since 1946 I joined the revolution and walked away from home. The damage both emotionally and economically I did to the family is undeniable, as the eldest son, it's not forgivable.

However, I could never agree with you that what I've done was entirely a mistake; and your accusation of crime is far from the truth. When we make a judgment of something, we can't remove it from the historical background and social environment.

As a family letter, let me start by recalling how I got myself into the revolution. It was when I had just entered WuHan University, studying English literature. At a sorority party I met your sister-in-law, my wife. By then, she had already participated in the Party's underground activities. Her purpose of coming to the sorority was to find more people to join the organization. I fell in love with her at first sight. In order to get closer to her, I found an excuse to borrow revolutionary books from her.

As I said, it was just an excuse, so to be honest, in the beginning I was not interested in Marx or Lenin, only reading a few pages to cope with questions from her. But she was very smart, every time she lent books to me she would leave something in some pages, a hair of hers or a leaf from a tree, or some pencil marks. That forced me to read the whole book, page by page. Gradually I became absorbed by the contents of the books and started to consciously study Max's theory. In order for this not to affect my English studies, I found some English versions of Marx and Engels' related books.

Worried they would be found, as at the time any Marx related books were forbidden, I wrapped the cover with Shakespeare. I can still clearly remember how one day one of the headmasters took my book in his hand, turned a few pages, obviously not understanding English but pretending he could, saying, "That's a very good book, I myself have read it twice already." Just like that, I knuckled down studying the revolutionary books. I became so serious that it even made my wife jealous, saying that I regarded the books as more important than her.

I was in my early twenties, a young man in his early adulthood, the period of time for his political ideology formation. Marx's "Das Kapital" made me question the society's system of Private Ownership.

Let us briefly recall the modern history of China: In the Qing Dynasty, many Chinese elites and intellectuals criticized the Qing government, saying the poverty and backwardness of the country was the result of corruption, therefore the only way to enrich China was to overthrow the Qing Dynasty. As a result, the Chinese people made a revolution and the Qing government was overthrown.

But the continuator of the BeiYang Government still could not make China rich and strong. Therefore, once again, the Chinese people organized to overthrow the BeiYang Government and established the Republic of China. But after decades of rule by a government lead by the National People's Party, still, China was no richer or stronger. This cruel fact gave me such an answer.

The problem was not that the governments were "no good", but that the Private Ownership social system was no good. Therefore, the only way to make China richer and stronger was to overthrow the Private Ownership Social System, and establish the Public Ownership Social System.

The Three People's Principles (1. nationalism; 2. democracy; 3. people's living) by the National People's Party, was proposing to overthrow imperialism along with feudal warlords and establish a bourgeois democratic republic. However, China was an agricultural country, therefore the bourgeoisie's strength was simply too weak.

It was Mao ZeDong who combined Marxism-Leninism with China's practical situation to create a series of theories about how to lead the Chinese revolution and establish the people's democratic dictatorship. This is what we call, "Mao ZeDong Thoughts", and that was Chairman Mao's greatest contribution to the Chinese people and the Chinese revolution.

Different from the majority of poor people who participated in the revolution simply for the purpose of overthrowing landlords and tyrants to get some land for a better life, I, like many intellectuals and elites, took part in the revolution because I understood and believed the theory of Socialist Public Ownership as scientific and advanced, one that would lead China in the inevitable direction of human development.

In short, it was because I believed, "Mao ZeDong Thoughts" and in the great Chinese Communist Party being correct, that I joined the Party and put my whole heart into the Chinese revolution. The Chinese Communist Party's rise and the fall of the People's National Party after World War II, proved the correctness of my choice.

As I had chosen my side with the proletariat class, I did feel shameful of our family at the time. Although our father was not a big landlord, but after all, "self-employed & small-land-renting" does not belong to the worker-peasant's class, nor the revolutionary class. Therefore, to transform myself into a true Bolshevik, the very first thing I needed to do was to betray my past, and the family I came from.

Just like all other Chinese Bolshevik's, I too started to hate our family, hate the education I had received and hate everything about my past. That was the real reason I lost contact with you all, just like all other typical and true revolutionaries.

Now let's talk about the ideology of socialism. Whether it is good or not, we should let the facts speak. Since in your letter you listed a lot of bad aspects of our Party and country, I will also list some indisputable facts to illustrate how our Party led the nation from the old China, the "one poor two white" (we were poor and had nothing) to become a complete, independent, industrialized, powerful, New China.

Before the liberation of 1949, the Chinese modern industry was almost zero. We couldn't even produce a match stick. Remember how we called the "match" a "foreign match", so it was also "foreign oil", "foreign nail", "foreign bucket", "foreign cup". Almost everything had a "foreign" in front.

But after the liberation, we first engaged our industry in the Northeast region. We manufactured our own aircraft, automobiles, heavy machinery, precision instruments... as many as six hundred projects. We built the New Wuhan Yangtze River Bridge; as well as more than thirty railways linking most areas of the country. Within ten years after liberation we built two Iron & Steel Bases in Wuhan and Baotou and Oilfields in Daqing, Shengli and Dagang.

By 1965, we were basically self-sufficient in oil supply. Our electric power industry also grew very fast, so that within ten years electrical supply increased by nearly seventy times in countryside areas. In addition, more than eight thousand kilometers of new railways were built including Baotou-Lanzhou railway. High technology also developed very quickly and successfully. In the year 1964, we had our first atomic bomb. The successful development of the crystalline bovine insulin was another achievement.

Despite the heavy loss to the national economy during the "Ten Years Disturbance" (Cultural Revolution), in which development slowed, still some achievements were made, such as the No. 2 car factory in Hubei Province; Nanjing Yangtze River Bridge; Chengdu-Kunming Railway; Hunan-Guizhou railway etc. In national defense technology, we developed our own missiles as well as the hydrogen bomb and an artificial earth satellite.

Since the 1980s "Reform & Open-Door" and the Party giving priority to the agricultural sector, grain and cotton production have steadily increased to No. 1 in the world.

In industry we have some projects that have reached the world's most advanced technology, such as Baoshan Iron & Steel base; Gezhouba Dam Project; the Daya Bay Nuclear Power Station and the Beijing-Kowloon railway; and in recent years, The Sanxia Dam Project and Qinghai-Tibet railway.

The foreign trade and cultural exchanges also have a new face. We have joined the World Trade Organization. Science and technology, education and culture also flourish. The living standard in both urban and rural areas have improved significantly. In space industry innovation, since 1979 we have successfully tested long-range rockets and built "Shenzhou V" and "Shenzhou VI", manned spacecraft's.

If we look back through modern Chinese history, we were a nation always being beaten by foreign powers. However, since the establishment of the New China in 1949, we said farewell to that part of our history. We built a strong military and national defense. From the Anti US Supporting the Korean War and other border conflicts with neighboring countries, we have never lost one inch of our land, maintaining the integrity and unity of our motherland.

In the early 50s we were not very strong, still we did not succumb to the pressure of the Soviet Union by tying ourselves to their chariot. We defeated all the foreign anti-China forces of isolation, blockade, interference and provocation to our nation and consolidated our political independence, courageously saying "No" to the world powers.

During the fall of the Soviet Union and drastic changes in Eastern Europe and the world, we withstood the instability and passed the test. Our nation now proudly stands among the leading nations of the world.

In the education field, before liberation, China was one of the world's most illiterate countries. Today, China has basically eliminated illiteracy. To follow Deng XiaoPing's policy in 1983, in which education must face modernization, the world and the future, universities reformed the entrance examination system. University enrollment increased from several hundred thousand to several million students.

In the diplomatic aspect, our government firmly carried out Comrade Mao ZeDong and Zhou EnLai's Foreign policy, opening a new era in our diplomatic history. As a member of the United Nations, our country has establish diplomatic relations with one hundred and twenty countries, keeping friendly relationships with many countries and regions in the field of economics, trade, cultural exchange and so on.

In health care, after liberation our government implemented the free medical care system, essentially eliminating severe infectious diseases. The death rate declined significantly. People's health greatly improved overall. Although there remain some problems in the health care reform areas, the great progress and improvement is undeniable.

In sports, we have successfully hosted the Beijing Olympics. Between 1984, in which our athletes won our first Olympic gold medal, to the 2008 Beijing Olympic Games, we have won a total of fifty-one gold medals, becoming the world's No. 1 gold medal winning country! In front of these hard facts, who dares to call us "sick Asians" again?

In your letter, you accused our Party of having harmed many people in the past few decades. I do not deny that our Party, in the process of leading the people to fight for a better life, did make some errors and detours, some even very serious, bringing harm to some people.

However, nothing is perfect. In this world, any person, any party, any government has its path towards maturation and perfection. As to China, according to the development of our society the main problem has been constantly changing. Our Party also constantly adjusts and improves itself. The maturation process of the Chinese Communist Party theory can be divided into three stages.

The first stage was to combine Marxism-Leninism's universal principles together with the reality of Chinese revolution. This is what I have said before regarding, "Mao ZeDong Thoughts". Mao thought of the representative theory to mainly deal with the problem of class struggle. Before liberation, the main social contradiction was between the poor and the rich; after liberation the main social contradiction became which road to follow in building our society, the socialist road, or the capitalist road.

The second stage took place in the year 1978, after the third session of the 10th Party Conference. Deng XiaoPing, as the core of the second generation of The Party's central leadership, created the Deng XiaoPing Theory. We found our own way to build our socialist country. Deng used very simple, symbolic language such as, "No matter if the cat is black or white, as long as it catches rats, it's a good cat" and "The hard thing is to develop our country's economy." During this period the principal contradiction in China has come to be between, "The people's increasing material and cultural needs and the backward productive ability." Deng XiaoPing Theory focused on solving the problems of, "How to build a socialist country."

The third stage, from the year 2000, our third generation Party leader, comrade Jiang ZeMin, put forward the theory of, "The three represents" (1. Our Party represents the need of China's advanced social productive force; 2. Our Party represents the direction of China's advanced culture; 3. Our Party represents the fundamental interests of the majority of people.)

It resolved the current historical problem of, "The nature of the Communist Party." Comrade Jiang formally announced, "Communism is not a goal we fight for, but a great and lofty ideal." He improved and emancipated our minds; putting the truth and facts before ideology. He also changed the slogan of, "Building a socialist country" to, "Building a Chinese characterized socialist country."

The, "Chinese characterized socialism theoretical system" is our Party's complete theory. It is the condensation of Marxism-Leninism, Mao ZeDong Thought, Deng XiaoPing theory and the "three represents", as well as the wisdom and untiring efforts of exploration and Chinese Communists leading the people for two generations.

The history of mankind has experienced the "three technology revolution": 1. The invention of the steam engine facilitated the commencement of the first industrial revolution; 2. The invention of electric power technology marked the second industrial revolution; 3. The Internet caused the rapid development of human society into the information age.

Compared with European capitalist countries we started late and our foundation was not solid, our economy was weak. However, we do not want to be left behind. In today's information age and globalization, our people, under the leadership of our Party, are studying and working hard to make our nation play an increasingly important role in the world.

Since China became a member of the WTO, more and more foreign enterprises are coming to China looking for cheap laborers. Now our country is called "The World's Factory". However, our nation will not be satisfied with being factory workers. We are only temporarily doing our studies, as if paying tuition to learn advanced foreign technology and management. We, eventually, will make our own brands and be proud to move from "Made in China" to "Created in China", so that we can gain the most profit and maximum economic benefit. We will be in an invincible position among world competition.

So far, I have given so many adequate examples of the greatness and correctness of our Party. At the same time you can also see that our Party is not an unchangeable stone. In fact, from the political policy to the members of the Party, for different needs in different periods of time, we have been changing continually and accordingly.

Our Party in the past, at present and in the future, will continue correcting our mistakes, adjusting our cause, ultimately leading the Chinese people toward prosperity. The whole world, only in the period of history with the Communist Party in power, has seen an independent, powerful, modern and strong China.

As a CCP member, I wish to say a few more words about our Party. Our Party is composed of the elites of our nation. This fact will never change. In China, there is no other political party which can compete with the Chinese Communist Party. So, no matter what changes occur inside the Party, now or in the future, as long as it doesn't change the title, "The Chinese Communist Party", it cannot be replaced. In other words, the Party can be changed, but cannot be overthrown. So, as the old saying goes: "Only to be a Party member, can one save China."

As in your letter you made a lot of complaints about some practical problems, difficult times we had after the liberation, I would say that some disasters were caused by natural and historical limitations, that could happen to any government, from any political party, in any social system. Therefore, everything must be analyzed accordingly, not simply put all blame on the Party.

Although our Party has to continue exploring and adjusting itself, I can already foresee in the future of half a century, China will have a huge change, will become one of the world's most important countries.

The people around the world will look at us, the "sick Asian" in a totally different light, and most borders will be open for Chinese citizens to go in and out freely…China, our motherland, used to be known as a sick, weak, poor country. In the near future, we will be a healthy, strong and rich country standing among the world's leading countries, countries such as the USA, Germany, UK, Japan etc.

Unfortunately I can't see the day with my own eyes, though I feel and strongly believe the day is very close. By that time, I hope you, my younger brother, can look at our Party and our nation, in a macro view, subjectively and comprehensively.

Take a good think and burn me a letter again when the time is coming, even if not for me, you should and need to do it for yourself, and for our generations to follow. I appreciate your patience to have read this long-winded letter.

This is a letter I write to you, as well write to the whole family and even to all our descendants. I also would like to take this letter as a review and summary of my faithful and hard work for the Party all my life.

Finally I would ask you for a favor. Next time you pay your visit to our father, please add some earth to his grave on my behalf.

Elder brother of yours

My Last Battle With Father

At last I finished reading such a long letter, I handed it back to him. But he gave no indication of taking it, instead looking at me as if waiting for me to make some comments.

How could I make any comments on such a long "political editorial"? Especially when much of the information appearing in it I had never heard of or thought about before. The more important thing was, before I came to the hospital I had already made up my mind, "This time, no matter what is going to happen I will endure, because there wouldn't be much chance left for me to show my maturity in front of Father."

Seeing me saying nothing Father couldn't help asking, "What do you think, any suggestions? "

I didn't expect Father to talk to me in such a discussing tone. I blurted out, "What you said, you certainly have your point."

Hearing that, Father released some tension that made his face look much more relaxed. At this moment, PanJie walked in. I suspected she had never really gone away, but waited outside the door. Despite PanJie's arrival, Father didn't move his eyes from me and said something vague to me.

"What?" I leaned in a little, my ear to him.

"Baba asked you to help him turn around." PanJie immediately interpreted. Looking at my hesitance, PanJie pushed me away and said, "Let me do it, I'm experienced."

"*I asked my son.*" This time Father's words were clearly discernible, startling PanJie. How could she be not startled? For all these years, PanJie had been much closer to Father than any of us brothers. Father talking to her like that, was extremely rare.

Though I was still hesitating as to whether I should help Father make a turn or not, I realized that that was not for me to choose, or to put it another way, it was unavoidable.

I stood up and clumsily embraced the pile of bones of my father's. Just about to help him make a turn around, unexpectedly Father hugged me, tightly. I was shocked; unconsciously I tried to get away, but gave up at the same time.

I seized this rare opportunity to ask the question that would have haunted me the rest of my life: "Baba, *why you don't like me by nature?* Is it because I don't resemble you, like a sheep's daddy, seeing his little sheep does not resemble him and gets frightened?"

Father didn't answer my question immediately. He used the last of his strength giving me a tight hug, and then gently released me. He paused for a moment, with a faint smile followed by a deep sigh, he shook his head, then patted me, telling me the reason why he didn't like me by nature. That reason stunned me. (If this were a TV drama, now should be commercial time)

My father said, "It was not because you don't resemble me, on the contrary, it was because you resemble me, resemble me too much. Aside from how you look, your character and temperament are just the same as me when I was young, say, your nature of showing-off; individual struggle, fighting to be rich and famous, those Bourgeoisie thoughts, just like me before I took part in the revolution.

Seeing all the old habits and foul problems that I got rid of through years of hard reform, appeared and proliferated all in you. How do you think I would feel? Therefore, when I said I disliked you by nature, 'nature' was not you, but me. Now, you see, when I said I disliked you, was actually I dislike me, myself."

Father paused a little, with a smile, one of the very few but the *nicest* smile I had ever seen from his face, he added: "Remember that song, 'Home, home, sweet home', was my favorite too when I was young. And also was the song, I captured your mother..."

He started to hum the melody of the song: Home, Home, Sweet Home...

Hearing the familiar melody that caused all the happenings, I was choked. I found no words to portray how I looked in that scene and the scene of the whole...

The mystery in the deep of my heart was then solved. I once again hugged my father, with decades of accumulated emotions gurgled into tears. Father was also immensely stirred.

It was then, on that spot and in that moment, the father and son both realized and felt: *"Family, is the most beautiful thing in the world!"*

If this is a movie, now is an emotional high climax, and should increase the background music, with a series of flashbacks: the sound of a moving train being overshadowed, recalling the scene when I was 6 years old, the first time Father took me on the train from Xinhua to Changsha; overlapping the scene that Father took me on his bike, riding me to school in snow when the water flowing out of a crack in my rain shoe turned to be ice; jumping to the scene that I was tailing a smoking adult for the moment to pick up his cigarette butt to give to Father; the next scene should be at my twelfth birthday, I scared my parents by asking them to buy me a violin; and the final scene would be Father smashing my white violin that I made by my own hands, into pieces... In short, to put carefully selected touching, moving scenes together, back and forth, to make the cinema into a pond of tears.

If the drama, "Father and Son" ended at this point, it could be a happy ending. But very unfortunately, when I got up about to leave Father, he pointed to the letter he wrote to Uncle Din and said to me, "Go make a copy for yourself and write some comments, let me see." Until then I hadn't realized that the letter Father wrote to Uncle Din was only part of it, in fact it was more meant for me. It seems I couldn't get away if I didn't make a clear and specific position.

I forced myself to smile a little and then said, "Baba, I really don't want to quarrel with you anymore. But it is you again pushing me, so don't blame me for it."

I stopped smiling, slowly spitting out, "Honestly most of what you wrote in your letter, such as your revolutionary principles or theories and so on, is just beyond my comprehension. I am just an ordinary person, a violin player and now a violin maker and repairman. My idea of life has never been high.

When I was small I only wished to suffer a little less from coldness and hunger, every meal time hoping to have some real and decent rice instead of cereals mixed with wild grasses, and on a rainy day to have rain shoes that wouldn't leak, in the cold winters to have a cotton-padded jacket to keep me warm; when I grew up, I just wanted to live a life with less spiritual suspense and the freedom to sing the songs I liked, to play a melody on my violin that I loved and be safe to say things I wanted to say, with no need to always worry someday a political punishment would suddenly come to my head.

Today, although I live in a foreign country, I still pray for my brother and that the shares he buys don't suddenly drop becoming valueless; pray for my sister-in-law to get her wage safely, fully and on time every month, and that she won't suddenly be out of job; pray for my friends returning home from work not to suddenly find themselves forced to move out due to a demolition; and more importantly that people can afford to send their children to school and the elderly can afford to have medication. "

Seeing me get more and more vigorous, Father's already ugly face twisted, becoming even worse. He raised his hand, sorry, he raised his bones and waved in the air, like an orchestra conductor to shut me up. Then gave a long sigh of despair and said, "It seems you have a very deep-rooted prejudice towards your motherland. But in any case you cannot deny the facts." Father raised his voice, very solemnly saying, "Who made you a violin artist? It was your socialist motherland that you dislike. And who made you from an artist into a businessman? It happens to be your favorite foreign capitalist country."

I stopped my father there, as I couldn't wait to make my point: "Oh no, my motherland did not make me a violin artist, but a tool and a weapon to educate the people against the enemy for your Party. It was the foreign capitalist countries that educated me in what real art and beauty is. Later, becoming a businessman was my choice; no one forced me to do it.

As for the reason I chose to give up violin performing, was because after re-educated by the western culture for some years, I realized there are more things I should and need to do other than violin playing in my life. For example, to grow a sense of responsibility and obligation to our nation, to read as many books as I could to continuously improve my quality and essence of thinking; or just say, to make enough money to support and help my family, particularly you, my dear father and the people around me..."

When I got excited, I couldn't avoid my old bad habit of quarreling with Father and forgot all of what I had decided about keeping quiet before I came to see Father.

"That's enough, more than enough; it's all the old tricks, that the moon is rounder in the West than in China." Father opened his eyes, coldly looked at the ceiling.

I know that was the peak of Father's maturity. However, since it has already come to the point, I decided to spit it all out, just to save myself regret for the rest of my life.

I continued: "It's true, the moon is rounder in the West than in China, if

China has a moon at all, as in the west the air is less polluted. Particularly for those of us who live in Norway, a high social welfare country, where every citizen is entitled to have free education and free medication. Everyone's human rights and freedom are protected by the law, freedom and rights including giving up living as an artist and choosing to be a businessman."

I quickly expressed my deepest feelings and thoughts before Father could make any action, "The biggest difference between the people in the West and China is: people in the West can *choose* and control their own lifestyle and destiny, while the life of Chinese people is basically controlled by the hands of bureaucrats, as least in the first few decades of the New China.

So tell me, as a human being, what is different from a slave, if one is not allowed to live in a place one wants to live, or not allowed to learn something or choose a favorite profession, but has to do things told to do?"

Father woodened, closed his eyes, never meaning to refute. I hope this time he was speechless, not just employing the Deng XiaoPing trick and playing "no debate".

Silence, it was sad and deadly quiet. At this point I obviously felt the small stool that I sat on, growing thorns and getting longer and harder, making my ass feel pain. I stood up and gently placed the letter on the small stool. I was about to say, "Take a good rest", to get away when Father opened his eyes again, and said with deep and heavy feeling, "The greatest regret of my life is I cannot live to see the day of proof that socialism is superior to capitalism. However, (my father raised his voice) I do believe that day will come."

As everything I needed to say had been said, and all the gas in my stomach I had also let out, I would be deadly stupid if I had not caught the chance to show my maturity. In order to ease the mood, and to lower myself in front of Father, I adopted a joking tone to express the great truth in my heart, "The greatest regret of my life is that I have not become the king of music, didn't see the result of my years of struggle and effort, seeing myself on the stage of a large concert hall, behind me an orchestra, in front of me people's eyes, camera flashes, flowers and applause and what is more, the television cameras shooting me…"

Father interrupted me and blurted out, "What, 'the king of music'? To the end, you walked a circle to the beginning, the same old stuff…" Father didn't finish what he was saying. I knew by then, even if he had, his determination of fighting with me to the end, he had no longer such strength.

We both avoided each other's eyes, in a state of profound thinking, plunged into a deeper confusion.

25: FAREWELL MY FATHER

A Special Family Reunion Meal

Family Reunion Meal is when all family members sit together around a table to have a meal. It's an important event for Chinese families, normally happening on the eve of Chinese New Year. But it wasn't a New Year's Eve on which our family had such a reunion meal, for our father could certainly not last until the next New Year's Eve.

Even though we made a huge effort to put everyone in the family together, still it wasn't as perfect as we wanted, since Father was too weak to sit by the table and therefore could only lean back on a sofa. Mother had an empty seat and a set of chopsticks on the table for Father. Next to Father's empty seat was another empty seat, which was for my younger brother DanHen. That is to say, DanHen was also absent from the table. However DanHen's ex-wife was present, as they had a deal. When DanHen could make more, or at least about the same money as the wife, they would marry again. Therefore, the divorce was only on paper. In reality, they still lived together as a family.

To borrow this opportunity, I really would like to say a few good words about my little sister-in-law, the youngest, the prettiest, the smallest, yet the biggest money maker in the family. Since the education reform had been carried out, her income was several times higher than that of my brother, given that she was working in the education field. In addition, she founded a private art school together with her partner. That meant extra cash. In China, parents compete with each other. Their private art school was never lacking in little customers.

What is the emancipation of women? Women's emancipation is the emancipation of economic strength. Therefore naturally, the financially stronger wife became increasingly more powerful in the family. My little brother (he wasn't little at all, not anymore) could not bear the shame as the man of the house; he decided to fight with the wife, economically. He swore he wouldn't be her husband until he made more or about the same. That was what the divorce was all about. Putting it in other words, LOVE had never been a problem between them. The problem was only one thing, one thing only, that was money, the money that the wife made too much of.

To express her emotion, Mother picked up a huge piece of fat pork with chopsticks, intentionally leaning in younger brother's wife direction (this is an old Chinese style, using one's own chopsticks to pick up food and give to another person, was a way to show respect to the person, though westerners might find it disgusting). When the young wife saw that piece of fat oily pork, she was disgusted and almost spit it out.

At this moment, the young wife's mobile phone rang. She immediately passed the phone to their daughter, saying, "Tell your father, starting from today, we will lock the door at 12 o'clock midnight." The daughter started to chat with her father and forgot all about "12 o'clock" thing. The wife was about to grab the phone back, but her daughter refused, handing the phone over to me instead saying, "My father is asking Uncle to answer the phone."

"What? Me?" what a surprise, I confirmed: "Your father really said for the 'Uncle', the *second*, not the eldest, to answer the phone?"

The wife again asked her daughter to pass the phone back to her, but the daughter wasn't joking, she passed the phone over to me.

As I wrote throughout the whole book, my younger brother and I had broken diplomatic relations (domestic relations may be more appropriate) since our childhood. Though recently, with effort, there were some signs of repair, yet not quite at a level of "Uncle", therefore it was unthinkable that he wanted to talk to me, directly. I took the courage and trembled a bit to receive the phone, busy thinking what nice words I should say: "Ai, is that DanHen ah?" But he cut all the shit, hit direct to the bush, "The Hunan Orchestra invited you to have a violin solo concert, they asked me to inform you."

Such a joke was *too sudden*, too much for me. I certainly didn't believe him. DanHen didn't bother to explain, but handed the phone to Conductor Xiao (He was by then the head of the Hunan Orchestra). Hearing Xiao's voice after so many years, I started to believe it was true. After I showed my appreciation, I told him the truth... that I had quit violin performance several years ago, therefore wasn't able to take the solo role.

Xiao encouraged me, "Quit! How could you? A man's value is the persistent pursuit of his goal. Of course, being able to achieve the goal is another matter."

Those wonderful words from the mouth of Conductor Xiao were

particularly inspiring. Recalling when I was a middle school student, how he made his comments about me, "Too many rhythm problems and too strong amateur habits, difficult to transform into a professional musician." And how did I write back to him? "I swear to you I will to be the No. 1 violinist in Changsha. One day I will become a professional violin soloist. Become the king of music. You will lead your orchestra, chasing after me with my rhythm, as my accompaniment."

Thinking of that, I couldn't help laughing. As the saying goes, "a man's revenge, even after ten years it wouldn't be too late." I waited for this moment for so many years, and finally I see the day I win the battle! Shouldn't I be satisfied and proud of myself?

However, now wasn't then. Time had gone by, nearly three decades; I was by then, after all, no longer a naive middle school kid. I, after many years in the west had become a gentleman, or more precisely, close to a gentleman. It would be a waste if I don't seize that opportunity to show my gentleman's quality.

After I once again tried to refuse the concert, Xiao suddenly said some words rather difficult to understand. He said "No need to put off again. Even if you don't think of your own interest, you should think of the orchestra colleagues' interest. You have business and should favor your old friends."

"Business? What business?" I quickly asked Xiao, and then to hand the phone back to my brother DanHen.

DanHen avoided answering my questions. He only said, "It's not easy to explain on the phone. Let's talk about it when we meet next time."

His wife seized the phone shouting, "The door will be locked at 12 o'clock…"

"Cough" the phone was cut off.

Seeing me in a state of extreme confusion, DanHen's wife revealed the truth of my recital. The truth was, Father gave the money I gave *him* for medical treatment to DanHen as the manager, to buy Hunan Orchestra's accompaniment for me in a recital. I thought it was my violin performing ability that conquered Conductor Xiao. What a sentimental and romantic fantasy!

"Oh no, no, how can I spend money to buy a concert? In addition, I haven't practiced violin for years and I no longer have the ability stand on the stage to give a solo concert." I said.

The young wife didn't agree, she said, "What age it is now? The world has changed and now money is level with ability. Look at those performing artists on TV, how many are really there because of their artistic talent and ability? Nowadays, people pay for their own concert, pay for publishing their own books, pay for their own names. If other people can, *why can't you*, my brother DanJiu?"

"Other people can, but your brother... I cannot, because I'm not other people." I tried to explain to my sister-in-law.

DanHen's wife made a, "knowing nothing about good or bad (you took people's good intentions to be bad)" expression, took her daughter and said, "It's getting late; let's go home to lock the door."

I Decided To Take The Recital Concert

After the family reunion meal, I recalled the whole history of my violin life, from the first time I saw the violin at brother Li's window; making my first violin under the instruction and help from Master Zhou; at middle school age going to the pond to practice violin in the early morning and by the side of the railway track practicing violin in the evening; when working at the construction company, hiding somewhere using a mute to practice violin during work-break time; when working at the Hunan Beijing Opera I practiced violin like crazy, every morning, even earlier than those martial arts actors; even that year I was sent to work in a rural area on behalf of the Government, with a dirty muddied face and empty stomach, I still did not stop practicing violin.

When studying at the Shanghai Conservatory of Music, at the beginning, even though I had no place to stay and wandered the whole night on the streets, I did not give up practicing violin.

It is for the violin, I trekked through dozens of countries, going halfway around the world. I had done all the hard work, day after day for decades, all so that one day I could stand on a big stage concert hall, accompanied by a big orchestra with flowers and applause from the audience, camera flashes the television cameras pointing at me. "To give a solo concert", which I thought was a very distant dream, suddenly fell from the sky in front of my eyes. That temptation was almost irresistible.

Although I had psychologically changed my social position and accepted the fact that I had become a "professional violin maker," a craftsman instead of a performing artist. Although, violin making is also a serious creative art, almost good enough to find peace of mind and satisfaction in vanity, but I was after all, a *VIOLINIST*.

Yes, I want to play violin, just give me a reason, even a small reason, if no reason then I only need an excuse... However, to give a concert, not because of my violin performing level and ability but money, that would be an insult to an *artist*! Oh no, absolutely not. It was not that I cared so much about the money, but...

Not sleeping well the whole night, I turned back and forth unable to figure out why Father suddenly changed his attitude, buying me an orchestra to give my solo concert? With a mind full of doubt, I went to see Father early the next morning.

"Do you think I can die in peace with my eyes closed if I don't see your brilliancy on the stage?" No matter what Father really meant it sounded to me that it was no more than sarcasm.

"What do you really want to do with me?" I almost begged.

"Alright, alright." Father waved his dry bones, "I just want to seriously listen to my son play the violin. Just count it as the last wish of my life. Wouldn't you do it for your father?"

With Father saying things like that, what else could I say? However, to recall the history I realized that Father, against his will, gave up his dignity, and even put aside his faith in communism and communist principles, buying me a concert, was just his way of saying "sorry". But at that time, I was so naïve, thinking Father really wanted to listen to my violin playing, or I'd rather *believe* that was the truth.

Meanwhile, a nurse asked me to go to Premier Liu's office. I went there and found a doctor was waiting for me instead of Premier Liu. Seeing me, the doctor said, "About your father, we have done all that we could, but the reality is cruel."

"Please, just tell me how much time's ...left?" I asked bluntly

"Say, a week, no more than 10 days…" the doctor answered.

I thanked the doctor, ran out of the hospital and immediately made a call to DanHen, asking him to tell Conductor Xiao that I accepted the concert and the sooner the better.

I took a taxi rushing to DanXin's home, took out my white violin, the violin I made when I was small, that Father smashed into pieces during the Cultural Revolution and later I brought to the US course to repair. Then I went out again to buy some tools. As quickly as possible, I had to have the violin, the violin of great historical significance, adjusted to performing condition. That feeling was just like a warrior preparing his weapon for the battle field!

The violin was soon ready, but my violin playing ability had been lost for years, not just my fingers, but also many violin works that I could no longer remember in full. To look for the music scores, there was no time, even if some scores could be found I wouldn't have time to practice.

With such a difficult situation, Conductor Xiao came up with a brilliant idea, "You don't need to remember the whole concerto, just play whatever you remember from all the concertos you've played before. The part you remember must be the part you like the most. I will put them together and call it, "The Best of Classical Violin Concertos".

"Teacher Xiao, you've got to be joking. Please be serious…" I said what I thought.

But Xiao said, "Do you see me *not* serious? Do you see me laughing? What the market needs, is what we do. Nowadays, one can do whatever one wants and likes, and we have new labels called 'innovative school', 'avant-garde'...." Conductor Xiao was getting more and more excited, he sighed and said sadly, "It's not that I'm not serious, it's that now we can't afford to only play serious classical music, for economic reasons."

As the result of discussion between Xiao and me, I listed all parts of violin concertos that I could remember, including Bach, Mozart, Beethoven, Bruch, Tchaikovsky, Wieniawski, Sibelius and others. Xiao linked all the parts of the different works by the different composers together, forming a new violin concerto and euphemistically called it, "The Best of the World's Classical Violin Concertos."

"Well, let's settle it this way." Xiao hastily looked at his watch and said, "Sorry, I have other business to negotiate, today I can't accompany you for a meal. When the scores are ready I will ask someone to pass them to your brother. Your solo part is your responsibility. When you practice; do pay attention to the rhythm. The orchestra only has one rehearsal for you before the concert."

"How come only one rehearsal?" I was rather surprised.

"Your brother has only paid that price." Conductor Xiao spoke as he opened his Jetta car door.

I had not yet fully awoke from that dialogue by the time the emissions from Xiao's car had dissolved as part of the city.

Dramatic Tragedy At The Concert Hall

After three days of hard practice with a metronome, the big day had come. At the concert hall, I took a look at all the orchestra members. I found quite a few old colleagues, but also new members I didn't know. I went to greet my old colleagues one by one. Yet I was disappointed to not see the person I wanted to see the most, my boyhood friend DuGuo. After asking, I learned that he was a violin professor teaching at a conservatory in the neighboring province.

Rehearsal started. Though Conductor Xiao did his best not to make things perfect, he still couldn't change his serious nature. He asked the orchestra to repeat some places over again and again, until some of the younger members started to grumble, "You said we only do once and pass. Why do it over and over again, like it's a real thing?"

The two hour rehearsal was soon over. The musicians all went back stage for a break. Left on the stage, were only Xiao and I. I went to shake hands with him and express my gratitude. Xiao with a helpless smile said, "After so many years, you still have not radically improved your rhythm problem." I laughed with pain and replied, "But you have improved a great deal in following-soloist skills."

Hearing that, Conductor Xiao, with a bitter smile (that smile was uglier than crying), said, "Yes, no matter how capable I am, I have to follow God.

Customers are our Gods; therefore I have to follow customers. Today you are our customer, our God, so I must follow you."

It seemed except for those sad topics, we had no other encouraging things to talk about therefore we were both about to go back stage and take a break. At *exactly* that moment the full-stage lighting came on. Two television cameras were shooting at me. That atmosphere suddenly made me feel like a star.

A female reporter holding a microphone came up to me and interviewed, "Mr. Daniel Chen, or should I call you Chen DanJiu, after more than thirty years, when you come back to your hometown Changsha, what is your biggest feeling?"

I blurted out with the Changsha dialect, "My biggest feeling back home is: I'm a foreigner."

The lady reporter smiled, "JiuGe, (Nine Brother in Changsha dialect) you have the same accent after so many years, rare, not easy." But immediately she switched back to working status, asking me, "Why do you feel like a foreigner? Can you explain?"

"Because, because great changes have taken place, both in my hometown and myself, especially my hometown…"

Not waiting until I finished my sentence, the TV director shouted "cut". The lights on stage switched off at once. Then I realized it wasn't a real interview but just a lighting and sound test.

I adjusted my eyesight for the sudden change, looked toward the audience, vaguely seeing my former violin teacher Guo in a wheelchair. The man pushing the wheelchair should be her son. I remembered her son was a genius violinist. That was also why she gave up the position as the concertmaster of the Hunan Orchestra and became a full time violin teacher, so she would have more time for teaching him. Why had so many years passed with nothing being heard about her son? Another thing that had always puzzled me was, if I was no more than her student, not even a good one, why did she take me so seriously, helping me and pushing me so hard to be a good violinist? That question must be answered, not now but in the end.

I gave my teacher a slight bow and walked toward backstage to take a break. But just as I walked by the side stage, I was surrounded by some old friends chatting. I socialized with them but my eyes were busy searching the audience down stage again, imagining another wheelchair, a wheelchair with my father in it, or him being carried by my younger brother DanHen… Meanwhile, an incredible scene appeared before me, as I saw my father not coming by wheelchair nor being carried, but walking in on his own feet! The only strange thing was that Father looked smaller and shorter in reality than he was in my mind.

Immediately I left all the friends and ran down stage toward my father.

To my major disappointment I found it was not my father at all but my aunt disgusted as my father, meaning she was wearing my father's clothes, especially my father's black woolen hat that was supposed to be his trademark. No wonder I mistook my aunt for my father!

Aunt complained to PanJie, "I said we should wait to come in after the concert started. You see, just like the people in the north say, 'It revealed the secret'." Then Aunt smiled and said to me, "The hospital wouldn't let your Dad come out in any case, therefore he asked me to come in his place."

"If my father didn't ask you, you as my Aunt wouldn't come to my concert?"

Aunt removed her hat and said, "Of course I would come. Wearing the hat I am on behalf of your father, with the hat off I am your aunt."

Knowing that Father couldn't come to the concert hall in person, a great sense of loss came to my heart. Fortunately, PanJie quickly comforted me by saying, "DanXin would move a TV set to Father's room, to let Father see me through the TV." This made me feel much better.

In the meantime, on the street outside, my brother DanXin was holding a big TV set and squeezed into a taxi. The always gentle DanXin, that day uncharacteristically, kept pushing the taxi driver, "Faster, more quickly!"

"Please don't push me. Driving a car is like that, the faster you want, the slower you get." The driver looked back at my brother when the taxi was just approaching an intersection. Seeing the yellow light, the driver floored the accelerator rushing out a few meters just as a small motorcycle crossed directly in front of the car. The driver slammed on the brake, followed by a crashing sound from behind! The taxi's ass was kissed by the car behind.

"Do you know how to drive a car!? How could you make such a sudden stop!?" The driver of the BMW behind examined the damage to his car as he cursed.

"You're talking crazy. It was you who hit *me*, how could you ask me if I know how to drive a car?" The taxi driver also checked the back of his car to see how badly it was damaged. But the taxi driver, seeing the car was a BMW, figured the driver must be somebody; therefore he dared not be too aggressive.

In only a short moment, the two crashed cars were surrounded by a crowd of curious spectators. "BMW eats fart! BMW eats fart!" The people were all gloating. DanXin took a look at the meter showing eight and a half RMB, immediately gave the taxi driver ten RMB and said, "Keep the change." He opened the taxi door, paying no attention to his big swollen head, and carried the TV set through the crowd and got into another taxi. This time, he asked the driver, "Don't hurry, take your time, the faster you want, the slower you will get."

But how do you think the driver responded? He said to DanXin, "My brother, I cannot afford to drive slowly. Time is money, money is life. You pay me by kilometer, not by time. Am I right?"

"Okay, okay, eyes front, don't look back. Just drive safely, as safely as you can.", DanXin asked the driver.

Finally DanXin reached the hospital. He carried the heavy TV set, climbing up to the first floor, second floor; he needed a rest, but tried to get to the third floor. Really unable to hold it longer, he put the TV on his leg, resting it against the wall for just a second to let his hands, one by one, have a short break, then he went on to the fourth floor.

As soon as he got to the fourth floor he ran into a nurse with a medicine cart. DanXin said, "borrow" in words but actually he seized the cart and put the TV set on it, regardless of the nurses objections, he pushed the TV heading to Father's room. As soon as he got into the room, DanXin put the TV on a chair, plugged it in, installed a temporary antenna, and adjusted the channel finally finding the channel broadcasting our live performance at the concert hall.

DanXin excitedly clapped his hands, about to call Father to get up, when the nurse called an on duty doctor to come and blame DanXin, saying that taking her cart was a barbaric action. DanXin had no time to talk to them; he tried to get Father up. But Father gave no response.

DanXin patted Father and once again with more force. The doctor realized something was wrong, he looked at Father and found all medical equipment connected to Father was off of him. The doctor checked Father's pulse and eyelids. With a sympathetic expression he looked at DanXin, and then covered Father's head with a blanket.

"Doctor, he robbed my cart..." The nurse insisted.

"Get out!" DanXin roared.

The doctor immediately covered the nurse's mouth and got her out of the ward.

"My cart..." that nurse was still watching the TV on the small cart.

"Go get another one." The doctor's voice and the body of the nurse both disappeared out of Father's room.

DanXin removed the blanket from Father's face and held Father's body, leaning against him, facing the TV. Premier Liu and the emergency service group arrived at Father's room. The rescue routine was performed.

At the Hall, the concert was about to begin. Meanwhile, I was in a dressing room back stage, doing a final check of my glorious image, got some saliva to sculpt the few remaining hairs on my forehead, stood up and walked to the door. I went out the door and stood by the side of the stage, ready to give the concert.

The concert finally began. I stood in front of the stage, back to the orchestra. This was the moment I wanted and fought for all my life. The concert started. Conductor Xiao was very serious and the orchestra too, not at all the same as during the rehearsal. The concert went very smooth.

At the same time in the hospital, my father was given an electric shock. It was purely a formality, but unexpectedly, my father gave a deep sigh and came back! It was such a great joy to DanXin. He turned up the volume to the highest level and held my father, sitting up, facing the TV. Everyone in the room stopped what they were doing, in astonishment or for other reasons not important enough to explain.

My father opened his eyes, looking at the TV. When my violin sound came out of the TV, he smiled a smile of satisfaction and everything, for the last time in his life...

All of this lasted only a few seconds. My father left us, left the world, terminating his life journey...

PanJie was backstage too, keeping contact with DanXin. When the first piece of music finished, I received huge applause, *including* from Teacher Guo. I was in an excellent mood, bowing once, twice, three times and then leaving the stage.

As soon as I returned backstage, waiting for my next piece, PanJie rushed to me.

"Baba, he..." PanJie's next words were interrupted by heavy breathing.

"What happened to Baba?" I guessed ninety percent sure my guess was right.

"Don't tell him now!" DanHen shouted to PanJie running toward us.

"It's too late." I banged the door of the dressing room with my fist.

Suddenly, my heart was being pressed by the weight a huge rock and I could hardly breathe. Though I was well prepared for my father's death, when the moment actually arrived, that feeling was difficult to accurately describe in words. I think, anyone who has lost a loved one would know this feeling from their own experience.

However, I had another feeling that I'm sure not everyone has the opportunity to experience. I was just about to play a violin solo onstage, *the moment I had dreamed of for several decades*. After all of the hard work and effort, I could finally show my magnificence in front of people and above all, to make my father proud of me and admit his defeat in front of me. But at this very key moment, Father suddenly left me. Making me feel like a warrior whose opponent is dead; he would find all the weapons in his hands no longer making sense for him, neither the martial arts training nor hard practice since childhood had its use.

It's like in a war, with no enemy aircraft, anti-aircraft will become a pile of scrap metal; or if there were no viruses attacking a computer, anti-virus software would become a pile of useless data occupying hard drive space; To think of it deeper, if a samurai lost his rival, he could even doubt the value of his own continued existence.

"It's show time again. Come quickly to the stage." someone knocked at the door of my room.

I woke up from the immersion of my contemplation and another question emerged, "Now I have no father, to whom do I play violin for?

"Everybody is waiting for you, come out quickly please." the stage manager called me again.

Even though Father no longer existed, I still had hundreds in an audience waiting for me. Yet even thousands or billions could not compare with one person, my father. However, even though I could ignore the audience, I couldn't let down my musician colleagues on the stage waiting for me half way into the concert.

My mind was busy with my own affairs while my legs were involuntarily out of the dressing room. The stage manager saw me with a strange look and asked, "Hey, I say, Mr. Chen, where's your violin?"

I realized I forgot my violin. With a bitter smile, I went back to my room to fetch the violin. When I came out again, the stage manager saw my red eyes and encouraged me, "Relax, you did well. Everything will be alright."

Seeing I looked as if I were going to fall to pieces, the stage manager held me and led me towards the stage and said again, "Relax, relax, you'll be alright." Then he pushed me to the stage. I went to the center of the stage again. Conductor Xiao nodded to me and then raised his baton. When he waved his hand, about to start the orchestra, I raised my right hand to signal him to stop. Xiao looked at me with great confusion and embarrassment.

I slowly lifted the violin, along with memories from my childhood, the tune from big brother Li's window, to children's songs, "Little Frogs" , "Iris" , "Only work is the most glorious" and Father's favorite, "Li-song", to my brother's most favorite songs, "The evening of Moscow Countryside" and "Troika". I went on and on up to the Beijing Opera's, "Go mountain to beat the tiger.", and finally, the song, "Home, Home Sweet Home"...

Conductor Xiao was completely bewildered and didn't know what to do. But the concertmaster led the orchestra, following me. Xiao realized that was the only way, so he gave a wink to the orchestra members meaning for everyone to follow me closely. That situation was acting out the letter I wrote to Xiao when I was a kid saying, *"I swear to you that someday I will become the No. 1 violinist in all of Changsha City. By then you will say I am a professional. When I play the solo in my style, you will have to lead your orchestra crawling and rolling to follow my rhythm."*

In that way, my music went on for probably half an hour. Throughout, Father's image constantly looming in front of me. I finally reached the limits of control, suddenly stopping. I held my violin with both hands, my face firmly affixed to the back of my violin, for a long, long pause.

Since the very first time I touched a violin, every day I dreamed of the moment I would stand on the stage. It was this dream that gave me unlimited power to overcome all obstacles, conquer all difficulties step-by-step, climbing to this point. Today, however, when this moment really came, I suddenly felt it was exceptionally dull.

Maybe like mountain climbing. During the climb, one has high spirits and feels full of confidence, but when they reach the top they look around only to find oneself surrounded by other, higher mountains, and what had been climbed was no more than a small slope. Or like crossing a desert, in a state of desperation, dying and suffering, then accidentally stumbling upon a lush green oasis. With the yearning to survive, one struggles to jump into the oasis only to find that under the beautiful green is an everglade that one cannot escape.

There could be many other reasons to feel apathetic when finally reaching a goal. However, I knew clearly why I felt that way when I at last took the stage.

"My father passed away! Comrades and friends, my father passed away!" I shouted out, even shouting hysterically to the public, to the point of drooling, was still not enough to vent the burning feeling in my heart. Suddenly, completely out of control, I raised my violin over my head, and then, I fainted. My violin was released from my hand, dropped on the stage, just as my father had done to her during the Cultural Revolution. My violin, "tennis... tennis ..." cried the final moan.

The entire Concert Hall, both musicians and audience were in a commotion. Soon I came to, sitting on the stage for a few seconds, a few more seconds. With help from the stage manager and Conductor Xiao, I stood up again.

I was about to leave the stage, but after just a half step I stopped. Quickly I adjusted my mood, turned toward the audience, "Please forgive me, I, I'm sorry." I crouched down and picked up my broken violin, piece by piece very carefully, trying incredibly hard to use the time to calm myself down.

Using a more moderate tone, again I addressed the audience, "We don't have chances to get together like this, in the future, probably no such chance ever again..." I paused for a moment and suddenly, increasing my volume, "Please allow me to take this opportunity to express my gratitude.

I would first like to thank the schools and work units which I have been a part of: the Changsha XinXiang Kindergarten; the Changsha DaTong Elementary school; the Changsha New River Elementary school; the Changsha No. 4 Middle School; the Changsha Construction Company; the Hunan Beijing Opera; the Hunan Radio and Television Orchestra; and the Hunan University; the Changsha Railway Institute; the Beijing Broadcasting Institute of Hunan Correspondence Center and of course, the most important, the Shanghai Conservatory of Music; as well as the Shanghai

Academy of Drama.

I want to thank those who taught me, trained me in my life journey, especially my teachers, such as Li ZengTao, my enlightened teacher who took the political risk, teaching me how to play the violin secretly in a church. Without him, I could never have taken the violin path in the first place.

My teacher Yu BoPing, the former concertmaster of Hunan Beijing Opera, who changed me from an amateur violin player to a professional. My teacher Guo ShuMing, who not only gave me a strict basic violin education, but also built for me a bridge from Hunan to Shanghai. My professor Sheng ZhongHua and Yu LiNa of the Shanghai Conservatory of Music, who gave me academic education and linked me to the outside world.

My professor Boyhansen of the Norwegian Academy of Music who polished me as a piece of rough material into a mature violin performing artist and many more I need to mention as my masters and teachers in the violin making field.

The last but not the least, I certainly want to thank my friends: Ma XiaoMao and Wang ShiYi, my school classmates and friends. It was they who stimulated and encouraged me get into the violin world.

I would also like to take this opportunity to thank everyone in my family: My aunt, thank you for giving all the love during my childhood; DongYa, my very first wife from Shanghai, without her selfless unconditional love and financial support, it was not likely I could have completed my studies in Shanghai.

Marianna, my family in Norway, it would have been impossible for me to change citizenship and become a free man of the world without her and all the western re-education I received from her. I especially want to thank my brother DanXin and his wife PanJie, for all the things they have done for me over many years, of course, including a tolerance to noise. In short, I want to thank everyone who gave me help growing up.

Finally and most importantly I greatly appreciate my father for his making my dream come true today. Decades of fighting with my father, and today I finally understand *everything* which was hidden deep in that battle, it is my father's deep love.

To put this love into sublimation we perhaps come to this conclusion: love my father; we should love my father's whole generation. In order to achieve an ideology, our predecessors created this period in history, created the history of the People's Republic of China.

From liberation, to land reform, the Great Leap Forward, the Cultural Revolution, Reform and Open-Door to the present Chinese Characterized Socialist Society. No nation and no period in the history of the world, has experienced as many social changes and rich life experiences in such a short period of time as our generation. From this sense, aren't we the most fortunate generation in human history?"

As my speech went on without knowing the time, about half an hour had passed. Conductor Xiao gently knocked the baton on the sheet music table, pointing to his watch. I knew he was trying to tell me, the two-hour concert only has one hour left. I nodded and smiled to tell Xiao that I understood. I cleared my voice and said, "Finally, I would like to thank Conductor Xiao and every colleague in the orchestra."

I stepped back and was about to leave the stage, but a very strong idea burst into my mind, I shouted with excitement "One more thing to announce, my comrades and friends, which is, I am here to publicly propose to a woman, who is present in the hall."

Hearing this, the audience made a huge noisy, noise of surprise, curiosity, shock and anger or perhaps impatience...

"Yes, ladies and gentlemen, colleagues and friends, I have a marriage proposal to announce, the woman I'm going to marry is the little lady selling my music CDs and books at the concert hall entrance."

As soon as I finished my announcement, the television lights went off. I saw a cameraman carrying the machine along with the hostess, running towards the concert hall entrance. Other people followed to see what was going to happen. Obviously, they all went to see MeiMei.

I looked at my watch, "Now there are 45 minutes left for the concert, my friends, let's dance." I put my violin's remaining pieces carefully on the lap of the concertmaster and took his violin, played a Strauss waltz, a wave of Conductor Xiao's baton and the orchestra colleagues immediately followed. The audience, one by one stepped out to dance, turning the concert hall into a ballroom.

I passed the violin back to the concertmaster, holding my violin remains; I went directly from the stage down to the audience. I took a flower from a flower basket and squeezed towards the entrance. Then several kind people shouted, "Please give way to the groom."

MeiMei, at this time, was taking a rest at the concert hall entrance for she was a little tired after selling my books and CDs before the concert. Seeing a crowd of people suddenly rushing toward her, she had absolutely no idea what was going on. The TV director ordered his crew, "Be ready, lights on, action."

The TV reporter asked MeiMei, "Are you the one Mr. Chen is going to marry? If yes, could I ask a few questions?" Then, the TV hostess pointed the microphone to MeiMei. No response from MeiMei, the cameraman caught a hand covered face. The TV hostess went on asking, "Will you accept the marriage proposal?"

This unexpected question threw MeiMei into a state of panic, she muttered, "What? I don't know what you're talking about?" She was trying to escape from the crowd.

The TV hostess immediately explained, "Mr. Chen, we call him JiuGe, just proposed to you publicly on the stage. Didn't he ask you before?"

"JiuGe just proposed to *ME* publicly on stage?" MeiMei stressed the word "ME", sounding full of surprise. "You, or he, must be out of his mind. Please let me out, I need to go to the ladies room."

26: THE ENDING

I *was* out of my mind. When I recall, I honestly have no idea why I did that to MeiMei. The only thing that could explain it was I needed some excitement after such a great loss.

Later at MeiMei's place, she talked with me like this: "I just had a dream, the same dream I've had many times, that you want to marry me." And then she started to cry silently, gradually bursting into tears. When she finally calmed down, very seriously and sincerely she said to me, "In fact, what you said on the stage, I have heard many times in my dreams, but every time I answered like this: It's better we keep things this way. To live together with me would drag your legs, for I don't belong to your life and your world. If one day you started to be dissatisfied with me and kick me out of your house, I'd rather stay outside your door, watching you, to feel I am with you; this would be enough for me. I can wait until you are old and return to your roots, just like your father lying in bed, with no energy to kick. I might then come into your house, looking after you…"

Father has passed away. A dead person, without a soul and feelings, it's only a pile of substance now. However, til today, I still can't find an accurate explanation of why I didn't go to the hospital to see my father's remains for the last time.

The date of Father's memorial service couldn't be decided easily due to various problems, such as the specification of memorial service level issues; the eulogy at Father's political evaluation; who should be invited to the memorial service; who should be the memorial service host and who was going to read the memorial letter… As the saying goes, when people die, everything finishes, but our Chinese people, especially the Chinese Communist Party members who are representing the Chinese people, even being dead, doesn't get them away from these complicated issues.

As a Norwegian citizen, borrowing a very ridiculous international excuse, "That is an internal affair of your country and I as a foreigner shouldn't interfere." got me out of all the trouble.

The whole family was busy with Father's memorial service. This time, no one saw me off at the airport, not even MeiMei who went to see me off abroad for the first time many years ago.

I said goodbye to my home country and once again boarded the flight to Norway. Just a moment into the cabin, I suddenly asked myself a question, "What's the reason I'm going to Norway again? And I have no reason to come back to China again."

My flight was in the air. I closed my eyes. My mind conjured up a song, such a song I had never heard before. The song went like this:

"I must hold the tears that I could not hold; I must stop thinking the love that I could not stop thinking; To tell you my love, my love to you; Even though I know you're in a different sphere that you cannot hear, cannot hear, But I will not end my telling, forever, forever. Because it is true love, a lifetime only once that kind of love…"

I suddenly opened my eyes and looked out the window to see if my father was there. After a while I closed my eyes again and felt a complete peace in my heart. Because one day, I will carry my violin, without aircraft, I will be in the sky. By that time, I will be somewhere meeting my father again. By then I will tell him the story of my life decades after that! But what story that would be, I didn't know yet. But one thing I know for sure, that is, I must follow fate to complete the rest of my mission, the essential and the most difficult part of that mission is: ***To live as a good human.***

27: EPILOGUE

After I left China, a week later Father's memorial service was finally held. My brother DanXin spoke on behalf of our family. In his speech he repeatedly thanked the socialist country.

MeiMei attended the memorial service as a family member of ours. She used the two hundred RMB that my parents gave to me when I went abroad the first time, the two hundred RMB my father saved from his cigarettes for many years, to buy a bunch of flowers dedicated to my father in my name.

MeiMei also put the remains of my white violin at my father's side and had them cremated together.

My violin became smoke, with Father's soul, floating into infinite time and space.

Later I was back to China several times. I have visited my first wife DongYa's mother twice in Shanghai. According to her mother, some years after our divorce, DongYa remarried, but had no children. Reminding me of that year, when I accompanied her for an abortion at the hospital and what she swore to me in extreme pain, "I will never have a child again."

Marianne sold our apartment in Oslo. After paying back the bank loan, she used the rest of the money to buy a small house in a remote area outside of Oslo. She must have concentrated all of her heart, soul and mind on theology studies. I never heard that she got remarried or had children.

Jiang LangSha, after getting out of China, became an influential net writer. Apart from many works in Chinese, he also writes in English. Just recently I received an e-mail from him telling me he had completed an autobiography titled, "My Father" in English, and is now trying to find a publisher.

Uncle Feng's self-built small shed, as illegal construction, was demolished. He hid in an abandoned room at a construction site, moving constantly from place to place; no one knows how many times they have moved. Of sickness and old age, Uncle Feng finally passed away. People could only assume Chu XiaoLin, the vegetable girl, without Uncle Feng's care, starved to death a few days after Uncle Feng's death.

After many twists and turns, I finally found Chu XiaoLin's Uncle's leather envelope that led to so many tragedies. I returned the envelope to Chu's aunt who was at the edge of her life. The aunt looked at the envelope, first burst into tears and then laughed. She opened the envelope in front of me. Guess what was hidden in the envelope that they wouldn't let anyone see? It was simply a wedding photo of Chu XiaoLin's aunt with her husband. That was all! (But during the Cultural Revolution if the photo had been seen, they could be in big trouble. Or they just wanted to keep the photo for themselves, so as no one would see it or destroy it.)

Ma XiaoMao immigrated to Japan. She married a Japanese man 30 years older than her. To find such a man, as old as her father to marry, the purpose was obvious (a marriage of convenience). But unexpectedly, after living together with her husband, she fell in love with the father-aged husband and together they have a handsome son. Now Ma is working full time in a company to earn money for the family during the day and taking care of the old and young in the evening, a very busy, but happy life.

Our schoolmate Flute Chen came back to Changsha from XinJiang with his child (the child looked like the mother but not him). He sells smoked mutton in the streets. He has been trying hard to get the benefits from the government that they think they are entitled to as members of the XinJiang Production and Construction Corps (it was said to be a part of the Chinese army. The truth is uncertain).

He was one of the petitioners who went to Beijing, but was arrested each time. Though I offered my help to him several times, it was refused each time. Finally, in order to put his child through school, Flute Chen accepted my private loan and together with other money sources he opened a very tiny, LanZhou Noodle House.

Wang ShiYi was one of those "got-rich-first", during the reform and open-door policy. He not only bought a car, but also bought a driver's license. Very sadly, he was killed in a car crash.

Lu XiaoBing worked as a judge. Ironically, the final Mao Team reunion took place in her court. The defendant was no other than the worker's representative Chuang who was in charge of our middle school Mao Team. He got himself implicated in a crime involving the bribing of an official. The case was in Lu's hands. *Somehow*, Chuang got away with his evident crime.

That unbelievable result must have hurt Lu very badly. It was after that,

that Lu retired as a judge and focused herself on some kind of research to do with the moon.

Teacher Li passed away quietly in peace. No student was informed about his death.

Teacher Guo also passed away. It was some years later that I found out why she took me so seriously and pushed me so hard.

I met her genius violin son in Shanghai. The son of my teacher Guo purposely used his left hand to shake my hand. It was then I noticed all his fingers were the same length. The story was that he didn't really like violin. He was much more into making transistor radios. As he couldn't endure the enormous pressure from his mother, *he flattened his fingers with a kitchen knife...* by the time we met, he was working as a computer expert. This explained why Teacher Guo put so much pressure and hope, all of which was originally on her own son, on me.

Now *my* family. My elder brother DanXin and his wife PanJie stayed in our hometown, taking care of our mother day and night for years, until recently when our mother went to see our father in heaven. Now DanXin and his wife live their lives just like the majority of compatriots in my motherland, a Chinese characterized life.

I suggested many times that they move from Changsha, China's worst polluted city, to another country, but they refused as they are used to the place and all of their friends are there. "Not dead proves livable", is my brother DanXin's well-known quotation.

My younger brother DanHen never managed to re-marry his wife. Yet the relationship stayed normal. He is now a British citizen living in the UK with their daughter. We have little direct contact, everything goes through DanXin.

Last but not least, MeiMei kept close to my family and looked after my mother until her end.

Remember the small Buddha I took out from the nunnery and passed to MeiMei as a doll when we were around 10 years old? Somehow, I also managed to get it back from my friend Jiang LangSha. About 30 years had passed when I handed it to MeiMei again.

I wonder if she got the wrong message, as we took the Buddha back to the same nunnery it came from, MeiMei said goodbye to me in front of the nunnery, holding the Buddha, walked into the nunnery and never walked out... I have never heard from her again.

After nine years living in Norway, I met a Japanese girl. With her I moved to Japan. There I lived the longest time in my life, almost twenty years. About my life in Japan, it could be my third autobiography titled, "Gaijin", in Japanese meaning "Foreigner".

My second autobiography's Chinese version was finished a long time ago. An English version is planned. The book is about my life in Australia and Norway, with the title, "A Saint, a Scholar and a Prostitute".

Now, I live all over the world, traveling, learning, exploring, experiencing and enjoying every moment of my life.

Daniel Olsen Chen (Chen DanJiu)

ABOUT THE AUTHOR

Daniel Chen is a world renowned maker of fine violins and bows, born in China twelve years before the Cultural Revolution. (Recently the author unexpectedly found out he happens to be the great nephew of Mao's teacher, Chen Runlin.)

Among his many honors and awards he is a partner in Hollywood Star winning musical group *"The BergenMusic"*, and is a diploma holder from *Mittenwald International Violin Making Competition*.

Daniel was featured on Chinese National TV series *"Outstanding Talents"* in 2012, a forty-minute documentary entitled *"Danny's Violin Life"* presented him as the highest of achievers in the violin field.

Writing is among Daniel's passions and he was awarded *"Writer of the Year 2002"* in Taiwan for his Mandarin language book *"Christian's Violin"*. He is a Norwegian citizen now residing in Japan, technically. Daniel is a citizen of the world which he explores continually sharing his vast knowledge of violin and travel adventures via his YouTube channel *AVDanielViolin*.

Coming Soon!

"Three WOMANS" (A Saint, a Scholar and a Prostitute) – A story of the culture shock when east meets west, his life story in Australia and Norway.

"Gaijin" (Foreigner) – The twenty years of my life spent living in Japan.

And Many More Including Novels, Short Stories And Essays

47925846R00209

Made in the USA
Columbia, SC
05 January 2019